A Reader of Handwritten Japanese

A Reader of Handwritten Japanese

P. G. O'Neill

KODANSHA INTERNATIONAL
Tokyo • New York • London

To

Amy 英美

Publication of this book was assisted by a grant from The Japan Foundation.

Distributed in the United States by Kodansha America, Inc., 114 Fifth Avenue, New York, N.Y. 10011, and in the United Kingdom and continental Europe by Kodansha Europe Ltd., Gillingham House, 38-44 Gillingham Street, London SW1V 1HU. Published by Kodansha International Ltd., 17-14 Otowa 1-chome, Bunkyo-ku, Tokyo 112, and Kodansha America, Inc. Printed in Japan.

LCC 84-81170
ISBN 4-7700-1663-8

First edition, 1984
First paperback edition, 1992
92 93 94 5 4 3 2 1

CONTENTS

Preface

The foreign student of Japanese is now well supplied with the means to take his study of the language to a high level in virtually all fields except one—handwritten Japanese. There is little or nothing to train him to read quite everyday types of handwriting, yet few things are more frustrating for him than to be unable to read a postcard, letter or routine business correspondence in Japanese, particularly if he knows that he otherwise has a good general ability in the language.

There are, of course, reasons for this. In the early stages of studying the language, the grammar, large vocabulary and range of characters used in written Japanese can be quite enough to keep a student occupied, to say nothing of the complications of respect language. On the other hand, once he has covered the basic grammar and learned *kana* and a few hundred characters, handwritten Japanese can provide him with a training in the language at least as good as that from most other written material and, at the same time, with experience in an important and useful area of language usage.

The two main requirements for reading handwritten Japanese are to have a reasonable reading ability in the language and a practiced eye with which to recognize the general shapes of written characters in their standard and variant forms. A general understanding of the system of respect language is also needed, since the level of politeness used in letters is always greater than would be used in conversation between the individuals concerned, but much of this kind of language appears in the form of stereotyped phrases which soon become familiar.

The aim of this book is to enable a student with the first of these requirements—an intermediate ability in the reading of Japanese—to develop the skills necessary to read a range of handwriting covering anything likely to be met in normal usage. To this end, a general introduction which includes an outline of the system of respect language is followed by one hundred handwritten items, each in a different hand. These are graded in order of difficulty, with romanized transcriptions and notes on grammatical points, etc., for them all; with translations and full vocabulary for the first twenty-five; and with unusual modern vocabulary not given in standard student dictionaries for the rest. This is supplemented by four appendices: the first presenting an outline of respect language; the second showing the old, full forms of characters with their modern simplifications; the third listing written forms of the sixty most important characters, and the fourth giving the main variant forms of *kana* found in handwritten Japanese. Readers with a good ability in the reading of printed Japanese will be able to work straight through the items, while those with less experience in the language can use the texts for reading practice in parallel with other material, safely working alone if necessary through the first twenty-five items which are provided with everything they should need. In either case, the type of language used in letters and the like will soon cause less and less difficulty, and the eye will gradually learn to take in groups of written signs in an impressionistic way, rather than as items to be laboriously identified and then pieced together to produce their meaning. The reader will also come to recognize the range of respect levels used according to the relationships among the people concerned and, finally, to be able to use similar phrasing, as appropriate, in his own correspondence.

I should here like to thank all the writers of the letters and postcards used in this book, which have been sent over a period of years to myself or one or other of my colleagues. Although most of them were intended as nothing more than casual personal communications and their writers had no thought of fine or careful handwriting, for present purposes their value lies in that very fact, and I here acknowledge my debt and my gratitude to the hundred original authors of this book.

P.G. O'Neill

London, November 1984

INTRODUCTION

GENERAL

Since the use of Chinese characters has given Japanese a largely non-phonetic script which has not easily lent itself to a printed form, handwriting has played an even larger part in Japanese life than it has in the West; and although word-processors are clearly making great headway in the business world in Japan today, they will be for her little more than the typewriter has long been for the rest of the world. This, and the high regard in which calligraphy is held in the countries of the Far East, mean that handwriting will continue to be a feature of Japanese life for the foreseeable future and that it will remain a form of the language which cannot be ignored.

The two main areas of handwritten Japanese may be described as, first, its wholly or mainly 'detached' use in such things as manuscripts intended for the printer, official forms, notices, general memoranda and diaries, where the writer and reader have little or no recognized social relationship; and, second, its use in personal communications between one individual and another, usually in the form of letters or postcards. The former type needs no special note here because the absence of any specific personal relationship means that it is essentially neutral in tone, and such variations as do occur arise from the same considerations of style as apply to printed material in newspapers and magazines, for example.

Personal communications, however, are necessarily handwritten and involve language which reflects primarily the relationship between the writer and addressee, but also their relationships with any third person who might be mentioned. As letters contain a range of formal expressions at their beginning and end which is considerably reduced in the case of postcards, it is convenient to give an account of letters first. (Some use of respect language is inevitably involved in this, and readers who are not familiar with this type of language are recommended to read through the "Outline of Respect Language" in Appendix I before going further. Explanations of respect forms will also be found in notes to the items in which they occur.)

LETTERS

Like other types of Japanese script, letters may be written either from left to right or from top to bottom. In either case they are most often written on plain paper, but when they are written vertically, paper with lines to separate the columns is also used (see, for example, the letter given as No. 3). This latter type of paper is distinct from squared paper (*genkō yōshi* 原稿用紙, "manuscript/copy paper"), which is used when it is important to know the exact length of a passage, as in the case of a text for the printer, or sometimes as an aid in writing practice. It is also considered polite to use more than a single sheet of paper, even for a short letter, and this can lead to the final lines being deliberately spread out to go over the page or even to a second, blank sheet of paper being enclosed.

Nowadays, the writing is usually done with a pen—in black or blue ink, since most Japanese would feel the use of other colours to be at least discourteous—but sometimes with a brush, using Indian ink. Brush writing carries with it an aura of dignity, so that it is regularly used for New Year cards, for example, and on formal occasions such as weddings and funerals. It also gives a feeling of traditional elegance and, for this reason, is often used for everyday purposes by people in the academic world or the arts and especially by women.

FORM OF LETTERS

The arrangement within a letter in Japanese follows a fixed sequence, which can be summarized as follows.

INTRODUCTION

1. Opening Word or Phrase: indicating respect, the safe receipt of a letter, that the present letter is written in haste, etc.
2. Preliminary Remarks: concerning the weather and concern for the health of the addressee, or thanks or apologies to him.

SUBSTANCE OF LETTER

3. Main Text: usually introduced by a word or phrase to indicate this new stage.

CONCLUSION

4. Concluding Phrases and Words: expressing some form of farewell or indicating the purpose of the letter, together with the respect of the writer.
5. Date and Names: of writer and addressee.
6. Postscript: if any.

The content of all these sections except 3 and 6 consists of variations on a fairly limited number of themes, the exact wording varying according to the particular circumstances in which the letter is written, especially the time of the year and the degree of respect used. Examples falling within the sections set out above will be found throughout the letters in this book, but typical ones are given below. Alternatives are separated by oblique strokes, and where they are used between different levels of respect, the first is the more respectful, suitable for use to someone being treated as of higher status than the writer, and the second appropriate for use to others; and words in parentheses may or may not be included.

1. Opening Word or Phrase

Nowadays letters sometimes begin with the recipient or recipients being addressed directly, in the case of an individual by name, followed by a title such as 様

sama, "Mr./Mrs./Miss." Such a direct, Western-style reference to the addressee means that the name is not then given at the end of the letter, as it would otherwise be, and it replaces the more usual and traditional openings. The most common of these are as follows.

Haikei 拝啓, *Haitei* 拝呈, *Kinkei* 謹啓, *Keijō* 啓上, all meaning "Respectfully (presented)."

Tsutsushinde mōshi-agemasu 謹んで申し上げます, "I respectfully send word to you."

When the letter is a reply: *Haifuku* 拝復, *Keifuku* 敬復, both meaning "In respectful reply."

When writing in haste: *Zenryaku* 前略, "Preliminaries omitted"; *Tori-isogi mōshi-agemasu* 取り急ぎ申し上げます, "I am sending word to you in haste."

There then often follows some such remark as *O-tegami haiken itashimashita/shimashita* お手紙拝見致しました/しました, "I have (respectfully) seen your letter"; *Itsumo go-busata bakari itashite orimasu/shite imasu* いつも御無沙汰ばかり致して居ります/しています, "(I am sorry that) I am always so remiss in writing to you."

2. Preliminary Remarks

(a) Seasonal Greetings

SPRING: *Daibu haru rashiku natte mairimashita/kimashita ga . . .*
大分春らしくなって参りました/きましたが……
"It has now become very spring-like, and . . ."

Shinshun no kō to natte mairimashita/kimashita ga . . .
新春の候となって参りました/きましたが……
"The season of early spring has come, and . . ."

Shundan no orikara, . . .
春暖の折柄……
"At this time of spring warmth, . . ."

SUMMER: *Shinryoku/Seika no kō to natte mairimashita/kimashita ga . . .*
新緑/盛夏の候となって参りました/きましたが……
The season of fresh greenery/high summer has now come, and . . .

Hi-goto ni natsu rashiku natte mairimashita/kimashita ga . . .
日毎に夏らしくなって参りました/きましたが……
"Day by day it has become more summery, and/but . . .

Mainichi atsusa ga tsuzukimasu ga . . .
毎日暑さが続きますが……
"Day after day the heat continues, but . . . "

AUTUMN: *Asa-yū wa sukoshi suzushiku narimashita ga . . .*
朝夕は少し涼しくなりましたが……
"It has now become cool morning and night, but . . . "

Suzushii aki-kaze ga fuku yō ni narimashita ga . . .
涼しい秋風が吹くようになりましたが……
"Cool autumn breezes have now started, but . . . "

Dan-dan yo-naga ni narimashita ga . . .
段々夜長になりましたが……
"The nights have gradually lengthened, but . . . "

WINTER: *Nan to naku fuyu chikaku kanjiru yō ni narimashita ga . . .*
何となく冬近く感じるようになりましたが……
"One somehow feels now that winter is not far away, but . . . "

Shotō no kō/Samui jikō to narimashita ga . . .
初冬の候/寒い時候となりましたが……
"The early-winter season/The cold season has now come, but . . ."

Reinen ni nai samusa de gozaimasu/desu ga . . .
例年にない寒さでございます/ですが……
"In normal years we never have such cold, but . . . "

(b) Solicitous Enquiries: usually follow the above; for example:

O-kawari (mo) gozaimasen/arimasen ka.
お変り（も）ございません/ありませんか。
"I trust that you are as well as ever."

Go-kinkyō ikaga de gozaimasu/desu ka.
御近況いかがでございます/ですか。
"How are things with you lately?"

Sono go, ikaga de irasshaimasu/desu ka.
その後，如何でいらっしゃいます/ですか。
"How are you since I saw/heard from you last?"

Mina-sama ni wa go-sōken ni o-sugoshi no koto to zonjimasu.
皆様には御壮健にお過ごしのことと存じます。
"I hope that you are all going along in good health."

Watakushi/Watashi mo buji ni kurashite orimasu/imasu kara, go-anshin kudasaimasu/kudasaru yō o-negai mōshi-agemasu/shimasu.
私/わたしも無事に暮して居ります/いますから，御安心下さいます/下さるようお願い申し上げます/します。
"I too am fit and well, so I ask you please not to worry."

(c) Apologies

Sono go wa go-busata ni uchi-sugite orimasu/imasu.
その後は御無沙汰にうち過ぎております/います。
"(I am sorry that) I have not written since then/for so long."

Kokoro ni kake-nagara, go-buin o kasanete orimasu/imasu.
心にかけながら，御無音を重ねております/います。
"Uneasy though I am about it, I have continually neglected to send word to you."

(d) Thanks

Heiso wa o-hiki-tate ni azukari, makoto ni arigatō zonjimasu.
平素はお引立てにあずかり，誠に有難う存じます。
"Thank you very much indeed for continuing to favour me with your kind consideration."

3. Main Text

The beginning of this part of a letter is usually indicated by an introductory word such as *Sate* さて/扨, *Tokoro de* 所で, both meaning "Well (then/now)," or *Sassoku de gozaimasu/desu ga . . .* 早速でございます/ですが, "This is (very) sudden, but . . . " The writer then goes on to set out the matter which prompted the letter.

4. Concluding Expressions

As with Western letters, it is usual to round off a letter with phrases or sentences which may simply indicate its approaching end, the reason for the letter being written, or express good wishes to the addressee and/or his family. Such expressions can therefore vary a great deal, but typical ones are:

Mazu wa migi go-tsūchi/o-negai made.
先ずは右御通知/お願いまで。
"The above, then, is to inform you/is my request to you."

Dōzo migi yoroshiku o-negai mōshi-agemasu/shimasu.
どうぞ右よろしくお願い申し上げます/します。
"I ask you to be kind enough to help me with the above matter."

Oku-sama ni yoroshiku (o-tsutae kudasai).
奥様によろしく（お伝え下さい）。
"(Please pass on) my best wishes to your wife."

A concluding word or short phrase then usually follows, written either at the bottom of a separate column (or of course at the righthand side of a line if the writing is done from left to right), or at the bottom of the column in which the above phrase or sentence ends. The most common of these concluding items are:

Sō-sō 草々/匆々 "In haste"
Keigu 敬具, *Haigu* 拝具 both meaning "Respectfully"
Keihaku 敬白 "Informing you respectfully"
Sayōnara さようなら "Goodbye"
(Sore) de wa mata （それ）ではまた "Well, then, (I will write) again" or, when the writer is a woman,
Kashiko かしこ "With reverence/respect."

5. Date and Names

The date is then written towards the top of a new column, often in the form of the month and day alone but sometimes proceded by the year, either the Western-style one or the year according to the Japanese era name. Note that, since the year when an emperor comes to the throne is the first one of his reign, the year-number specified in this type of date must be added to the year *before* his reign began in order to arrive at the Western year. Thus, because the emperor whose reign was given the name Shōwa came to the throne in 1926, "Shōwa 59," for example, is 1925+59=1984.

The writer's name is then given at the bottom of a column without any form of title but occasionally with a following character, 拝 *hai*, "respectfully," or, when the writer is a man, 生 *sei*, "(your) junior," as an indication of humility. A seal may also be used here, when the letter is a formal one or from an institution.

The name of the addressee, on the other hand, is always written at the top of a column (or, of course, on the extreme left in horizontal writing) and followed by some respectful suffix. The most common of these is *-sama* 様 "Mr./Mrs./Miss," but others are:

Sensei 先生 literally "teacher," for a person in the teaching world, the arts or public life, to whom the term is felt to be appropriate;
-kun 君 in this situation, used exclusively between men who are close friends, or to a subordinate, close relation, etc.;
-dono 殿 a formal, official term, much like English "Esq."; and

Kakui 各位 when referring to a group or corporate body, much like "Messrs."

Finally, after the addressee's name and title there may be, written just to the side (or below in horizontal writing), a further respectful word or short phrase, such as:

Jishi 侍史 literally "(to your) secretary";
Gyokuanka 玉案下 "below your revered desk"; or
On-moto e 御許/下へ (alternatively, *O-moto e* お許/下へ) literally "to your residence," when the writer is, almost without exception, a woman.

6. Postscript

A postscript will normally be introduced by a word describing it as such, most commonly *Tsuishin* 追伸, *Nishin* 二伸, , or *Tsuikei* 追啓.

ENVELOPES

Virtually all the letters given in this book follow the sequence outlined above, and there will be no difficulty in identifying the various sections, but there are conventions about the use of envelopes which are worth special notice.

Briefly, the most important thing is that, in the address on the envelope, the name and title of the addressee should be put in a separate column down the center. They are also often set higher and written in slightly larger characters than the address to the right.

On the reverse side of the envelope, the name and address of the sender are written in smallish characters towards the bottom, with the date rather higher up, and the flap is sometimes "secured" by writing over it a character such as 〆 *shime* or 封 *fū,* both meaning "sealed," or more formally by affixing a personal or official seal. See Figure 1 for the two sides of a typical envelope.

Fig. 1. Two sides of an envelope.

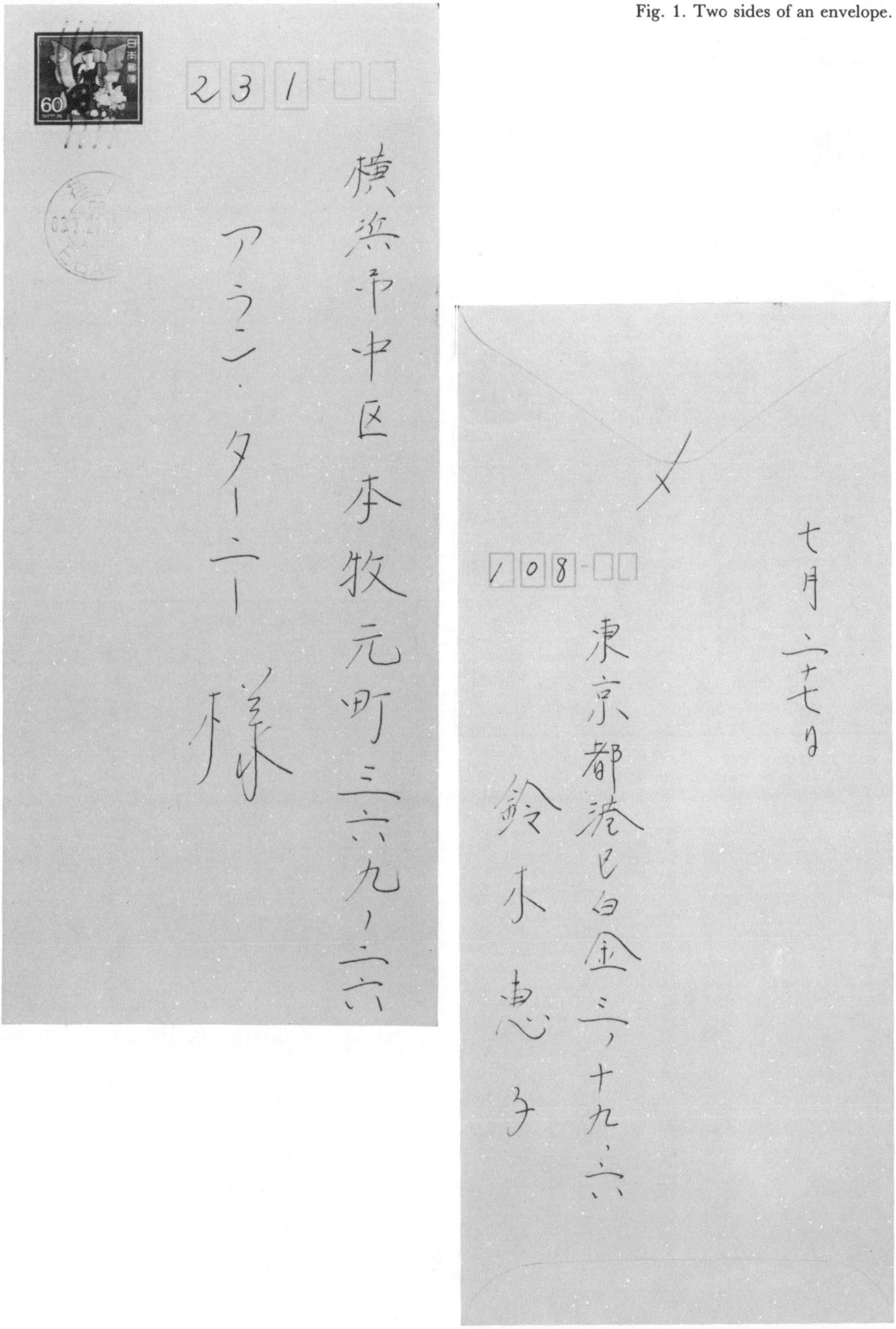

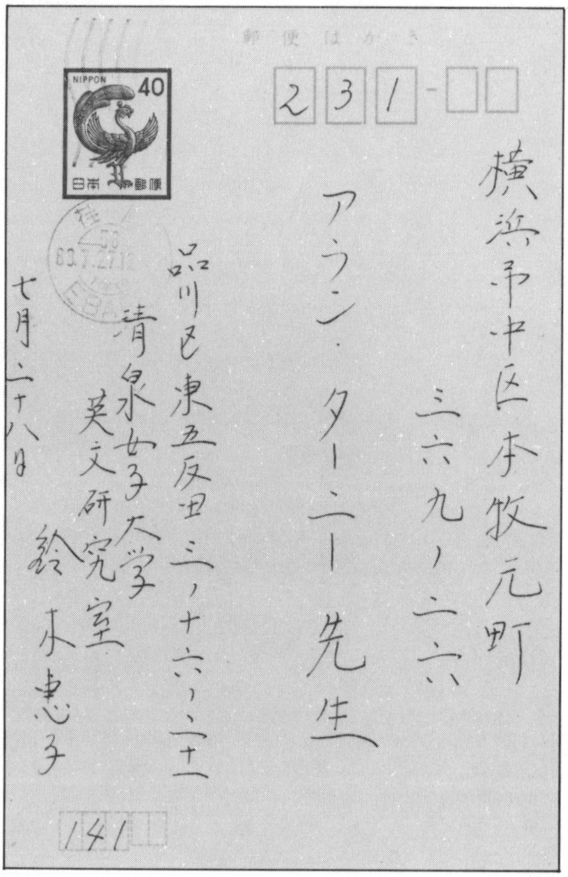
郵便はがき

231-

NIPPON 40

日本郵便

横浜市中区本牧元町
三六九ノ二六
アラン・ターニー 先生

品川区東五反田三ノ十六ノ二十一
清泉女子大学
英文研究室
鈴木恵子

七月二十八日

141

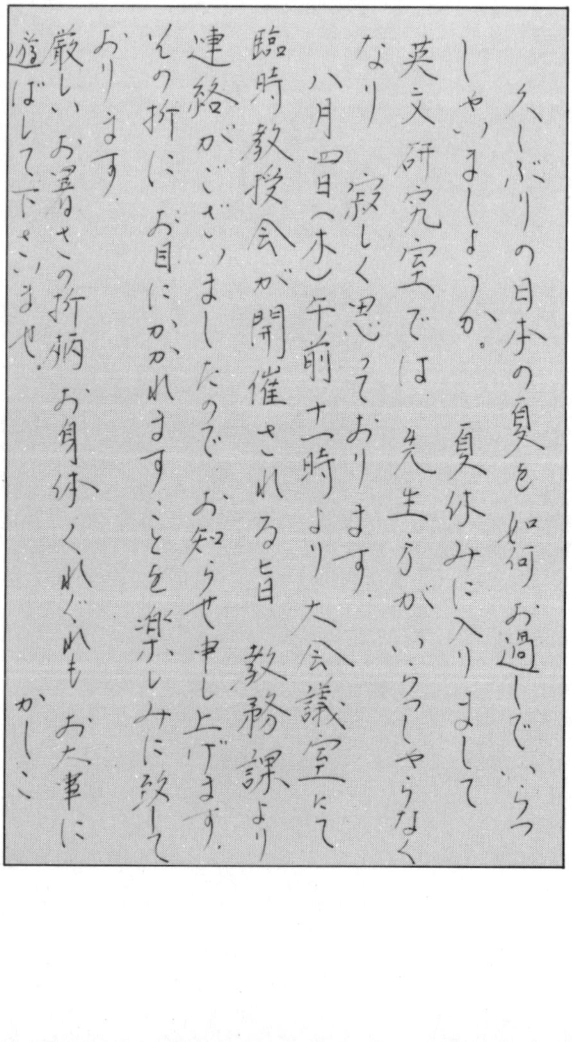
久しぶりの日本の夏を如何お過しでいらっ
しゃいましょうか。 夏休みに入りまして
英文研究室では 先生方がいらっしゃらなく
なり 寂しく思っております。
八月四日(木)午前十一時より大会議室にて
臨時教授会が開催される旨 教務課より
連絡がございましたので お知らせ申し上げます。
その折に お目にかかれますことを楽しみに致して
おります。
厳しいお暑さの折柄 お身体くれぐれも お大事に
遊ばして下さいませ。 かしこ

Fig. 2. Two sides of a postcard.

POSTCARDS

The writing of postcards usually follows the same sequence as that for letters set out above, but in an abridged form because of limitations of space. There will, however, normally be an introductory word or phrase (as in Section 1 above) or, instead, a preliminary remark (as in Section 2); the substance of the communication (Section 3); and finally a concluding expression (as in Section 4). Names and the date are not usually given at the end of the text, as in a letter, but on the address side of the card (or in the address half in the case of a picture postcard), together with the addresses of both sender and recipient. See Figure 2 for the two sides of a typical postcard.

The hundred items in this book have been arranged as far as possible in an order of increasing difficulty. Handwritten material in Japanese has, however, a number of different aspects—legibility, of course, but also such things as the range of characters used, the occurrence of old forms of characters and old *kana* spellings, and the style of language—and what is difficult for one person may not be so for another. The arrangement was therefore based primarily on the legibility or otherwise of the writing, and then modified by consideration of other aspects. Any unevenness there may be for a particular reader should in any case confirm him in his progress when an 'easy' item is met.

In using this book, readers are recommended to begin by going through the early items taking full advantage of the transcriptions to confirm or provide readings, and of the notes for guidance on the grammar, etc. The transcriptions give three indications of where to find information on the relevant word, phrase or syllable:

UPPER CASE LETTERS
: indicate an item explained in a note to that particular text.

<u>Underlining</u>
: indicates an item explained in a note or notes and listed with the note references in the Index and Glossary.

Bold Type
: indicates words and names not given in standard dictionaries and therefore listed in the Index and Glossary.

Some Japanese words have more than one possible reading when writttten in characters. The most common example is 私 which, although its only officially recognized reading as a single character is *watakushi*, is widely used to write the less formal *watashi* also. Similarly, 貴方 is frequently used as a way of writing *anata*, but it also has the much stiffer reading *kihō* with the same meaning of "you." In such cases, the transcriptions give what seemed to be the appropriate reading in the particular context, but in general *watakushi* and *anata* have been the preferred readings for those particular examples.

The careful reader will also find that, here and there, the usage of characters and *kana* in a written piece may not correspond with the standard or official one. In some cases the characters used are acceptable alternatives to the regular ones, but it must be realised that outright "spelling" mistakes occur in Japanese as in other languages. Such mistakes have to be taken in one's stride in the real world, and it is hoped that readers finding lapses in the present material will be both enouraged and consoled by their discoveries.

It is unlikely that the writing itself in the twenty-five Introductory Texts of the first section will cause any difficulty, but if necessary the printed form of any particular character can be seen under the relevant word in the Index and Glossary. The printed forms of characters in later items can be found in any standard Japanese-English dictionary (including the "Index by Readings" in Nelson's *Japanese-English Character Dictionary*) or, when they occur in unusual words, again by referring to the Index and Glossary. The translations were intended to be helpful rather than elegant; that is to say, their main purpose was to aid an understanding of the Japanese and, where there was a choice, they were therefore made literal rather than literary. Similarly, the punctuation in the romanized transcriptions does not rigorously follow the sometimes wayward usage of the originals, but is given to clarify as far as possible the structure of the Japanese.

By the time the Introductory Texts have been read, many of the stock expressions used in letters and the like will have been met, and it will often be possible to decide from the context as much as from the writing itself what a particular word, phrase or clause must be. In reading handwritten Japanese it is in any case important to get into the habit of looking ahead in order to see a related sequence as a whole, so that the various elements in it can combine to suggest the reading, and not to try to decipher isolated elements if this can possibly be avoided. As increasingly cursive forms of characters come to be met, it will be useful to look through the written forms of common characters given in Appendix III. These will show that there are standard cursive forms for various elements, most of which occur repeatedly in different characters, and a familiarity with them will go a long way towards training the eye to recognize these other characters when they are met. This, with the help of the context, should eventually extract the reading and meaning even from writing which at first glance looks quite undecipherable. As with most other aspects of language learning, progress in the reading of handwritten Japanese may sometimes seem slow and uncertain, but it must be remembered that the items are intended to be progressively more advanced. This means that, while none may seem easy on a first reading, reassurance can be found by looking back over earlier items which may themselves have seemed difficult at the time.

INTRODUCTORY TEXTS

Nos. 1–25

With transcriptions, notes and translations,
and a full vocabulary in the Glossary.

1. Circular from a Bookshop

1981年4月

書籍購入担当各位御中

この度、当書店メイルオーダー部では、日本関係出版物（和・洋）を広範囲に取扱うようになり、現在各種カタログ製作等、準備がすゝめられています。

研究活動に必要な資料・書籍を選択、購入する担当者、購読者の側に立って、個々の必要に充分お応えする、役立つ書店として工夫、努力をかさねる方針です。

つきましては、個々の専門分野の詳細、メイルオーダーによる購入に際しての具体的要望、ご用命、ご意見等、何でも率直にお聞かせ下さるようお願い致します。お答えいただいた際には、積極的にできるだけの便宜をはからせていただきます。

恵美子 Wise

1981nen shigatsu

Shoseki Kōnyū Tantō KAKUI ONCHŪ,

Kono tabi, TŌ-shoten meiru ōdā bu de wa, Nihon kankei shuppanbutsu (wa, yō) o kōhan'i ni tori-atsukau YŌ NI NARI, genzai kakushu katarogu seisaku nado, junbi ga SUSUMERARETE IMASU.

Kenkyū katsudō ni hitsuyō na shiryō, shoseki o sentaku, kōnyū suru tantōsha, kōdokusha no gawa ni tatte, ko-ko no hitsuyō ni jūbun O-KOTAE SURU, yaku-datsu shoten to shite kufū, doryoku o kasaneru hōshin desu.

TSUKIMASHITE WA, ko-ko no senmon bun'ya no shōsai, meiru ōdā ni yoru kōnyū ni saishite no gutai-teki yōbō, go-yōmei, go-iken nado, nan de mo sotchoku ni O-KIKASE KUDASARU YŌ O-NEGAI ITASHIMASU. O-KOTAE ITADAITA sai ni wa, sekkyoku-teki ni dekiru dake no bengi o HAKARASETE ITADAKIMASU.

Emiko Wise

Notes

a. KAKUI ONCHŪ Both are respectful words, *kakui* referring particularly to a number of individuals (cf. colloquial *mina-sama*), and *onchū* collectively to the members of a company or other organization, like the English "Messrs." The character for the *i* of *kakui* is 位 in printed form.

b. TŌ- Means "this (present)" or "the . . . in question," thus, here = "this/our (bookshop)."

c. YŌ NI NARI The phrase *yō ni naru* means literally "become so that, turn out in such a way that," and hence "come about that." Grammatically, *nari* is the verb-stem (i.e. the form which takes *-masu*, etc., and always ends in either *-i* or *-e*), and when this form occurs at the end of a clause, the absence of an ending means that the verb is left in suspense and can therefore be said to be in the "suspensive form." Such verbs depend for their full form (and thus for their tense and full meaning) on some following parallel verb or adjective. In this case this is *(susumerare)te imasu*, and this *nari* is therefore equivalent to *natte imasu*, "it has come about that."

d. SUSUMERARETE IMASU A passive form from *susumeru*; thus, "are being advanced."

e. O-KOTAE SURU The *o* + vb. stem *suru/itasu/mōshi-ageru* construction is a humble one used to show respect to the other person or persons concerned in the action of the verb, here the addressees. Since the *o* + vb. stem makes a verbal noun and *suru*, *itasu* and *mōshi-ageru* can all mean "do, make," the construction means literally "humbly do a . . . ing." Thus, here, "a bookshop which will (humbly) respond."

f. TSUKIMASHITE WA A polite, *-masu* form equivalent of *tsuite wa*, "in this connection."

g. O-KIKASE KUDASARU YŌ O-NEGAI ITASHIMASU *Kikase* is the stem of the verb *kikaseru*, "cause to hear, inform," used here as a verbal noun (like *o-kotae* in e. above) meaning "informing, notification"; and since *kudasaru* means "condescend," i.e., "give (from a 'superior' to an 'inferior')," *o-kikase kudasaru* means "kindly give (us) notification, kindly inform (us)." Since *yō (ni)* means "(in a) way, manner" (cf. c. above) and the *o* + vb. stem *itasu* construction is a humble one, as explained in e. above, the whole phrase means "we (humbly) request (in such a way) that you kindly inform us."

h. O-KOTAE ITADAITA The same verbal-noun form as in e. and g. above + *itadaku* = "humbly receive a . . . ing"; thus, in this case, "(when) we have received your reply." Note that, since this construction takes the standpoint of the "receiver" of the action of the verb, it is the opposite of the *o* + vb. stem *kudasaru* construction mentioned in g. above, in which the "giver" is the subject.

i. HAKARASETE ITADAKIMASU A causative form *(sa)sete* + *itadaku* "(humbly) receive" makes a very humble equivalent of the preceding verb, meaning more or less literally "receive your permission to . . . " The basic verb here being *hakaru*, "plan, aim at, strive for," the meaning is "we trust you will allow us to aim at . . . "

Translation

To All Those in Charge of Book Purchases,

The mail order department of this bookshop has now come to deal with a wide range of publications concerned with Japan, and preparations are at present under way for such things as the production of various types of catalogues.

It is our policy, by putting ourselves at the side of subscribers and those responsible for selecting and purchasing the material and books necessary for research activity, to increase our plans and efforts as a bookshop which will fully respond and be of service to your individual needs.

In this connection, we ask you to be kind enough to tell us frankly such things as the details of your individual fields of specialization, and your concrete wishes, instructions and views when making purchases by mail order, no matter what these may be. When we have received your replies, we shall strive to accommodate you in a positive way to the best of our ability.

Emiko Wise

Dear Professor Doctor O'Neill

前略、その後先生におかれましては おかわりなく おすごしのことと存じあげます。7月の1日には 御多忙の中、私のために わざわざ お時間をくだされ、御親切な御教示 まことにありがとうございました。実を申しますと先生にお逢いするまでの不安の蓄積は相当なもので、私としてこれから三ヶ月程 英国に滞在する不安で一杯でございました。先生のあたたかなおもてなしに 本当に目頭の熱くなる思いでございました。個人的な仕事はこれから先 こつこつと積み上げてゆくつもりです。下宿住いにもようやく慣れ、日本に居た時と同じ生活のパターンがもどりつつあります。

その後まだ ロンドン大学には 行っていないのですが、来週早々にも 図書室入室許可をもらいに 行こうと考えております。ロンドン大学、大英図書館、ケンブリッジ大学 この三ヶ所で 仕事をするつもりでいますが、その計画は目下考慮中です。先生にお目にかかれる 又の日を楽しみにしております。とり急ぎ お礼の言葉をおくらせていただきました。御健勝におすごし下さい。 敬具

加藤 裕一

Dear Professor Doctor O'Neill,

ZENRYAKU. Sono go sensei NI OKAREMASHITE WA o-kawari naku o-sugoshi no koto to ZONJI-AGEMASU. Shichigatsu no tsuitachi ni wa go-tabō no naka, watakushi no tame ni waza-waza o-jikan o KUDASARE, go-shinsetsu na go-kyōji makoto ni arigatō GOZAIMASHITA. Jitsu o MŌSHIMASU to, sensei ni o-ai suru made no fuan no chikuseki wa sōtō na mono DE, watakushi to shite kore kara sankagetsu hodo Eikoku ni taizai suru fuan de ippai DE GOZAIMASHITA. Sensei no atataka na o-motenashi ni hontō ni megashira NO atsuku naru omoi de gozaimashita. Kojin-teki na shigoto wa kore kara saki kotsu-kotsu to tsumi-agete yuku tsumori desu. Geshuku-zumai ni mo yōyaku NARE, Nihon ni ita toki to onaji seikatsu no patān ga modori-TSUTSU arimasu.

Sono go mada Rondon Daigaku ni wa itte inai no desu ga, raishū sō-sō ni mo toshoshi-tsu nyūshitsu kyoka o MORAI NI IKŌ to kangaete ORIMASU. Rondon Daigaku, Dai-Ei Toshokan, Kenburijji Daigaku kono sankasho de shigoto o suru tsumori DE IMASU ga, sono keikaku wa mokka kōryo-chū desu. Sensei ni O-ME NI KAKARERU mata no hi o tanoshimi ni shite orimasu. Tori-isogi o-rei no kotoba o OKURASETE I-TADAKIMASHITA. Go-kenshō ni o-sugoshi kudasai.

KEIGU

KATŌ HIROKAZU

Notes

a. ZENRYAKU "Preliminaries omitted"; an introductory word commonly used in letters to apologize for the omission of conventional phrases about the weather, the health of the addressee, etc.

b. NI OKAREMASHITE WA A very respectful equivalent for the formal *ni oite wa*, which can itself be regarded as a weightier equivalent for the particle *wa*. Thus, "as for you, sir, . . ."

c. ZONJI-AGEMASU *Zonji-ageru* is a somewhat humbler form of *zonjiru*, which is itself a humble equivalent for *omou*, "think, feel, hope" or *shiru*, "know."

d. KUDASARE The suspensive form (see 1 c) of *kudasareru* (a formal written equivalent for *kudasaru*), which here takes its tense from the following parallel verb *gozaimashita*. Thus, "you kindly gave me." Note that *o- /go-* noun combinations such as *o-jikan* here are used like the *o-* verb stems in 1 egh to make similar respect forms with the relevant verbs.

e. GOZAIMASHITA A polite (i.e., respectful to the person addressed) equivalent for *arimashita*. When "*-i* adjectives" (as distinct from "*na* adjectives") are used before forms of *gozaimasu*, they take the long-vowel form ending in *-ō* or *-ū*, as here.

f. MŌSHIMASU A humble equivalent for *iimasu*, "say." Since a person is always more respectful to another in letters than he would be in speaking to him, it is not unusual to have a *-masu* form of a verb in a non-final position, as here, instead of (*Jitsu o*) *mōsu/iu to* (see also 1f).

g. DE The suspensive form (or sometimes, in other contexts, the *-te* form) of *da/desu*. The following parallel verb here is *de gozaimashita* (= *deshita*: see h. below), and the meaning of *de* here is therefore "was . . . and . . ."

h. DE GOZAIMASHITA Since *gozaimashita* is a polite equivalent for *arimashita* (see e. above), *de gozaimasu/gozaimashita* = *de arimasu/arimashita* = *desu/deshita*.

i. NO Here = *ga*: when a phrase consisting of subject + verb or adjective is used attributively before a noun (here *megashira* + *atsuku naru*, describing *omoi*), the subject can be followed by either *no* or *ga*. Thus, "my feelings (which) become moved (to tears), I am deeply moved."

j. NARE The suspensive form of *nareru*, "become accustomed (to)," parallel here to *modori(-tsutsu arimasu)*. Since *-tsutsu arimasu* (see k. below) therefore applies to both verbs, the meaning of *nare* here is "I am (in the process of) getting used (to) . . . and . . ."

k. -TSUTSU A suffix used in the written language, with a form of the verb *aru* where appropriate, with the meaning "while, (be) in the process of . . .ing."

l. MORAI NI IKŌ A verb stem + *ni* + verb of motion = "(go/come) in order to . . ."

Morau, "receive," is a less humble equivalent of *itadaku*, and is used here because the impersonal context does not require great humility.
m. ORIMASU A humble equivalent for *imasu*, "be, be present."
n. DE IMASU An equivalent for *desu*, used after certain nouns when the subject is animate. Earlier in this letter *tsumori desu* is used, but it is common to meet *tsumori de iru*, "be in a mind to . . ."
o. O-ME NI KAKARERU The potential form of *o-me ni kakaru*, which is a humble equivalent of *au*, "meet (a person)." Thus, "(when) I can meet you."
p. OKURASETE ITADAKIMASHITA "I have taken it that you will allow me to send, I respectfully send you"; cf. 1i.
q. KEIGU A respectful concluding word in letters: "Yours truly/respectfully."
r. KATŌ HIROKAZU The readings of Japanese names can be very difficult to determine, because each character usually has a number of possible readings and the one used in any particular case is often uncertain, depending as it does on the individual person, place, etc. The problem is especially acute with personal, given names, since someone whose name is officially and normally read in the *kun* may on occasion prefer to use the more formal-sounding Sino-Japanese *on* reading. Here, for example, other possible readings for the given name would include Michihito, Sukekazu or, more formally, Yūichi. For a guide to name readings, see O'Neill: *Japanese Names*, Weatherhill, 1972.

Translation

Dear Professor Doctor O'Neill,

Please excuse the omission of preliminary greetings. I trust that you have been keeping well, sir, since I saw you last. On 1 July, you went out of your way to give time up for my sake when you were so busy, and I am truly grateful for your kind guidance. To tell you the truth, my apprehension before meeting you had built up into something quite considerable, and I was full of apprehension at what was to be, for me, a stay of some three months in England. I was truly very moved at the cordial reception you gave me. From now on I intend to work hard to do more and more of my personal work. I am even gradually becoming used to living in lodgings, and am getting back to the same life-style as I had when I was in Japan.

I have not yet been to London University since I saw you, but I am thinking of going there early next week to obtain my library entry permit. My idea is to work at three places—London University, the British Library, and Cambridge University—and I am at present considering my plans. I am looking forward to being able to see you another day. Meanwhile, I am taking this early opportunity to send you these words of thanks. Please keep well.

Yours respectfully,
Katō Hirokazu

3. Letter from a University Official Not Known to Addressee

各大学の視察旅行に出ますが、
貴大学には、八月三日(金)午後、参りますので、できますれば、その時、候補者と面談いたしたく存じます。
なお、貴大学に該当者無き場合には、オックスフォード大学、ケンブリッジ大学等にご照会の労をおとり下さいますなら、誠に幸甚に存じます。
ついでながら、我々は八月三日から八月六日午前九時頃まで、ロンドンのホテルに投宿いたします。
(ホテルの名は八月三日に申し上げます。)
どうぞ宜しくお願いいたします。

敬具

一九七九年 六月二十九日

四天王寺女子大学
学長 藤田清

O'Neill 先生

O'Neill 先生！

突然卑簡を差し上げますこと、お許し下さい。
私の奉職する女子大学は、日本最古の仏教寺院
四天王寺の設置する大学でございますが、
来年四月より向う三ヶ年できれば貴大学
日本語学科のDoktorandin（またはそれに類する
女の方）を英会話の講師として迎えたく存じま
すので、御紹介お願い申し上げます。
当大学には、英米文学科の他に史学科（東洋史、
日本史を含む）、日本文学科、仏教学科等があり、
日本文化を研究する人には、何かと便利に存
じます。
我々一行は、七月十七日から八月六日までヨーロッパ

O'Neill Sensei!

Totsuzen HIkan o sashi-agemasu koto, o-yurushi kudasai. Watakushi no hōshoku suru joshi daigaku wa, Nihon saiko no Bukkyō jiin Shitennōji no setchi suru daigaku de gozaimasu ga, rainen shigatsu YORI mukō sankanen dekireba KI-daigaku Nihongo gakka no Doktorandin (mata wa sore ni rui-suru onna no KATA) o Ei-kaiwa no kōshi to shite mukaeTAKU ZONJIMASU NO DE, go-shōkai O-NEGAI MŌSHI-AGEMASU.

Tō-daigaku ni wa Ei-Bei bungaku-ka no hoka ni shigaku-ka (Tōyō-shi, Nihon-shi o fukumu), Nihon bungaku-ka, Bukkyō gakka nado ga ARI, Nihon bunka o kenkyū suru hito ni wa nani-ka to BENRI NI zonjimasu.

WARE-WARE ikkō wa shichigatsu jūshichinichi kara hachigatsu muika made Yōroppa kaku-daigaku no shisatsu ryokō ni demasu ga,

KI-DAIGAKU ni wa hachigatsu mikka (KIN) gogo MAIRIMASU no de, DEKIMASUREBA, sono toki, kōhosha to mendan ITASHITAKU ZONJIMASU. Nao, ki-daigaku ni gaitōsha NAKI baai ni wa, Okkusufōdo Daigaku, Kenburijji Daigaku nado ni go-shōkai no rō o o-tori kudasaimasu NARA, makoto ni kōjin ni zonjimasu.

Tsuide-NAGARA, ware-ware wa hachigatsu mikka kara hachigatsu muika gozen ku-ji-goro made Rondon no hoteru ni tōshuku itashimasu. (Hoteru no na wa hachigatsu mikka ni MŌSHI-AGEMASU.)

DŌZO YOROSHIKU o-negai itashimasu.

Keigu

1979nen rokugatsu nijūkunichi

Shitennōji Joshi Daigaku
Gakuchō Fujita Kiyoshi

Notes

a. HI- Meaning "humble, wretched," this is used as a prefix with certain Sino-Japanese words to mean "my/our." Cf. *ki-* under c. below.

b. YORI A stiff, formal equivalent for *kara*, "from, since."

c. KI- Meaning "valuable, precious," this prefix is used with Sino-Japanese words to mean "your (university, etc.)." Cf. *hi-* under a. above.

d. KATA A respectful equivalent for *hito*, "person."

e. -TAKU ZONJIMASU *-taku* is the adverbial form of *-tai*, "want to," and *zonjiru* is a humble equivalent for *omou*, "think, feel, hope" or *shiru*, "know." This phrase therefore means the same here as the neutral-level *-tai to omoimasu*, which itself means not "I think I want to" but "I feel I want to," i.e., simply "I would like to."

f. NO DE "It being that, . . . and so."

g. O-NEGAI MŌSHI-AGEMASU "I (humbly) request"; see 1e.

h. ARI Suspensive form (see 1c) of *aru*, here parallel to *zonjimasu*.

i. BENRI NI "(We think of it) as being convenient."

j. WARE-WARE *Ware* is a formal pronoun for "I," and has the plural forms *ware-ware* and *ware-ra*.

k. KI-DAIGAKU Although this comes in the middle of a sentence, because it means "your university" it was felt more respectful to put it at the top of a new column rather than near the bottom of the previous one.

l. KIN An abbreviation for *Kin'yōbi*, "Friday."

m. MAIRIMASU *Mairu* is a humble equivalent for *kuru* or, as here, *iku*.

n. DEKIMASUREBA The *-eba* conditional form of *dekimasu*, equivalent to the neutral-level *dekireba*. On *-masu* forms in non-final positions, see 1f and 2f.

o. ITASHITAKU ZONJIMASU Being a humble equivalent for *suru*, *itasu* means "(humbly) do." This and e. above will thus show that the whole phrase is equivalent to *shitai to omoimasu*, "I would like (to hold interviews)."

p. NAKI The literary attributive ending *-ki* means that this word is equivalent to colloquial *nai* used before a noun.

q. NARA Like its alternative form *naraba*, a conditional verb form meaning "if it were/should be (that)."

r. -NAGARA Like its alternative form

-nagara mo, this is a suffix corresponding to English "while," both in the sense of "during the time that" and, as here, "although"; i.e., *tsuide-nagara* = "although it is in passing/incidental," i.e., "incidentally."

s. MŌSHI-AGEMASU Although *mōshi-ageru* is a humble equivalent for *suru* in some structures (see 1e and g. above), like *mōsu* itself it is basically a humble equivalent for the neutral-level *iu*, "say," and it is in this meaning that it is used here.

t. DŌZO YOROSHIKU Meaning respectively, "please," and "well, in a good/kindly way," these words are regularly used with a verb, to ask someone to do or say something on the speaker's behalf. (They are also used, normally on their own, to commend oneself to a senior person when meeting him for the first time.)

Translation

Dr. O'Neill!

Please forgive me for sending you this letter of mine so unexpectedly. The women's university in which I serve is a foundation of the Shitennōji, the oldest Buddhist temple in Japan, and since it would like to invite, if possible, a woman doctoral candidate from the Japanese Department of your university (or a similar kind of woman) as an instructor in English conversation for the next three years from April next year, we would like to ask you for introductions.

Apart from courses in English and American Literature, this university has courses in History (including Oriental and Japanese history), Japanese Literature, Buddhist Studies, etc., and we feel that it would be convenient in all kinds of ways for someone doing research on Japanese culture.

A group of us will be setting out on a tour of inspection of European universities from 17 July to 6 August, and since we shall be going to your university on the afternoon of (Friday) 3 August, we would if possible like to interview candidates on that occasion. Also, should there be no one applicable at your university, we would be most happy if you would take the trouble to make enquiries at Oxford, Cambridge and other universities.

Incidentally, we shall be staying in a London hotel from 3 August until about 9 a.m. on 6 August. (We shall tell you the name of the hotel on 3 August.)

We ask you for your kind help in this matter. Yours respectfully,

29 June 1979

Fujita Kiyoshi
President, Shitennōji
Women's University

Dr. O'Neill

4. First Letter from a Man Introduced by a Mutual Acquaintance

打ち合わせるのはいかがでしょうか。そのためにはお手数ながら電話番号をお知らせいただきたく存じます。いずれにしてもまだかなり日数がございますのでご都合のよい時にご一報くださるようお願い申しあげます。

ではしたしくお目にかかる日を待ち望んでおります。

草々

七月二十一日

西尾寅弥

P・G・オニール先生

Hajimete O-TAYORI O ITASHI, GO-AISATSU O MŌSHI-AGEMASU. Go-REImei wa kanete yori UKETAMAWATTE orimashita. Kono tabi wa Nomoto-san o tsūjite o-negai o mōshi-agete orimashita TOKORO, konshū ki-daigaku o o-tazune suru koto o kokoroyoku go-shōdaku itadak-i, makoto ni URESHIKU kōei ni zonjite orimasu.

KITARU jūgatsu nanuka (Kayōbi) ni Rondon-chaku no yotei DE ARIMASU ga, sono go no nittei wa mada tatete orimasen. Ni-sannichi kyūyō YA shinai kenbutsu o shite nochi ni o-tazune shitai to omotte orimasu. Tōkakan-gurai Igirisu ni TAIZAI dekimasu no de, sono koro no go-tsugō no yoi hi o go-shitei ITADAKE-MASU deshō ka. Aruiwa mada kanari saki no koto de go-tsugō mo kimaranai TO SUREBA, watakushi ga Rondon ni tsuite kara o-denwa shite hi o uchi-awaseru NO WA IKAGA

はじめてお便りをいたし、ごあいさつを申し
あげます。ご令名はかねてよりうけたまわって
おりました。このたびは野元さんを通じてお願い
を申しあげておりましたところ、今秋貴大学をお訪
ねすることを快くご承諾いただき、まことにうれしく
光栄に存じております。
来る十月七日(火曜日)にロンドン着の予定であり
ますが、その後の日程はまだ立てておりません。二、三日
休養や市内見物をして後にお訪ねしたいと思って
おります。十日間ぐらいイギリスに滞在できますので、
そのころのご都合のよい日をご指定いただけますでしょ
うか。あるいは、まだかなり先のことでご都合も決まらない
とすれば、私がロンドンに着いてからお電話して日を

deshō ka. Sono tame ni wa o-tesū-nagara denwa bangō o o-shirase itdakitaku zonjimasu. IZURE NI SHITE MO mada kanari nissū ga gozaimasu no de, go-tsugō no yoi toki ni GO-IPPŌ KUDASARU yō o-negai mōshi-agemasu.

De wa shitashiku o-me ni kakaru hi o machi-nozonde orimasu.

SŌ-SŌ

Shichigatsu nijūichinichi

Nishio Toraya

P.G. Oniiru Sensei

Notes

a. O-TAYORI ITASHI *Itashi* being the suspensive form (see 1c) of *itasu*, parallel to *mōshi-agemasu*, the meaning of the phrase here is "I make contact with you/I write a letter to you . . . and . . . "

b. GO-AISATSU O MŌSHI-AGEMASU *Mōshi-ageru* being a humble equivalent for *suru* here, this structure is the same as that in the preceding clause (see a. above), and both can be expressed as a single *o-* /*go-* noun *suru*/*itasu*/ *mōshi-ageru* construction. (Note that this same construction applies when the noun is a verb stem, as described in 1e, or when the verb is *kudasaru* or *itadaku*, as mentioned in 2d.)

c. REI- This is to be found used in a number of Sino-Japanese compound words in the sense of "your (esteemed)"; e.g., *go-reisoku*, "your son."

d. UKETAMAWATTE *Uketamawaru* is a humble verb equivalent to neutral-level *kiku* in the meaning "hear" as here, or "receive (information/orders, etc.)."

e. TOKORO As well as "place," this word can mean "point of time, stage (in a process)" as here, and "aspect, point, matter." Thus, here "when (I made a request)."

f. URESHIKU The suspensive form of true-Japanese adjectives (i.e., those of Japanese origin ending in a vowel + *i*) is the same as the adverbial *-ku* form, as here. Since it is parallel here to the immediately following *kōei ni*, the meaning is "(I feel) happy (and honoured)."

g. KITARU Note the reading of this character when it is used attributively (i.e., adjectivally) to mean "this coming . . . , the next . . . " In this use it should strictly be written 来たる.

h. DE ARIMASU A formal equivalent for *desu*; see 2h and cf. the standard colloquial negative form *de wa arimasen*.

i. YA As one of the particles meaning "and," *ya* suggests that there may be items other than those listed. (This suggestion is all the stronger when *toka* is used between items in a list, which therefore often ends with *nado*, "etc." Conversely, the use of *to* indicates that the list is complete as given.)

j. TAIZAI The character used here for *tai* is the old full form 滯 instead of modern standard 滞.

k. ITADAKEMASU Note that this is not *itadakimasu*, but from the potential form *itadakeru*. Thus, "(do you think) I could have. . . ?"

l. TO SUREBA Following a statement, conditional forms of *to suru* make it hypothetical from the basic meaning of "make/treat/consider as." Thus, *to sureba* here means "if it should be that, if we take it that."

m. NO WA IKAGA Used after a verb or adjective, *no* can mean "the one(s) who/which"; or alternatively, as here, "the fact/matter of." In this case, it simply makes a noun form: "(as for) arranging (a day)." Since *ikaga* is a polite equivalent for *dō*, "how," the meaning of the whole phrase is "how about arranging a day."

n. IZURE NI SHITE MO *Izure* here being the equivalent of *dochira* or *dore*, the meaning is "whichever way we take it, in any event."

o. GO-IPPŌ KUDASARU "To kindly send word/write to me." Note that this is part of the same *go-* /*o-* noun (*o*) *kudasaru* construction as the *o-kikase kudasaru* of 1g.

p. SŌ-SŌ "In haste." The character here is the most common one used to write this concluding phrase in letters, and is an elegant variant for 早 *SŌ* "fast, quick."

Translation

This is my first letter to you, and with it I send you my compliments. I have heard about you for some time past, and now that you have readily agreed to my visiting your university this autumn when I asked you to do so through Mr. Nomoto, I am indeed pleased and honoured.

I expect to arrive in London (Tuesday) 7 October next, but my schedule from then on is not yet fixed. I would like to call on you after resting and sightseeing in the town for two or three days. Since I shall be able to stay in England for about ten days, do you think you could specify for me the day that would suit you best during that time? Alternatively, if it should still be too far ahead for your arrangements to be made, how would it be if I were to arrange a day with you by telephoning after I arrive in London? I am sorry to trouble you, but I would like you to let me know your telephone number in order to do this. Either way, there is still plenty of time left, so please let me know about this at your convenience.

I am, then, very much looking forward to the day when I shall meet you in person.

In haste,
Nishio Toraya

21 July
Dr. P.G. O'Neill

P. G. O'neill 先生

東京都港区芝西久保桜川町1ボ4森ビル
国際交流基金.日本語教育学会
日本語教育国際会議準備委員会
佐都栗　暁

拝啓　国際交流基金および社団法人日本語教育学会は.「日本語教育国際会議」を下記の要領で共催することになりました。つきましては 貴殿をこの会議に御招待申しあげたいと存じます. 往復旅費および滞在費は当方で負担させていただきます.

なお 御出席いただける場合には.研究発表または公開講演およびシンポジウムの講師を御引き受けいただきたいと存じます. また.研究発表.講演.シンポジウムの内容を会議後.出版いたしたいと思いますが.その際.原稿をお出しいただきたいと存じます。

また.会議用語は日本語といたします.

以上の点を御諒承の上.至急御返事くださいますようお願い申しあげます。

日本語教育国際会議

1. 期日.場所　1978年3月16日(木)～3月20日(月)
東京および大阪.

2. プログラム.　研究発表,シンポジウム.公開講演など

敬具.

P.G. O'Neill Sensei

Tōkyō-to Minato-ku Shiba Nishikubo Sakuragawa-machi 1
DAI-yon Mori Biru
KOKUSAI KŌRYŪ KIKIN, Nihongo Kyōiku Gakkai
Nihongo Kyōiku Kokusai Kaigi Junbi Iinkai
Nitoguri Akira

HAIKEI. Kokusai Kōryū Kikin oyobi Shadan Hōjin Nihongo Kyōiku Gakkai wa, "Nihongo Kyōiku Kokusai Kaigi" o kaki no yōryō de kyōsai suru KOTO NI NARIMASHITA. Tsukimashite wa, KIDEN o kono kaigi ni go-shōtai mōshi-age-tai to zonjimasu. Ōfuku ryohi oyobi taizai-hi wa tōhō de futan sasete itadakimasu.

Nao, go-shusseki itadakeru baai ni wa, kenkyū happyō mata wa kōkai kōen oyobi shinpojiumu no kōshi o o-hiki-uke itadakitai to zonjimasu. Mata, kenkyū happyō, kōen, shinpojiumu no naiyō o kaigi-go, shuppan itashitai to omoimasu ga, sono sai genkō o o-dashi itadakitai to zonjimasu.

Mata, kaigi yōgo wa Nihongo to itashimasu.

Ijō no ten o go-ryōshō no UE, shikyū go-henji kudasaimasu yō o-negai mōshiagemasu.

Nihongo Kyōiku Kokusai Kaigi

1. Kijitsu, Basho 1978nen sangatsu jūrokunichi (Moku)—sangatsu hatsuka (Getsu). Tōkyō oyobi Ōsaka.
2. Puroguramu Kenkyū happyō, shinpojiumu, kōkai kōen nado.

Keigu

Notes

a. DAI- The character 才 used here is an abbreviation for 第. It is common in handwriting, and is found occasionally even in print.
b. KOKUSAI KŌRYŪ KIKIN Literally "The International Exchange Foundation," the official English name is "The Japan Foundation."
c. HAIKEI A formal introductory word in letters; "Respectfully."
d. KOTO NI NARIMASHITA *Koto ni naru* means "come about that, turn out that." It thus has much the same meaning as *yō ni naru* (see 1c) but gives a more specific and definite impression.
e. KIDEN A man's word for "you," used in letters to show respect to another man.
f. UE Here means "after, following."

Translation

P.G. O'Neill

Organizing Committee of the International Conference on Japanese-language Education
The Japan Foundation, The Society for Japanese-language Education, Inc.
No. 4 Mori Building, 1 Sakuragawa-machi, Shiba Nishikubo, Minato-ku, Tokyo
Nitoguri Akira

Respectfully,

The Japan Foundation and the Society for Japanese-language Education, Inc. will jointly hold an "International Conference on Japanese-language Education" along the lines noted below. In this connection, we should like to invite you to this conference. We on our side will bear the cost of return travel and your stay here.

Furthermore, should we be able to have you attend, we would like you to undertake a presentation of your research or a public lecture, together with speaking at a symposium. Also, we would like to publish after the conference the research presentations, the public lectures, and the content of the symposium, and at that time we would like you to produce your manuscript.

Also, we shall make Japanese the language to be used in the conference.

We ask you to give your reply with the utmost urgency following your appreciation of the points above.

The International Conference on Japanese-language Education

1. Time, Place (Thurs.) 16 March 1978—(Mon.) 20 March. Tokyo and Osaka.
2. Programme Research presentations, symposium, public lectures, etc.

Yours truly

6. Letter from a Middle-aged Man after a Brief Acquaintance

大いに成果が上ったと思います。昨夜江藤淳氏に電話で話をして、ロンドン大学の雰囲気を伝えておきました。

また近い将来どこかでお目にかかりたいと思いますが、どうかお元気でお過しになるよう念じております。

ダン、ストロング両先生をはじめ、日本文学研究室の皆様に宜しくお伝え下さい。もし日本へおいでになることがあれば、ぜひ御一報下さいますようお願い致します。

敬具

二月六日

感謝をこめて

入江隆則

パトリック・オニール先生

Haikei.

O-genki desu ka. Rondon taizai-chū wa taihen SHINSETSU NI SHITE ITADAK-I, makoto ni arigatō gozaimashita. Nihon e kaette kara, kazoku o tsurete Izu no hō e hoyō ni IKI, KINŌ yatto moto no sumai e ochitsuita tokoro desu. Rondon Daigaku de no seminā wa taihen TANOSHIKU, mata SHINKEN DE kōdo na kenkyū ga NASARETE IRU no o SHIRI, ŌI NI URU TOKORO ga arimashita. Toshokan o TSUKAWASETE ITADAITA no mo taihen benri DE, kokoro kara kansha mōshi-agemasu. Sara ni saigo ni HIRAITE itadaita pāti wa, watashi no kokoro ni yoi omoide to shite nagaku nokoru NI CHIGAI ARIMASEN.

Ichigatsu ni wa Amerika de Koronbia Daigaku no Aiban Morisu-SHI ni aimashita ga, YOROSHIKU to itte ORAREMASHITA. Watakushi ga Rondon e mairimashita no wa moto-moto gendai no Igirisu o kenkyū suru tame deshita ga, KOCHIRA NO HŌ

拝啓
お元気ですか。ロンドン滞在中は大変親切にしていただき、まことにありがとうございました。日本へ帰ってから、家族をつれて伊豆の方へ保養に行き昨日やっともとの住居へ落ち着いたところです。
ロンドン大学でのセミナーは大変楽しく、また真剣で高度な研究が為されているのを知り、大いに得るところがありました。図書館を使わせていただいたのも大変便利で心から感謝申し上げます。さらに最後に開いていただいたパーティは、私の心によい思い出として長く残るに違いありません。
一月にはアメリカでコロンビア大学のアイバン・モリス氏に会いましたが、宜しくと云っておられました。
私がロンドンへ参りましたのは、もともと現代のイギリスを研究するためでしたが、こちらの方も

MO ōi ni seika ga agatta to omoimasu. Yūbe Etō Jun-shi ni denwa de hanashi o shite, Rondon Daigaku no fun'iki o tsutaeTE OKIMASHITA.

Mata chikai SHŌRAI doko-ka de o-me ni kakaritai to omoimasu ga, DŌKA o-genki de O-SUGOSHI NI NARU yō nenjite orimasu.

Dan, Sutorongu ryō-sensei O HAJIME, Nihon Bungaku Kenkyūshitsu no mina-sama ni yoroshiku o-tsutae kudasai. MOSHI Nihon e OIDE NI NARU koto ga areba, zehi go-ippō kudasaimasu yō o-negai itashimasu.

Keigu

Nigatsu muika
Kansha o komete

Irie Takanori

Patorikku Oniiru Sensei

a. SHINSETSU NI SHITE ITADAKI The *-te itadaku* construction, literally "(humbly) receive a . . .ing," is used when someone kindly does something for the speaker (cf. *(sa)sete itadaku*, explained under 1i, which is used when the speaker is "kindly allowed" to do something). Since *shinsetsu ni shite* means "doing (things) in a kind way" and *itadaki* is a suspensive form parallel to *gozaimashita*, the whole phrase means "you were good enough to treat me kindly and . . ."

b. IKI A suspensive form, parallel here to *ochitsuita*. Since both words qualify *tokoro*, "point of time, stage" (see 4e), the meaning is "I am at the stage where I went . . . and settled down . . ."

c. KINŌ The characters used also have the more formal Sino-Japanese reading *sakujitsu*, which would have been more appropriate in a stiffer style. (Similarly, the characters 昨夜 occurring in the second paragraph with the reading *yūbe* also have the more formal reading *sakuya*.)

d. TANOSHIKU The suspensive form of *tanoshii* (see 4f), parallel here to *arimashita* and therefore equal to *tanoshikatta* in a separate sentence. Thus, " . . . was/were enjoyable and . . ."

e. SHINKEN DE The suspensive form of "*na* adjectives" is the first word + *de*, as here. Since *shinken de* is parallel to the following verbal (*kōdo*) *na*, the meaning is "(research) which is serious and (high-level)." Also, the character 眞 used here for *shin* is the old form of modern standard 真 (see App. II, Table I).

f. NASARETE IRU A passive form of *nasu*, which is a literary equivalent for *suru*, "do," or *okonau*, "carry out"; hence, "is being done/carried out."

g. SHIRI Like *tanoshiku*, a suspensive form parallel to *arimashita*.

h. ŌI NI URU TOKORO Literally, "points/matters where I gain greatly," i.e., "(matters of) considerable benefit."

i. TSUKAWASETE ITADAITA *Tsukawasete* being a causative form from *tsukau*, "use," the meaning is "(the fact that) you were kind enough to allow me to use"; see 1i.

j. DE Either the suspensive form or the *-te* form of *da/desu/na* (see 2g and e. above). Strictly speaking, there are thus two alternative interpretations: since the suspensive is normally only a written form and is correctly used when there is no strong causal connection with the following part of the sentence, the first would be "it is/was convenient and I thank you"; and since the *-te* form, when correctly used in written Japanese, suggests a strong connection with what follows, like the English *-ing* ending, the other would be "it being/having been convenient, I thank you." (Note that, in spoken Japanese, the *-te* form is normally used to cover both these cases and so its connection with what follows can vary greatly.)

k. HIRAITE In handwriting, the gate element 門 (radical 169) is often abbreviated to 门 or something similar, as here in the character 開.

l. NI CHIGAI ARIMASEN Literally, "there is no difference from," i.e., "there is no doubt that, (it) will surely/certainly."

m. -SHI An honorific suffix, a formal written equivalent for *-sama/-san*.

n. YOROSHIKU When a verb signifying "say, tell, pass on," etc., is used or, as here, merely understood after *yoroshiku*, the meaning is "(speak, etc.) well for me" (see 3t); i.e., "give my best wishes/regards (to) . . ."

o. ORAREMASHITA The combination of a humble verb (here *oru* = neutral-level *iru*, "be") with an honorific passive/potential ending (*-(ra)reru*) is used when the speaker wishes to express respect for both the third person, the subject of the verb, and the person he is addressing: the use of the humble verb indicates respect for the person addressed, and the honorific ending shows respect for the third person. The phrase here thus = *(itte) imashita*. The only other verbs commonly used in this way are *mōsareru*, "(he) says," and *mairareru*, "(he) goes/comes."

p. KOCHIRA NO HŌ MO "On this side too," i.e., "in this respect also."

q. -TE OKIMASHITA As well as the literal meaning of "(do something) and leave it," the *-te oku* construction can mean "do something beforehand (in preparation for some future use)." Here the implication is that what the writer told Mr. Etō was for his future reference.

r. SHŌRAI The form used here for the character *rai* is a variant of the modern standard 来.

s. DŌKA = *dōzo*, "please."

t. O-SUGOSHI NI NARU The *o* + vb. stem *ni naru* (or *nasaru*) construction is an honorific one and therefore shows respect for the subject of the verb. It is thus equivalent here to the neutral-level *sugosu*, "spend one's time, go along in life," and is comparable to the humble *o* + vb. stem *suru/itasu/mōshi-ageru* construction explained under 1eg.

u. O HAJIME Also sometimes simply . . . *hajime*, this means "beginning with . . ." or, more naturally, ". . . and also . . ."

v. MOSHI Usually, *moshi* introduces and strengthens a conditional verb or adjective (here *areba*) with the meaning "if (it should be that . . .)"; but occasionally it is found used with such words as *toki*, *baai* in a similar meaning: "if there should be a time when/case in which . . ."

w. OIDE NI NARU Like *irassharu*, an honorific equivalent for *iru*, *iku* or, as here, *kuru*. (In origin, it is the standard *o* + vb. stem *ni naru* honorific construction mentioned in t. above.)

Translation

Respectfully,

How are you keeping? I am truly grateful for the kindness you showed me while I was staying in London. After returning to Japan, I went to Izu for a rest, taking my family with me, and finally settled down yesterday in my own home. The seminars at London University were very enjoyable. I also learned that serious and high-level research is being carried on there, and I benefited a great deal. It was also very convenient to have been allowed to use the library, and I thank you sincerely for this. Furthermore, the party which you gave at the end will certainly remain with me for a long time as a happy memory.

In January in America I met Mr. Ivan Morris of Columbia University, and he asked to be remembered to you. My visit to London was basically for the sake of doing research into present-day England, and I feel that in this direction too I achieved a great deal. Last night I spoke to Mr. Etō Jun on the telephone and advised him of things in general at London University.

I hope to meet you again somewhere in the near future, and trust that you will continue to go along in good health.

Please pass on my good wishes to Drs. Dunn and Strong, and also to everyone in the Japanese Literature Research Section. If you should come to Japan, do please be sure to send me word.

Yours truly,
Irie Takanori

6 February
With grateful thanks
Dr. Patrick O'Neill

7. Letter from the Married Daughter of Old Family Friends

早速に　ご親切に　お手紙を　頂き
感激しております。　本当に有難うございました。
皆様　お元気そうで　何よりと　存じます。
母や祖母も　喜んでおります。
今日は　桃の節句　‥‥　うちの店でも
おひなさま用の　特別の　お菓子を　作りました。
最近　だんだん　日本古来の　行事の　影が
薄くなりつつありますが、　大切にしたい
ものです。　伝統や　慣習は、「それに
縛られるもの」では　なく　「それを楽しむ
もの」であるはずで、私は時々　その驚くべき
合理性に　目を　見はらされます。　もっとも
こんな　悠長な　事を　言ってはいられない
時が　くるかも　しれませんね。
梅や桃の花が　ほころぶのを見て
春の　訪れを　感じるかと　思うと　翌日は
雪，　といった　具合に　ちっとも　気候
が　定まりませんが　これこそが　春の入り
なのでしょうか。
黒崎さんの方には　私からも　手紙を
出して　Pat の　御助言を　伝えますが、
もし　何か　言ってきたら　どうぞよろしく　お願い
致します。　大学のしくみについては　私も
お手紙で　わかりました。
これから　祖母が　遊びにきます。

先日は　お誕生日のお祝いを　上野もの
母の所で，竹田様はじめ　数人のお友達を
お招きして致しました。　前，よく　代田の
二階で　天ぷら屋さんをよんで　お祝い
をしたのを　おもいだします。
　私の方は　もっか春休みですが，4月から
また学校が忙しくなります。　赤ちゃんが
産まれても　学校は休みたくないと思って
いるのですが，　何しろ経験がないので
どうなるのか　見当もつきません。丁度
7月から　9月まで　夏休みなので　運が
良かったと思っています。「休学」は避け
たいのですが・・・。母が「おばあちゃん」
では気の毒みたい。でも，Diana, Pat
も　うかうかしているうちに　すぐ「おばあ
ちゃん」「おじいちゃん」になってしまう
かもしれませんよ。

　それでは　また．
　　　　　'80年　3月3日
　　　　　　　　　　　　由紀子

Sassoku ni go-shinsetsu ni o-tegami o itadak-i kangeki shite orimasu. Hontō ni arigatō gozaimashita. Mina-sama o-genki-SŌ de NANI-YORI to zonjimasu. Haha ya sobo mo yorokonde orimasu.

Kyō wa momo no sekku.... UCHI NO mise de mo o-hinasama-yō no tokubetsu no o-kashi o tsukurimashita. Saikin dan-dan Nihon korai no gyōji no kage ga usuku nari-tsu-tsu arimasu ga, taisetsu ni shitai mono desu. Dentō ya kanshū wa, "Sore ni shibarareru mono" de wa naku "Sore o tanoshimu mono" DE ARU hazu de, watakushi wa toki-doki sono odoroku-BEKI gōri-sei ni ME O MI-HARASAREMASU. Mottomo KON-NA YŪCHŌ NA KOTO O ITTE WA IRARENAI toki ga kuru KA MO SHIREMASEN ne.

Ume ya momo no hana ga HOKOROBU no o mite haru no otozure o kanjiru KA TO OMOU TO, yokujitsu wa yuki, to itta guai ni chitto mo kikō ga sadamarimasen ga, kore KOSO ga haru no iri na no deshō ka.

Kurosaki-san no hō ni wa watakushi kara mo tegami o dashite Pat no go-jogen o tsutaemasu ga, moshi nani-ka itte KITARA dōzo yoroshiku o-negai itashimasu. Daigaku no shikumi ni tsuite wa watakushi mo o-tegami de wakarimashita.

Kore kara sobo ga asobi ni kimasu. Senjitsu wa o-tanjōbi no O-IWAI O Kaminoge no haha no tokoro de, Takeda-sama hajime sūnin no o-tomodachi o o-maneki shite itashimashita. Mae, yoku Daita no nikai de tenpuraya-san o yonde o-iwai o shita no o omoi-dashimasu.

Watakushi no hō wa mokka haru-yasumi desu ga, shigatsu kara mata gakkō ga isogashiku narimasu. Aka-chan ga umarete mo gakkō wa yasumitaku nai to omotte iru no desu ga, nani-shiro keiken ga nai no de dō naru NO KA kentō mo tsukimasen. Chōdo shichigatsu kara kugatsu made natsu-yasumi NA NO DE un ga yokatta to omotte i-masu. "Kyūgaku" wa saketai no desu ga . . . Haha ga "o-bā-chan" de wa ki-no-doku mitai. De mo, Diana, Pat mo uka-uka shite iru uchi ni sugu "o-bā-chan" "o-jii-chan" ni NATTE SHIMAU ka mo shiremasen yo.

Sore de wa mata.

'80nen sangatsu mikka

Yukiko

Notes

a. -SŌ This suffix means "looking (like), seeming (to be)," and is added to the stems of verbs and *-i* type adjectives (e.g., *naki-sō*, "look like crying," *taka-sō*, "expensive-looking") or, as here, to words used as *na*-type adjectives.
b. NANI-YORI ="(better/more) than anything." Thus, here, "I feel it (to be) better than anything that. . . , I am truly delighted that . . ."
c. UCHI NO "My/our (own)."
d. DE ARU A written or formal equivalent to *desu*, it is used here to link two nouns, *mono* and *hazu*, "likelihood, obligation."
e. -BEKI An attributive suffix meaning "which can/should/will/might"; thus, *odoroku-beki* = "at which one will (etc.) be surprised" or, simply, "surprising."
f. ME O MI-HARASAREMASU The basic phrase is *me o mi-haru* "stretch/open wide one's eyes (in astonishment, etc.)." The *-sareru* form used here is a passive of the causative (i.e., "be made/allowed to . . ."), and thus gives the meaning "I am made to stare, I cannot help staring."
g. KONNA YŪCHŌ NA KOTO O ITTE WA IRARENAI Meaning "I cannot go on saying such leisurely/relaxed things as this," the phrase is sometimes used more generally to mean "I cannot go on wasting time like this, I have no time to lose." N.B. *-te (wa) irarenai*, "(I) cannot go on . . .ing."
h. KA MO SHIREMASEN Literally, "it is not even known whether . . . ," thus, "it may be that . . ."

i. HOKOROBU = *hokorobiru,* "(flowers) break into bloom."
j. KA TO OMOU TO "When one wonders whether . . . ," usually, as here, in the sense of "No sooner does one think . . . (than . . .)."
k. KOSO The most emphatic particle in Japanese, with the force of "It is *this* that . . ."
l. KITARA Literally, "if she should come to you (saying . . .)." The *-tara* form of verbs and adjectives is either more hypothetical than other conditionals, as here, or is used in a past sense: "if one had (come, etc.)."
m. O-IWAI O This is the object of the final verb of the sentence *itashimashita;* hence, "we held a celebration (at . . . by inviting . . .)."
n. NO KA An interrogative often used at the end of a subordinate clause, as here, for euphony.
o. NA NO DE The *na* is verbal, meaning "who/which is" as in the *na*-type adjectives and is in some respects comparable to *da/desu/de aru;* and *no de* ≐ "it being that, and so." Thus, "since it is."
p. NATTE SHIMAU The use of *shimau* after a *-te* form gives a feeling of finality to the preceding verb and can sometimes be translated, if at all, by "utterly, completely, . . . and that was the end of it," etc.

Translation

I appreciate very deeply having received your kind letter so promptly. Thank you very much indeed. I am delighted that you all seem to be well. My mother and grandmother are also pleased at this.

Today is the Peach Festival.... In our shop, as elsewhere (= *de mo*), we have made special cakes for use in this Dolls' Festival. Recently Japan's ancient ceremonies have been gradually fading away, but they are things I would like to cherish. Traditions and customs should be things to enjoy and not to be bound by, and I am sometimes amazed at the surprising logic in them. Of course, the time may come when I shan't be able to take such a relaxed view of things.

No sooner do I see the plum and peach blossoms beginning to break and feel that spring is coming than the next day brings snow—with things being like that, the weather is not at all settled, but perhaps that is just how the beginning of spring is.

I too will send a letter to Miss Kurosaki and pass on your advice, but I would like to ask you to help her if she should contact you. I myself understood about the structure of the university from your letter.

Grandmother is now going to pay us a visit. The other day we celebrated her birthday at my mother's place at Kaminoge by inviting Mrs. Takeda and a number of other friends. I often recall how, in earlier times, we used to celebrate it on the upper floor at Daita by bringing in a *tenpura* man.

I for my part have a spring holiday at present, but will become busy with school again from April. I feel that I don't want to take time off from school even when the baby is born but, after all, I have no experience and so I can't even guess how things will turn out. From July to September is exactly the summer holiday, so I feel I've been lucky. I want to avoid taking "university leave" but. . . . It seems a shame that my mother will be "Granny." Still, you and Diana too may suddenly end up as "Granny" and "Grandad" before you realise what is happening, you know.

Well, then, until I write again.

3 March 1980

Yukiko

8. Letter from the Wife of a New Teacher Coming from Japan

大人二人でございましたら全く不安がないのでございますが子供がおりますと可能な限り良い教育環境においてやりたいと思いますし又病気その他の突発事故でお金が要ることが多いと思われます。又お金のためだけでなく英国を知ると云う目的のためにも家にだけとじこもっていることはよくないと思われますのでお忙がしい先生に個人的な御願いをして大変恐縮でございますがどうかよろしく御配慮下さいませ

右御願いまで　敬具

一月十八日

吉平陽子

オニール先生

Zenryaku gomen kudasaiMASE.

Kono tabi wa shujin no to-Ei no koto ni tsukimashite sensei o hajime mina-sama no go-shinsetsu na o-kokorozukai NI AZUKAR-I, hontō ni ARIGATAKU kansha shite orimasu. SAKUJITSU Owada Sensei kara jissai no go-TAIKEN o kuwashiku kaita o-tegami o itadakimashita. Sore ni yorimasu to, ikkagetsu no seikatsu-hi ga watakushi-DOMO no futari no kodomo no kyōiku-hi sono ta o iremasu to, kanari kakaru YŌ NI OMOWAREMASU. Sore de watakushi mo nani-ka pāto-taimu no shigoto o SASETE ITADAKE-TARA, taihen shiawase to zonjimasu. Izen ni Dan Sensei ni mo kono koto ni tsuite o-negai mōshi-ageta koto ga gozaimasu ga, kono sai mō ichido Oniiru Sensei ni mo o-negai shitaku zonjimasu. Watakushi no shokureki wa kyōin de gozaimasu ga, tosho no seiri de mo nan de mo YATTE MI-TAKU omoimasu. (Dekireba gakunai no shigoto DE) sensei ga watakushi ni mo deki-sō da to o-kangae ni naru koto ga arimashitara, dōzo yarase-TE KUDASAImase.

前略ごめん下さいませ。
このたびは主人の渡英のことにつきまして先生をはじめ皆様の御親切な御心づかいにあづかり本当にありがたく感謝しております。昨日小和田先生から実際の御体験をくわしく書いたお手紙をいただきました。それによりますと一ケ月の生活費が私共の二人の子供の教育費その他を入れますとかなりかかるように思われます。それで私も何かパートタイムの仕事をさせていただけたら大変しあわせと存じます。以前にダニー先生にもこのことについて御願い申し上げたことがございますが、この際もう一度オニール先生にも御願いしたく存じます。私の職業は教員でございますが、図書の整理でも何でもやってみたく思います。(出来れば学内の仕事で)先生が私にも出来そうだとお考えになることがありましたらどうぞやらせて下さいませ。

Otona futari de gozaimashitara, mattaku fuan ga nai no de gozaimasu ga, kodomo ga orimasu to kanō na kagiri yoi kyōiku kankyō ni OITE YARITAI to omoimasu SHI, mata byōki sono ta no toppatsu jiko de o-kane ga iru koto ga ōi to omowaremasu. Mata o-kane no tame dake de naku, Eikoku o shiru to iu mokuteki no tame ni mo uchi ni dake toji-komotte iru koto wa yoku nai to omowaremasu no de.

O-isogashii sensei ni kojin-teki na o-negai o shite taihen kyōshuku de gozaimasu ga, dōka yoroshiku go-hairyo kudasaimase.

Migi o-negai MADE

Keigu

Ichigatsu jūhachinichi

Yoshihira Yōko

Oniiru Sensei

Notes

a. -MASE An imperative form of the polite ending *-masu*.

b. NI AZUKARI In expressions referring to another's kindness, etc., *ni azukaru* means "partake in," i.e., "be given, receive, enjoy." Note that, in the *kana* spelling, the writer uses the traditionally correct づ for *zu*, instead of the modern standard ず.

c. ARIGATAKU The adverbial form of *arigatai*, meaning "thankfully, with gratitude." (Incidentally, *arigatō*, "thank you," is a contraction of this form.)

d. SAKUJITSU The more formal, *on* reading of the characters, which also have the more colloquial reading *kinō*; cf. 6c.

e. TAIKEN The character used here for *-ken* is the old full form for modern standard 験. (Conversely, the form 厂 used in l.12 for the *reki* of *shokureki*, "professional career" is an abbreviation for 歴.)

f. -DOMO Usually, as here, a humble plural suffix, it is occasionally used to mean rather "(I) and the likes of (me), people such as (I)."

g. YŌ NI OMOWAREMASU The passive/potential form *omowareru* means "get the feeling, cannot help feeling" and, with *yō ni*, "in (such) a way," gives the meaning "(I) cannot help feeling that."

h. SASETE ITADAKETARA "If I could receive your allowing me to do," i.e., "If I could be allowed to do, if you could allow me to do." On *sasete itadaku*, see 1i; on *itadakeru*, 4k; and on *-tara*, 7l.

i. YATTE MITAKU The *-te miru* construction means either literally "do something and see/look" or, more commonly, "do something and see what happens," i.e., "try doing something."

j. DE Here the suspensive form (see 1c) of *da/desu* (see 2g), parallel to (*o-kangae ni*) *naru*. Since both verbs qualify *koto*, the meaning is "things which are work . . . and which you think . . ."

k. -TE KUDASAI Since *kudasaru* means "condescend" (see 1g), the *-te kudasaru* construction can be understood as meaning "condescend by . . .ing," i.e., "be kind enough to/kindly . . . " Thus, since it is here used with a causative, *yarasete kudasaimase* means "kindly/please allow me to do it."

l. OITE YARITAI The *-te yaru* construction is a less respectful equivalent to *-te ageru*, "do something for someone else," and is used here because the writer is talking about her own children to an outsider. Thus, "I would like to put them..."

m. SHI A conjunction meaning "and (what is more)."

n. MADE Equivalent here to *to shite*, "as"; thus, "(I send this) as a request." The alternative form *made ni* is also found sometimes.

Translation

Please excuse the omission of preliminary greetings.

Now that my husband is to go to England, in this connection I express here my truly grateful appreciation of the kind consideration we have enjoyed from you and everyone concerned. Yesterday we received from Dr. Owada a letter in which he wrote in detail about his own practical experience. According to this, I cannot help feeling that our monthly living expenses will come to a considerable amount, if we include the education and other expenses for our two children. I would therefore feel very happy if I too could be allowed to do some part-time work. I have previously also asked Dr. Dunn about this matter, but I should like on this occasion to make another request to you, Dr. O'Neill. My professional career is as a teacher, but I would be willing to try my hand at sorting books or anything else. If there should be something which you think looks as if it could be done by me (and which, if possible, is within the university), do please allow me to do it.

If we were just two adults, there would be absolutely no concern on our part, but when there are children one would like to put them in as good an educational environment as possible, and one cannot help feeling also that there will be many cases when we shall need money because of illness or other unforeseen circumstances. Also, it is not simply because of the money, but because I cannot help feeling that, for the sake of my aim to learn about England too, it would not be good just to shut myself up at home.

I am very reluctant to make this personal request of you when you are so busy, but do please give it your kind consideration.

I send you this request,

Respectfully,

18 January

Yoshihira Yōko

Dr. O'Neill

9. Letter from a Visitor after His Return to Japan

拝啓　日本はすっかり秋になって、空が澄んで美しくなってまいりました。

先生はお元気のことと拝察いたします。私の方は、先生にごあいさつする機会もないままに帰国いたしてしまいました。ご無礼をお許し下さい。夏のヨーロッパとイギリスの旅を楽しみましたが、ロンドン大学の方へはあまり足を向けないままに終ってしまいました。しかし、先生にお逢いできてとても幸でございました。おいそがしいところをありがとうございました。

ジパニーズセクションの他の先生方とBAWDEN先生にもよろしくお伝え下さるようお願い申上げます。

それでは先生のご健勝をお祈り申上げます。

頓首再拝

昭和五十四年十月十日　中川幸廣

オニール先生　玉案下

Haikei. Nihon wa sukkari aki ni natte, sora ga sunde utsukushiku natte mairimashita.

Sensei wa o-genki no koto to HAIsatsu itashimasu. Watakushi no hō wa sensei ni go-aisatsu suru kikai mo nai mama ni kikoku itashite shimaimashita. Go-burei o o-yurushi kudasai. Natsu no Yōroppa to Igirisu no tabi o tanoshimimashita ga, Rondon Daigaku no hō e wa amari ashi o mukenai mama ni owatte shimaimashita. Shikashi, sensei ni o-ai dekite totemo saiwai de gozaimashita. O-isogashii tokoro o arigatō gozaimashita.

Jipaniizu Sekushon no hoka no sensei-GATA to Bawden Sensei ni mo yoroshiku o-tsutae kudasaru yō o-negai mōshi-agemasu.

Sore de wa sensei no go-kenshō o o-inori mōshi-agemasu.

TONSHU SAIHAI

Shōwa gojūyonen jūgatsu tōka

Nakagawa YukiHIRO

Oniiru Sensei GYOKUANKA

Notes

a. HAI- Meaning "worshipfully," it is used as a humble prefix; e.g., *haiken suru*, "humbly see." Thus, *haisatsu itasu* is a humble equivalent for *sassuru*, "(I humbly) presume/trust that."
b. -GATA A respectful plural suffix; cf. 8f.
c. TONSHU SAIHAI Literally, "With obeisance and my repeated respects," this is a very respectful and formal concluding phrase.
d. HIRO This character is the full, old form of 広.
e. GYOKUANKA "Below your revered desk"; a formal concluding phrase originally signifying "to be presented at your desk."

Translation

Respectfully,

Japan has become beautiful now that autumn has fully arrived and the skies are clear.

I trust that you are in good health, sir. I for my part returned to this country without having any opportunity to pay my respects to you. Please forgive my rudeness. I enjoyed my summer travels in Europe and England, but it all ended up without my making my way very much to London University. However, I was very happy to have been able to meet you, sir. Thank you for this, when you were so busy.

I ask you to be kind enough to give my regards to the other teachers in the Japanese Section and to Dr. Bawden.

With my best wishes for your good health, then.

Yours very respectfully,
Nagakawa Yukihiro

10 October 1979
Dr. O'Neill, with respect

10. Letter from an Older Man

P・G・オニール先生

五月二十二日付のお手紙を拝見いたしました。日本へおいでになりました由、お目にかかれなかったのは残念です。ロンドンで親切にしてくださった御礼を申上げたかったことです。今度おいでになる時は是非私のために時間を作ってくださいますよう、お願いいたします。

私は目下「古典俳文学全集」という、日本の俳句の全集を編修することに全力を尽くして居ります。今年の九月に第一回配本を出します。二ヶ年で全巻を刊行の予定です。私の大学の研究室で出して居ります「国文」という雑誌は、これからずっと先生にお送りいたします。次号は八月頃に刊行の予定です。劇文学の論文もたまには載るはずです。

御承知の通り日本の大学も学生騒動が起って居ります。私の大学は割合静かですが、それでも余波があり、そのために会議が多くて十分研究ができません。これは世界的傾向のようですが、困ったものです。

一層の御清安を祈ります。

敬具

一九六九年六月十五日

井本農一

P.G. Oniiru Sensei,

Gogatsu nijūninichi-zuke no o-tegami o haiken itashimashita. Nihon e oide ni narimashita YOSHI o-me ni kakarenakatta no wa zannen desu. Rondon de shinsetsu ni shite kudasatta o-rei o mōshi-agetakatta koto desu. Kondo oide ni naru toki wa, zehi watashi no tame ni jikan o tsukutte kudasaimasu yō o-negai itashimasu.

Watashi wa mokka "Koten Haibungaku Zenshū" to iu, Nihon no haiku no zenshū o henshū suru koto ni zenryoku o tsukushite orimasu. Kotoshi no kugatsu ni DAI-ikkai haihon o dashimasu. Nikanen de ZENKAN O KANKŌ NO YOTEI desu. Watashi no daigaku no kenkyūshitsu de dashite orimasu "Kokubun" to iu zasshi wa, kore kara zutto sensei ni o-okuri itashimasu. Jigō wa hachigatsu-goro ni kankō no yotei desu. Gekibungaku no ronbun mo tama ni wa noru hazu desu.

Go-shōchi no tōri Nihon no daigakû mo gakusei sōdō ga okotte orimasu. Watashi no daigaku wa wariai shizuka desu ga, sore de mo yoha ga ari, sono tame ni kaigi ga ōkute jūbun kenkyū ga dekimasen. Kore wa sekai-teki keikō no YŌ desu ga, komatta mono desu.

Issō no go-seian o inorimasu.

Keigu

Imoto Nōichi

1969nen rokugatsu jūgonichi

Notes

a. YOSHI Here means "hearing/having heard that, it being said that," as an extension of one of its basic meanings "news, fact, matter."

b. DAI- On this form of the character, see 5a.

c. ZENKAN O KANKŌ NO YOTEI Grammatically there is no verb expressed for the accusative particle *o* to go with, but the phrase can be regarded as a variant for *zenkan o kankō suru yotei*.

d. YŌ DESU When *yō da/desu*, etc., follow the final form of a verb or adjective or, as here, a noun + *no*, the meaning is "general appearances are that . . . , it seems that . . ."

Translation

Dr. P.G. O'Neill,

I have seen your letter dated 22 May. Hearing that you have been to Japan, I am disappointed that I was not able to see you. I wanted to repay the kindness you showed me in London. I do ask you to be good enough to make time for me without fail when you next come here.

11. Letter from a Younger Colleague on His Return to Japan

この三年間余り、言葉に尽くせない御親切にあずかりありがとうございました。本当に楽しい滞英生活でした。又、いろいろ学ぶことが多かったですが、これも全て、いい同僚にかこまれて働くことができたおかげです。幾重にもくりかえし、御礼申しあげます。

今日はとりいそぎ御礼のみ記しました。奥様にどうかよろしくお伝え下さい。又 諸先生方にも何とぞよろしく願いあげます。

さようなら

四月二十日

松村進

オニール先生

I am at present putting all my efforts into editing a complete collection of Japanese haiku called "A Complete Collection of Classical Haiku Literature." I shall bring out the first volume to be distributed in September this year. It is expected that all the volumes will be published in two years.

The magazine "Kokubun (National Literature)," which we publish from my university seminar room, I shall always send you from now on. The next number is expected to be published around August. It is likely to carry articles on dramatic literature too from time to time.

As you will know, student riots are also happening in Japanese universities. My university is comparatively quiet but, even so, there are side-effects and there are so many meetings because of these that we cannot carry out our research to the full. This seems to be a world-wide tendency, but it does cause difficulties.

With best wishes for ever more peace for you.

Respectfully,
Imoto Nōichi

15 June 1969

桜の盛りに帰国しましたが、今はもうすっかり散ってしまいました。あちこちに鯉のぼりが見えはじめた今日このごろです。

もっと早くお便りをするはずでしたが、こんなにおそくなり相すみませんでした。どうかお許し下さい。

私共は、飛行機がおくれて、三月三十一日に、神戸につきました。最初の印象は、人が多いこと、太陽が強烈なこと、緑がないことでした。又、騒音や人々の大声に悩まされました。すりぬけるように走る自動車にびくびくし、道端に大きな口をあけている溝に恐怖を感じました。上をむくと、空は青いけれど、電柱・電線が視界をさえぎります。はじめの二週間ほどは、疲れきってしまいましたが、このごろ、ようやく馴れてきたようです。元気を出す事が必要です。

さて、上の二人の子供は、幸いにも、年齢相当学年にもどることが出来ました。しかし、クラスでは可なり緊張しているらしく、帰宅すると疲れてぐったりしています。下の赤ん坊は、英語の世界から出ようとしません。

家内と私とは、家の中を整えたり、教えたり、多忙です。

今ここで思い出すのは、英国の静かな暮らしと、広い緑地とです。特にサリー州のあそこやここを恋しく思います。また、BBCを、むやみに恋しく思います。

Sakura no sakari ni kikoku shimashita ga, ima wa mō sukkari chitte shimaimashita. Achi-kochi ni koi-nobori ga mie-hajimeta kyō-konogoro desu.

Motto hayaku o-tayori o suru hazu deshita ga, konna ni osoku nari ai-sumimasen deshita. Dōka o-yurushi kudasai.

Watashi-domo wa, hikōki ga okurete, sangatsu sanjūnichinichi ni, KŌBE ni tsukimashita. Saisho no inshō wa, hito ga ōi KOTO, taiyō ga kyōretsu na koto, midori ga nai koto deshita. Mata, sōon ya hitobito no ōgoe ni NAYAMASAREMASHITA. Suri-nukeru yō ni hashiru jidōsha ni biku-biku shi, michibata ni ōki na kuchi o akete iru mizo ni kyōfu o kanjimashita. Ue o muku to, sora wa aoi keredo, denchū densen ga shikai o saegirimasu. Hajime no nishūkan hodo wa, tsukare-kitte-shimaimashita ga, konogoro, yōyaku narete kita YŌ DESU. Genki o dasu koto ga hitsuyō desu.

Sate, ue no futari no kodomo wa, saiwai ni mo, nenrei sōtō gakunen ni modoru koto ga dekimashita. Shikashi, kurasu de wa kanari kinchō shite iru RASHIKU, kitaku suru to tsukarete guttari shite imasu. Shita no akanbō wa, Eigo no sekai kara DEYŌ TO SHIMASEN.)

Kanai to watashi to wa, uchi no naka o totonoeTARI, oshieTARI, tabō desu. Ima koko de omoi-dasu no wa, Eikoku no shizuka na kurashi to, hiroi ryokuchi to desu. Toku ni Sarii-shū no asoko ya koko o koishiku omoimasu. Mata, BBC o muyami ni koishiku omoimasu.

Kono sannenkan amari, kotoba ni TSUKUSENAI go-shinsetsu ni azukari arigatō gozaimashita. Hontō ni tanoshii tai-Ei seikatsu deshita. Mata, iro-iro manabu koto ga ōkatta desu ga, kore mo subete, ii dōryō ni KAKOMARETE hataraku koto ga dekita o-kage desu. Ikue ni mo kuri-kaeshi, o-rei mōshi-agemasu.

Kyō wa tori-isogi o-rei NOMI shirushimashita.

Oku-sama ni dōka yoroshiku o-tsutae kudasai. Mata sho-sensei-gata ni mo nani-tozo yoroshiku NEGAI-AGEMASU.

Sayōnara

Shigatsu hatsuka

Matsumura Susumi

Oniiru Sensei

Notes

a. KŌBE Note the unusual reading of the characters in this important placename (a corruption of *kami* + *he*), and that in this letter the 113th radical as a lefthand element is written in full as 示, instead of in its simplified form as ネ.

b. KOTO When a noun at the end of a phrase is not followed by a particle, it is almost certainly part of a list which will conclude with an appropriate particle or some form of *da/desu*. Here, for example, the construction is . . . *koto*, . . . *koto*, . . . *koto deshita*.

c. NAYAMASAREMASHITA The passive form of the verb *nayamasu*, "afflict, annoy, trouble." Thus, "was afflicted (by)."

d. YŌ DESU "It seems, looks (like), be probable." See 10d.

e. RASHIKU The suspensive form (see 4f), parallel here to *imasu* and thus equivalent to *rashii desu* as a sentence-final form. *Rashii* can follow various parts of speech, with the meaning "seems, look (like), be probable."

f. DEYŌ TO SHIMASEN The *-ō to suru* construction covers two main meanings: (i) "try to . . ."; (ii) "be about to . . ."

g. -TARI . . . -TARI The multiple use of this frequentative suffix means that one thing is done and then another, or that various actions take place in a random sequence; and even when only one *-tari* is used, the implication is that other actions also occur. Strictly, the construction should be completed by some form of *suru*, but this is sometimes omitted, as here, where *shite* can be understood.

h. BBC Abbreviation for "British Broadcasting Corporation."

i. TSUKUSENAI A potential form of

tsukusu, "exhaust"; thus, "which cannot be exhausted/fully covered (in words)"; i.e., "inexpressible."

j. KAKOMARETE A passive form of *kakomu*, "surround; enclose"; thus, "being surrounded (by)."

k. NOMI A written-style word for "only, solely."

l. NEGAI-AGEMASU A respectful equivalent for *negaimasu*.

Translation

I returned to this country when the cherry blossom was at its height, but already now it has completely fallen. It is now the time when carp streamers have begun to appear.

I should have sent word to you earlier, and I am sorry that it has become as late as this. Please forgive me.

The plane being late, we arrived in Kobe on 31 March. My first impressions were of the large numbers of people, the fierceness of the sun, and the lack of greenery. Also, I was troubled by the noise and people's loud voices. I quaked at cars rushing along so that they just scrape through, and felt frightened at the roadside drains with their great gaping holes. When I look up, the sky is blue, but telegraph poles and electric cables interrupt the view. At first, for two whole weeks I was utterly exhausted, but recently I seem to have got used to it at last. You just have to keep your spirits up.

Well now, the two older children have fortunately been able to go back into a grade corresponding to their age, but they seem to be pretty tense in class and when they come home they are absolutely worn out. The youngest one, the toddler, makes no attempt to leave his English-speaking world.

My wife and I are very busy getting things straight at home and teaching. What we now recall here is the peaceful life and the expanses of green land in England. We particularly miss various places in Surrey, and we also desperately miss the BBC.

For the past three years and more we have enjoyed kindness from you which I can't find words to describe. It was a truly happy life we led staying in England. I also learned a great many things and it was entirely due to the fact that I was able to work surrounded by excellent colleagues. Time and again I thank you for this.

In my haste today I have simply written to thank you.

Please pass on my regards to your wife. I also ask you to give my regards to all the teachers.

Goodbye.

20 April

Matsumura Susumi

Dr. O'Neill

1979.4.19.

ロンドン大学SOAS教授
P.G. オニール殿

国立国語研究所
日本語教育センター
高田　誠

拝啓
突然御手紙差し上げる失礼お許し下さいませ。小生
国立国語研究所より派遣され、当地のドイツ語研究
所に参っているものです。
このたび、ロンドンを訪問する機会を得ましたので、上司の
野元菊雄よりかねがねおうわさをうかがっております
貴日本語学科を見学させていただきたく、御手紙差し上げ
ました。
5月の7日より1週間ロンドンに滞在いたす予定です。
その間にぜひ一度訪問をお許し下さいますよう御願い
申しあげます
また重ねての御願いにて恐縮に存じますが、御返事、
御都合、小生の出発日の5月4日以前にお聞かせ下されば
幸甚に存じます。

敬具

1979. 4. 19

Rondon Daigaku SOAS Kyōju
P.G. Oniiru-DONO

Kokuritsu Kokugo Kenkyūjo
Nihongo Kyōiku Sentā
Takada Makoto

Haikei,

Totsuzen o-tegami sashi-ageru shitsurei o-yurushi kudasaimase. SHŌSEI Kokuritsu Kokugo Kenkyūjo yori haken sar-e, tōchi no Doitsugo Kenkyūjo ni maitte iru MONO desu.

Kono tabi, Rondon o hōmon suru kikai o emashita no de, jōshi no Nomoto Kikuo yori kane-gane o-uwasa o UKAGATTE orimasu ki-Nihongo Gakka o kengaku sasete itadakitaku o-tegami sashi-agemashita.

Gogatsu no nanuka yori isshūkan Rondon ni taizai itasu yotei desu. Sono aida ni zehi ichido hōmon o o-yurushi kudasaimasu yō o-negai mōshi-agemasu.

Mata kasanete no o-negai NITE kyōshuku ni zonjimasu ga, go-henji, go-tsugō, shōsei no shuppatsu-bi no gogatsu yokka izen NI o-kikase kudasareba kōjin ni zonjimasu.

Keigu

Notes

a. SOAS Abbreviation for "School of Oriental & African Studies."
b. -DONO A formal written suffix used of men, most often in addressing them by letter; thus = "Esq."
c. SHŌSEI A humble written term used by men in referring to themselves.
d. MONO A humble equivalent for *hito*.
e. UKAGATTE *Ukagau* is a humble equivalent for *kiku* and *tazuneru*.
f. NITE A literary particle equivalent to colloquial *de*.
g. NI The writer made a slip here by beginning to write the character 前 again, but then inserted the *kana* sign *ni* underneath.

Translation

19 April 1979

London University SOAS Professor
P.G. O'Neill, Esq.

National Language Research Institute
Japanese Language Education Centre
Takada Makoto

Respectfully,

Please forgive my rudeness in sending this letter to you so unexpectedly. I have been sent by the National Language Research Institute, and have come to the German Language Research Institute over here.

Since I have now been given the opportunity of visiting London, I am sending you this letter from a desire to be allowed to inspect your Japanese Language Department which I have already heard about from my superior Nomoto Kikuo.

I expect to stay in London for one week from 7 May, and I would like to ask you to allow me to visit you without fail during that time.

I feel reluctant to make yet another request of you, but I would be very much obliged if you could let me have your reply and tell me about your arrangements before 4 May, the day of my departure.

Yours sincerely

13. Circular from a Bookshop

No.

各位殿

拝啓

日頃は お引立てを賜わり 有難度く

御礼申上げます。

さて 早速で恐縮ですが 弊社古書目録

113号（前篇）を お送り致します

尚 後篇は教育学関係の目録として

発行致しておりますので 御入要の節は

お知らせ下さい。 折返し 御送り申上げます。

以上。目録送付の御案内のみですが

今後共 宜しく お願い申上げます。

1982年4月2日

株式会社 文生書院 代表取締役 小沼良成

Kakui-dono

Haikei,

Higoro wa o-hikitate o TAMAWAR-I, ARIGATAKU o-rei mōshi-agemasu.

Sate, sassoku de kyōshuku desu ga, HEIsha kosho mokuroku 113-gō (zenpen) o o-okuri itashimasu.

Nao kōhen wa kyōikugaku kankei no mokuroku to shite hakkō itashite orimasu no de, go-nyūyō no SETSU wa o-shirase kudasai. Ori-kaeshi o-okuri mōshi-agemasu.

Ijō, mokuroku sōfu no go-annai nomi desu ga, kongo-tomo yoroshiku o-negai mōshi-agemasu.

1982nen shigatsu futsuka

Kabushiki-gaisha Bunsei Shoin
Daihyō Torishimari-yaku
Konuma Yoshinari

Notes

a. TAMAWARI *Tamawaru*, "(humbly) receive, be granted" is a humble verb much like *itadaku*.

b. ARIGATAKU Since the first two characters of this word themselves give the reading *arigata(i/ku)*, the third character 度 (= *ta* (*i/ku*), "want to") is superfluous.

c. HEI The character 幣 used here is a mistake for 弊, also read HEI, a prefix much used to mean "my/our (humble)"; cf. *hi-* under 3a, and *ki-* under 3c.

d. SETSU "time, occasion" or, as here, rather "in the case of."

Translation

To All Concerned

Respectfully,

Having enjoyed your patronage for so long, we express to you our grateful thanks.

Now, we regret that this is without prior notice, but we are sending you our company's catalogue of old books No. 113 (vol. 1).

Also, since we have published Volume 2 as a catalogue relating to the science of education, we ask you to kindly let us know if you require this. We shall then send it to you by return.

The above is simply an information note to accompany the catalogue, but we trust that you will continue to favour us with your patronage in the future.

2 April 1982

Bunsei Shoin, Inc.
Representative Director:
Konuma Yoshinari

14. Letter from an Official of an Academic Society

親愛なる Dr.Patric Geoffrey O'Neill.

「桜花賞(さくら)」授与式典を終えてから、もう10か月がすぎました。

あなたは、その後ちも元気で勉学に励んでおられることとお察しいたします。

わが全国日本学士会では、あなたの健康であることを祝福するとともに、貴地での活躍を期待しております。

あの、「桜花賞(さくら)」の授与については、当時報道機関の発表により、全国民の注目するところとなり、日本語を世界の各国に普及することの関心が高まりつつあります。

そこで本会では、あなたの活動状況を本会の発行する学術新報「アカデミア」誌に掲載して、一般に知らせたいと存じますので、最近のあなたの日本語教育、研究ならびに普及等に関する状況をお知らせ賜りますれば幸甚に存じます。

あなたは、お忙しいことと存じますが、日本のみなさんにあなたの仕事を認識してもらう為にも是非近況を来る1977年10月31日迄にお知らせくださいますようお願い申し上げます。

二伸

「桜花賞(さくら)」授与式典の記念写真帖を別便(航空便)で送りましたからお受け取りください。

1977年10月5日

社団法人全国日本学士会

編集部 井上栄司

Shin'ai NARU Dr. Patric Geoffrey O'Neill,

"Sakura-shō" juyo shikiten o oete kara, mō jikkagetsu ga sugimashita. Anata wa, sono nochi mo genki de bengaku ni hagende ORARERU koto to o-sasshi itashimasu.

Waga Zenkoku Nihon Gakushikai de wa, anata no kenkō de aru koto o shukufuku suru to tomo ni, ki-chi de no katsuyaku o kitai shite orimasu.

Ano, "Sakura-shō" no juyo ni tsuite wa, tōji hōdō kikan no happyō yori, zenkokumin no chūmoku suru TOKORO to nari, Nihongo o sekai no kakkoku ni fukyū suru koto no kanshin ga takamari-tsutsu arimasu.

Soko de HONkai de wa, anata no katsudō jōkyō o honkai no hakkō suru gakujutsu shinpō "Akademia"-shi ni keisai shite, ippan ni shirasetai to zonjimasu no de, saikin no anata no Nihongo kyōiku, kenkyū narabi ni fukyū nado ni kan-suru jōkyō o o-shirase TAMAWARIMASUREBA kōjin ni zonjimasu.

Anata wa, o-isogashii koto to zonjimasu ga, Nihon no mina-san NI anata no shigoto o ninshiki SHITE MORAU tame ni mo zehi kinkyō o kitaru 1977nen jūgatsu sanjūichinichi made ni o-shirase kudasaimasu yō o-negai mōshi-agemasu.

Nishin

"Sakura-shō" juyo shikiten no kinen shashin-chō o betsubin (kōkūbin) de okurimashita kara o-uke-tori kudasai.

1977nen jūgatsu itsuka

Shadan Hōjin Zenkoku Nihon Gakushikai
Henshūbu: Inoue Eiji

Notes

a. NARU Meaning "who/which is/are," this is the attributive form of the old literary copula *nari*, "be" (= modern *da*, *de aru*). This form is thus equivalent in contexts such as this to the *na* used with "*na* adjectives."

b. ORARERU This passive/potential form is intended here as a simple honorific showing respect to its subject (cf. the usage under 6o), and can therefore be taken as equivalent to *irassharu*, an honorific for *iru*.

c. TOKORO "Aspect, matter"; see 4e.

d. HON- As well as "main, original," this can mean, as here, "this, the present, the . . . in question."

e. TAMAWARIMASUREBA On *tamawaru*, see 13a; and on *-masureba*, see 3n.

f. NI . . . SHITE MORAU = "receive/get/have (an understanding of . . .) by (someone)." This is a less humble equivalent of the *-te itadaku* construction (see 6a), and being therefore less respectful to whoever else is concerned in the action, is much used when this other person is not the person addressed but a third party, as here.

Translation

Dear Dr. Patrick Geoffrey O'Neill,

Already ten months have passed since the end of the award ceremonies of the "Sakura (Cherry) Prize." I presume that you have continued to devote yourself to your studies in good health since then.

As well as rejoicing in your sound health, our All-Japan Graduates Association trusts that you are still continuing your activities in your country.

With regard to the award of this "Sakura Prize," through the announcements of the information media at the time this came to the attention of all the Japanese people, and interest in the spread of the Japanese language to all the countries of the world is now on the increase.

We in this Association would therefore like to make the state of your activities generally known by carrying it in the magazine "Academia," a new learned publication put out by the Association; and so we would be greatly obliged if we could have information about the state of such things as the education work, research and popularization you have done lately on the Japanese language.

I expect that you are busy, but I do request you to be sure to let us have the information about the recent situation by 31 October 1977 next, so that we can have your work appreciated by everyone in Japan.

P.S. We have sent under separate cover (airmail) an album of commemorative photographs of the "Sakura Prize" Award Ceremonies, so please accept this from us.

5 October 1977

All-Japan Graduates Association,
Inc.
Editorial Department: Inoue Eiji

15. A Covering Letter from a University Official

O'Neill, P.G. 殿

昭和57年2月1日
新堀通也

謹啓

御清栄のこととお慶び申し上げます
先日は貴殿からのアンケートを受け取りました
お忙しいところ，たいへんありがとうございました
さて，貴殿からの指示通り，貴機関の他の
日本研究者にアンケートを実施してもらうために，
アンケート用紙を15通お送り致しました．
御協力下さいます様，よろしくお願いします
最後に，貴殿の御健康と御活躍を
お祈り致します

敬具

O'Neill, P.G. -dono

Shōwa 57nen nigatsu tsuitachi
Shinbori Michiya

KINKEI,

Go-seiei no koto TO o-yorokobi mōshi-agemasu.

Senjitsu wa kiden kara no ankēto o uke-torimashita. O-isogashii tokoro, taihen arigatō gozaimashita.

Sate, kiden kara no shiji-dōri, ki-kikan no hoka no Nihon kenkyūsha ni ankēto o jisshi shite morau tame ni, ankēto yōshi o jūgo-tsū o-okuri itashimashita. Go-kyōryoku kudasaimasu yō, yoroshiku o-negai shimasu. Saigo ni, kiden no go-kenkō to go-katsuyaku o o-inori itashimasu.

Keigu

Notes

a. KINKEI A respectful introductory word, similar to *Haikei* (see 5c).

b. TO When used with verbs like *yorokobu*, this *to* can be regarded either as the same "quotative *to*" as in *to iu/omou*, "say/think thus: . . . ," or as equivalent to *to omotte*, "thinking that . . ." In any case, *koto to* can conveniently be translated as "(I am delighted) at the fact that."

Translation

P.G. O'Neill, Esq.

1 February 1982
Shinbori Michiya

Respectfully,

I am delighted that you are keeping well.

I received the questionnaire from you the other day. Thank you very much for this, when you are so busy.

Now, as was indicated by you, I have sent you fifteen copies of the questionnaire sheets in order to have these completed by the other people doing research on Japan at your institution. I ask you to be kind enough to give us your cooperation in this. Finally, I pray that you will continue in your activities in the best of health.

With respect

16. Letter of Thanks from an Official

オニール先生

国際交流基金
ロンドン駐在員
中村　聰

前略、
　本日は私に貴大学日本学部の授業を参観する機会をお与え下さり、御多忙中にもかかわらず種々御案内を賜った上に、結構な昼食のおもてなしまで頂き、誠にありがとうございました。
　おかげさまでかねて念願しておりました貴学部の授業を拝見することができ、日本語教育がどのように行われているかを具体的に知ることができてうれしく思うと共に、学生諸君が難しい教材をさして難儀な様子も見せずに消化しているのを見たのは大きな驚きでした。
　私の任期はもう残り少なではありますが、もし幸い秋になっても当地に滞在しているようでしたら、新装成った図書館を拝見にもう一度参上致したいと考えております
　末筆ながらダン先生に宜しく御鳳声のほどお願い申し上げます。
草々

Oniiru Sensei

Kokusai Kōryū Kikin
Rondon Chūzai-in
Nakamura Satoshi

Zenryaku,

Honjitsu wa watashi ni ki-daigaku Nihon Gakubu no jugyō o sankan suru kikai o o-atae kudasar-i, go-tabō-chū NI MO KAKAWARAZU shu-ju go-annai o tamawatta ue ni, kekkō na chūshoku no o-motenashi made itadak-i, makoto ni arigatō gozaimashita.

O-kage-sama de, kanete nengan shite orimashita ki-gakubu no jugyō o haiken suru koto ga deki, Nihongo kyōiku ga dono yō ni okonawarete iru ka o gutai-teki ni shiru koto ga dekite ureshiku omou to tomo ni, gakusei shokun ga muzukashii kyōzai o SASHITE nangi na yōsu mo miseZU NI shōka shite iru no o mita no wa ōki na odoroki deshita.

Watashi no ninki wa mō nokori-sukuna de wa arimasu ga, moshi saiwai aki ni natte mo tōchi ni taizai shite iru yō deshitara, shinsō NATTA toshokan O HAIKEN NI, mō ichido sanjō itashitai to kangaete orimasu.

Mappitsu-nagara Dan Sensei ni yoroshiku go-hōsei no HODO o-negai mōshi-agemasu.

Sō-sō

Notes

a. NI MO KAKAWARAZU Usually following a noun form, this phrase means "despite, in spite of (the fact that)." Thus, here, "despite your being so busy."

b. SASHITE . . . -ZU NI Used before a negative, *sashite* means "(not/without) particularly." The negative ending *-zu*, sometimes + *ni* as here, is equivalent to the more colloquial *-nai de* or *-naku* "without . . .ing" and is used with the same negative form of the verb. (It is itself seldom used in the colloquial language except in *omowazu*, "without thinking, unconsciously.") Thus, "without (showing any) particular (sign . . .)."

c. NATTA Since this here means "completed, achieved," *shinsō natta* can be translated as "newly completed."

d. O HAIKEN NI Being a *suru*-type verbal noun, *haiken* here takes its own object (*toshokan*) like a normal verb; thus, the meaning is "to see, for a look at."

e. HODO In such contexts, *hodo* is little different from *koto* and simply makes a more rounded phrase of the previous noun.

Translation

The Japan Foundation
London Representative
Nakamura Satoshi

Dr. O'Neill,

Please excuse the omission of preliminary greetings.

Today, in addition to providing me with the opportunity to see the teaching in the Japanese Department at your university and, in spite of being very busy, showing and telling me all kinds of things, you even gave me the hospitality of an excellent lunch, and I am truly grateful to you.

Thanks to you, I feel happy at having been able to see the teaching in your department which I had already wished to do, and to learn in a concrete way how Japanese language studies are carried on there. As well as this, it was a great surprise to me to have seen the students absorbing difficult teaching material apparently without any great problem.

My tour of duty is now coming to an end, but one of the things (= *nado*) I am thinking is that if, happily, it should appear that I will be here in your country in the autumn, I should like to visit you once again to see your newly completed library.

Last but not least, I ask you to be kind enough to pass on my best wishes to Dr. Dunn.

In haste

17. First Letter from a Professor Introduced by a Mutual Acquaintance

謹啓

はじめて、突然、私が あなたに お便りを 差上げる 失礼を お許し下さいませ。

私は 水谷謙吾と申します。あなたを 私の恩師、日本音声学会会長大西雅雄博士からご紹介をいただきました。

私は 日本語音声学を専攻しております。そして、私は、30年間、発音の悪い日本人に、正しい日本語の発音や、上手な話術を教え、全国の放送局へ 多くのアナウンサーを教育して、送り出しました。そして、又、国立の大阪外国語大学や、他の大学などで、たくさんの留学生に日本語を教えて来ました。そして、私は、その功績により、1981年7月3日、全国日本学士会から、名誉会員に推挙せられ、同時に、アカデミア賞を授けられました。

私は、このような経験を基に、現在、2冊の日本語教本と、それに必要な発音練習カセット、テープ各5本（合計10本）を完成し、それを別便で、あなたのもとへ お送りいたしました。（これらの本は、将来、7冊まで完成の予定です。）これは、私が、あなたに、謹んで 差上げるものです。

どうぞ、これらの本やテープを、あなたの日本語の研究や、学生の教育に、実験的に、お使い下さい。そして、あなたから、私の本とテープに対するご批評や、ご批判を 私に頂けたならば、私は誠に幸せに存じます。

最後に、私は、あなたのご健康とご多幸をお祈りいたします。ありがとうございました。

1981年9月

日本語専門学園
関西放送文化連盟 理事長 水谷謙吾

Kinkei,

Hajimete, totsuzen, watakushi ga anata ni o-tayori o sashi-ageru shitsurei o o-yurushi kudasaimase. Watakushi wa Mizutani Kengo to mōshimasu. Anata o watakushi no on-shi, Nihon Onseigakkai Kaichō Ōnishi Masao Hakushi kara go-shōkai o itadakimashita.

Watakushi wa Nihongo onseigaku o senkō shite orimasu. Soshite, watakushi wa, san-jūnenkan, hatsuon no warui Nihonjin ni, tadashii Nihongo no hatsuon ya, jōzu na wajutsu o oshie, zenkoku no hōsōkyoku e ōku no anaunsā o kyōiku shite okuri-dashimashita. Soshite, mata, kokuritsu no Ōsaka Gaikokugo Daigaku ya, hoka no daigaku nado de, takusan no ryūgakusei ni Nihongo o oshiete kimashita. Soshite, watakushi wa, sono kōseki ni yori, 1981nen shichigatsu mikka, Zenkoku Nihon Gakushikai kara, Meiyo Kaiin ni suikyo serar-e, dōji ni, Akademia-shō o sazukararemashita.

Watakushi wa, kono yō na KEIKEN O MOTO NI, genzai futatsu no Nihongo kyōhon to, sore ni hitsuyō na hatsuon renshū kasetto, tēpu kaku gohon (gōkei jippon) o kansei shi, sore o betsubin de, anata no moto e o-okuri itashimashita. (Korera no hon wa, shōrai, nanasatsu made kansei no yotei desu.) Kore wa, watakushi ga, anata ni, tsutsushinde sashi-ageru mono desu.

Dōzo, korera no hon ya tēpu o, anata no Nihongo no kenkyū ya, gakusei no kyōiku ni, jikken-teki ni o-tsukai kudasai. Soshite, anata kara, watakushi no hon to tēpu ni tai-suru go-hihyō ya, go-hihan o watakushi ni ITADAK-ETA NARABA, watakushi wa makoto ni shiawase ni zonjimasu.

Saigo ni, watakushi wa, anata no go-kenkō o o-inori itashimasu. Arigatō gozaimashita.

1981nen kugatsu

Nihongo Senmon Gakuen
Kansai Hōsō Bunka Renmei
Rijichō
Mizutani Kengo

Notes

a. KEIKEN O MOTO NI The character used for *kei-* is an abbreviation for 經. This phrase is incomplete in having no verb, but it can be understood as ending with *shite*; thus, "making experience a basis, on the basis of experience."

b. ITADAKETA NARABA "If it has been possible (for me) to receive . . . (I shall feel)," that is, "If I could have . . ." On *itadakeru*, see 4k, and on *naraba*, 3q.

Translation

Respectfully,

Please forgive my rudeness in sending you a letter for the first time without warning. I am called Mizutani Kengo. I have kindly been given an introduction to you by my respected teacher, Dr. Ōnishi Masao, President of the Japan Phonetics Association.

I specialise in the pronunciation of Japanese, and for thirty years I have taught the correct pronunciation of Japanese and the art of good talking to Japanese with poor accents, and I have trained and sent out many announcers to broadcasting stations all over the country. Also, I have taught Japanese to many foreign students in Japan at such places as the national Foreign Languages University in Ōsaka and other universities. Then, for these achievements, on 3 July 1981 I was proposed by the All-Japan Graduates Association as an Honorary Member and, at the same time, I was awarded the Academia Prize.

On the basis of this kind of experience, I have now completed two Japanese-language textbooks and five each (ten in all) of the pronunciation cassettes and tapes necessary for these, and I have sent these to your address under separate cover. (The expectation is that these books will be complete in seven volumes in the future.) These I beg to give to you.

Do please use these tapes experimentally for your research into the Japanese language and for the education of your students. I would then be very happy if I could have your comments and criticisms about these books and tapes.

Finally, I wish for your good health and great happiness. With thanks.

September 1981

Mizutani Kengo
Chairman, Specialist Academy for the
Japanese Language and the Kansai
Broadcast Culture Federation

前略　昨年、五月には大変お世話に成りました。井上先生からメッセージ（伝言書）があったと思いますが、この十月十二日（月曜）に英国に行きます。十月十三日（火曜）にロンドン大学のオニール教授先生の研究室をたずねます。午後一時の予定です。かってなお願いですみませんが、よろしくお願いいたします。
ロンドンではフレミング・ホテル（Flemings Hotel…
Half moon Street W2 … TeL 499-2964）に宿泊いたします。
すみませんが、よろしく、よろしくおねがいいたします。

9月1日

萩野浩基

オニール教授

Zenryaku. Sakunen no gogatsu ni wa taihen o-sewa ni narimashita. Inoue Sensei kara messēji (dengonsho) ga atta to omoimasu ga, kono jūgatsu jūninichi (Getsuyō) ni Eikoku ni ikimasu. Jūgatsu jūsannichi (Kayō) ni Rondon Daigaku no Oniiru Kyōju Sensei no kenkyūshitsu o tazunemasu. Gogo ichiji no yotei desu. Katte na o-negai de sumimasen ga, yoroshiku o-negai itashimasu.

Rondon de wa Furemingu Hoteru (Flemings Hotel . . . Half roon Street W1 . . . Tel 499-2964) ni shukuhaku itashimasu.

Suminasen ga, yoroshiku, yoroshiku o-negai itashimasu.

Jūgatsu tsuitachi

Hagino Kōki

Oniiru Kyōju

Translation

Please excuse the omission of preliminary greetings.

Thank you for all your help in May last year. I think that you will have had a message from Dr. Inoue, but I shall be coming to England on the 12th of this month (Monday). I shall call in at your research centre at London University, Professor O'Neill, on 13th October (Tuesday). I expect it to be at 1 p.m. I am sorry to make such an arbitrary request of you, but I do hope that you will kindly agree to this.

In London I shall be residing at Flemings Hotel (Flemings Hotel . . . Half roon (sic) Street W1.... Tel 499-2964).

I am sorry to ask this of you, but I hope and hope that you will kindly agree.

1 October

Hagino Kōki

Professor O'Neill

19. Letter of Request from a Lady to a Professor under Whom She Had Worked

拝啓

オックスフォード大学のボードリアン図書館が、そのオリエンタル、ブック部の司書助手を募集している事を、タイムズ・ハイアー・エジュケイション・サプルメントに依り知り、早速履歴書を提出し、応募致しました。履歴書に、照会者の一人として貴教授の御名前を挙げました。事後承諾ではございますが、若し図書館より問い合わせが有れば御怱忙中誠に恐れ入りますが御手紙を書いて下さいませ。謹んでお願い申し上げます。

尚、トロントのヨーク大学のジュニア・ジャパン・スペシャリストへの就職志願書は、同じく貴教授の御名前を照会者の一人として挙げました履歴書を添えて一月十四日に投函致しました。

敬具

昭和五十二年一月二十日

ストラウド・ドリンクウォーター 真澄

ダン教授

Haikei,

Okkusufōdo Daigaku no Bōdorian Toshokan ga sono Orientaru Bukku-bu no shisho joshu o boshū shite iru koto o Taimuzu Haiā Ejukeishon Sapurumento ni yori shiri, sassoku rirekisho o teishutsu shi, ōbo itashimashita. Rirekisho ni, shōkaisha no hitori to shite ki-kyōju no o-namae o agemashita. Jigo shōdaku de wa gozaimasu ga, moshi toshokan yori toi-awase ga areba, go-sōbō-chū makoto ni osore-irimasu ga o-tegami o kaite kudasaimase. Tsutsushinde o-negai mōshi-agemasu.

Nao, Toronto no Yōku Daigaku no Junia Japan Supesharisuto e no shūshoku shigan-sho wa ONAJIKU ki-kyōju no o-namae o shōkaisha no hitori to shite agemashita rirekisho o soete ichigatsu jūyokka ni tōkan itashimashita.

Keigu

Sutoraudo-Dorinkuuōtā Masumi

Shōwa gojūninen ichigatsu nijūichinichi

Dan Kyōju

Notes

a. ONAJIKU A literary adverbial form from *onaji*, equivalent to the colloquial *onaji yō ni*, "similarly."

Translation

Respectfully,

I learned from the Times Higher Educational Supplement that the Bodleian Library of Oxford University is recruiting a library assistant for its Oriental Books Department, and I immediately sent my curriculum vitae and applied for this. In the curriculum vitae I gave your name, Professor, as one of the referees. This is indeed asking for agreement after the event, but if there should be an enquiry from the Library, do please write a letter for me, even though I am truly reluctant to ask you to do this when you are so busy. I do humbly beg you to do this for me.

Also, on 14 January, I posted off my application as a Junior Japan Specialist at York University in Toronto, together with a curriculum vitae in which I likewise gave your name as one of the referees.

Yours respectfully,
Masumi Stroud-Drinkwater

21 January 1977
Professor Dunn

20. Letter from a Previously Unknown Woman

ごろまでロンドンに滞在し、あと、五日ほど、中部イングランド
を歩く予定でございます。誠に、恐縮でございますが、八日
から十二日までの間に御都合よろしければ、お目にかかりとう
ございます。どうぞ、よろしくお願い申しあげます。
なお、お目にかかれます場合はお電話番号を、教えていた
だきたく、重ねてお願い申しあげます。
かしこ

六月八日　　高橋慶子

オニール先生

Haikei. Totsuzen o-tegami shitsurei itashimasu. Watakushi-KOTO Nihongo kyōshi no shikaku o totta bakari no mono de gozaimasu ga, shichigatsu ni Eikoku e ryokō suru yotei de gozaimasu. Nomoto Sensei ni o-hanashi shimashita tokoro, Oniiru Sensei ga Nihon no chūsei bungaku go-senmon DE IRASSHAIMASU koto o oshiete kudasaimashita. Watakushi wa naga-nen shuppansha ni tsutome, ''Kokusho Sōmokuroku'' no kōsei o hete, tadaima ''Koten Bungaku Zenshū'' no henshū ni jūji shite orimasu. Tōkyō Joshi Daigaku de wa NŌ-KYŌGEN no Furukawa Hisashi Sensei no kōgi o kikimashita.

Iro-iro go-tayō no koto to wa zonjimasu ga, sukoshi no jikan o itadake-masu naraba, Eikoku NI OKERU Nihon bungaku no JUYŌ, mata, kore kara Nihongo kyōshi o kokorozasu mono e no adobaisu nado, o-kikase itadakereba URESHŪ gozaimasu.

Yūjin ga Kenburijji ni, Eigo o benkyō suru tame, ryūgaku shite imasu no de, Rondon

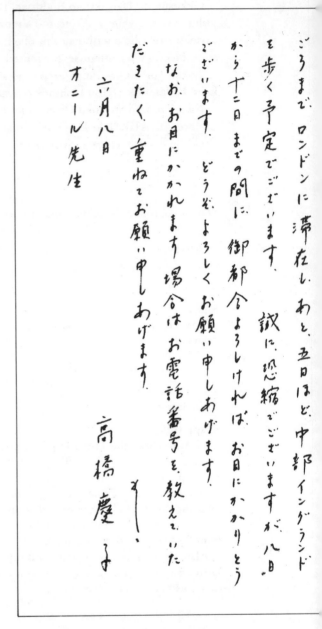

拝啓　突然お手紙失礼いたします。私こと、日本語教師の資格をとったばかりの者でございますが、七月に英国へ旅行する予定でございます。野元先生にお話しましたところ、オニール先生が、日本の中世文学御専門でいらっしゃいますことを、教えて下さいました。私は長年、出版社につとめ、「国書総目録」の校正を経て、只今は「古典文学全集」の編集に従事しております。東京女子大学では、能狂言の古川久先生の講義を聴きました。

いろいろ、御多用の事とは存じますが、少しの時間をいただけますならば、英国における日本文学の受容、また、これから日本語教師を志す者へのアドバイスなど、お聞かせいただければうれしゅうございます。

友人が、ケンブリッジに、英語を勉強するため留学していますので、ロンドンに宿をとってくれました。七月八日から七月十二日

ni yado o totte KUREMASHITA. Shichigatsu yōka kara shichigatsu jūninichi-goro made, Rondon ni taizai shi, ato, itsuka hodo, chūbu Ingurando o aruku yotei de gozaimasu. Makoto ni kyōshuku de gozaimasu ga, yōka kara jūninichi made no aida ni, go-tsugō yoroshikereba, o-me ni KAKARITŌ gozaimasu. Dōzo yoroshiku o-negai mōshi-agemasu.

Nao, o-me ni kakaremasu baai wa, o-denwa bangō o oshiete itadakitaku, kasanete o-negai mōshi-agemasu.

KASHIKO

Takahashi Keiko

Rokugatsu yōka
Oniiru Sensei

Notes

a. -KOTO In this use as a suffix, *-koto* means "in speaking of . . . , as far as . . . is concerned."
b. DE IRASSHAIMASU An honorific equivalent for *desu*, used when the subject is a person and respect is to be shown to him. Since *irassharu* is an honorific for *iru* (see 6w), this is directly equivalent to *de imasu*.
c. NŌ-KYŌGEN The Kyōgen comic plays long associated with Nō drama and performed traditionally between Nō plays.
d. NI OKERU A literary phrase equivalent to colloquial *ni aru* or *de no*, "(which is/are) in."
e. JUYŌ See 11b; in this case the particle which governs *juyō* and its following parallel noun is *nado*.
f. URESHŪ Japanese *-i* adjectives are used in their "long-vowel" form before *gozaimasu* and related forms. Since the long-vowel forms are a contraction of the *-ku* adverbial form, resulting from the disappearance of the *k*, those ending in *-ii* went via *-i(k)u* to *-ū*, as here; and those ending in *-oi* and *-ai* went via *-o(k)u* and *-a(k)u* to *-ō*, as in *o-hayō gozaimasu* (see also 8c).
g. KUREMASHITA This less respectful word for "condescend" is used here, rather than *kudasaimashita*, because the writer's own friend is being referred to when addressing an outsider, and the greater level of respect was therefore felt to be inappropriate.
h. KAKARITŌ On this *-tō* ending, from *-tai*, "wish to," via *-taku*, see f. above.
i. KASHIKO The stem of a word meaning "revered, awe-inspiring," it is used by women as a formal conclusion to letters.

Translation

Respectfully. It is rude of me to write to you like this without warning, but I am someone who has just obtained qualifications as a teacher of Japanese and expects to travel to England in July. When I talked to Dr. Nomoto, he kindly told me that you

21. Letter from the Wife of an Acquaintance in Japan

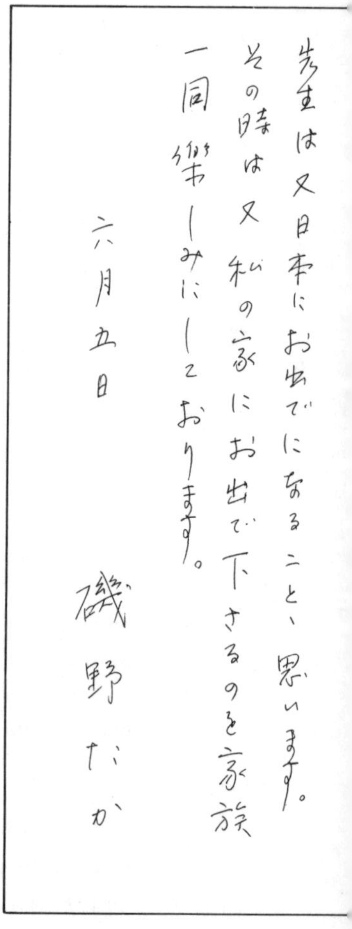
先生は又日本にお出でになることゝ思います。
その時は又私の家にお出で下さるのを家族
一同楽しみにしております。
六月五日
磯野たか

are a specialist in medieval Japanese literature. I have worked for many years in publishing and, with the proofs of "A Comprehensive Catalogue of Japanese Books" behind me, I am at the moment engaged in editing "A Complete Collection of Classical Literature." At Tokyo Women's University, I heard lectures from Dr. Furukawa Hisashi on Nō Kyōgen.

I expect that you are busy with all kinds of things, but if you could spare me a little time, I would be happy to hear from you about such things as the reception of Japanese literature in England and your advice to someone who aims from now on to be a teacher of Japanese.

As I have a friend who is studying in Cambridge in order to learn English, she has arranged somewhere for me to stay in London. I expect to be staying in London from the 8th to about the 12th July, and then to go around the Midlands for about five days. I am truly hesitant to ask you, but I would like to meet you in the period between the 8th and the 12th, if this would be convenient for you. I do ask you to be kind enough to do this for me.

Furthermore, if I should be able to meet you, I also ask to be informed, if you please, of your telephone number.

Yours humbly,
Takahashi Keiko

8 June
Dr. O'Neill

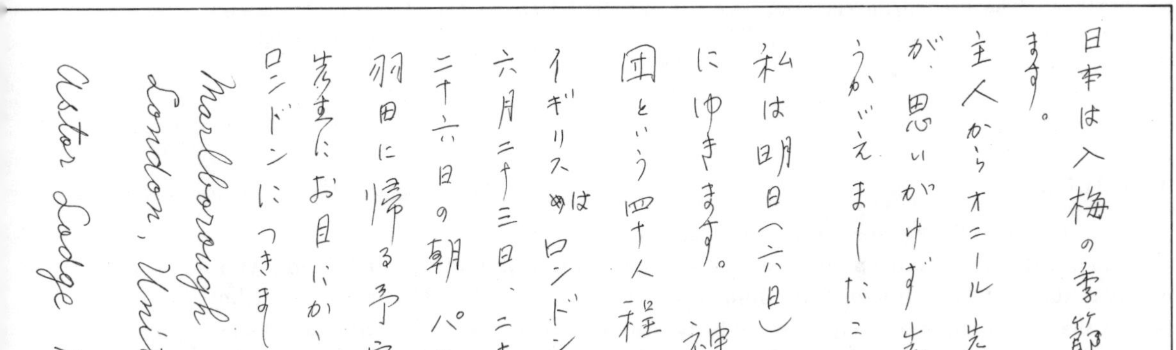
日本は入梅の季節に入り毎日雨が降っております。
主人からオニール先生のことを聞いておりましたが、思いがけず先生にお目にかかりお話をうかがえましたことを幸せに思っております。
私は明日（六日）の飛行機でヨーロッパ旅行にゆきます。神奈川県私立学校教育視察団という四十人程の教員の団体で参ります。
イギリスではロンドンだけに泊ります。
六月二十三日、二十四日、二十五日と三日泊り二十六日の朝パリにゆき二十九日パリから羽田に帰る予定です。団体旅行ですので、先生にお目にかかれるかどうかわかりませんが、ロンドンにつきましたら電話をおかけします。
Marlborough place N.W.8
London, United Kingdom Tel 624-0181
Astor Lodge Hotel に泊ります。

Nihon wa nyūbai no kisetsu ni hairi, mainichi ame ga futte orimasu.

Shujin kara Oniiru Sensei no koto o kiite orimashita ga, OMOIGAKEZU sensei ni o-me ni kakar-i o-hanashi o ukaga-e-mashita koto o shiawase ni omotte orimasu. Watakushi wa ASHITA (muika) no hikōki de Yōroppa ryokō ni yukimasu. Kanagawa-ken Shiritsu Gakkō Kyōiku Shisatsu-dan to iu yonjūnin hodo no kyōin no dantai de mairimasu. Igirisu wa Rondon dake ni tomarimasu.

Rokugatsu nijūsannichi, nijūyokka, nijūgonichi TO mikka tomari, nijūrokunichi no asa Pari ni yuki, nijūkunichi Pari kara Haneda ni kaeru yotei desu. Dantai ryokō desu no de, sensei ni o-me ni kakareru ka dō ka wakarimasen ga, Rondon ni tsukimashitara denwa o o-kake shimasu.

Marlborough place N.W. 8, London, United Kingdom, Tel. 624–0181, Astor Lodge Hotel ni tomarimasu.

Sensei wa mata Nihon ni oide ni naru koto to omoimasu. Sono toki wa mata watakushi no uchi ni OIDE KUDASARU no o kazoku ichidō tanoshimi ni shite orimasu.

Rokugatsu itsuka

Isono Taka

Notes

a. OMOIGAKEZU Equivalent to the more colloquial *omoigakenaku*, "unexpectedly"; on *-zu*, see 16b.

b. ASHITA The two characters used here also have the readings *asu* and, more stiffly, *myōnichi*.

c. TO In this usage *to* can be understood as signifying a preceding adverbial phrase, with a meaning like "thus" or, here "namely."

d. OIDE KUDASARU Literally, "condescend a coming," that is, "be kind enough to come"; see 1g.

Translation

Japan is now in the early-summer rainy season, and it rains every day.

I had heard about you from my husband, and I am happy that unexpectedly I met you and was able to talk with you. I am going on a trip to Europe by plane tomorrow (the 6th). I shall be going in a group of some forty teachers known as the Kanagawa Prefecture Private-School Teachers Inspection Group. In England, we shall be staying only in London.

We expect to stay there for the three days of the 23rd, 24th and 25th June, to go to Paris on the morning of the 26th, and to return from Paris to Haneda on the 29th. Since it is group travel, I do not know whether I shall be able to meet you, but I shall telephone you when we have arrived in London.

We shall be staying in the Astor Lodge Hotel, Marlborough Place, London N.W. 8, United Kingdom, Tel.: 624–0181.

I expect you will be coming to Japan again. When you do so, all the family will be looking forward to you coming to our house again.

5 June

Isono Taka

22. Letter from a Visitor after His Return to Japan

突然、大学にお邪魔しましてから、早一年余り、無音に打ち過ぎました
ことを、誠に心苦しく思っております。併し、面識もない私共を、心温く
迎えて戴きました御好意の程、折にふれ思い起しては、感謝の念を
新にしている次第でございます。外遊の報告、粗末なものでございま
すが、活字に付しましたので、同封致しました。御笑覧戴ければ、
何よりの幸いかと存じます。
尚、京都にお出での節はもとより、日頃の御研究の資料の件なり
とも、御一報戴けますならば、出来うる限りの御便宜をはかりたいと
考えております。御遠慮なく御用命下さるよう、お待ち申し上げて
おります。

四月二一日

鷹津義彦
拝

オニール教授
机下

Totsuzen, daigaku ni o-jama shimashite kara, haya ichinen amari, buin ni uchi-sugimashita koto o, makoto ni kokoro-gurushiku omotte orimasu. Shikashi, menshiki mo nai WATAKUSHI-DOMO o, kokoro-atatakaku mukaete itadakimashita go-kōi no HODO, ori ni fure omoi-okoshite wa, kansha no nen o arata ni shite iru SHIDAI de gozaimasu. Gaiyū no hōkoku, somatsu na mono de gozaimasu ga, katsuji ni fu-shimashita no de, dōfū itashimashita. Go-SHŌRAN itadakereba, nani-yori no saiwai ka to zonjimasu.

Nao, Kyōto ni oide no setsu wa motoyori, higoro no go-kenkyū no shiryō no ken

NARI TOMO, go-ippō itadake-masu naraba, deki-URU kagiri no go-bengi o hakaritai to kangaete orimasu. Go-enryo naku go-yōmei kudasaru yō, o-machi mōshi-agete orimasu.

Shigatsu nijūichinichi

Takatsu Yoshihiko

HAI

Oniiru Kyōju

KIKA

Notes

a. WATAKUSHI-DOMO Here *-domo* means "someone like (myself)" rather than being a simple plural suffix; see 8f.
b. HODO Here, "the fact/matter (of your kindness)"; see 16e.
c. SHIDAI Meaning basically "sequence, reason, circumstances," this word is often used before *desu*, etc., at the end of a sentence without any strong meaning, serving merely to round off the sentence; but it sometimes has a more positive meaning of "the situation is that, what happened was that," depending on the context.
d. SHŌRAN "Laughingly see"; i.e., "look at (my poor effort)."
e. NARI TOMO Meaning "even if/though it is," this is a rather formal phrase equivalent to the more colloquial *de atte mo*.
f. -URU This verbal suffix, a variant of the verb *eru*, "gain, obtain, be able to," indicates capability; thus, here, "(to the extent) I can manage."
g. HAI A word usable after the name of the writer to mean "with reverence/humility."
h. KIKA Literally "below your desk," this is a formal phrase used after the name of the addressee and very similar to *gyokuanka* (see 9e).

Translation

I feel very badly indeed about the fact that already more than a year has passed without a word from me, since I unexpectedly imposed on your time at the university. However, I have felt renewed gratitude on remembering from time to time how kind you were to receive with such cordiality someone like myself who was a stranger to you. My report of my travels abroad is nothing very much, but since I have put it into print, I am enclosing it for you. I would be very happy if you would kindly look at it.

Also, if I could have word from you should you come to Kyoto, of course, or even if it is a matter of material for your regular research, I would like to meet your requirements to the limit of my ability. I look forward to having you ask me freely for what you need.

21 April

Takatsu Yoshihiko
With respect

Professor O'Neill

23. Letter from a Schoolboy Met While Travelling

拝啓

今日この頃身にしみる寒さが続きますね。当地岩手県は随分寒くなりました。

その後お変り有りませんか。僕は元気で毎日通学しております。

突然ですみませんが五月に岩手県平泉でP・G・オニールさんと撮りました写真をお送り致します　笑って見て下さい。

写真が着きましたら御返事下さい。おまちしております。

あまりにも勝手ではございますが左の所へお送って下されば幸いとぞんじます。

住所「岩手県胆沢郡前沢町

岩手県立前沢高等学校

第三学年7組」

菊地勲

P・G・オニール様

十月十三日記。

Haikei,

Kyō-konogoro mi ni shimiru samu-SA ga tsuzukimasu ne. Tōchi Iwate-ken wa zuibun samuku narimashita. Sono go o-kawari arimasen ka. BOKU wa genki de mainichi tsūgaku shite orimasu.

Totsuzen de sumimasen ga, gogatsu ni "Iwate-ken Hiraizumi" de P.G. Oniiru-san to torimashita SHASHIN o o-okuri itashimasu. WARATTE MITE kudasai.

Shashin ga tsukimashitara go-henji kudasai. O-machi shite orimasu.

Amari ni mo katte de wa gozaimasu ga, hidari no tokoro e O-OKUTTE kudasareba saiwai to zonjimasu.

Jūsho: "Iwate-ken Isawa-gun Maezawa-chō
Iwate-kenritsu Maezawa Kōtō Gakkō-NAI
Dai-san Gakunen B Gumi"

P.G. Oniiru-sama

Kikuchi Isao

Jūgatsu jūsannichi ki

Notes

a. -SA A noun-forming suffix added to the stem of true Japanese adjectives (e.g., *naga-sa*, "length") or to most words used as *na* adjectives (e.g., *tabō-sa*, "business, pressure of work").

b. BOKU A male word for "I" used by boys virtually to the exclusion of all other pronouns, and by men in informal situations.

c. SHASHIN The old full form 眞 has been used here for the second character, now usually 真 (see App. II, Table I).

24. Letter from a Professor During a Visit to England

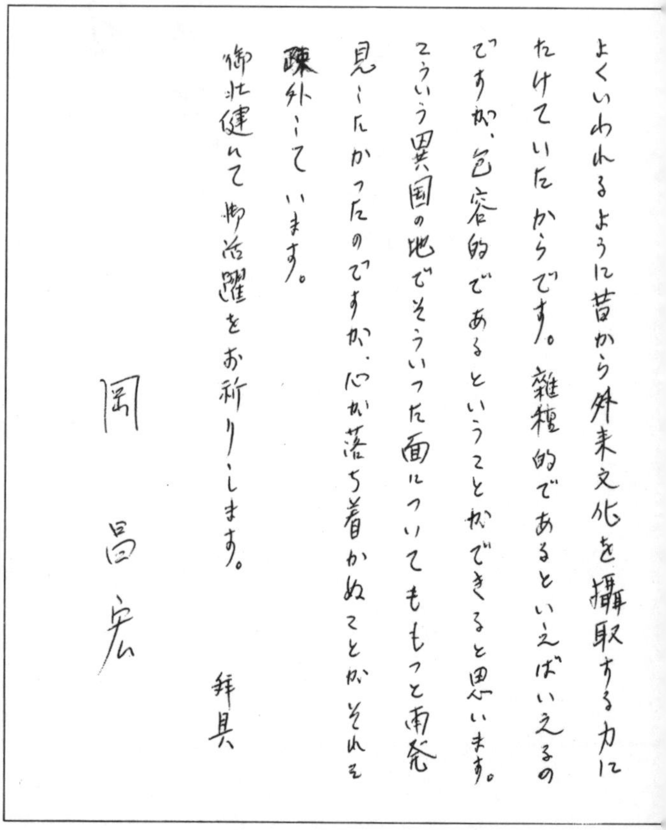
よくいわれるように昔から外来文化を摂取する力に
たけていたからです。雑種的であるといえばいえるの
ですが、包容的であるということができると思います。
こういう異国の地でそういった面についてももっと再発
見したかったのですが、心が落ち着かぬことがそれを
疎外しています。
御壮健にて御活躍をお祈りします。
拝具
岡昌宏

d. WARATTE MITE "(Please) laughingly look"; cf. *shōran* 22d.
e. O-OKUTTE Either *okutte kudasareba* or *o-okuri kudasareba* would be grammatically preferable here.
f. -NAI This suffix, meaning "within," can be used in addresses after the name of an institution or organization to which the addressee belongs.

Translation

Respectfully,

At this time of year, there is a continual piercing cold, isn't there. Here in Iwate Prefecture, it has become very cold. Are you still well since I saw you? I am in good health and attend school every day.

I am sorry that this is unexpected, but I am sending you the photograph taken with you, Mr. O'Neill, at Hiraizumi in Iwate Prefecture. Please amuse yourself by having a look at it.

Please send me a reply when the photograph arrives. I shall look forward to it.

This is very presumptuous of me, but I would be glad if you would please send it to the place below.

Address: B Group, Third Grade, Iwate Prefectural High School at Maezawa, Maezawa-chō, Isawa-gun, Iwate Prefecture.

Mr. P.G. O'Neill

Kikuchi Isao

Written 13 October

前略
その後お変りなくお過しのことと存じます。
さて小生居をKensington High Streetのすぐ近くに移しました。フラットですが、静かな一室です。こうしていることのできるのも僅かになってきたようですが、その幸いを喜ばねばなりません。
先日(四月)マインツ(西独)にまいりました。国際カント学会に出席するためでしたが、そこの書店で、俳句、禅、生花などの独訳本を多く見ました。以前からJapanologieがドイツではかなり取り上げられていることを聞いていましたが、その一端を見たような気がいたしました。イギリスでの感じ(といって、一、二の東洋の宗教について論じた書物から受けた感じ)では、東洋に関する研究のなかで日本に関する部分の比重が少し小さいのではないかという風に思われました。私ののぞいたほんの僅かな部分に過ぎませんので、もっと詳細に調べねばならぬとは思いますが。
日本の文化はたしかに多様な要素を含んでいます。

Zenryaku,

Sono go o-kawari naku o-sugoshi no koto to zonjimasu. Sate shōsei kyo o Kensington High Street no sugu chikaku ni utsushimashita. Furatto desu ga, shizuka na isshitsu desu. Kō shite iru koto no dekiru no mo wazuka ni natte kita yō desu ga, sono saiwai o YOROKOBANEBA narimasen.

Senjitsu (shigatsu) Maintsu (Sei-DOKU) ni mairimashita. Kokusai Kanto Gakkai ni shusseki suru tame deshita ga, soko no shoten de, haiku, ZEN, ikebana nado no Dokuyakubon o ōku mimashita. Izen kara Japanologie ga Doitsu de wa kanari tori-agerarete iru koto o kiite imashita ga, sono ittan o mita yō na ki ga itashimashita. Igirisu de no kanji (to itte, ichi-ni no Tōyō no shūkyō ni tsuite ronjita shomotsu kara uketa kan-ji) de wa, Tōyō ni kan-suru kenkyū no naka de Nihon ni kan-suru bubun no hijū ga sukoshi chiisai no de wa nai ka to iu fū ni omowaremashita. Watashi no nozoita hon no wazuka na bubun ni sugimasen no de, motto shōsai ni SHIRABENEBA NARANU to wa omoimasu ga.

Nihon no bunka wa tashika ni tayō na yōso o fukunde imasu. Yoku iwareru yō ni mukashi kara gairai bunka o sesshu suru chikara ni takete ita kara desu. Zasshu-teki de aru to ieba ieru no desu ga, hōyō-teki de aru to iu koto ga dekiru to omoimasu. KŌ IU ikoku no chi de SŌ ITTA men ni tsuite mo motto SAI-hakken shitakatta no desu ga, kokoro ga OCHI-TSUKANU koto ga sore o SOGAI shite imasu.

Go-sōken nite go-katsuyaku o o-inori shimasu.

HAIGU

Oka Masahiro

Notes

a. YOROKOBANEBA The ending *-neba* is a negative conditional equivalent to standard *-nakereba*.
b. DOKU Being the first of the characters with which *Doitsu* was written, 独 is used to mean "Germany" in the same way as 米 *Bei* for "America," 英 *Ei* for "England/Britain," 仏 *Futsu* for "France," etc.
c. ZEN The writer has used the old full form of the character 禪 here, instead of the modern simplified form 禅. Similarly, the last paragraph contains the old forms 攝 (摂) and 雜 (雑). See App. II, Table I.
d. SHIRABENEBA NARANU The *-neba naranu* combination is a mainly Kansai equivalent of standard *-nakereba naranai*, "(one) must." See a. above and note that *-nu* = *-nai*.
e. KŌ IU = *konna*, *kō shita*, "like this, such (as this)."
f. SŌ ITTA = *sonna*, *sō shita*, "like that, such (as that)."
g. SAI- As a first element, the character 再 is usually translatable as "re-(discover, etc.)."
h. OCHI-TSUKANU = *ochi-tsukanai* (see d. above).
i. SOGAI Written with the characters 疎外 used here, *sogai suru* means "shun, alienate," but the context gives much the same meaning as the *sogai* written 阻害 and meaning "obstruct, impede."
j. HAIGU A formal, concluding word, similar to *keigu* (see 2q).

Translation

Please excuse the omission of preliminary greetings.

Well now, I hope that you have been as well as ever since I saw you last. I have changed my accommodation to the immediate vicinity of Kensington High Street. It is a flat, but a single quiet room. Even places where one can be as I am now seem to have become scarce, and I shall have to be glad of my good fortune.

The other day (in April) I went to Mainz (West Germany). It was in order to attend an International Kant Conference, and in the bookshops there I saw many books in German translation on such things as haiku, Zen, and flower arrangement. I had heard previously that Japanology has been taken up a good deal in Germany, and I felt that I had seen a glimpse of this. From the feeling I have got in England (by which I mean the feeling from one or two books which discussed Oriental religions), I could not help thinking that the proportion of the parts concerning Japan among studies concerning the Orient was perhaps rather small. What I have glanced at is no more than a mere trifling part of the whole, and so I do feel that I ought to go into this in more detail, though. . . .

Japanese culture certainly contains many kinds of elements. As is often said, this is because from olden times Japan has been well endowed with the capacity to take over culture from abroad. It can indeed be said that it is hybrid, but I feel that it can be said to be comprehensive. In such a foreign land as this I did want to rediscover more about such aspects, but being so unsettled in my mind has kept me from this.

I hope that you are continuing your activities in good health.

With respect,
Oka Masahiro

25. Letter from a Previously Unknown Man

突然お手紙をさしあげます
別紙の野元先生の紹介状にありますように、私は
日本語インスティチュートというところで日本語を教えて
いるものです。かねてより先生のお名前を存じ上げて
おり、一度お目にかかりたいと願っておりましたが
このたびたまたま、ロンドンを訪問する機会を得まし
たので、ぜひお目にかからせていただきたいと思い、野元
先生の紹介状をいただきました。どうぞご便宜を
はかっていただきたくお願い申しあげます。
ロンドン滞在は五月四、五、六の三日間で、たいそう
短かいため、うまくスケジュールをお合わせいただくのが
むつかしいことと存じますが、どうぞよろしくご配慮
の上、日時をご指定いただけばさいわいでございます。
右記の日ならどの時間でも結構でございます。
なお、日本から持っていけるものがございましたら、
なんなりとお申しつけください。突然に、まことに
勝手なお願いでございますが、どうぞよろしくお願い
申し上げます。

三月二十日

オニール先生

Totsuzen o-tegami o sashi-agemasu.

Besshi no Nomoto Sensei no shōkaijō ni arimasu yō ni, watakushi wa Nihongo Insutichūto to iu tokoro de Nihongo o oshiete iru mono desu. Kanete yori sensei no o-namae o zonji-agete or-i, ichido o-me ni kakaritai to negatte orimashita ga, kono tabi tama-tama, Rondon o hōmon suru kikai o emashita no de, zehi o-me ni kakarasete itadakitai to omo-i, Nomoto Sensei no shōkaijō o itadakimashita. Dōzo, go-bengi o hakatte itadakitaku o-negai mōshi-agemasu.

Rondon TAIZAI wa gogatsu shi, go, roku no mikka-kan de, taisō mijikai tame, umaku sukejūru o o-awase itadaku no ga mutsukashii koto to zonjimasu ga, dōzo yoroshiku go-hairyo no UE, nichiji o go-shitei itadakeba saiwai de gozaimasu. Uki no hi nara dono jikan de mo kekkō de gozaimasu.

Nao, Nihon kara motte ikeru mono ga gozaimashitara, NAN NARI TO o-mōshi-tsuke kudasai. Totsuzen ni, makoto ni katte na o-negai de gozaimasu ga, dōzo yoroshiku o-negai mōshi-agemasu.

Sangatsu hatsuka

Yokohagi Michihiko

Oniiru Sensei

Notes

a. TAIZAI On the form of the character used here for *tai*, see 4j.
b. UE Here means "after, following," (see also 5f).
c. NAN NARI TO This can be regarded as a simple vocabulary item meaning "anything, whatever," but its alternative form is *nan nari tomo* (see 22e) and it is strictly equivalent to *nan de atte mo*, and hence equals *nan de mo*.

Translation

I am sorry for sending you this letter without notice.

As is to be found in the separate letter of introduction from Dr. Nomoto, I am teaching Japanese at a place called the Japanese Language Institute. I have known your name for some while and had hoped to meet you at some time; and since I now by chance have an opportunity to visit London, I felt that I would certainly like to be allowed to see you and obtained the letter of introduction from Dr. Nomoto. I do ask you, please, to be kind enough to arrange this for me.

My stay in London will be for the three days of the 4th, 5th and 6th June, and because this is very short, I realise that it will be difficult to have you fit your schedule in so precisely; but I would be happy if you would give this your kind consideration and then specify a day and a time for me. If it is one of the above days, any time would be fine for me.

Also, if there is something I can bring you from Japan, do please tell me, no matter what. This is a very selfish request I am suddenly making of you, but I beg you for a kind response.

20 March

Yokohagi Michihiko

Dr. O'Neill

INTERMEDIATE TEXTS

Nos. 26–60

With transcriptions and notes, and uncommon vocabulary in the Glossary.

26. Letter from a Professor Following a Visit to England

大変ごぶさた致しました　お変りございませんか
私も元気です　早く　お礼を申しあげねば
ならぬと思いながらも　学年始めの忙しさに
追われて　遅れたことを　お詫び申しあげ
ます
ロンドン大学訪問の際は　突然であるのにも
拘らず　ご親切にいろいろ　ご教示下さいまして
まことに有難うございました　また手厚く
おもてなし下さいまして　これまた有難うござい
ました　おかげさまで　イギリスのすぐれた
日本学の現状と実績がわかりまして　私の
今後の研究に役立ったことを　厚く御礼申し
あげます
これからも　先生がたが　業績をあげられるよう
願って止みません
私はあれから四ヶ国をまわり視察して
日本へ帰りました　多くの点で　わが国が
今後一層　励まねばならぬことを　痛感いたし
ました
同封のものは　明治時代の古銭で　現在
こちらでは　ブームを起しているものです　明治
時代が古典化しつつあるためと、国力を
のばした時代であるためでしょう　明治百年
祭は終りましたが　その感激は　現在　この
ような形になって現れております　プレゼント
致しますので　お受けとり下さい

Taihen go-busata itashimashita. O-kawari gozaimasen ka. Watakushi mo genki desu. Hayaku o-REI o mōshi-age-neba naranu to omoi-nagara mo, gakunen-hajime no isogashi-sa ni owarete okureta koto o o-wabi mōshi-agemasu.

Rondon Daigaku hōmon no sai wa totsuzen de aru no ni mo kakawarazu, go-shinsetsu ni iro-iro go-kyōji kudasaimashite makoto ni arigatō gozaimashita. Mata te-atsuku o-motenashi kudasaimashite, kore mata arigatō gozaimashita. O-kage-sama de, **Igirisu** no sugureta Nihongaku no genjō to jisseki ga wakarimashite, watakushi no kongo no kenkyū ni yaku-datta koto o atsuku o-rei mōshi-agemasu.

Kore kara mo sensei-gata ga gyōseki o AGERARERU yō negatte yamimasen.

Watakushi wa are kara yonkakoku o mawari, shisatsu shite Nihon e kaerimashita. Ōku no ten de waga kuni ga kongo issō hagemaneba naranu koto o tsūkan itashimashita.

Dōfū no mono wa **Meiji** jidai no KOSEN de, genzai kochira de wa būmu o okoshite iru mono desu. **Meiji** jidai ga koten-KA shi-tsutsu aru tame to, kokuryoku o nobashita jidai de aru tame deshō. **Meiji** hyakunen-sai wa owarimashita ga, sono kangeki wa genzai kono yō na katachi ni natte arawarete orimasu. Purezento itashimasu no de, o-uke-tori kudasai.

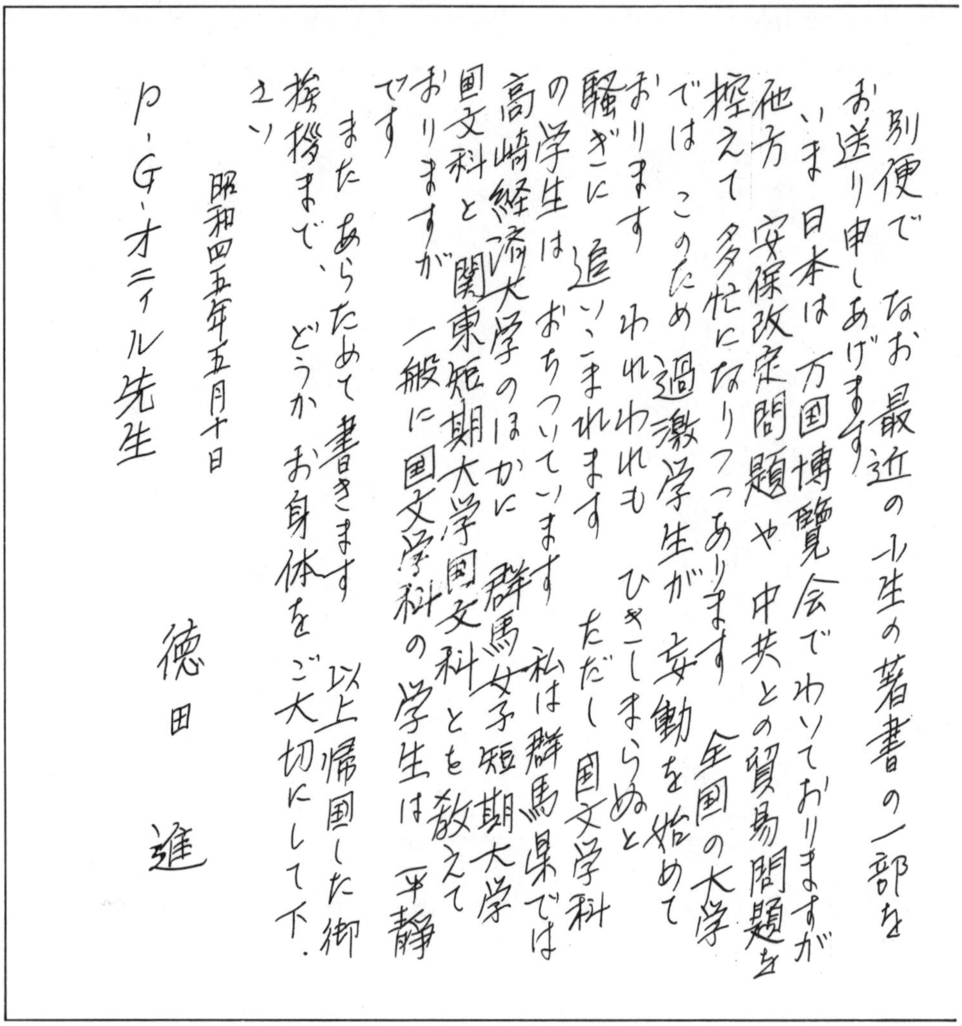
別便で なお最近の小生の著書の一部を
お送り申しあげます
いま日本は万国博覧会でわいておりますが
他方 安保改定問題や中共との貿易問題を
控えて多忙になりつつあります 全国の大学
では このため過激学生が妄動を始めて
おります われわれも ひきしまらぬと
騒ぎに追いこまれます ただし 国文学科
の学生は おちついています 私は群馬県では
高崎経済大学のほかに 群馬女子短期大学
国文科と関東短期大学国文科とを教えて
おりますが 一般に国文学科の学生は 平静
です
また あらためて書きます 以上帰国した御
挨拶まで どうか お身体をご大切にして下
さい
昭和四五年五月十日
徳田 進
P・G・オニイル先生

Betsubin de, nao saikin no shōsei no chosho no ichibu o o-okuri mōshi-agemasu.

Ima Nihon wa Bankoku Hakurankai de waite orimasu ga, tahō ANPO kaitei mondai ya CHŪKYŌ to no bōeki mondai o HIKAETE tabō ni nari-tsutsu arimasu. Zenkoku no daigaku de wa kono tame kageki gakusei ga **mōdō** o hajimete orimasu. Ware-ware mo HIKI-SHIMARANU TO sawagi ni oi-komaremasu. Tadashi kokubungaku-ka no gakusei wa ochi-tsuite imasu. Watakushi wa **Gunma**-ken de wa **Takasaki** Keizai Daigaku no hoka ni **Gunma** Joshi Tanki Daigaku Kokubunka to **Kantō** Tanki Daigaku Kokubunka to o oshiete orimasu ga, ippan ni kokubungaku-ka no gakusei wa heisei desu.

Mata aratamete kakimasu. Ijō kikoku shita go-aisatsu made. Dōka o-KARADA o go-taisetsu ni shite kudasai.

Shōwa yonjūgonen gogatsu tōka

Tokuda Susumu

P.G. **Oniiru** Sensei

Notes

a. REI In this letter, several old forms of characters or components of characters occur (here, e.g., 禮 for 礼). Henceforth, no special mention will be made of such forms, or of old *kana* spellings when they are used, but when necessary reference can be made to the lists of these forms and spellings in Apps. I and II.

b. AGERARERU The passive/potential form used as an honorific; it is thus equivalent in meaning to *ageru*.

c. KOSEN The character used for *sen* is an abbreviation for 銭.

d. -KA As a suffix, this is used to mean "change into, move towards" and hence is often translatable as "-ize." Here, however, *koten-ka shi-tsutsu aru* could be translated as "is becoming part of our classical past."

e. ANPO An abbreviation of *Anzen Hoshō Jōyaku*, "Security Pact," being a combination of the first characters of the first two words.

f. CHŪKYŌ An abbreviation of *Chūka Jinmin Kyōwakoku*, "The People's Republic of China."

g. HIKAETE "Having, being faced with."

h. HIKI-SHIMARANU TO "Unless (we) stand firm/are strong-minded."

i. KARADA Another reading of this compound would be *shintai*, but the characters are often used simply for *karada* and the use of the honorific prefix *o-* shows that this reading was intended here.

27. Letter from a Previously Unknown Woman

初めてお手紙を差し上げます失礼をお許し下さいませ。私は郡司正勝先生の御指導のもとで早稲田大学の修士課程を終え、以来、日本の近代演劇の研究を續けて来た者でございます。昨年十一月に、十年余を費しました明治期の演劇観の変遷についての研究を一応完成し、六年前に出版いたしました「明治前期演劇論史」に續いての「明治演劇論史」を出版いたしました。これでひとまず、日本の近代の演劇思想の歴史に終止符を打ち、西洋に於ける日本演劇観についての研究を始めたいと思っております。それで、四月末頃にロンドンに参りまして、主に、the British Museumの図書館と新聞図書館で資料を調査する計画でございます。

実は、私は大学の学部(under-graduate)は慶応義塾大学の図書館学科(現在の図書館情報学科)を卒業しておりまして、一九五三年(卒業時)から六年間、東京のthe British Councilで図書館司書として働らきました。それでこの度の訪英につきまして、the British Councilにも御相談に伺いまして、ロンドンでの調査については出来るだけ便宜を計っていただけることになりましたが、やはり、高名なSchool of Oriental & African Studiesの先生方の御指導をいただきたいと思っておりましたところ、郡司先生より、オニール先生に御紹介下さるとのお話を戴きました。私としましては、これ以上の幸運はないと喜んでおります。もちろん、先生が大変にお忙しいことはよく承知しておりますので、あまりお邪魔をいたすつもりはございませんが、一度でもお目にかかって何らかの御示唆を戴ければ幸せに存じます。

先生は私の研究には御興味をお持ちでないかとも存じましたが、一応、私の二冊の研究書をお送り申し上げました。船便でございますので私のロンドン着の前にお手もとに届くかどうか、心配でございます。私は英語にはあまり不自由はございません。近代演劇研究の他に、舞踊（歌舞伎舞踊と上方舞）の批評を専門誌に執筆しております。以前は、坂東流の名取りでございましたが、流派にちょっとした争いごとがございまして、名前を返えし、それからは上方舞（地唄舞）に力を入れまして、神崎流の名取りとなっております。舞は能の動きととても似た処がございますので、私はよく能は拝見いたしております。先生のお噂は郡司先生から よく伺っておりますので、お目にかかれますのを楽しみにいたしております。

三月六日

松本伸子

P・G・オニール先生

Hajimete o-tegami o sashi-agemasu shitsurei o-yurushi kudasaimase. Watakushi wa **Gunji Masakatsu** Sensei no go-shidō no moto de **Waseda** Daigaku no shūshi katei o OE, IRAI, Nihon no kindai engeki no kenkyū o tsuzukete kita mono de gozaimasu. Sakunen jūichigatsu ni, jūnen-yo o tsuiyashimashita **Meiji**-ki no engeki-kan no hensen ni tsuite no kenkyū o ichiō kansei shi, rokunen mae ni shuppan itashimashita "**Meiji** Zenki Engeki-ron Shi" ni tsuzuite no "**Meiji** Engeki-ron Shi" o shuppan itashimashita. Kore de hitomazu, Nihon no kindai no engeki shisō no rekishi ni shūshi-fu o uchi, Seiyō ni okeru Nihon engeki-kan ni tsuite no kenkyū o hajimetai to omotte orimasu. Sore de, shigatsumatsu-goro ni **Rondon** ni mairimashite, omo ni, The British Museum no Toshokan to SHINBUN Toshokan de shiryō o chōsa suru keikaku de gozaimasu.

Jitsu wa, watakushi wa daigaku no gakubu (undergraduate) wa **Keiō Gijuku** Daigaku no Toshokan Gakka (genzai no Toshokan Jōhō Gakka) o sotsugyō shite orimashite, 1953nen (sotsugyō-ji) kara rokunen-KAN, **Tōkyō** no The British Council de toshokan shisho to shite HATARAKIMASHITA. Sore de, kono tabi no **hō-Ei** ni tsukimashite,

The British Council ni mo go-sōdan ni ukagaimashite, **Rondon** de no chōsa ni tsuite wa dekiru dake bengi o hakatte itadakeru koto ni narimashita ga, yahari, kōmei na School of Oriental and African Studies no sensei-gata no go-shidō o itadakitai to omotte orimashita TOKORO, **Gunji** Sensei yori, **Oniiru** Sensei ni go-shōkai kudasaru TO NO o-hanashi o itadakimashita. Watakushi to shimashite wa, kore ijō no kōun wa nai to yorokonde orimasu. Mochiron, sensei ga taihen ni o-isogashii koto wa yoku shōchi shite orimasu no de, amari o-jama o itasu tsumori wa gozaimasen ga, ichido de mo o-me ni kakatte nanra-ka no go-shisa o itadakereba shiawase ni zonjimasu.

Sensei wa watakushi no kenkyū ni wa go-kyōmi o o-mochi de nai ka to mo zonjimashita ga, ichiō, watakushi no nisatsu no kenkyūsho o o-okuri mōshi-agemashita. Funabin de gozaimasu no de, watakushi no **Rondon**-chaku no mae ni o-temoto ni todoku ka dō ka shinpai de gozaimasu. Watakushi wa Eigo ni wa amari fu-jiyū wa gozaimasen. Kindai engeki kenkyū no hoka ni, buyō (Kabuki buyō to **Kamigata-mai**) no hihyō o senmon-shi ni shippitsu shite orimasu. Izen wa, **Bandō**-ryū no natori de gozaimashita ga, ryūha ni chotto shita arasoi-goto ga gozaimashite, namae o kaeshi, sore kara wa **Kamigata-mai (Jiuta-mai)** ni chikara o iremashite, **KANZAKI**-ryū no natori to natte orimasu. Mai wa Nō no ugoki to totemo nita tokoro ga gozaimasu no de, watakushi wa yoku Nō wa HAIKEN itashite orimasu.

Sensei no o-uwasa wa **Gunji** Sensei kara yoku ukagatte orimasu no de, o-me ni kakare-masu no o tanoshimi ni itashite orimasu.

Sangatsu muika

Matsumoto SHINKO

P.G. **Oniiru** Sensei

Notes

a. OE The suspensive form (see 1c) of *oeru*, vt., "finish." Being parallel here to *kita*, both verbs qualify the following *mono*, "person."

b. IRAI On the form of the character for *rai* used here and later in this letter, see 6r.

c. SHINBUN On this handwritten form of the character for *bun*, see 6k.

d. -KAN See c. above.

e. HATARAKIMASHITA The character used here is an abbreviation for the modern standard 働.

f. TOKORO Here, "(at the point/time) when"; see 4e.

g. TO NO = *to iu*, "saying that, to the effect that."

h. KANZAKI This reading is a corruption of *kamisaki*.

i. HAIKEN "Humbly seeing"; see 9a.

j. SHINKO A more common reading of these name characters is "Nobuko."

28. Letter from a Lady, a Family Friend for Many Years

保守党が圧勝をして日本を驚かせています。
その後御元気ですか。
日本にいらっしゃる時は、自分の思う様に
お訪ねも、お手伝いも出来ず ダイアナとも
テニスすら出来なかったのが残念に思います。
皆様お元気ですか。
ペラはどういらっしゃいますか。
今度コターチさんが大使になられるので
皆で 九月の御来日を待っています
さて、由紀子の友人 黒崎さんのことで
大変お世話になりましたことを
心から 厚く御礼申し上げます
黒崎さんから ドクター！オニールに
推せん状を書いて頂いたり、大変お世話に
なったとのことで感謝していらっしゃいました。
私共からも 厚く感謝致します。
彼女が 何か 日本からいらしゃったお客の
案内役でも何でもオニール先生の
お役に立てることがあったらおっしゃって
頂きたい！と 喜こんでいらしゃいました。
四年〜五年の間 かんばって勉強するそうです。
ありがとうございました。
由紀子は九月にBabyが出来るので早くも
我々は おじいさん・おばあさんになります。
月日 年月の経つのが早いとお思いになりませんか…
おめにかかれる日を楽しみにしております。

パット
ダイアナ

六月二十三日

Hoshu-tō GA ASSHŌ NO nyūsu ga Nihon o odorokasete imasu.

Sono go, o-genki desu ka.

Nihon ni irassharu toki wa, jibun no omou yō ni o-tazune mo, o-tetsudai mo dekizu, **Daiana** to mo tenisu SURA dekinakatta NO GA zannen ni omoimasu.

Mina-sama o-genki desu ka.

Pera wa DŌ SHITE irasshaimasu ka.

Kondo **Kotāchi**-san ga taishi ni narareru no de, mina de kugatsu no go-rai-Nichi o matte imasu.

Sate, **Yukiko** no yūjin **Kurosaki**-san no koto de, taihen o-sewa ni narimashita koto o kokoro kara atsuku o-rei mōshi-agemasu. **Kurosaki**-san kara, Dokutā **Oniiru** NI suisen-jō o kaite ITADAITARI, taihen o-sewa ni natta to totemo totemo kansha shite irasshaimashita. Watakushi-domo kara mo atsuku kansha itashimasu.

Kanojo ga nani-ka Nihon kara irasshatta o-kyaku no annai-yaku de mo nan-demo **Oniiru** Sensei no o-yaku ni tateru koto ga attara OSSHATTE itadakitai to yorokonde irasshaimashita. Yonen-gonen no aida ganbatte benkyō suru SŌ DESU.

Arigatō gozaimashita.

Yukiko wa kugatsu ni Baby ga dekiru no de hayaku mo ware-ware wa o-jii-san o-bā-san ni narimasu. Tsukihi, toshitsuki no TATSU no ga hayai to o-omoi ni narimasen ka....

O-me ni kakareru hi o tanoshimi ni shite.

Ayako

Patto
Daiana

Rokugatsu nijūsannichi

Notes

a. GA ASSHŌ NO No verb is expressed for the subject-particle *ga* to go with, but the phrase can be seen as an abbreviation of . . . *ga asshō shita to no (nyūsu)* (cf. 17a). Thus, "the news that the Conservative Party had an overwhelming victory."

b. SURA A literary word for "even," equivalent to *sae* or *made*.

c. NO GA Although *dekinakatta no ga zannen ni omoimasu* seems acceptable to some Japanese, *dekinakatta no* "not having managed" (see 4m) cannot logically be the subject of *omoimasu*. The writer seems to have fallen between . . . *no wa/o zannen ni omoimasu* and . . . *no ga zannen ni omowaremasu*.

d. DŌ SHITE Note that here the sense is not *dō-shite irasshaimasu ka*, "how/why is she here?" but *dō shite-irasshaimasu ka*, "how is she getting along?"

e. NI . . . ITADAITARI With the *-te itadaku/morau* construction, the person who does the favour is indicated by the particle *ni* (or, occasionally, *kara*), giving the literal meaning "receive a . . .ing by (/from) someone"; see also 14f.

f. OSSHATTE The verb *ossharu* is an honorific equivalent for *iu*, "say."

g. SŌ DESU When *sō da/desu*, etc., follows a final form of a verb or adjective, the meaning is "word has it that, he/she/they say that, I hear/read that"; cf. the more comprehensive *yō desu* under 10d and 11d.

h. TATSU The character 圣 used here is an abbreviation for 経.

29. Unsigned Letter from a Man after a Visit to London

た。そして、こうした経験は日本におりましては体験できないものでした。私どものように日本からこちらへ参る者にとりましては、一度御地に参ったら、二度ともうこられないだろうという正に「一生に一度」の思いで、やって参りますので、失礼とは存じながら、ついついご好意に甘えさせて頂くことになってしまいます。ストロング先生が快く出させて下さったこと、又、寛大にもそういう機会をお与え下さいました主任の先生に対しても、深く感謝申し上げる次第です。

先ずは御礼のみ申し上げます。

敬具

一九七四・三・十三

オニール先生　机下

拝啓

昨日（十二日）はお忙しいところを又、お邪魔致しまして失礼致しました。又、来週の先生のご授業を聴講させて頂けるとのこと、私の方の一方的なお願いを心よくお許し下さいまして、重々、厚く御礼申し上げます。

正式な手続も取らずに、大切な授業に出させて頂けるということは、全く先生のご好意に甘えた「日本式なやり方」であることも承知致しております。又、先生方のお立場からすれば、「外来者」が深い考えもなく他人の授業に顔を出すということは余り感心することでないということも存じております。そういうことを承知した上で、なお、敢えてお願いしたわけは、私にとりまして、異国の地、ロンドンで、日本語というものを、外国人の立場から眺める絶好の機会が得られるからでございます。ストロング先生の現代日本文学の授業を二度ほど聴講させて頂きましたことは、この間も申し上げましたように、私がロンドンで得た最大の収穫でし

Haikei,

Sakujitsu (jūninichi) wa o-isogashii tokoro o mata o-jama itashimashite shitsurei itashimashita. Mata, raishū no sensei no go-jugyō o chōkō sasete itadakeru to no koto, watakushi nó hō no ippō-teki na o-negai o kokoroyoku o-yurushi kudasaimashite, jū-jū atsuku o-rei mōshi-agemasu.

Seishiki na tetsuzuki mo torazu ni, taisetsu na jugyō ni desasete itadakeru to iu koto wa, mattaku sensei no go-kōi ni amaeta "Nihon-shiki na yari-KATA" de aru koto mo shōchi itashite orimasu. Mata, sensei-gata no O-TACHIBA KARA SUREBA, "gairaisha" ga fukai kangae mo naku tanin no jugyō ni kao o dasu to iu koto wa amari kanshin suru koto de nai to iu koto mo zonjite orimasu. SŌ IU koto o shōchi shita ue de, nao, aete o-negai shita wake wa, watakushi NI TORIMASHITE, ikoku no chi, **Rondon** de, Nihongo to iu mono o, gaikokujin no tachiba kara nagameru zekkō no kikai GA erareru kara de gozaimasu. **Sutorongu** Sensei no gendai Nihon bungaku no jugyō o nido hodo chōkō sasete itadakimashita koto wa, kono aida mo mōshi-age-mashita yō ni, watakushi ga **Rondon** de eta saidai no shūkaku deshita. Soshite, kō shita keiken wa Nihon ni orimashite wa taiken dekinai mono deshita. Watakushi-domo no yō ni Nihon kara kochira e mairu mono ni torimashite wa, ichido **on-chi** ni maittara, nido TO mō korarenai darō to iu masa ni "isshō ni ichido" no omoi de, yatte mairimasu no de, shitsurei to wa zonji-nagara, tsui tsui go-kōi ni amaesasete itadaku koto ni natte shimaimasu. **Sutorongu** Sensei ga kokoroyoku desasete kudasatta koto, mata, kandai ni mo sō iu kikai o o-atae kudasaimashita shunin no sensei ni taishite mo, fukaku kansha mōshi-ageru shidai desu.

MAZU WA o-rei nomi mōshi-agemasu.

1974. 3. 13 Keigu

Oniiru Sensei kika

Notes

a. -KATA Following the stem of a verb, *-kata* means "way of. . . .ing."

b. O-TACHIBA KARA SUREBA "If one takes/considers it from the standpoint (of . . .)"; on *suru* understandable as "treat/consider," etc., cf. *to suru* under 41.

c. SŌ IU "Like that, such (as that)"; cf. 24ef.

d. NI TORIMASHITE The polite *-masu* form of *ni totte (wa)* "for/to (me), for (my) part, in (my) case."

e. GA This particle can be used to indicate the subject of a potential verb (here *erareru*), which would be the object of the ordinary active verb; e.g., *kikai o eru*, "gain/obtain an opportunity," can have as a passive either *kikai ga erareru,* "an opportunity is obtainable/can be gained," or *kikai o erareru*, "(one) can gain an opportunity"; see, e.g., *jikan o itadakemasu* in No. 20, paragraph 2.

f. TO This is the adverbial *to* (as in *hakkiri to*, "clearly," etc.), describing here the way in which the writer cannot come, i.e., "for a second time"; cf. the similar use under 21c.

g. MAZU WA In such contexts, this phrase or *mazu* alone is used without any strong meaning, with much the same feeling as "well now, then," etc., in English.

30. Letter of Thanks from a University Official

20. 12. 1963

Dr. P. G. Oneill
University of London
W. C. 1.

新年おめでとうございます。

一層寒さが厳しくなりましたが　お変りなく　お過しのことゝ拝察致します。
御地滞在中は一方ならぬ　お世話になりありがとうございました。心からお礼を申上げます。
御好意により初めて接する御地で心安く有意義に過すことが出来ました。
そして大きな収穫を得ました。
又、お忙がしい時にもかゝわらず体育学校の資料を　お送り頂き有難とうございました。　私共の体育学校は設立準備中で一年後に開校の予定です。
帰国後の多忙さから　お礼状の遅れましたことを　お詫びするとゝもにとりあえず書中をもって　お礼申し上げます。

不一

浪商学園理事長
野田三郎

Shinnen o-medetō gozaimasu.

Issō samu-sa ga kibishiku narimashita ga, o-kawari naku o-sugoshi no koto to haisatsu itashimasu. **On-chi** taizai-chū wa HITOKATA-NARANU o-sewa ni nari, arigatō gozaimashita. Kokoro kara o-rei o mōshi-agemasu.

Go-kōi ni yori, hajimete sessuru **on-chi** de kokoro-zuyoku yūigi ni sugosu koto ga dekimashita. Soshite ōki na shūkaku o emashita.

Mata, o-isogashii toki ni mo kakawarazu taiiku gakkō no shiryō o o-okuri itadak-i, arigatō gozaimashita. Watakushi-domo no taiiku gakkō wa setsuritsu junbi-chū de, ichinen-go ni kaikō no yotei desu. Kikoku-go no tabō-sa kara o-reijō no okuremashita koto o o-wabi suru to tomo ni, tori-aezu **shochū** O MOTTE o-rei mōshi-agemasu.

FUITSU

Namishō Gakuen Rijichō
Noda Saburō

Notes

a. HITOKATA-NARANU Since *hitokata* means "ordinary, usual," and *naranu*, the negative attributive form of the literary copula *nari*, "be" (see 14a), is equivalent to colloquial *de nai*, the meaning of the phrase is "(which is) out of the ordinary/extraordinary/considerable."

b. O MOTTE A literary phrase equivalent to colloquial *de*, "with, by means of."

c. FUITSU Literally "incomplete," this word is used at the end of a letter to indicate that it is only an inadequate expression of the writer's true feelings.

31. Business Letter from a Bookshop

ヨーロッパ日本研究協会
P.G オニール 様

前略
今度は大変御世話に成り誠に有難うございます 御指示の通り着本次第貴方様宛の送金小切手にて代金£14.－を御送り申し上げます

御多忙の所色々と御配慮賜わり有難うございました今後共何卒宜敷く御願い申し上げます.

以上簡単ですが御礼のみにて失礼申し上げます.

敬具
(株)文生書院
小沼良成

Yōroppa Nihon Kenkyū Kyōkai
P.G. **Oniiru**-sama

Zenryaku,
Kondo wa taihen o-sewa ni nari, makoto ni arigatō gozaimasu. Go-shiji no tōri **chakuhon** shidai ANATA-sama ate no sōkin kogitte nite daikin £14- o o-okuri mōshi-agemasu.

Go-tabō no tokoro iro-iro to go-hairyo tamawar-i, arigatō gozaimashita. Kongo-tomo nani-tozo yoroshiku o-negai mōshi-agemasu.

Ijō kantan desu ga, o-rei nomi nite shitsurei mōshi-agemasu.

Keigu
(KABU) **Bunsei** Shoin
Konuma Yoshinari

Notes

a. ANATA These characters also have the more formal reading *kihō*, "you."

b. KABU Abbreviation for *kabushiki-gaisha* "a stock company," i.e., "Co. Ltd., Inc."

32. Letter from a Lady Formerly Employed as a Language Instructor

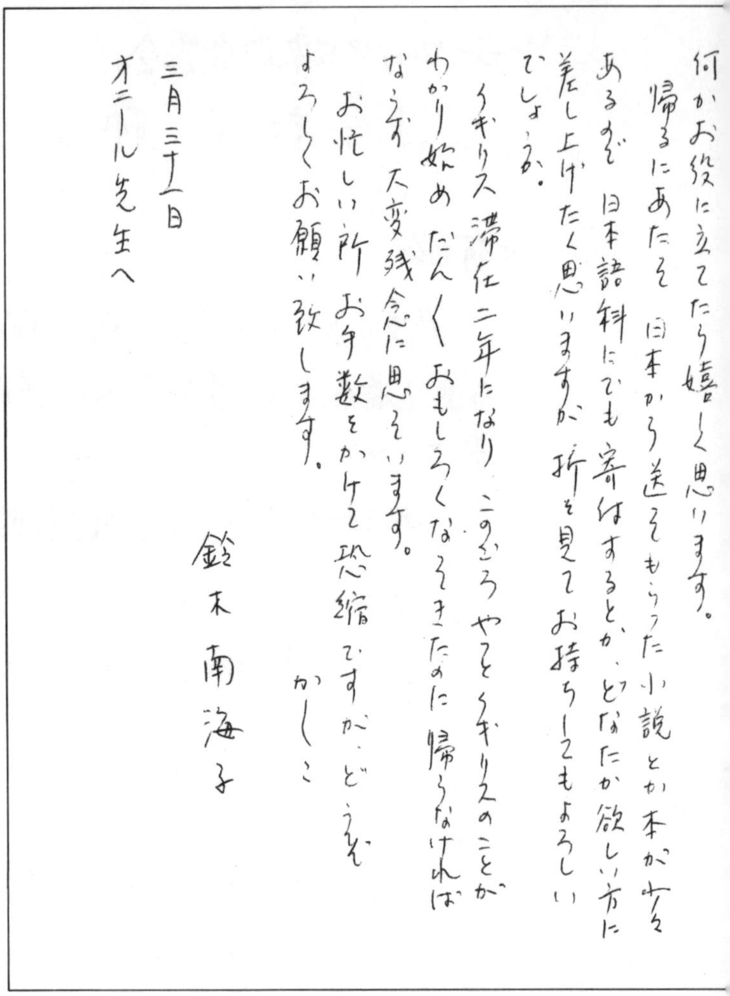

何かお役に立てたら嬉しく思います。
帰るにあたって日本から送ってもらった小説とか本が少々
あるので日本語科にでも寄付するとか、どなたか欲しい方に
差し上げたく思いますが折を見てお持ちしてもよろしい
でしょうか。
イギリス滞在二年になりこのごろやっとイギリスのことが
わかり始めだん〱おもしろくなってきたのに帰らなければ
ならず大変残念に思っています。
お忙しい所お手数をかけて恐縮ですがどうぞ
よろしくお願い致します。
かしこ
鈴木南海子
三月三十一日
オニール先生へ

Go-busata shite orimasu ga, o-kawari naku o-sugoshi deshō ka. Mō sugu **Iisutā** de, watakushi mo **Iisutā** o machi-kogarete imasu. Ninen **Igirisu** ni ite, konogoro yatto **Iisutā** o machi-kogareru mina-san no kimochi ga wakatte kita tokoro desu. Nagai fuyu ni toji-komerarete yatto haru ga **Iisutā** to tomo ni kuru no desu kara.

Watakushi wa yatto genki ni nari, UCL no Day Nursery no seki mo tore, gakkō ni korareru yō ni narimashita ga, taihen zannen na koto ni kyū ni shujin no kaisha no hō de henkō ga ari kikoku suru koto ni narimashita. Mada hakkiri kimatte imasen ga, gogatsu ka rokugatsu-goro ni nari-sō desu. Sore de o-negai ga atte kono tegami o kaite imasu. Nihon ni kaette mata doko-ka de oshieru tsumori desu ga, sono toki no tame ni Soas no Nihongo-ka de 1974nen kugatsu kara jūnigatsu made oshieta koto o shōmei suru tegami o kaite itadake-tara taihen ureshiku omoimasu. Suisen-jō de nakute, jōki no kiKAN oshieta to kaite areba yoroshii no desu. Eibun de kekkō desu. Taihen tankikan de, o-negai suru no ga jibun to shite wa hazukashii no desu ga, kore ga areba tsugi no shūshoku ni ii no de wa nai ka to omoi, o-negai suru shidai desu. Kyaria ni ninen-han no buranku ga aru no de.

Nihon ni kaette kara, Soas no tame ni nani-ka watakushi de o-yaku ni tatsu koto ga arimashitara nan-demo itashimasu no de, o-shirase kudasaimase. Nani-ka o-yaku ni tatetara ureshiku omoimasu.

ごぶさたしておりますが お変わりなくおすごしでしょうか。
もうすぐイースターで 私もイースターを待ちこがれています。
二年イギリスに居て このごろやっとイースターを待ちこがれる
皆さんの気持がわかってきたところです。長い冬にとじこめられて
やっと春がイースターと共に来るのですから。
　私はやっと元気になり UCLのDay Nurseryの席もとれ
学校に来られるようになりましたが、大変残念なことに
急に主人の会社の方で変更があり 帰国することになり
ました。まだはっきり決まっていませんが 五月か六月ごろに
なりそうです。それでお願いがあってこの手紙を書いています。
日本に帰ってまたどこかで教えるつもりですが その時のために
SOASの日本語科で1974年九月から十二月まで教えたことを
証明する手紙を書いていただけたら大変嬉しく思います。
推せん状でなくて、上記の期間教えたと書いてあればよろしい
のです。英文で結構です。大変短期間で、お願いするのが
自分としては恥かしいのですが、これがあれば 次の就職に
いいのではないかと思い、お願いする次第です。キャリアに
二年半のブランクがあるので。
　日本に帰ってから SOASのために何か私でお役に立つ
ことがありましたら 何でも致しますので お知らせ下さいませ。

Kaeru ni atatte, Nihon kara okutte moratta shōsetsu toka hon ga shō-shō aru no de, Nihongo-ka ni DE MO kifu suru toka, DONATA-ka hoshii kata ni sashi-agetaku omoimasu ga, ori o mite o-mochi shite mo yoroshii deshō ka.

Igirisu taizai ninen ni nari, konogoro yatto **Igirisu** no koto ga wakari-hajime, dan-dan omoshiroku natte kita NO NI kaeranakereba narazu taihen zannen ni omotte imasu.

O-isogashii tokoro o-tesū o kakete kyōshuku desu ga, dōzo yoroshiku o-negai itashimasu.

Kashiko

Sangatsu sanjūichinichi

Suzuki Namiko

Oniiru Sensei e

Notes

a. UCL Abbreviation for "University College, (University of) London."

b. -KAN On this form of the character, see 27d.

c. DE MO Literally "even being, be it even," this combination can indicate a suggestion or possibility, as here; e.g., *kōhii de mo ikaga*, "how about a coffee or something?"

d. DONATA A respectful equivalent for *dare*, parallel to *kata* for *hito* (see 3d).

e. NO NI Following a verb or adjective, *no ni* can mean "even though, in spite of," as here; cf. *no de*, "it being that, since."

33. An Air-Letter Form (Hence Without Signature to the Letter Itself) from an Older Man of Long Acquaintance

名勝などガイドしてやって下さい。彼女は私も親しくしていますので、ダン氏にも日本に来ない前に依頼したのでしたが、九月末まで滞在、帰英は十月になる由ですから、アナタを頼るほかありません。何れ本人からも旅宿決定次第、お知らせしますから、都合してやっていただくと大変結構です。末尾ですが奥さん、お娘さんにも呉々もよろしくお伝え下さい。

草々

五月十五日

Haikei. Kunpū sawayaka na nenkan saiteki no gogatsu o mukaeta Nihon desu ga, o-taku mina-san, go-yōsu ikaga desu ka, o-ukagai shimasu. Go-shōchi no yō ni mokka **Dan-shi** fusai, **Kyōto Kita-Shirakawa** no taihen shizuka na kankyō no **sanaka** ni aru **Shirakusō** ni taizai-chū desu ga, senjitsu hōmon, yokujitsu BUNRAKU ni annai shimashita. (**Dan** Fujin no **Amerika** no yūjin—**rō-fujin** mo dōkō, watashi no kanai mo kuwawatte, ikkō gomei. Oshiego de genzai Bunraku no jūchin ni natte imasu **Moji-DAYŪ** no annai de gakuya o kuwashiku kengaku sasemashita. **Amerika** fujin wa koto-no-hoka KYŌMI o idaki, shūshi, me o maruku shite wandafuru o KURI-KAESHITE imashita.

Tokoro de, kono shichigatsu jōjun kara nijūgonichi-kan hodo, **Kenburijji** Daigaku no kaki kōshū ni sanka shimasu **Matsuura Satoko-JŌ** (**Kansei** Gakuin Daigaku Eibunka sannen zaigaku) ga **Rondon** Daigaku ni anata o tazuneru yotei de imasu no de, sono se-tsu wa go-yakkai-nagara yoroshiku daigaku kōnai sono ta meishō nado gaido SHITE YATTE KUDASAI. Kanojo wa watashi mo shitashiku shite imasu no de, **Dan-shi** ni mo Nihon ni KONAI MAE NI irai shita no deshita ga, kugatsumatsu made taizai, **ki-Ei** wa jūgatsu ni naru yoshi desu kara, anata o tayoru hoka arimasen. Izure honnin kara mo ryoshuku kettei shidai, o-shirase shimasu kara, tsugō SHITE YATTE ITADAKU to

拝啓　薫風さわやかな年間最適の五月を
迎えた日本ですが、お宅みなさん、ごようすいかが
ですか、お伺いします。ご承知のように目下
ダン氏夫妻、京都北白川の大変静かな環
境のさ中にある紫洛荘に滞在中ですが、先日
訪問、翌日文楽に案内しました。（ダン夫人のアメ
リカの友人、老夫人も同行、私の家内も加わって、一
行五名。教え子で現在文楽の重鎮になっていま
す文字大夫の案内で楽屋を詳しく見学さ
せました、アメリカ夫人は殊の外興味を抱き、
終始、眼を丸くしてワンダフルを繰していました。
ところで、この七月上旬から十五日間程、ケンブリッヂ
大学の夏期講習に参加します松浦智子（サト）
嬢（関西学院大学英文科三年在学）がロンドン
大学にアナタをたずねる予定でいますので、その
節（せつ）はご厄介ながらよろしく大学構内その他

taihen kekkō desu. Matsubi desu ga, oku-san, o-jō-san ni mo kure-gure mo yoroshiku o-tsutae kudasai.

Sō-sō

Gogatsu jūgonichi

Notes

a. BUNRAKU The traditional Bunraku puppet theatre, based in Ōsaka.

b. -DAYŪ A suffix which, like the noun-form *tayū*, can also be written 太夫 and is a title used of certain types of fully fledged professional entertainers and geisha.

c. KYŌMI The character used here for *kyō* is an abbrevation for the standard 興.

d. KURI-KAESHITE The reading intended here must be *kuri-kaeshite*, but this would normally be written with a second character: 繰返して.

e. -JŌ A respectful suffix used of a young unmarried woman; hence, "Miss."

f. SHITE YATTE KUDASAI "Please do . . . for her"; on *-te yaru/ageru*, see 8k.

g. KONAI MAE NI Like *kuru mae ni* and *konai uchi ni*, this means simply "before one comes," though the phrases with the negative verb forms usually carry an implication of haste in trying to do something before the action of the negative verb takes place; e.g., *tomodachi ga kaeranai uchi ni denwa suru*, "telephone before one's friend goes home."

h. SHITE YATTE ITADAKU Here "receive from you (*itadaku*) a doing . . . for her (*yatte*)"; i.e., "have you do . . . for her." On *-te yaru*, see 8l, and on *-te itadaku*, 6a.

34. Letter from a Former Colleague and Friend

拝啓その後お元気にお過しのことと存じます。本日は東方学会から頼まれましてこの手紙を書いております。実は本年6月16日と17日に第23回国際東方学者会議(The 23rd International Conference of Orientalists in Japan)が開催されますが、その第1日目の16日に特別講演として外国人学者1名と日本人学者1名の方にお願いすることになりました。

いつもお願いばかりで申しわけございませんが、この特別講演(16日午前中)をお引受け願えませんでしょうか。題目は御専門の能について適当なものがあれば幸です。また、招聘されて日本にいらっしゃるので他にも講演を頼まれているかと思いますが、それと同じ演題であってもよいかとも思います。(数年前ケンブリッジのミルズさんが東方学会の招待で来日なさった折の講演は同じ題目のものを他所にもなさりました)是非お願いしたいのですがいかがでしょうか。

御専門の研究の成果ではなくとも、例えばヨーロッパなどにおける能の受容などについてお話し下さっても結構だと思います。

日本人はどうもすぐ外国人の先生方に講演をお願いしてしまいます。ご迷惑だということはよくわかっているのですが、イギリスの先生というと色々なことを頼まれてしまいます。

今年はケンブリッジのミルズさんが国文学資料館の招聘で来日します。皆さんにお会い出来るのが楽しみです。S.O.A.S の Old Boys のパーティをやりたいと思います。5月頃には今建築中の私の新しい家が完成しますのでご招待致しましょう。

ではご返事をお待ちしております。草々

3月5日　池田重

P.G.オニール様

Haikei. Sono go o-genki ni o-sugoshi no koto to zonjimasu. Honjitsu wa Tōhō Gakkai kara tanomare-mashite kono tegami o kaite orimasu. Jitsu wa honnen rokugatsu jūrokunichi to jūshichinichi ni Dai-nijūsan-kai Kokusai Tōhō Gakusha Kaigi (The 23rd International Conference of Orientalists in Japan) ga kaisai saremasu ga, sono daiichinichi-me no jūrokunichi ni tokubetsu kōen to shite gaikokujin gakusha ichimei to Nihonjin gakusha ichimei no kata ni o-negai suru koto ni narimashita.

Itsu mo o-negai bakari de mōshi-wake gozaimasen ga, kono tokubetsu kōen (jūrokunichi gozen-chū) o o-hiki-uke negaemasen deshō ka. Daimoku wa go-senmon no Nō ni tsuite tekitō na mono ga areba saiwai desu. Mata, shōhei sarete Nihon ni irassharu no de hoka ni mo kōen o tanomarete iru ka to omoimasu ga, sore to onaji endai de atte mo YOI KA TO MO OMOIMASU. (Sūnen mae **Kenburijji** no **Miruzu**-san ga Tōhō Gakkai no shōtai de **rai-Nichi** NASATTA ori no kōen wa onaji daimoku no mono o hoka ni mo nasaimashita.) Zehi o-negai shitai no desu ga, ikaga deshō ka. Go-senmon no kenkyū no seika DE WA NAKU TOMO, tatoeba **Yōroppa** nado ni okeru Nō no juyō nado ni tsuite o-hanashi kudasatte mo kekkō da to omoimasu.

Nihonjin wa dōmo sugu gaikokujin no sensei-gata ni kōen o o-negai shite shimaimasu. Go-meiwaku da to iu koto wa yoku wakatte iru no desu ga, **Igirisu** no sensei to iu to iroiro na koto o tanomare-te shimaimasu.

Kotoshi wa **Kenburijji** no **Miruzu**-san ga Kokubungaku Shiryōkan no shōhei de **rai-Nichi** shimasu. Mina-san ni o-ai dekiru no ga tanoshimi desu. Soas no Old Boys no pāti o yaritai to omoimasu. Gogatsu-goro ni wa ima kenchiku-chū no watashi no atarashii ie ga kansei shimasu no de go-shōtai itashimashō.

De wa go-henji o o-machi shite orimasu.

Sō-sō

Sangatsu itsuka **Ikeda Tadashi**

P.G. **Oniiru**-sama

Notes

a. YOI KA TO MO OMOIMASU "I think/feel too that it will perhaps/probably be all right."

b. NASATTA *Nasaru* is an honorific equivalent for *suru*, "do,"—hence the standard honorific *o-* vb. stem *nasaru* form, in contrast to the *o-* vb. stem *suru* humble form (see 6t). Since there is a parallel construction with *go*-noun (e.g., *go-benkyō nasaru*, "you/they, etc., study"), the whole range of these respect forms can be summarized as "*go- /o-* noun + verb in respect expressions"; see *o- noun* . . . entries in the Index for references.

c. DE (WA) NAKU TOMO = *de (wa) nakute mo*, "even though/if it is not." The *-ku* form is regularly used before *tomo* in this sense; e.g., *sukunaku tomo*, "even if it is few," i.e., "at the least."

35. Letter from a Woman on the Editorial Staff of a Periodical

第2回目を載せたいと思っておりますが
もし、来年早々に先生の原稿をいただけ
るようでしたら、紙面をあけてお待ち
しております。御予定お知らせ下さ
れば幸いです。
執筆条件は左記の通りです。
① 400字詰原稿用紙15枚内外(略歴を含む)
(付) 顔写真1枚 (13〜 1枚)
② 稿料は400字詰原稿用紙1枚1,000円(税込)
送金は、雑誌掲載後1か月以内に(日本発送)小切手で送る(特に指定が
あれば銀行振り込みで)
③ 原稿の当着日によってすぐ次の号には
掲載できない場合もあります。
以上です。専門雑誌で発刊後日が浅
いため、余り高い稿料をお支払いできな
くて申し訳なく思っております

Hajimete o-tegami o sashi-agemasu.

Nagakawa Reiji-shi o tōshite genkō o o-negai itashimashita zasshi "Gekkan Gengo" no henshūbu no mono desu. Kokoroyoku o-hiki-uke kudashaimashita sō de, arigatō gozaimasu.

Nagakawa-shi no hanashi de wa, kotoshi wa o-isogashikute muri da ga, rainen sō-sō ni wa kaite itadakeru to no koto deshita ga, ichigatsu-goro ni kaite itadake-masu deshō ka?

Kono "Nihongo To Watakushi" shiriizu wa, fu-teiki ni sankagetsu ni ichido-gurai no keisai o meyasu ni, keikaku shimashite, dai-ikkai o jūnigatsu-gō (11/25 hatsubai) kara hajimemashita. Narubeku hayaku dai-nikai-me o nosetai to omotte orimasu ga, moshi rainen sō-sō ni sensei no genkō o itadakeru yō deshitara, shimen o akete o-machi shite orimasu. Go-yotei o-shirase kudasareba saiwai desu.

初めてお手紙を差し上げます。
永川玲二氏を通して原稿をお願い致しました雑誌『月刊言語』の編集部の者です。快くお引き受け下さいましたそうでありがとうございます。
永川氏の話では、今年はお忙しくて無理だが、来年早々には書いていただけるとのことでしたが、一月頃に書いていただけますでしょうか？
この「日本語と私」シリーズは、不定期に、3か月に1度位の掲載を目安に、計画しまして、第1回を12月号（11/25発売）からはじめました。なるべく早く

Shippitsu jōken wa saki no tōri desu.

1. 400ji-zume genkō yōshi 13–15 mai (ryakureki ichimai o fukumu). Tsuki: kaojashin ichimai.

2. Kōryō wa 400ji-zume genkō yōshi ichimai 1,000 en (zei-komi). Sōkin wa zasshi keisai-go ikkagetsu inai ni (Nihon hassō) kogitte de okuru. (Toku ni shitei ga areba, ginkō furi-komi de.)

3. Genkō no tōchaku-bi ni yotte, sugu tsugi no gō ni wa keisai dekinai baai mo arimasu.

Ijō desu. Senmon zasshi DE hakkan-go hi ga asai tame, amari takai kōryō o o-shi-harai dekinakute mōshi-wake naku omotte orimasu.

別便で『言語』を三、四冊お送り致し
ましたので、どのような雑誌かおわかり
いただけると存じます。12月号（第
1回目のシリーズ掲載）は発売次第、
航空便でお届け致します。
執筆を引き受けて下さって本当に
ありがとうございました。

十月十五日

日高美南子

Betsubin de "Gengo" o san-yonsatsu o-okuri itashimashita no de, dono yō na zasshi ka o-wakari itadakeru to zonjimasu. Jūnigatsu-gō (dai-ikkai-me no shiriizu keisai) wa hatsubai shidai, kōkūbin de o-todoke itashimasu.

Shippitsu o hiki-ukete kudasatte hontō ni arigatō gozaimashita.

Jūgatsu jūgonichi

Hidaka Minako

Notes

a. DE Here the suspensive form of *da/desu*, parallel to *asai*. Since both qualify *tame*, the meaning is "because it is a specialised magazine and it is early days . . ."

36. Letter from a Visitor Following His Return to Japan

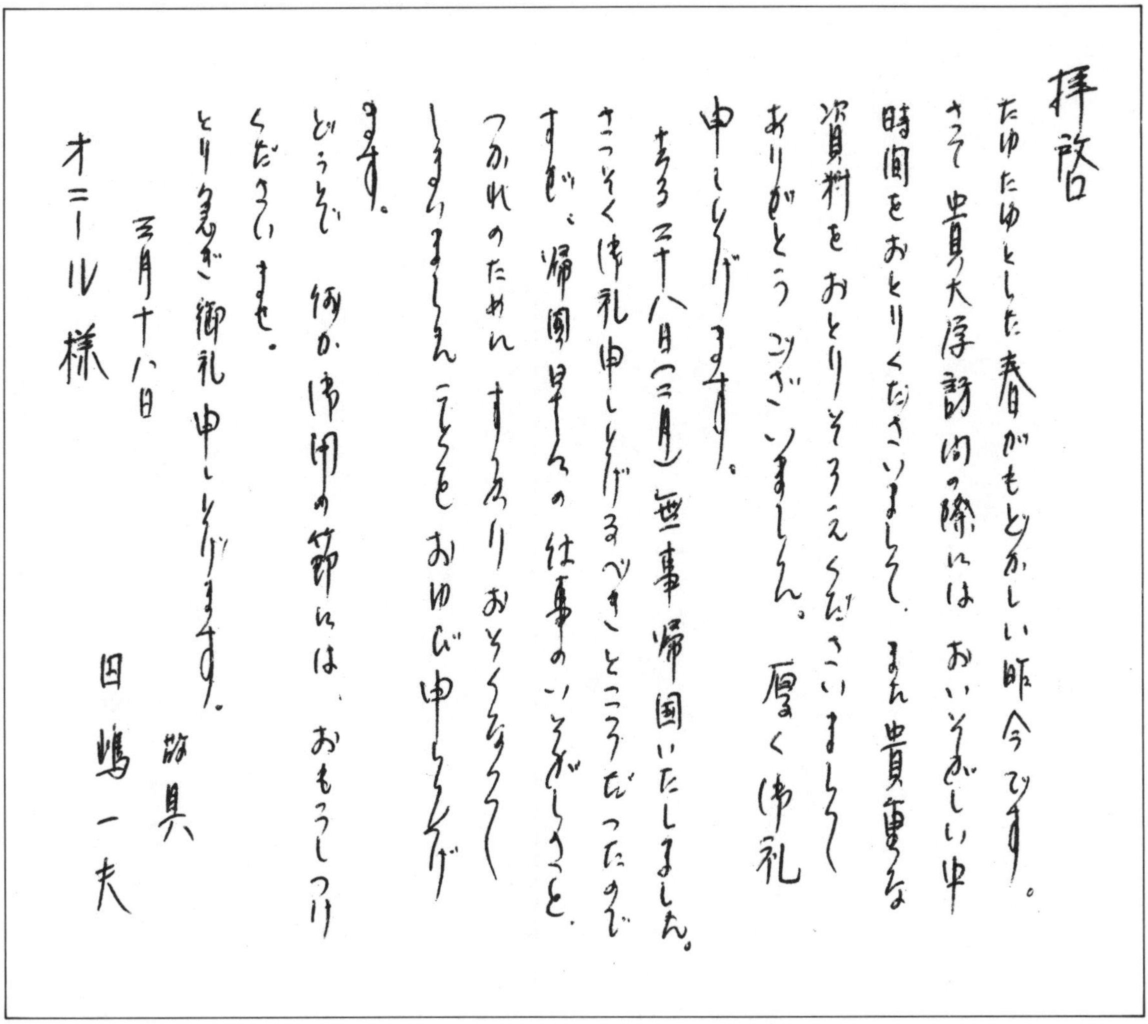

拝啓
たゆたゆとした春がもどかしい昨今です。
さて貴大学訪問の際にはおいそがしい中
時間をおとりくださいまして、また貴重な
資料をおとりそろえくださいまして
ありがとうございました。厚く御礼
申しあげます。
去る二十八日(二月)無事帰国いたしました。
さっそく御礼申しあげるべきところだったので
すが、帰国早々の仕事のいそがしさと
つかれのためすっかりおそくなってし
まいましたことをおわび申しあげ
ます。
どうぞ何か御用の節にはおもうしつけ
くださいませ。
とりいそぎ御礼申しあげます。
敬具
三月十八日
田嶋一夫
オニール様

Haikei,

Tayu-tayu to shita haru ga modokashii sakkon desu.

Sate, ki-daigaku hōmon no sai ni wa, o-isogashii naka jikan o o-tori kudasaimashite, mata kichō na shiryō o o-tori-soroe kudasaimashite, arigatō gozaimashita. Atsuku o-rei mōshi-agemasu.

Saru nijūhachinichi (nigatsu) buji kikoku itashimashita. Sassoku o-rei mōshi-agerubeki tokoro datta no desu ga, kikoku sō-sō no shigoto no isogashi-sa to tsukare no tame ni sukkari osoku natte shimaimashita koto o o-wabi mōshi-agemasu.

Dōzo, nani-ka go-yō no setsu ni wa o-mōshi-tsuke kudasaimase.

Tori-isogi o-rei mōshi-agemasu.

Keigu

Tajima Kazuo

Sangatsu jūhachinichi
Oniiru-sama

37. Short Letter from a Lady Employed as a Part-Time Teacher

オニール先生

では右簡単ながらお返事申し上げます。

草々

一九八十年十二月十五日

笙子・コーニシ拝

HAIFUKU,

Jūnigatsu tōka-zuke o-tayori itadakimashita. Arigatō gozaimashita. Go-irai itadakimashita ken ni tsuki,

1. Jūrai-dōri no Suiyō gogo niji-kan ni tsukimashite wa hiki-tsuzuki oshiesasete itadakimasu.

2. Shinki **daikō-bun** no Mokuyō gozen niji-kan jūji kara jūniji made no niji-kan mo tsugō ga tsukimasu no de, hiki-ukesasete itadakimasu.

Tadashi, **konpojishon** ni tsuite no keiken ga asō gozaimasu no de, shin-gakki hajimarimashite kara de mo shiryō nado ni tsuki go-shidō itadakereba saiwai ni zonjimasu. Chikara ga oyobimasu ka dō ka shinpai de gozaimasu ga, dekiru kagiri no koto o shite miru TSUMORI de gozaimasu.

拝復

十二月十日付お便りいただきました。有難うございました。

ご依頼いただきました件につき、

一、従来通りの水曜午後二時間につきましては引続き教えさせていただきます。

二、新規代講分の木曜午前二時間十時から十二時までの二時間も都合がつきますので引受けさせていただきます。

但しコンポジションについての経験が浅うございますので新学期始まりましてからでも資料等につきご指導いただければ幸いに存じます。力が及びますかどうか心配でございますが、出来る限りのことをしてみる心算でございます。

De wa, migi kantan-nagara o-henji mōshi-agemasu.

Sō-sō

1980nen jūnigatsu jūgonichi

Takako Kōnishi hai

Oniiru Sensei

Notes

a. HAIFUKU "A respectful response"; a polite term used to introduce a reply.

b. TSUMORI The characters used here also have the more stiff and formal reading *shinsan*.

拝啓　過日は折角、平泉へお誘いをいただき、
社の仕事の都合で伺えませんでした。大変残念に
思っています。いつか、お会いしたときに、色々とお
話を伺います。
さて、同封の写真は先日の仕事のなかで
スナップしたものです。オニールさんの真面目
~~勤勉~~な性格がでているのではないかと
思っています。
公務の繁多の確実な日と時間が判ったら
御一報くださいますようお願いします。
右お願いまでに。

五月二十日

サナに

高橋正雄

オニール様

Haikei. Kajitsu wa sekkaku **Hiraizumi** e o-sasoi o itadak-i, sha no shigoto no tsugō de ukaga-emasen deshita. Taihen zannen ni omotte imasu. Itsu ka, o-ai shita toki ni, iro-iro to o-hanashi o ukagaimasu.

Sate, dōfū no shashin wa senjitsu no kisha no naka de **sunappu** shita mono desu. **Oniiru**-san no majime na seikaku ga dete iru no de wa nai ka to omotte imasu.

Hiroshima no HAYASHIDA no kakujitsu na hi to jikan ga wakattara, go-ippō kudasaimasu yō o-negai shimasu.

Migi o-negai made ni.

Gogatsu hatsuka

Sō-sō

Takahashi Masao

Oniiru-sama

Notes

a. HAYASHIDA 囃田; a large-scale rice-planting festival held annually in the northern part of Hiroshima Prefecture.

39. Letter from an Older Man, Met a Few Times through a Mutual Acquaintance

余をロンドンで過します。詳細のスケジュールもホテルもまだ分かりませんが。その間にオリヴィエの「オセロ」や野外劇場での「ヴェローナの二紳士」、ストラットフォードオンエイヴォンのローヤル・シェイクスピア劇場で「ヘンリー五世」を、またエディンバラへ飛んで、音楽祭の「ロメオとジュリエット」を聴き、シアターワークショップで「ヘンリー四世」を見る予定になってゐます。

右のやうな団体行動のほかに、可成り自由な時間も持てるだろうと思ってゐますが、何分にも私は英語もよく話せませんし、英国の知識も乏しいので、大した望みは持てないにしても、できるだけ収穫を得たいものと努めて居ります。いづれ、詳しいスケジュールが決り次第、申上げます。

ちょうど、夏休みの期間中なので、あなたもどこかへ旅行をなさってゐるかも知れないし、また御研究で余暇もお持ちにならないかも知れぬと思ひますが、もし無理なく貴重なお時間を私のために割いて頂けるなら、たいへん幸福と存じます。

先年、九州旅行を御一緒に行ったチャールズ・ダンさんにも、同様に手紙を出しました。

どうぞよろしく。お目にかかれるのを楽しみにしてゐます。

北岸佑吉

P.G.オニール様

お元気でいらっしゃいますか。久しぶりのお手紙を日本語で書くことをお許し下さい。

私も五年前に朝日新聞社を定年退職しましたが、引續き、客員の待遇を受けて、今も随時、新聞に演劇の評論を書いてゐます。また五年前から、大阪の浪速短期大學教授として、演劇の講義をしてゐます。杉本藤次郎君も出てゐる大學です。一昨年から京都で藝能史研究会が結成されたので、各地の民俗藝能の探訪に行ったりしてゐます。兵庫縣下の農村歌舞伎舞台、三河花祭、播磨の鴨川住吉祭、山形縣の黒川能などへ行きました。

ことしの夏はヨーロッパ旅行に出ることになりました。日本演劇協会のシェイクスピア生誕四百年記念祭参加、ヨーロッパ演劇界視察団に一員として参加するのです。一行には、歌舞伎の市川團十郎夫妻、新劇女優の夏川靜江、劇作家の北條秀司夫妻らも参加します。

八月十二日朝、東京出發、十三日朝ロンドン着、それから二十一日朝アムステルダムへ向って出發するまでの一週間

Kitagishi Sukeyoshi

P.G. **Oniiru**-sama,

O-genki de irasshaimasu ka. Hisashi-buri no o-tegami o Nihongo de kaku koto o o-yurushi kudasai.

Watashi mo gonen mae ni Asahi Shinbun-sha o teinen taishoku shimashita ga, hiki-tsuzuki, kyakuin no taigū o ukete, ima mo zuiji, shinbun ni engeki no hyōron o kaite I-MASU. Mata gonen mae kara, **Ōsaka** no **Naniwa** Tanki Daigaku kyōju to shite, engeki no kōgi o shite imasu. **Sugimoto Tōjirō**-KUN mo dete iru daigaku desu. Issakunen kara **Kyōto** de Geinō-shi Kenkyū-kai ga kessei **sareta no de**, kakuchi no minzoku geinō no tanbō ni ittari shite imasu. **Hyōgo-kenka** no nōson Kabuki butai, MIKAWA HANA-MATSURI, HARIMA NO KAMOGAWA SUMIYOSHI matsuri, **Yamagata**-ken no **Kurokawa** Nō nado e ikimashita.

Kotoshi no natsu wa **Yōroppa** ryokō ni deru koto ni narimashita. Nihon Engeki Kyōkai no **Sheikusupia** seitan yonhyakunen kinen-sai sanka, **Yōroppa** engeki-kai shisa-tsu-dan ni ichiin to shite sanka suru no desu. Ikkō ni wa, Kabuki no **Ichikawa Danjūrō** fusai, Shingeki jōyū no **Natsukawa Shizue**, geki-sakka no **Hōjō Hideji** fusai-ra mo sanka shimasu.

Hachigatsu jūninichi asa, **Tōkyō** shuppatsu, jūsannichi asa **Rondon**-chaku, sore kara nijūichinichi asa **Amusuterudamu** e mukatte shuppatsu suru made no isshūkan amari o **Rondon** de sugoshimasu. Shōsai no sukejūru mo hoteru mo mada wakarimasen ga, sono aida no **Orivie** no "**Osero**" ya yagai gekijō de no "**Verōna** no Ni-shinshi," **Sutorad-dofōdo-on-Eivon** no **Rōyaru Sheikusupia** Gekijō de "**Henrii** Gosei" o, mata **Edin-bara** e tonde, ongaku-sai no "**Romeo** to **Jurietto**" o kiki, **Shiatā Uākushoppu** de "**Henrii** Yonsei" o miru yotei ni natte imasu. Migi no yō na dantai kōdō no hoka ni, kanari jiyū na jikan mo moteru darō to omotte imasu ga, **nanibun ni mo** watashi wa Eigo mo yoku hanasemasen shi, Eikoku no chishiki mo toboshii no de, taishita nozomi wa motenai NI SHITE MO, dekiru dake shūkaku o etai mono to negatte orimasu. Izure kuwashii sukejūru ga wakari shidai, mōshi-agemasu. Chōdo, natsu-yasumi no kikan-chū na no de, anata mo doko-ka e ryokō o nasatte iru ka mo shirenai shi, mata go-kenkyū de yoka mo o-mochi ni naranai ka mo shire-nu to omoimasu ga, moshi muri naku kichō na o-jikan o watashi no tame ni saite itadakeru nara, taihen kōfuku to zonjimasu.

Sennen, **Kyūshū** ryokō o go-issho ni itta **Chāruzu Dan**-san ni mo, dōji ni tegami o dashimashita.

Dōzo yoroshiku. O-me ni kakareru no o tanoshimi ni shite imasu.

Notes

a. IMASU In this letter, the writer uses the old *kana* spelling of ゐ *(w)i* for the *i* of *iru*, etc.

b. -KUN A term used by men in reference to others junior to themselves. Being a good deal less respectful than *-san*, it can be regarded as much the same as not using any term of address with a Western name and simply calling someone "Brown," etc.

c. MIKAWA HANA-MATSURI 三河花祭; the "Flower Festivals" which take place in mid-winter in Mikawa, an area covering the eastern part of modern Aichi Prefecture.

d. HARIMA NO KAMOGAWA SUMIYOSHI 播磨の鴨川住吉; Harima is an area covering the western part of modern Hyōgo Prefecture.

e. NI SHITE MO Being much the same as *to shite mo* (see 4l), the meaning is "even if one takes it that"; cf. *izure ni shite mo* under 4n.

40. Letter from a Former Colleague in a Research Institute

ただいま お手紙拝見しました
先日は、ほんとうに思いがけず お会いすることができ、嬉し
く思いました
比較的涼しい夏のようですが、もう落ちつかれた由、
大慶に存じます
さて、お申し越しの一件、承知いたしました 早速
コピーして同封いたします。いちおう全部コピー
致しましたので、適宜御利用ください
今後とも、当方でお役に立てることがありましたら、何なり
とお申しつけください
南山大学は、以前、私の遠縁にあたる水谷一雄教授
(経済学専攻、現在、神戸大学名誉教授)が教鞭を
とっていたところなので、とてもなつかしい気がいたします
それでは 御発表の御成功をお祈り申しあげます

八月一日

西野春雄

P.G. オニール様

P.S. もうすぐ八月八日、世阿弥忌がきますね もっとも旧暦
でかぞえないと、いけませんが

Tadaima o-tegami haiken shimashita.

Senjitsu wa hontō ni omoi-gakezu o-ai suru koto ga deki, ureshiku omoimashita.

Hikaku-teki suzushii natsu no yō desu ga, mō ochi-tsukareta yoshi **taikei** ni zonjimasu.

Sate, o-mōshi-koshi no ikken, shōchi itashimashita. Sassoku copii shite dōfū itashimasu. Ichiō zenbu copii itashimashita no de, tekigi go-riyō kudasai.

Kongo-tomo, tōhō de o-yaku ni tateru koto ga arimashitara, nan nari to o-mōshi-tsuke kudasai.

Nanzan Daigaku wa, izen, watashi no tōen ni ataru **Mizutani Kazuo** Kyōju (keizaigaku senkō, genzai, **Kōbe** Daigaku meiyo kyōju) ga kyōben o totte ita tokoro na no de, totemo natsukashii ki ga itashimasu.

Sore de wa, go-happyō no go-seikō o o-inori mōshi-agemasu.

Hachigatsu tsuitachi

Nishino Haruo

P.G. **Oniiru**-sama

P.S. Mō sugu hachigatsu yōka, ZEAMI-ki ga kimasu ne. Mottomo kyūreki de kazoenai to, ikemasen ga.

Notes

a. ZEAMI 世阿弥; the most famous figure in the history of Nō drama, an actor and playwright who lived 1363?–1443?

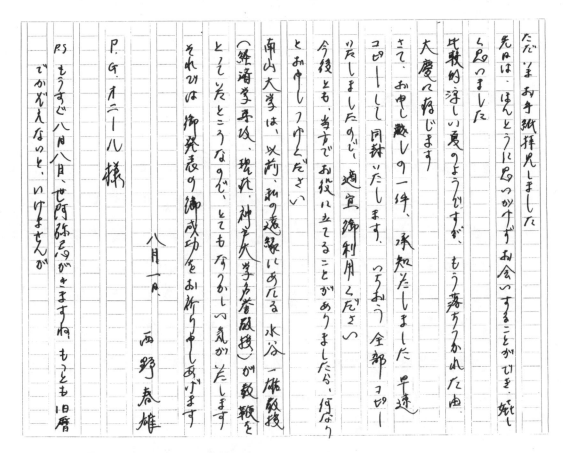

41. Letter from a Professor after His Return to Japan

拝啓　厳寒の候となりましたが、先生にはその後おかわりなくご活躍のことと存じます。

さて、昨年10月、貴大学にお邪魔した時には、お忙しい中にもかかわらず、楽しいひと時を過させていただき、まことにありがとうございました。厚くお礼申しあげます。遅ればせながら、その時の写真および私の家庭の写真を一枚同封しました。どうぞご笑納下さい。後者は、右から、長男（大学1年）、妻、次女（大学4年）、私、長女（昨年5月に結婚）の順です。

なお、拙著「東西文化の交流」を1冊、船便にてお送りしました。お手許に届くまで2,3か月かかるかと存じますが、ご一読いただければ幸いです。

最後に、先生のご健勝とご発展をお祈り申しあげます。

敬白

1月19日　　　伊瀬仙太郎

オネイル先生

Haikei. Genkan no **kō** to narimashita ga, sensei ni wa sono go o-kawari naku go-katsuyaku no koto to zonjimasu.

Sate, sakunen jūgatsu, ki-daigaku ni o-jama shita toki ni wa, o-isogashii naka ni mo kakawarazu, tanoshii hito-toki o sugosasete itadak-i, makoto ni arigatō gozaimashita. Atsuku o-rei mōshi-agemasu. **Okurebase**-nagara, sono toki no shashin oyobi watashi no katei no shashin o ichimai dōfū shimashita. Dōzo go-**shōnō** kudasai. Kōsha wa, migi kara, chōnan (daigaku ichinen), tsuma, jijo (daigaku yonen), watashi, chōjo (sakunen gogatsu ni kekkon) no jun desu.

Nao, **SETCHO** "Tōzai Bunka No Kōryū" o issatsu, funabin nite o-okuri shimashita.

O-temoto ni todoku made ni-sankagetsu kakaru ka to zonjimasu ga, go-ichidoku itadakereba saiwai desu.

Saigo ni, sensei no go-kenshō to go-hatten o o-inori mōshi-agemasu.

KEIHAKU

Ise Sentarō

Ichigatsu jūkunichi
Oneiru Sensei

Notes

a. SETCHO *Setsu-*, "unskilful, clumsy," is used as a humble prefix, mainly and correctly in conjunction with a person (almost always oneself) or thing which can be described as showing no skill or ability (cf. *hei-* under 13c, which is used of something inherently poor or wretched). Thus, *setcho* means "my (poor) book."

b. KEIHAKU "Respectfully stated"; a formal concluding word in letters, like *keigu*.

42. Two Postcards from a Professor Following a Research Leave in London

55. 3. 26.

拝啓

うららかな陽春の好季節となって参りました。
オニール先生には、お変りなく、お元気でお過しでしょうか。
奥様も、日本で唯一度お目に掛かっただけですが、お丈夫でいらっしゃいますか。

さて、私はSOASで満五ケ月の間、勉強をいたしていましたが、いよいよ、此の3月27日に、日本へ、帰らねばならなくなりました。先生を始め、ダン教授、ストロング先生、井上さん等から頂きました御親切なお教えと、御厚情とは、ほんとうに有難く、どんなに深く感謝しても、感謝し尽くせません。
まことに有難うございました。研究室で頂いたシェリー酒の味と、先生の御好意は、決して忘れません。お元気で御活躍を！

---

55. 3. 26

Haikei,

Uraraka na yōshun no **kō-kisetsu** to natte MAIRIMASHITA.

Oniiru Sensei ni wa, o-kawari naku, o-genki de o-sugoshi deshō ka. Oku-sama mo, Nihon de tada ichido o-me ni kakatta dake desu ga, o-jōbu de irasshaimasu ka.

Sate, watashi wa Soas de man-gokagetsu no aida, benkyō o itashite imashita ga, iyo-iyo, kono sangatsu nijūshichinichi ni, Nihon e KAERANEBA NARANAKU NARI-MASHITA. Sensei o hajime, **Dan** Kyōju, **Sutorongu** Sensei, **Inoue**-san-ra kara itadakimashita go-shinsetsu na o-oshie to go-kōjō to wa, hontō ni arigataku, DONNA NI fukaku kansha shiTE MO, kansha shi-tsukusemasen.

Makoto ni arigatō gozaimashita. Kenkyūshitsu de itadaita **sherii-shu** no aji to, sensei no go-kōi wa, kesshite wasuremasen. O-genki de go-katsuyaku o!

4. 4. 1980

Oniiru Sensei,

Yōshun no yoi kikō to natte mairimashita.

O-kawari mo naku, o-genki de o-sugoshi deshō ka.

Kokoro kara, o-kigen-ukagai no kotoba o mōshi-agemasu.

Sate, watashi no Soas kenkyū ryūgaku-chū wa, taihen iro-iro to, go-

オニール先生　4.4.1980.
陽春の良い気候となって参りました。
お変りも無く、お元気でお過ごしでしょうか。
心から、お機嫌伺いの言葉を申し上げます。
さて、私のSOAS研究留学中は、たいへんいろいろと、
御親切な御指導を頂きまして、本当にありがたく、
重ねて深く感謝の言葉を申し述べます。
有難うございました。ダン先生や稲垣さん、ストロング先生や
ボルハチット、ドハッティ両女史にも、どうぞよろしくお礼の気持を
お伝え下さいますように。ラッセル・スクエヤーとSOASの図書館そして
先生方の御厚情が忘れられません。気持の良い、いい大学で
ありました。有難うございました。
ではくれぐれもお大事にお過ごし下さいませ。さよなら
もし御来日の節は、ぜひお電話を賜わりますように。

---

shinsetsu na go-shidō o itadakimashite, hontō ni arigataku, kasanete fukaku kansha no kotoba o mōshi-nobemasu.

Arigatō gozaimashita. **Dan** Sensei ya **Inagaki**-san, **Sutorongu** Sensei ya **Boruhachitto**, **Dohatti** ryō-JOSHI ni mo, dōzo yoroshiku o-rei no kimochi o o-tsutae kudasaimasu yō ni. **Rasseru Sukueyā** to Soas no toshokan, soshite sensei-gata no go-kōjō ga wasureraremasen. Kimochi no yoi, ii daigaku de arimashita. Arigatō gozaimashita.

De wa, kure-gure mo o-daiji ni o-sugoshi kudasaimase. Sayonara.

Moshi go-**rai-Nichi** no setsu wa, zehi o-denwa o tamawarimasu yō ni.

Notes

a. MAIRIMASHITA Equivalent here to neutral-level *kimashita*. Thus, "it has turned into/become."

b. KAERANEBA NARANAKU NARIMASHITA Since *-neba* = *-nakereba* (see 24ad), *kaeraneba naranai* means "(I) must return." The *-naku naru* combination means "become/turn out that . . . is/does/will not . . ." and can therefore normally be translated as "no longer . . . , stop . . .ing," etc. Here, however, it is part of the *-neba naranai*, "must," construction and gives the phrase the meaning "It has come about that I must return, I must now return."

c. DONNA NI . . .-TE MO An interrogative word + . . . *-te mo/(-)de mo* can always be translated into English by a word ending in ". . .ever." Here, for example, "however profoundly I (may) thank you." Similarly, *dare ga kite mo*, "whoever comes," *dono hon de mo*, "whichever book it is," etc.

d. JOSHI A respectful term for a woman who is a public figure or has academic or artistic standing.

43. Letter from the Son of Old Family Friends

P.G. ONeill 先生

拝啓　永らく御無沙汰致しまして、申訳ございません。
その後皆様お元気のことと存じます。
私達の家族も大阪の両親も元気にしております。
昨秋Dunn先生が、National Museum of Ethnology (Senri EXPO Park. Suita) においでになり、私の研究室でお話しました。そのあと、大阪の家も訪ねて下さったとのことです。
私は、今夏、EuropeのOpen-Air Museum研究のため2カ月Europe各地をまわる予定です。7月2日、Narita (大変危険空港、1.5万人の警官が守っています) 発、アエロフロートでParisへ。Brusselasに友人がいますので、荷物をキープしてもらい、Denmark. Sweeden. Finland. NorwayのOpen-Air. Museumをまわり、あとWest Germany. Austria. のO.A.Mを見学します。そして8月15日頃Brusselasにもどり、OOstendeからドーヴァ海峡を渡ってEnglandへ。イギリスではCambridgeに友人が留学(客員研究員)していますので20日以後はそちらへ行く予定です。イギリスから3日間ほどIrelandを訪ね、Brunratty castleのFolk Parkにある古い民家を見る予定です。
突然厚かましいお願いですが、8月17～8日頃Londonについた時、1−2泊もし可能なら、お訪ねしようと思っています。荷物(かばん1個)をキープして頂いて、Irelandへ行き、英国に戻って(20日か21日)、Cambridgeの友人のところへ行くつもりです。友人は19日までEdinburghで経済史学会があり、不在なので、厚かましいお願いをした次第です。ONeill先生の御都合、御予定を御教示頂ければ幸いです。

よろしくお願い申し上げます。

奥様、ぺろさんにもよろしくお伝え下さい。

御健康お祈り致します。

1978・6・1　杉本尚次

P.G. O'Neill Sensei,

Haikei. Nagaraku go-busata itashimashite, mōshi-wake gozaimasen.

Sono go mina-sama o-genki no koto to zonjimasu.

Watashi-tachi no kazoku mo **Ōsaka** no ryōshin mo genki ni shite orimasu. Sakushū Dunn Sensei ga National Museum of Ethnology (Senri Expo Park, Suita) ni oide ni nari, watashi no kenkyūshitsu de O-HANASHI SHIMASHITA. Sono ato, **Ōsaka** no uchi mo tazunete kudasatta TO NO KOTO desu.

Watashi wa, **konka**, Europe no Open-Air Museum kenkyū no tame, nikagetsu Europe kakuchi o mawaru yotei desu. Shichigatsu futsuka, **Narita** (taihen kiken kūkō, 1.5mannin no keikan ga mamotte imasu) hatsu; **Aerofurōto** de Paris e. Brussels ni yūjin ga imasu no de, nimotsu o **kiipu** shite mora-i, Denmark, Sweden, Finland, Norway no Open-Air Museum o mawari, ato West Germany, Austria no O.A.M. o kengaku shimasu. Soshite hachigatsu jūgonichi-goro Brussels ni modori, Oostende kara **Dōvā** Kaikyō o watatte England e. **Igirisu** de wa Cambridge ni yūjin ga ryūgaku (kyakuin kenkyūin) shite imasu no de, hatsuka igo wa sochira e iku yotei desu. **Igirisu** kara mikkakan hodo Ireland o TAZUNE, Brunratty Castle no Folk Park ni aru furui minka o miru yotei desu.

Totsuzen atsukamashii o-negai desu ga, hachigatsu 17–8nichi goro London ni tsuita toki, 1–2 haku moshi kanō nara, o-tazune shiyō to omotte imasu.

Nimotsu (kaban ikko) o **kiipu** shite itadaite, Ireland e iki, Eikoku ni modotte (hatsuka ka nijūichinichi), Cambridge no yūjin no tokoro e iku tsumori desu. Yūjin wa jūkunichi made Edinburgh de KEIZAI-SHI gakkai ga ari, fuzai na no de, atsukamashii o-negai o shita shidai desu. O'Neill Sensei no go-tsugō, go-yotei o go-kyōji itadakereba saiwai desu.

Yoroshiku o-negai mōshi-agemasu.

Oku-sama, **Pera**-san ni mo yoroshiku o-tsutae kudasai.

Go-kenkō o-inori itashimasu.

Sugimoto Hisatsugu

1978. 6. 1

Notes

a. O-HANASHI SHIMASHITA Being a humble form (see 1e), this part of the sentence clearly indicates a change of subject; that is, "Dr. Dunn came . . . and we talked . . ."

b. TO NO KOTO Equivalent to *to iu koto* (see 27g) or, here, to *sō (desu)*; thus, "I understand that . . ."

c. TAZUNE The character used here is a rather extreme form of 訪. See line 8 for an intermediate form of the same character.

d. KEIZAI-SHI On the form of the character for *kei*, see 28h.

44. Letter from a Man Known When He was in Business in London

私の昼間の仕事（?）が広報であり、日頃新聞
記者の方々のお相手をする仕事なので、できれば
大学のどなたかを紹介して欲しい旨、依頼された、
という次第です。
ご多用の際に、恐縮に存じますが、二、三言学内の
事情をご説明いただければ幸甚に存じます。
先生にはすっかりご無沙汰し、先生のお宅にお招
きに預ったことなど、家内とまことになつかしく思い
だしております。
奥様それから大変美しいお嬢様はお元気で
いらっしゃいますか。
もし東京にご出張の機会でもございましたら、ぜ
ひお目どおりの機会を得たいと切望致しております。
日本学の皆様によろしくお伝え下さいませ

深田 拝

昭和五十一年九月

オニール先生

Haikei,

Hisashiku go-busata o kasanete orimasu.

Sensei ni wa ai-kawarazu o-genki de go-**kenSAN** no koto to zonjimasu.

Nihon ni kikoku itashimashite kara, shūkyū futsuka-sei no fukyū o yoi koto ni, shūmatsu o riyō shimashite "Seiyō Taiken" o bō-gekkan-shi ni rensai, sono go shuppan itashimashita tokoro, hakarazu mo "**Ōya Sōichi** Non-fikushon" SHŌ NARU MONO o Bungei Shunjū-sha yori chōdai suru, to iu kōun ni megumaremashita. Go-**shōnō** itadakereba makoto ni kōjin to zonjimasu.

Sate, honjitsu wa **Sankei** Shinbun no Fujin-bu kisha no **Yoshida**-san o go-shōkai mōshi-agemasu.

Go-zonji no **Tōkyō** no Kokusai Kirisuto-kyō Daigaku o sotsugyō shi, fujin kisha to shite wadai o otte katsuyaku sarete ita no desu ga, kondo ichinen hokki sar-e, ichinen Eikoku ni ryūgaku, **Rondon** Daigaku de chōkō no kibō mo motte orareru yō desu.

Watashi no hiruma no shigoto (?) ga kōhō de ar-i, higoro shinbun kisha no kata-gata no o-aite o suru shigoto na no de, dekireba daigaku no donata-ka o shōkai SHITE HOSHII mune, irai sareta, to iu shidai desu.

Go-tayō no sai ni, kyōshuku ni zonjimasu ga, ni-sangon gakunai no jijō o go-setsumei itadakereba kōjin ni zonjimasu.

拝啓
久しくご無沙汰を重ねております。
先生には相変らずお元気でご研鑽のことと
存じます。
日本に帰国致しましてから、週休二日制の
普及をよいことに、週末を利用しまして「
西洋体験」を某日刊誌に連載、その後出版
致しましたところ、計らずも大宅壮一ノ
ンフィクション賞なるものを文芸春秋社よ
り頂戴する、という幸運に恵まれました。
ご笑納いただければ誠に幸甚と存じます。
さて本日はサンケイ新聞の婦人部記者の吉田
さんをご紹介申しあげます。
ご存知の東京の国際キリスト教大学を卒業
し、婦人記者として話題を追って活躍されて
いたのですが、今度一念発起され、一年英国
に留学、ロンドン大学で聴講の希望を持ってお
られるようです。

Sensei ni wa sukkari go-busata shi, sensei no o-taku ni o-maneki ni azukatta koto nado, kanai to makoto ni natsukashiku omoi-dashite orimasu.

Oku-sama, sore kara taihen utsukushii o-jō-sama wa o-genki de irasshaimasu ka.

Moshi **Tōkyō** ni go-shutchō no kikai de mo gozaimashitara, zehi o-medōri no kikai o etai to setsubō itashite orimasu.

Nihon-gaku no mina-sama ni yoroshiku o-tsutae kudasaimase.

Shōwa gojūichinen kugatsu

Fukada hai

Oniiru Sensei

Notes

a. -SAN Note that this writer tends to omit the "legs" in character elements such as 貝 and 頁 (as in the *chō* of *chōdai* in line 10). The word is thus 研鑽 *kensan*, "study, research."

b. SHŌ NARU MONO The character here is 賞 *shō*, "prize," with the "legs" omitted (see a. above). Since *naru mono* (= *de aru mono*, see 14a) seems only to add a little more substance or euphony to the preceding noun, the meaning is "(what is) the . . . prize."

c. SHITE HOSHII Literally, "a doing is desired," i.e., "(I) would like (something) done." This *-te hoshii* construction has much the same meaning as *-te itadakitai/moraitai*, but note that it is a neutral expression that avoids the feeling of "(humbly) receiving."

45. Letter from an Older Acquaintance of a Colleague

なほ寒さに向ふ折柄愈〻御自愛
下さいますやう切に祈り上げます
先は略儀乍ら寸楮を以て右御礼の
御挨拶を申し上げます　不宣
一九七四年十一月念八日
帆足図南次
ロンドン大学教授
オニール先生
硯北
追伸　帆足萬里に関する小冊子
別送致しましたので
何卒御高覧の栄を賜はり
ますれば幸甚でございます

Haikei. Nihon no **sanga** wa **kinshū** no aki kara hayaku mo shotō no fuzei ni utsuri-kawarō to shite imasu ga, **on-chi** no shizen mo ichidan to banshū no **fūshu** o fukamete iru koto to omowaremasu orikara

SENSEI ni wa GO-KASHŌ NO DAN taikei shigoku ni zonji-agemasu. Sate, kono tabi wa watakushi-tachi no keikaku shita "**Hoashi Banri** No Kagaku Shisō No Kenkyū" ni go rikai o tamawari-i, "**Inoue Eimei**-kun no kyōdō kenkyū e no sanka o go-kaidaku kudasar-e, makoto ni arigataku, atsuku o-rei mōshi-agemasu. **Inoue**-kun mo sensei no go-**kontoku** naru go-shidō no moto ni gakumon no taisei o ki-shite iru koto to omowaremasu ga, kongo-tomo DŌkun ni tai-suru go-**yūeki** no hodo o kongan shi-TATEMATSURU shidai de gozaimasu.

Nao samu-sa ni mukau orikara iyo-iyo go-jiai kudasaimasu yō setsu ni inori-agemasu. Mazu wa ryakugi-nagara sunchō O MOTTE migi o-rei no go-aisatsu o mōshi-agemasu.

FUSEN

Hoashi Tonaji

1974nen jūichigatsu NEN-yōka
Rondon Daigaku Kyōju
Oniiru Sensei
KENPOKU

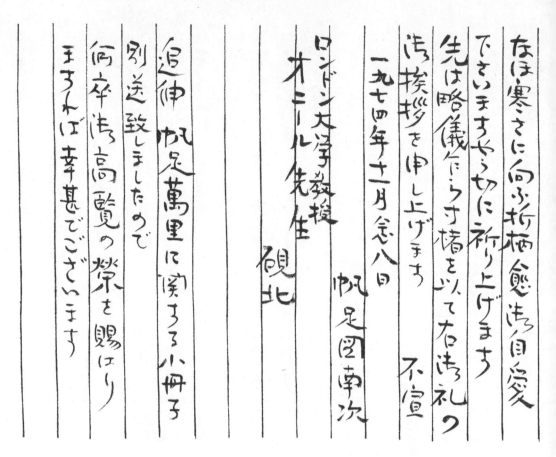

拝啓日本の山河は錦繍の秋から早くも初冬の風情に移り変らうとしてゐますが御地の自然も一段と晩秋の風趣を深めてゐることと想はれます折柄
先生には御佳勝の段大慶至極に存じ上げます さてこの度は私たちの計画した帆足萬里の科学思想の研究に御理解を賜はり井上英明君の協同研究への参加を御快諾下され洵に有難く厚く御礼申上げます
井上君も先生の御懇篤なる御指導の下に学問の大成を期してゐることと思はれますが今後とも同君に対する御誘掖の程を懇願し奉る次第でございます

Tsuishin: **Hoashi Banri** ni kan-suru shō-sasshi **bessō** itashimashita no de, nani-tozo go-kōran no ei o tamawarimasureba kōjin de gozaimasu.

Notes

a. SENSEI This word is put at the head of a new column merely to indicate respect (cf. *ki-daigaku* under 3k) and the following clause is grammatically part of the first sentence. The basic structure of this is thus "... but, at this time (*orikara*) when I imagine ..., I am delighted that ..."

b. GO-KASHŌ NO DAN *Kashō* is a rare word: meaning literally "fine excellence," it is used of scenery and, as here, reputation or standing. *Dan* in this kind of use has the same meaning as *koto* or *ken*, "matter, case." Thus, "(the matter of) your success" is a possible translation.

c. DŌ- A prefix meaning "this same"; thus, here, *dōkun* can be translated as "this same man" or simply "him."

d. -TATEMATSURU Meaning originally "offer, present," this is used as the second part of a compound verb to indicate that the action is done with respect.

e. O MOTTE "With, through, by means of"; see 30b.

f. FUSEN Literally, "not (fully) expressed," this is a conventional concluding word in letters (cf. *fuitsu* under 30c).

g. NEN- In this abstruse use of the character 念, the meaning is "twenty," on the basis of a similarity in the Chinese readings of it and the character 廿 ("two tens" =) "twenty." An alternative reading for the date would therefore be *nijūhachinichi*.

h. KENPOKU Literally, "north of the ink-stone," this means "at one's desk" (since writers would normally face south in order to catch the light) and is used like *kika*, *gyokuanka*, etc., as a respectful word after the name of the addressee.

46. Letter from an Employee of a Printing Firm

前略、
「漢字表」の清刷りが出来ましたので、今日、別便
航空便にて、お送りします。
元原稿も同封致しましたので、お受け取り下さい。
尚、清刷りは七部入っております。
先ずは、御連絡のみにて失礼致します。

笠井出版印刷社
係、長谷川.

一月十一日.
オニール博士

Zenryaku,

"Kanji-hyō" no KIYO-ZURI ga dekimashita no de, kyō, betsubin kōkūbin nite o-okuri shimasu.

Moto-genkō mo dōfū itashimashita no de, o-uke-tori kudasai. Nao, kiyo-zuri wa shichi-bu haitte orimasu.

Mazu wa go-renraku nomi nite shitsurei itashimasu.

Kasai Shuppan Insatsu-sha
Kakari: **Hasegawa**

Ichigatsu jūichinichi
Oniiru Hakushi

Notes

a. KIYO-ZURI A "clean printing" (as opposed to proof copies) prepared on good-quality paper for reproduction.

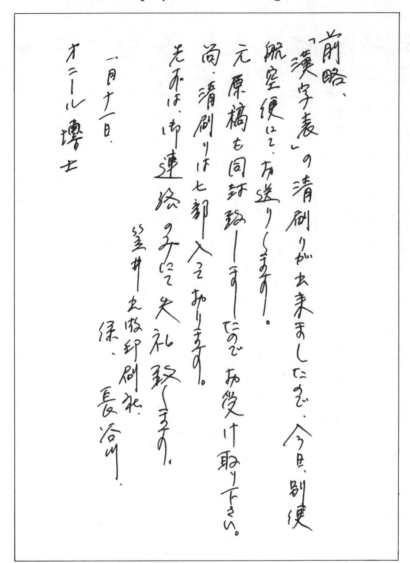

47. Letter from the Colleague of a Good Friend Who Had Died

七月八日。

オニール先生

先日は、ご馳走になったうえ、故アダムズさんのお話をいろいろ伺って貴重でした。おくればせながら改めてお礼申上げます。あの後早速、アジア経済研究所の東畑会長・小倉所長あてに手紙を認めました。そのあと、東京からの指令で大陸にゆき会議に出席したり、研究機関を訪問したり、二週間をこす出張を終えて帰ってまいりましたが、案に相違して東京からは、アダムズさんの問題については何も申して参りません。事務的には来年度予算の編成にかかる頃なので調査がおくれてるとも思えますが、厚生年金その他の受取りに問題のあることも考えられます。あるいは、もっと詳細な事情を知りたがっているとも考えられますが、死亡証明その他の請求もないところからすれば、故アダムズ氏のかけていた各種社会保険・年金の類から ご遺族に支払わられる分はないということかも知れません。保険や年金の加入年月が短かすぎた、ということも考えられます。けれども、私の推測にすぎません。あれから、随分日がたちましたので、気をもんではおりますが、一先ず状況をご報告しておきます。

パリに日本橋三越が店を出しまして、別添のようなものをおいてきました。

ご笑納下さい。

林　武拝。

Shichigatsu yōka

Oniiru Sensei,

Senjitsu wa, go-chisō ni natta ue, ko-**Adamuzu**-san no o-hanashi o iro-iro ukagatte kichō deshita. **Okurebase**-nagara aratamete o-rei mōshi-agemasu. Ano yo sassoku, Ajia Keizai Kenkyūjo no **Higashibatake** Kaichō, **Ogura** Shochō ate ni tegami o shitatamemashita. Sono ato, **Tōkyō** kara no shirei de tairiku ni yuki, KAIGI ni shusseki shitari, kenkyū KIKAN o hōmon shitari, nishūkan o kosu shutchō o oete kaette mairimashita ga, an ni sōi shite **Tōkyō** kara wa, **Adamuzu**-san no mondai ni tsuite wa nani-mo mōshite mairimasen. Jimu-teki ni wa **rai-nendo** yosan no hensei ni kakaru koro na no de chōsa ga OKURETERU to mo OMOEMASU ga, kōsei nenkin sono ta no uke-tori ni mondai no aru koto mo KANGAERAREMASU. Aruiwa, motto shōsai na jijō o shiritaGATTE IRU to mo kangaeraremasu ga, shibō shōmei sono ta no seikyū mo nai TOKORO KARA SUREBA, ko-**Adamuzu**-shi no kakete ita kakushu shakai hoken, nenkin no rui kara go-izoku ni shi-harawarareru bun wa nai to iu koto ka mo shiremasen. Hoken ya nenkin no kanyū nengetsu ga mijika-SUGITA to iu koto mo kangaeraremasu. Keredomo, watashi no suisoku ni sugimasen. Are kara, zuibun hi ga tachimashita no de, ki o monde wa orimasu ga, hitomazu jōkyō o go-hōkoku shite okimasu.

Pari ni **Nihonbashi Mitsukoshi** ga mise o dashimashite, betten no yō na mono o OITEMASHITA.

Go-**shōnō** kudasai.

Hayashi Takeshi hai

Notes

a. KAIGI Instead of using the standard form of the second character 議, the writer has abbreviated it by giving the radical 言 and *katakana* ギ, *gi*, for the phonetic part.

b. KIKAN As it stands, the first character looks like 桟, SAN (Nelson no. 2252), but in fact it is used as an abbreviation of the standard 機.

c. OKURETERU A colloquial-type contraction of *okurete iru*.

d. OMOEMASU *Omoeru* is the short potential form (as opposed to the full passive/potential form *omowareru*) from *omou*; thus, "(I/one can think (too that . . .)"

e. KANGAERAREMASU Being the passive/potential form from *kangaeru*, this is literally "(the fact that . . . is also) conceivable," i.e., "it can/might (also) be thought."

f. -GATTE IRU To avoid being dogmatic about other people's emotions and sensations, the Japanese use the verbal suffix *-garu* in such direct statements (when they do not avoid them by the use of a final *deshō*, *ka mo shiremasen*, etc.). It is possible to use it after the stems of some hundred adjectives, including *ita(i)*, "painful," *kowa(i)*, "fearful," and *omoshiro(i)*, "enjoyable"; but the most common use is, as here, after the desiderative suffix *-ta(i)*, "wish/want to." The use of the suffix in Japanese does not in fact affect the translation, which would here be simply "they want to know."

g. TOKORO KARA SUREBA "If we take/consider it from the aspect that . . ."; cf. 29b.

h. -SUGITA The verb *sugiru*, "exceed, pass" can be used after the stems of verbs and adjectives with the meaning "(do/be . . .) to excess."

i. OITEMASHITA Another colloquial-type contraction, here for *oite imashita*.

48. Letter from the Colleague of a Mutual Acquaintance

言語変化研究部長
飯豊毅一

オニール先生.

7月9日付のお手紙 および フローレンスの会議の紹介のある
E.A.J.Sの会報を ありがたく拝見いたしました。
様子がよくわかって、安心しました. 厚く御礼申し上げます.
申し込み書を同封します. 間に合うように お手許に
届くことを願っています.
渡航手続は 順調に進んでいますので 19日中に
フローレンスに着けるだろうと存じます。皆さんの発表を聞くことを
楽しみにしています. ただし, 私の語学力では, それに着いた
ばかりで、まだ聞く方も満足ではないでしょうから, 理解できるか
どうか 心配です。
9月25日にロンドンに着く予定にしています。リーズ大学と
S.F. Sanderson先生
エディンバラ大学の H. Speitel 先生に連絡がつきました。
中旬以降はそちらに参る予定にしています.
その他はまだ十分に予定ができていません。
何かと お世話になることと存じますが, どうぞ
先生のお力添えをお願いいたしたく存じます.
いずれ お目にかかって お教えをいただきたいと
存じますので, 何分ともよろしく, 伏してお願い
申し上げます.

敬具

Gengohenka Kenkyūbu-chō
Iitoyo Kiichi

Oniiru Sensei,

Shichigatsu kokonoka-zuke no o-tegami oyobi **Furōrensu** no kaigi no shōkai no aru E.A.J.S. no kaihō o arigataku **haiju** itashimashita.

Yōsu ga yoku wakatte, anshin shimashita. Atsuku o-rei mōshi-agemasu. Mōshi-komisho o dōfū shimasu. Ma ni au yō ni o-temoto ni todoku koto o negatte imasu.

Tokō tetsuzuki wa junchō ni susunde imasu no de jūkunichi-chū ni **Furōrensu** ni tsukeru darō to zonjimasu. Mina-san no happyō o kiku koto o tanoshimi ni shite imasu. Tadashi, watashi no **gogakuryoku** de wa, SORE NI tsuita bakari de, mada kiku hō mo manzoku de wa nai deshō kara, rikai dekiru ka dō ka shinpai desu.

Kugatsu nijūgonichi ni **Rondon** ni tsuku yotei ni shite imasu. **Riizu** Daigaku (S.F. Sanderson Sensei) to **Edinbara** Daigaku no H. Speitel Sensei ni renraku ga tsukimashita. Chūjun ikō wa sochira ni mairu yotei ni shite imasu.

Sono hoka wa mada jūbun ni yotei ga dekite imasen. Nani-ka to o-sewa ni naru koto to zonjimasu ga, dōzo sensei no o-chikara-zoe o o-negai itashitaku zonjimasu. Izure o-me ni kakatte o-oshie o itadakitai to zonjimasu no de, **nanibun tomo** yoroshiku, FUSHITE o-negai mōshi-agemasu.

Keigu

Notes

a. E.A.J.S. "The European Association for Japanese Studies."
b. SORE NI Here means "on top of that, in addition."
c. FUSHITE Literally, "prostrating oneself," i.e., "humbly, respectfully."

49. Letter from a University Teacher Met Previously Once or Twice

御無沙汰致しました。御変りなく御健勝のことと存じます。最近タトル社から先生の著作出版されたようで、おめでとうございました。二、三ヶ月とかにあれ「芥川の文学」という本に拙稿が発表され、今又来年出る同様の本「川端文学、特に山の音」にも寄稿します。私の「源氏物語」の訳は少しずつながら進んでおります。

扨、来月のペン大会に御出席なさる旨の朗報が入りましたが、私も行きますので、是非共東京で御会いしたいものです。楽しみにしています。

ではお御あいさつかたがた、失礼致します。

奥さまにくれぐれもよろしく

敬具

十月三十一日

堀井和也

オニール先生

Go-busata itashimashita. O-kawari naku go-kenshō no koto to zonjimasu. Saikin **Tatoru**-sha kara sensei no chosaku shuppan sareta yō de, o-medetō gozaimashita. Ni-sankagetsu mae ni deta "AKUTAGAWA No Bungaku" to iu hon ni **sekkō** ga happyō sar-e, ima mata rainen deru dōyō no hon "KAWABATA Bungaku, Toku Ni 'Yama No Oto' " ni mo kikō shimasu. Watashi no "GENJI MONOGATARI" no yaku wa sukoshi zutsu-nagara susunde imasu.

Sate, raigetsu no PEN Taikai ni GO-shusseki NASARU mune no rōhō ga hairimashita ga, watashi mo ikimasu no de, zehi tomo **Tōkyō** de o-ai shitai mono desu. Tanoshimi ni shite imasu.

De wa go-aisatsu kata-gata, shitsurei itashimasu.

Oku-sama ni kure-gure mo yoroshiku.

Keigu

Sakai Kazuya

Jūgatsu sanjūichinichi
Oniiru Sensei

Notes

a. AKUTAGAWA Akutagawa Ryūnosuke 芥川竜之介 (1892–1927), one of the most famous twentieth-century writers, noted especially for his short stories.

b. KAWABATA Kawabata Yasunari 川端康成 (1899–1972), another of the most famous modern Japanese writers.

c. GENJI MONOGATARI 源氏物語 "The Tale of Genji," the classic novel of early court life in Japan, written by Lady Murasaki Shikibu at the beginning of the eleventh century.

d. PEN The P.E.N. (Poets, Essayists and Novelists) Club.

e. GO- . . . NASARU The *go-* noun *ni naru/nasaru* construction is an honorific one corresponding exactly to the *o-* + vb. stem *ni naru/nasaru* construction (see 6t and 34b). The phrase here is thus equivalent to neutral-level *shusseki suru*.

オニール教授殿　　1974.5.2

拝啓

陽春の候となりました。御地ロンドンにも一年中で一番過しよい春がやって来たことと存じます。その後、先生には愈々御壮健にて御研究のことと遠察申し上げます。

さて、小生ロンドン大学University Collegeにて研究中は、度々貴大学の食堂におもむき、昼食をとりましたが、その際には、大変御馳走様になり、有難うございました。衷心より厚く御礼申し上げます。3月17日、1ヶ年のロンドン生活に別れを告げ、ヒースロー空港を後にし、途中モスクワにも立ち寄り、3月23日、帰国いたしました。丁度甲南大学の岡教授とも同じ日に離英したわけです。1ヶ年振りの日本は、全くの狂乱物価で、大学には沢山の郵便物が山積しており、それらのことにいささか圧倒されているうちに、1ヶ月がまたたく間に過ぎ去ってしまいました。そして、4月15日の入学式に続いて新年度が始まり、毎日を講義に追われている始末です。

次にお願いがございます。私がSOASに昼食をとりに行った際、御会いした2年の学生にMALLORY FROMM君がおります。彼は現在"宮沢賢治"の"銀河鉄道の夜"という童話(どうわ)を英訳中とのことですが、彼から私に質問があり　その童話の中に出てくる"天気輪の柱"とは

どんな意味かということでした。しかし、生憎、その時は
御質問に答えられませんでした。3月末、日本へ帰り、私の
学部の藤多（フジタ）助教授（国文学専攻）に尋ねましたところ、
同封のものをいただきました。御質問の御答えになって
いるかどうかわかりませんが、御送りしますので、大変御
手数ですがM. FROMM君に御渡し願います。なお、
朝日新聞を見ていましたら、"後生車"というのが出ていましたので
同じ用紙中に印刷しておきました。何かの御参考になると
思います。もし、不明な点がございましたらお手紙下さるよう
お伝へ願います。

先ずは取急ぎ御礼旁々御願いまで。末筆ながら
M. FROMM君やJ. P. BARRON君にも何卒よろしく
御伝へ願います。

敬具

懐かしいロンドンを偲びつつ
吉田三郎

1974. 5. 2

Oniiru Kyōju-dono

Haikei,

Yōshun no **kō** to narimashita. **On-chi Rondon** ni mo ichinen-jū de ichiban sugoshi-yoi haru ga yatte kita koto to zonjimasu. Sono go, sensei ni wa iyo-iyo go-sōken nite go-kenkyū no koto to **ensatsu** mōshi-agemasu.

Sate, shōsei **Rondon** Daigaku University College nite kenkyū-chū wa, tabi-tabi ki-daigaku no shokudō ni omomuki, chūshoku o torimashita ga, sono sai ni wa, taihen go-chisō-sama ni nari, arigatō gozaimashita. Chūshin yori atsuku o-rei mōshi-agemasu. Sangatsu jūshichinichi, ikkanen no **Rondon** seikatsu ni wakare o tsuge, **Hiisurō** kūkō o ato ni shi, tochū **Mosukuwa** ni mo tachi-yori, sangatsu nijūsannichi, kikoku itashi-mashita. Chōdo, **Kōnan** Daigaku no **Oka** Kyōju to mo onaji hi ni **ri-Ei** shita wake desu. Ikkanen-buri no Nihon wa, mattaku no kyōran bukka de, daigaku ni wa takusan no yūbinbutsu ga sanseki shite or-i, sorera no koto ni isasaka attō sarete iru uchi ni, ikkage-tsu ga matataku ma ni sugi-satte shimaimashita. Soshite, shigatsu jūgonichi no nyūgaku-shiki ni tsuzuite shin-nendo ga hajimari, mainichi o kōgi ni owarete iru shimatsu desu.

Tsugi ni o-negai ga gozaimasu. Watashi ga Soas ni chūshoku o tori ni itta sai, o-ai shita ninen no gakusei ni Mallory Fromm-kun ga orimasu. Kare wa genzai "MIYA-ZAWA KENJI" no "Ginga Tetsudō No Yoru" to iu dōwa o Eiyaku-chū to no koto desu ga, kare kara watashi ni shitsumon ga ari, sono dōwa no naka ni dete kuru "**tenkirin** no hashira" to wa donna imi ka to iu koto deshita. Shikashi, ainiku, sono toki wa go-shi-tsumon ni kotaeraremasen deshita. Sangatsumatsu, Nihon e kaeri, watashi no gakubu no **Fujita** Jo-kyōju (Kokubungaku senkō) ni tazunemashita tokoro, dōfū no mono o itadakimashita. Go-shitsumon no o-kotae ni natte iru ka dō ka wakarimasen ga, o-okuri shimasu no de, taihen o-tesū desu ga M. Fromm-kun ni o-watashi negaimasu. Nao, Asahi Shinbun o mite imashitara, "**goshō-guruma**" to iu no ga dete imashita no de, ona-ji yōshi-chū ni insatsu shite okimashita. Nani-ka no go-sankō ni naru to omoimasu. Moshi, fumei na TEN ga gozaimashitara o-tegami kudasaru yō o-tsutae negaimasu.

Mazu wa tori-isogi o-rei kata-gata o-negai made. Mappitsu-nagara M. Fromm-kun ya J.P. Barron-kun ni mo nani-tozo yoroshiku o-tsutae negaimasu.

Keigu

Natsukashii **Rondon** o shinobi-tsutsu.

Yoshida Saburō

Notes

a. MIYAZAWA KENJI 宮沢賢治 (1896–1933), a poet and writer of chidren's stories.

b. TEN The character here is a variant of the modern standard 点.

51. Letter from a Young Lady Researching at Another University

さって下さり又、図書館の案内、お食事
まで 本当に 有難うございました。
論文にとりかかるのはまだまだ先ですが
又先生のご意見など拝聴できれば幸福に
思います。 めっきり 春らしく なったとは
いえ、まだまだ風の冷たい今日この頃。
私も 下火になったとはいえ 油断をすると
追いかけてきそうな勢いはまだもっているようです。
どうぞ お身体には じゅうぶんご留意 遊ばし
ますように…

まずは お礼 まで。

かしこ

二月二十九日

藤原 有功 先生へ

オニール先生へ。

春を思わせるように暖かな日が続いているシェフィールドですが、ロンドンはいかがでしょうか？、ロンドンの街からどうも風邪を拾って帰ってきたらしく、帰ってそうそうfluで寝こんでしまいました。一、二日のつもりが結局丸一週間ベッドに釘づけにされることになります。シェフィールドの冬にはめずらしい程明るくはれた空をながめながら、「ペイシャント」はペイシャントにしていなければなりませんよ」などと自分にいいきかせたりして、お陽様の誘惑と戦った一週間でした。

というわけでお礼のお手紙もずいぶんおそくなってしまいました。ずいぶんお忙しいスケジュールのなか、貴重なお時間、私のような者のために

Oniiru Sensei e,

Haru o OMOWASERU yō ni atataka na hi ga tsuzuite iru **Shefiirudo** desu ga, **Rondon** wa ikaga deshō ka.

Rondon no machi kara dōmo kaze o hirotte kaette kita RASHI-KU, kaette sō-sō flu de ne-konde shimaimashita. Ichi-ninichi no tsumori ga kekkyoku maru-isshūkan beddo ni kugi-zuke ni sareta koto ni narimasu.

Shefiirudo no fuyu ni wa mezurashii hodo akaruku hareta sora o nagame-nagara, "**Peishanto** wa **peishanto** NI SHITE inakereba narimasen yo" nado to jibun ni ii-kikase-tari shite, O-HI-SAMA no yūwaku to tatakatta isshūkan deshita.

TO IU WAKE DE o-rei no o-tegami mo zuibun osoku natte shimaimashita. Zuibun o-isogashii sukejūru no naka, kichō na o-jikan, watashi no yō na mono no tame ni saite kudasar-i, mata, toshokan no annai, o-shokuji made, hontō ni arigatō gozaimashita.

Ronbun ni tori-kakaru no wa mada mada saki desu ga, mata, sensei no go-iken nado **haichō** dekireba kōfuku ni omoimasu. Mekkiri haru rashi-ku natta TO WA IE, mada mada kaze no tsumetai **kyō-konogoro**, flu mo shitabi ni natta TO WA IE yudan o suru to oi-kakete ki-sō na ikioi wa mada motte iru yō desu. Dōzo o-KARADA ni wa jūbun go-ryūi ASOBASHIMASU yō ni . . .

Mazu wa o-rei made.

Kashiko

Fujiwara Makiko

Nigatsu nijūkunichi

Notes

a. OMOWASERU A causative form from *omou*; thus "(so that they) make you think (of spring)."

b. RASHIKU Since *-ku* is the suspensive form, parallel here to the final *shimaimashita*, *rashiku* is here equivalent to *rashikatta desu* in a separate sentence and gives the meaning "it seemed that (I came back)."

c. NI SHITE From the literal meaning "make (someone/something) into," the meaning of *ni suru* here is "act/behave as, treat/regard (someone/something) as." It is thus very similar to *to suru* (see 41 and 39e).

d. O-HI-SAMA This polite word for "sun" is usually written お (or 御) 日様, but the choice of 陽 here is understandable from its use in 太陽 *taiyō*, "sun."

e. TO IU WAKE DE At the beginning of a sentence, as here, this phrase cites what has been said or written previously as the explanation of what follows. Thus, "for the above reason(s), because of this."

f. TO WA IE Also occurring as *to wa iedo (mo)* this phrase is very like the colloquial *to (wa) itte mo*, "even though (one may say that)."

g. KARADA On this reading of the characters alternatively readable as *shintai*, see 26i.

h. ASOBASHIMASU *Asobasu* is an extremely honorific equivalent for *suru*, "do," more respectful even than *nasaru*. It survives mainly in the language of very genteel ladies, and even then mostly as an elegant imperative, e.g., *gomen asobase*, "please excuse me."

52. Note from the Wife of a Colleague

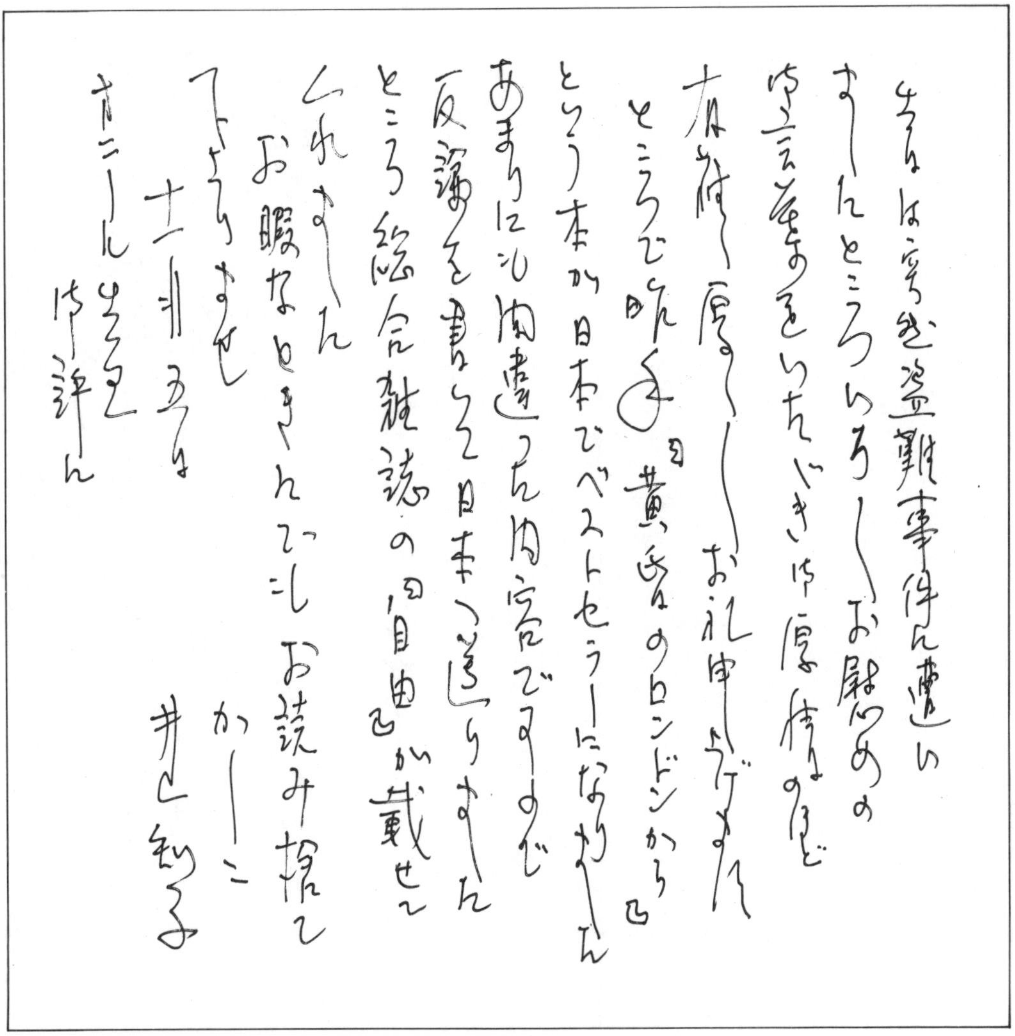

先日は突然盗難事件に遭いましたところいろいろお慰めの御言葉をいただき御厚情のほど有難く厚く厚くお礼申し上げます

ところで昨年「黄昏のロンドンから」という本が日本でベストセラーになりました
あまりにも間違った内容ですので反論を書いて日本へ送りましたところ総合雑誌の「自由」が載せてくれました

お暇なときにでもお読み捨て下さいませ

かしこ

十一月五日

井上知子

オニール先生

御許に

Senjitsu wa totsuzen tōnan jiken ni aimashita tokoro, iro-iro o-nagusame no o-kotoba o itadak-i, go-kōjō no hodo arigataku atsuku atsuku o-rei mōshi-agemasu.

Tokoro de, sakunen "Tasogare No **Rondon** Kara" to iu hon ga Nihon de besuto serā ni narimashita. Amari ni mo machigatta naiyō desu no de, hanron o kaite Nihon e okurimashita tokoro, sōgō zasshi no "Jiyū" ga nosete kuremashita.

O-hima na toki ni de mo o-yomi-sute kudasaimase.

Kashiko

Jūichigatsu itsuka

Inoue Tomoko

Oniiru Sensei

O-MOTO NI

Notes

a. O-MOTO NI *O-moto* (and the alternative reading *on-moto*) being elegant words for "your place," *o-* /*on-moto* (*ni*) is used almost exclusively by women after the name of the addressee in letters as a polite phrase indicating "(sent) to you/where you are."

53. Letter from a Previously Unknown Man Teaching in Japan

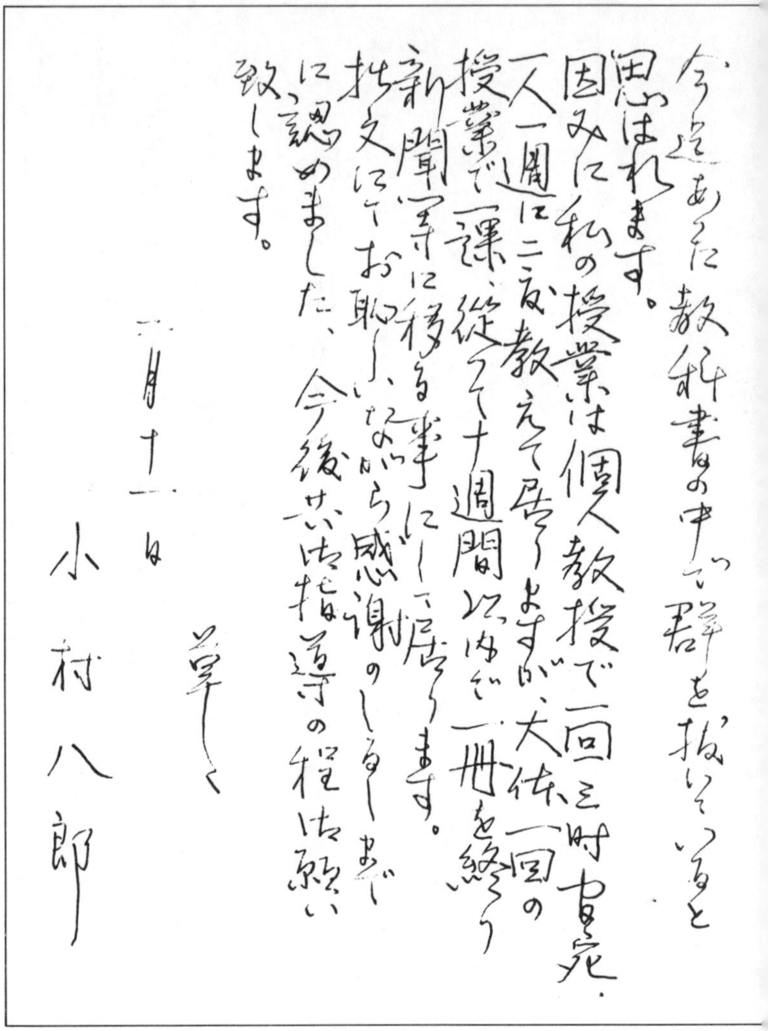
今迄あった教科書の中で群を抜いていると
思はれます。
因みに私の授業は個人教授で一回三時間宛
一人一週に二回教えて居りますが、大体一回の
授業で一課、従って十週間ぐらいで一冊を終り
新聞等に移る事にして居ります。
拙文にてお恥しいながら感謝のしるしまで
に認めました。今後共御指導の程お願い
致します。

草々

二月十一日

小村八郎

Zenryaku,

Watashi wa **Tōkyō** de Nihongo no KYŌSHI O SHITE orimasu ga, sensei no o-kaki ni natta hon ''Nihonbun Nyūmon'' ni tsuite kansha no i o arawashitaku pen o totta shidai desu.

Watashi wa Eikoku Taishikan no GOGAKUSEI ni oshiete orimasu ga, seito ga Eikokujin da kara to iu riyū de naku, makoto ni tekitō ni omowareru no de hajime ni ''**Chiichi Yuaserufu**'' tsuide ''Nihonbun Nyūmon'' o erabimashita.

Jitsu wa ima made bunpō o oshieta ato shinbun aruiwa ippan-teki na Nihon no bunshō o yomu ni itaru made no tekitō na tokuhon ga naku komari-**nuite** orimashita. ''Jibun de kakanakereba dame ka na'' to made kono namake-mono no watashi ga omotta hodo deshita ga gūzen ni sensei no hon o mitsuke, sono nayami ga ichidoki ni kaiketsu itashimashita.

Makoto ni arigatō gozaimashita.

Shikamo, hajime no hon ''**Tiichi Yuaserufu**'' to no kanren mo yoku, kanji no erabi-kata, bunshō no naga-sa mo jugyō no jikan ni teki-shi, toku ni bun no naiyō ga subarashiku, mada o-ai shita koto no nai sensei no fūkaku ga ukagawarete, ima made atta kyōkasho no naka de gun o nuite iru to omowaremasu.

前略
私は東京で日本語の教師をして居りますが
先生のお書きになった本「日本文入門」に
就いて感謝の意を表したくペンを取った
次第です。
私は英国大使館の語斈生に教えて居ります
が生徒が英国人だからという理由でなく甚
に適当に思われるので始めに「チーチェンバレン」
次で「日本文入門」を選びました。
実は今迄文法を教えた後新聞或は一般的
な日本の文章を読むに至る迄の適当な
読本がなく困り抜いて居りました。自分で
かかなければ駄目かなとまで この愚者の私が
思った程でしたが偶然に先生の本を見つけ
その悩みが一時に解決致しました。
誠に有難く存じ居りました。
然も始めの本「チイチェンバレン」との関連もよく
漢字の選び方、文章の長さも授業の時
間に適し、特に文の内容が素晴しくまだ
お会いした事のない先生の風格が窺われて

Chinami ni watashi no jugyō wa kojin kyōju de ikkai sanjikan zutsu, hitori isshū ni nido oshiete orimasu ga, daitai ikkai no jugyō de ikka, shitagatte jisshūkan inai de issatsu o owari, shinbun nado ni utsuru KOTO NI SHITE orimasu. Setsubun nite o-hazukashii-nagara, kansha no shirushi made ni shitatamemashita. Kongo-tomo go-shidō no hodo o-negai itashimasu.

Sō-sō

Komura Hachirō

Nigatsu jūichinichi

Notes

a. KYŌSHI O SHITE Words indicating professions and occupations can be followed directly by *o suru* to indicate "work as . . ." Thus, here, "I am (working as) a teacher."
b. GOGAKUSEI For *gaku* in this word, the abbreviated form 斈 is used for the modern standard 学.
c. KOTO NI SHITE Used after a verb, *koto/yō ni suru/itasu*, etc., means that the speaker takes steps to see that the action of the verb takes place. The translation is therefore often "see/decide that," but here "I arrange things so that" would be reasonable. Cf. this active meaning with *suru* with the involuntary implication of *yō/koto ni naru* explained under 1c and 5d.

54. Letter from the Wife of a Colleague

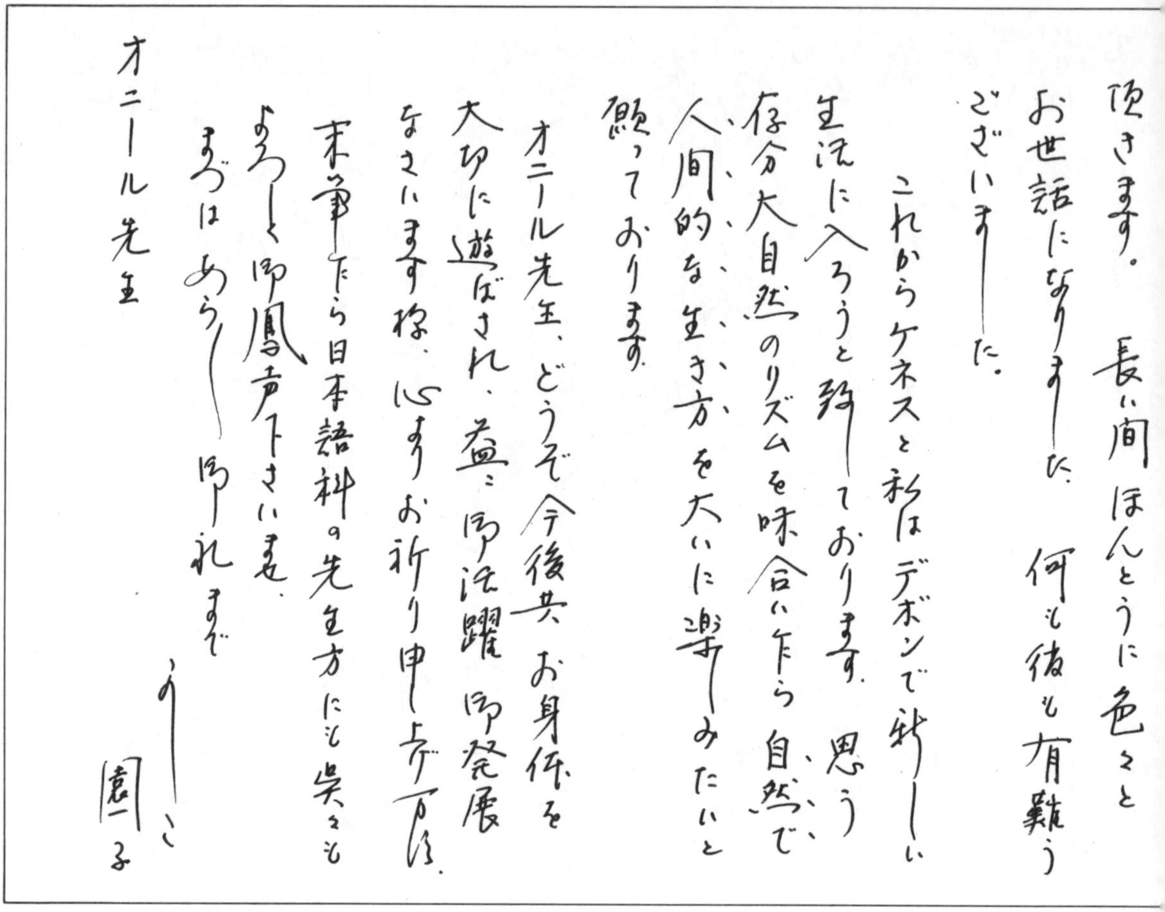

頂きます。長い間ほんとうに色々と
お世話になりました。何も彼も有難う
ございました。
これからケネスと私はデボンで新しい
生活に入ろうと致しております。思う
存分大自然のリズムを味合い乍ら自然で
人間的な生き方を大いに楽しみたいと
願っております。
オニール先生、どうぞ今後共お身体を
大切に遊ばされ、益々御活躍御発展
なさいます様、心よりお祈り申し上げます。
末筆乍ら日本語科の先生方にも呉々も
よろしく御鳳声下さいませ。
まずはあらあら御礼まで
かしこ
園子
オニール先生

Bara no hana ga niwa ni utsukushiku saki-midareru rokugatsu no YOKI kisetsu to narimashita.

Sakuyū wa **Kenesu** to watakushi o Chūka ryōri no zen ni o-maneki kudasaimashite, **Chārusu Bōdon** Kyōju o hajime Nihongo-ka no sensei-gata ga go-shinsetsu ni mo watakushi-domo no tame ni sōbetsu no en o mōkete kudasar-i, makoto ni kyōshuku ni zonjimasu. Go-ichidō-sama-gata no go-kōjō, kokoro yori atsuku o-rei mōshi-agemasu.

Mata, purezento to shite taihen rippa na denshi rajio-dokei o o-megumi kudasar-e, makoto ni arigataku, atsuku atsuku o-rei mōshi-agemasu. Mai-asa kore kara tanoshimi ni tsukawasete itadakimasu to dōji ni mata itsu mo **Oniiru** Sensei o hajime Nihongo-ka no sensei-gata no go-kōjō o omoi-dasu yosuga to sasete itadakimasu. Nagai aida hontō ni iro-iro to o-sewa ni narimashita. Nani-mo ka-mo arigatō gozaimashita.

Kore kara **Kenesu** to watakushi wa **Debon** de atarashii seikatsu ni hairō to itashite orimasu. Omou zonbun daishizen no rizumu o ajiwai-nagara shizen de ningen-teki na iki-kata o ōi ni tanoshimitai to negatte orimasu.

バラの花が庭に美しく咲きみだれる
六月の良き季節となりました。
昨夕はケネスと私を中華料理の
膳にお招き下さいまして、チャールス・ボードン
教授を始め日本語科の先生方がご親切
にも　私共の為に送別の宴をもうけて
下さり　誠に恐縮に存じます。
御一同様方の御厚情、心より厚く
御礼申し上げます。

尚、プレゼントとして大変立派な
電子ラヂオ・時計をお恵み下され、
誠に有難く厚く〳〵御礼申し
上げます。毎朝これから、楽しみに
使わせて頂きますと同時に尚いつも
オニール先生を始め日本語科の先生方
の御厚情を想い出すよすがとさせて

Oniiru Sensei, dōzo kongo-tomo o-karada o taisetsu ni asobasar-e, masu-masu go-katsuyaku go-hatten nasaimasu yō, kokoro yori o-inori mōshi-agemasu.

Mappitsu-nagara Nihongo-ka no sensei-gata ni mo kure-gure mo yoroshiku go-**hōsei** kudasaimase.

Mazu wa **ara-ara** o-rei made.

Kashiko

Sonoko

Oniiru Sensei

Notes

a. YOKI The classical literary attributive form ending in *-ki* (see 3p), equivalent here to colloquial *yoi/ii*.

55. Letter from a Girl High-School Student

拝啓

はじめまして

私達は日本の女子です　四月からは　みんな　大学．専門学校．就職

あるいは　家事手伝いと違った道を行きます

さて．私達は貴方の国に　とても興味を持っております

それで．あつかましいこととは　わかっておりますが．．貴方の大学の学生さんたちと

文通を通じて　より　イギリスについて　色々学びたいと思うのです

文通の際の使用言語は　出来れば　日本語にして下さらないでしょうか．

私達は　英語は　堪能では　ございませんし．それに日本語でしたら

貴方の　学生さんたちの　勉強にも　色々力を　お貸しすることも　出来るでしょう

しかし．どうしてもと　おっしゃるのでしたら　英語でもよろしいです

（でも　ほんの　２～３人に限ります）

さて　こちらには　文通を希望している者は　１０人程おります

もし了解して下さるのでしたら　文通を希望しておられる方の　住所．氏名

年令　そして　簡単な　自己紹介を　お書きになり　こちらに送り返して下さい

１０人以上でありましても　私が．．必ず　全員の方に素晴らしい

ペンパルを　御紹介　いたします　御希望される方は．男女を

問いませんが．．こちらは全て女子です　年令は　みんな　１８才

（あるいは１７か１９）です

では　すぐにお返事のあることを願いつつ．．．．

さようなら．

敬具

代表者．．．市原いづみ．

Haikei,

Hajimemashite.

Watashi-domo wa Nihon no joshi desu. Shigatsu kara wa minna daigaku, senmon gakkō, shūshoku aruiwa kaji tetsudai to chigatta michi o ikimasu.

Sate, watashi-domo wa anata no kuni ni totemo kyōmi o motte orimasu. Sore de, atsukamashii koto to wa wakatte orimasu ga anata no daigaku no gakusei-san-tachi to buntsū o tsūjite, YORI Igirisu ni tsuite iro-iro manabitai to omou no desu. Buntsū no sai no shiyō-gengo wa dekireba Nihongo ni shite kudasaranai deshō ka. Watashi-domo wa Eigo wa tannō de wa gozaimasen shi, sore ni Nihongo deshitara anata no gakusei-san-tachi no benkyō ni mo iro-iro chikara o o-kashi suru koto mo dekiru deshō. Shikashi, dō shite mo to ossharu no deshitara Eigo de mo yoroshii desu.

(De mo, hon no 2–3nin ni kagirimasu.)

Sate, kochira ni wa buntsū o kibō shite iru mono wa 10nin hodo orimasu. Moshi ryōkai shite kudasaru no deshitara, buntsū o kibō shite ORARERU kata no jūsho, shimei, nenrei, soshite kantan na jiko shōkai o o-kaki ni nar-i, kochira ni okuri-kaeshite kudasai. 10nin ijō de arimashite mo watashi ga kanarazu zèn'in no kata ni subarashii pen paru o go-shōkai itashimasu. Go-kibō sareru kata wa DANJO O TOIMASEN ga, kochira wa subete joshi desu. Nenrei wa minna 18sai (aruiwa 17 ka 19) desu.

De wa, sugu ni o-henji no aru koto o negai-tsutsu . . .

Sayōnara
Keigu

Daihyōsha
Ichihara Izumi

Notes

a. YORI This mainly written use of *yori*, "(rather/more) than," gives a comparative meaning to the following word or phrase, in the same way as *motto*, "more." It usually immediately precedes the word to which it applies, but here this word is *manabitai*; thus, "we would like to learn more (about all kinds of things)."

b. ORARERU Here, as in 14b, clearly intended as a simple honorific equivalent to *irassharu*.

c. DANJO O TOIMASEN "One does not ask (whether) male or female," i.e., "we do not mind whether they are male or female." Cf. the common adverbial phrase *danjo o towazu*, "regardless of sex."

56. Letter from an Intending Visitor to London

英文で書くべきなのですが、日本語の手紙で
失礼いたしました。
御身御自愛くださるようお祈り申しあげます。　敬具

八月十三日　　越智（おち）治雄（はるお）

P.G.オニール先生

Haikei,

Tōkyō wa kibishii atsu-sa no mainichi de gozaimasu ga, **on-chi** wa ikaga deshō ka.

Kono tabi wa, watakushi no katte na o-negai o o-kiki-todoke kudasaimashite, o-maneki no o-tegami o-okuri itadak-i, arigatō gozaimashita.

Nishi-Doitsu no **Boffumu** de jūgatsu kara rainen no kugatsu made kōgi o itashimasu ga, NATSUME SŌSEKI no kenkyū o shite orimasu no de, zehi **Rondon** de Sōseki yukari no tochi o arukitai to omotte orimashita ga, sono negai ga kanai, konna ureshii koto wa gozaimasen.

Ki o mite **on-chi** e ukaga-i, go-aisatsu sasete itadaku tsumori desu ga, tori-aezu o-rei made ni shitatamemashita.

Nao, ima made ni kakimashita Sōseki-ron ga hon ni matomarimashita no de, goran itadakitaku, o-okuri suru yō shoten ni tanomimashita. O-osame itadak-ereba saiwai de gozaimasu.

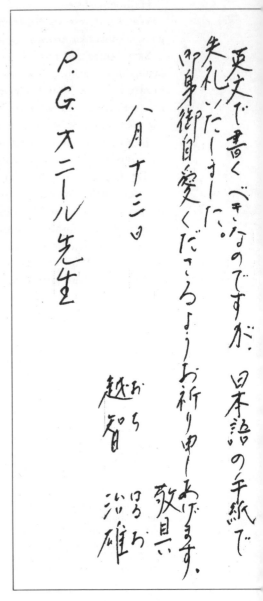

拝啓
東京はきびしい暑さの毎日でございますが、
御地はいかがでしょうか。
このたびは、私の勝手なお願いをお聞き届け
下さいまして、お招きのお手紙、お送りいただき、
ありがとうございました。
西ドイツのボッフムで十月から来年の九月まで
講義をいたしますが、夏目漱石の研究をして
おりますので、ぜひロンドンで漱石ゆかりの土地
を歩きたいと思っておりましたが、その願いが
ない、こんなうれしいことはございません。
機をみて御地へうかがい、ごあいさつさせていた
だくつもりですが、とりあえず御礼までにし
たためました。
なお、今までに書きました漱石論が本にまと
まりましたので、ごらんいただきたく、お送りする
よう書店に頼みました。おおさめいただければ
さいわいでございます。

Eibun de kaku-beki na no desu ga, Nihongo no tegami de shitsurei itashimashita. O-karada go-jiai kudasaru yō o-inori mōshi-agemasu.

Keigu

Ochi Haruo

Hachigatsu jūsannichi
P.G. **Oniiru** Sensei

Notes

a. NATSUME SŌSEKI 夏目漱石; a famous novelist who lived 1867–1916 and studied in London for nearly three years.

57. First Letter from a Publisher

8月25日

P.G.オニール様

日本アイ・ビー・エム
広報
前野昭吉

拝啓　時下益々ご清栄のこととお慶び申し上げます。
さて，突然お手紙を差し上げましたのは，同封の
J.クライナー先生のお手紙にもあるとおり，弊誌
「無限大」へのご寄稿をお願いするためです。
J.クライナー先生と面識を得ましたのは，「無限大」
が一連の企画——「日本人とは何か」，「われわれの
祖先は何語を話していたのか」，「日本学の方法」を特集
したことがきっかけです。　そして，一夕 住谷一彦
先生，J.クライナー先生，パウアーご夫妻と談笑中，

P.G. Oniiru-sama

Hachigatsu nijūgonichi

Nihon **Ai Bii Emu**
Kōhō
Maeno Shōkichi

Haikei. Jika masu-masu go-**seiei** no koto to o-yorokobi mōshi-agemasu.
Sate, totsuzen o-tegami o sashi-agemashita no wa, dōfū no J. **Kurainā** Sensei no o-tegami ni mo aru tōri, hei-shi "**Mugendai**" e no go-kikō o o-negai suru tame desu. J. **Kurainā** Sensei to menshiki o emashita no wa, "**Mugendai**" ga ichiren no kikaku—"Nihonjin To Wa Nani Ka," "Ware-ware No Sosen Wa Nani-go O Hanashite Ita No

一つの企画が生まれました。さきに上げた「日本学」の
特集の系譜に「知られざる日本研究」(仮)を加えたら
どうかというものです。これは、日本ほど理解しずらい
国はないと思い込んでいる日本の読者に、外国での
日本研究のひろがりを知らせるのがねらいです。

　先生に原稿をお願いするにいたったいきさつは以上の
ようなものです。「無限大」の性格、特集「知られざる
日本研究」のあらまし、先生へお願いする原稿の要領
を下記いたしましたので、ぜひご寄稿いただけます
ようお願い申し上げます。なお、「無限大」の
バック・ナンバーは別便にてお送りいたしました。
お返事をお待ちしております。　　敬具

Ka,'' ''Nihongaku No Hōhō'' o tokushū shita koto ga kikkake desu. Soshite, isseki **Sumiya Kazuhiko** Sensei, J. **Kurainā** Sensei, **Pauā** go-fusai to danshō-chū, hitotsu no kikaku ga umaremashita. Saki ni ageta ''Nihongaku'' no tokushū no keifu ni ''Shirare-ZARU Nihon Kenkyū'' (kari) o kuwaetara dō ka to iu mono desu. Kore wa, Nihon hodo rikai shi-ZURAI kuni wa nai to omoi-konde iru Nihon no dokusha ni, gaikoku de no Nihon kenkyū no hirogari o shiraseru no ga nerai desu.

Sensei ni genkō o o-negai suru ni itatta ikisatsu wa ijō no yō na mono desu. ''**Mugendai**'' no seikaku, tokushū ''Shirare-zaru Nihon Kenkyū'' no aramashi, sensei e o-negai suru genkō no yōryō o kaki itashimashita no de, zehi go-kikō itadake-masu yō o-negai mōshi-agemasu. Nao, ''**Mugendai**'' no bakku nanbā wa betsubin nite o-okuri itashimashita. O-henji o o-machi shite orimasu.

Keigu

記

1. 「無限大」
日本アイ・ビー・エムが、日本のオピニオン・リーダー、マスコミ関係者、IBMユーザーの経営者層に配布している隔月刊の雑誌で、発行部数は23,000部。とり上げているテーマは人間と科学・技術、異文化間の交流など。

2. 先生へのご寄稿のお願い

・題名：　英国における日本研究
（貴国におけるこれまでの日本研究のあらましと、現在どのような方がどのような問題について研究されているかをご紹介いただきたいと思います。どのような点に特徴があるかについてもご執筆いただければ幸いです。）

・文章：　日本語、英語、仏語、独語のいずれでも結構です。最も書きやすい言語でお願いいたします。ただし、日本語

Ki

1. **"Mugendai"**

Nihon **Ai Bii Emu** ga, Nihon no **opinion riidā**, masu-komi kankeisha, IBM **yūzā** no keieisha sō ni haifu shite iru **kakugekkan** no zasshi de, hakkō busū wa 23,000bu. Tori-agete iru **tēma** wa ningen to kagaku gijutsu, **i-bunka-kan** no kōryū nado.

2. Sensei e no go-kikō no o-negai

Daimei: Eikoku ni okeru Nihon Kenkyū
(Ki-koku ni okeru, kore made no Nihon kenkyū no aramashi to, genzai dono yō na kata ga dono yō na mondai ni tsuite kenkyū sarete iru ka o go-shōkai itadakitai to omoimasu. Dono yō na ten ni tokuchō ga aru ka ni tsuite mo go-shippitsu itadakereba saiwai desu.)

Bunshō: Nihongo, Eigo, **Futsugo**, **Dokugo** no IZURE DE MO kekkō desu. Mottomo kaki-yasui gengo de o-negai itashimasu. Tadashi, Nihongo igai no baai, koyū meishi, shomei, ronbun-mei, in'yōbun nado wa Nihongo o

以外の場合、固有名詞、
書名、論文名、引用文などは
日本語を付け加えて下さい。
翻訳は当編集部にご一任
下さい。

・枚　数：　日本語に訳して400字×10枚
前後（ただし、これは本文のみ。
研究一覧表などは別）。

・締　切：　1980年　11月　10日

・お　礼：　8万円
（どこへ、どのような方法で
お送りすればよいか　お教え
下さい。）

以上

---

tsuke-kuwaete kudasai. Hon'yaku wa tō-henshūbu ni go-ichinin kudasai.

Maisū: Nihongo ni yaku-shite 400ji×10mai zengo (tadashi, kore wa honbun nomi; kenkyū ichiranhyō wa betsu.)

Shime-kiri: 1980nen jūichigatsu tōka

O-rei: 8man'en (Doko e, dono yō na hōhō de o-okuri sureba yoi ka, o-oshie kudasai.)

Ijō

Notes

a. -ZARU This is a literary form which, being a contraction of *-zu* (see 16b) + *aru*, is negative and attributive. Thus, its meaning is "which/who (is) not."

b. -ZURAI The voiced form of *tsurai*, "hard, painful, cruel," which, like any other appropriate adjective, can be used with the stem of a verb; e.g., *wakari-yasui*, "easy to understand," and, here, *rikai shi-zurai*, "hard/difficult to comprehend."

c. IZURE DE MO A literary equivalent for *dore de mo*, "whichever (it is)"; cf. *izure ni shite mo* under 4n.

をお知らせしようと筆をとった次第でございます。
どうぞ御一読下さいませ。（或は誰方かがもうお送り下さって
お手許におありかもしれませんが……）
また、大変おくればせながら、三年前の研究室で撮らせていただき
ました先生のお写真、お送りいたします。お手数を
かけますが、一枚はダン先生におわたし下さいませ。
例年ならば残暑厳しい東京も、今年は天候不順で、九月に入り
肌寒いような曇天がつづいております。
大学も始まり、あわただしい日々がまたまた続きそうでございます。
どうぞ御体御大切になさいまして御活躍下さいませ。

九月十二日　かしこ

里川知恵子

オニール先生

台風の影響で毎日、はっきりしない天候が続いております。
御無沙汰しておりますが、先生にはますますお元気で
おすごしの御様子、およろこび申し上げます。
ダニエルズ先生の御紹介で大学の研究室に先生をお訪ね
しましてから三年、時の流れの早さにおどろくばかりで
ございます。 先日、ダニエルズ先生からお便りいただき、
ロンドンの街々を思いうかべなつかしく思いながら夕刊を
手にしてみますと、英紙「タイムズ文芸付録」の「日本文学
特集を見て」が掲載され、その中に先生のお名前を
見ました時は、本当に感慨無量でございました。
早速、この新聞をお送りして先生の御研究の日本での反響

Taifū no eikyō de mainichi hakkiri shinai tenkō ga tsuzuite orimasu. Go-busata shite orimasu ga, sensei ni wa masu-masu o-genki de o-sugoshi no go-yōsu, o-yorokobi mōshi-agemasu.

Danieruzu Sensei no go-shōkai de daigaku no kenkyūshitsu ni sensei o o-tazune shimashite kara sannen, toki no nagare no haya-sa ni odoroku bakari de gozaimasu. Senjitsu, **Danieruzu** Sensei kara o-tayori itadak-i, **RONDON** no machi-machi o omoi-ukabe, natsukashiku omoi-nagara, yūkan o te ni shite mimasu to, **Eishi "Taimuzu Bungei Furoku"** no "Nihon Bungaku Tokushū O Mite" ga keisai sar-e, sono naka ni sensei no o-namae o mi-idashita toki wa, hontō ni kangai muryō de gozaimashita.

Sassoku kono shinbun o o-okuri shite, sensei no go-kenkyū no Nihon de no hankyō o o-shirase shiyō to fude o totta shidai de gozaimasu. Dōzo go-ichidoku kudasaimase. (Aruiwa, donata-ka ga mō o-okuri kudasatte o-temoto ni O-ARI ka mo shiremasen ga . . .)

Mata, taihen **okurebase**-nagara, sannen mae, kenkyūshitsu de torasete itadakimashita sensei no o-shashin, o-okuri itashimasu. O-tesū o kakemasu ga, ichimai wa **Dan** sensei ni o-watashi kudasaimase.

Reinen nara zansho kibishii Tōkyō mo, kotoshi wa tenkō fujun de, kugatsu ni hairi, hada-samui yō na donten ga tsuzuite orimasu.

Daigaku mo hajimari, awatadashii hi-bi ga mata mata tsuzuki-sō de gozaimasu.

Dōzo o-karada o-taisetsu ni nasaimashite go-katsuyaku kudasaimase.

Kashiko

Tagawa Chieko

Kugatsu jūninichi
Oniiru Sensei

Notes

a. O-ARI This is part of the regular *o-* + vb. stem *ni naru* honorific construction (see 6t), but the nature of the verb *aru*, "exist," means that, when it is used in an honorific construction to express the idea of "have, possess," the respect is directed to the possessor and not to the grammatical subject (which would here be *shinbun*) as is otherwise the case with honorifics. In other words, respect is being shown here to the addressee and not to the copy of the newspaper which he may already have.

59. Letter from an Older Man of Long Acquaintance

年末なのに、郵便局の誤配ではやばやと
お年賀状を頂きました。日本でのお正月をお二人
で楽しくお過し下さい。
先日はわざわざお出で頂きありがたく
ございました。その時の写真、今度は
どうやらうつりましたので、同封致し
ます。家は今基礎工事に入って
居り、新しい年になってから建物が立つ
ようです。明二十三日から、始めてハワイ四島廻り
見物に出かけ、二十九日に帰って来ます。
一月二日NHK第二放送(ラジオ)新春五流謡曲の会
春流石橋(午前十時と三時)、一月十六日NHK
教育テレビ(3チャンネル)九時(午前?)金剛流船
弁慶に出演いたしますので、おひまでし
たらどうぞ。一月になったらまた機会を
作ってお目にかかりたいと思って居ります。
学生の卒業論文審査や期末試験やらで
ごたごたしては居りますが。

十二月二十二日

田中允

P・G オニール様

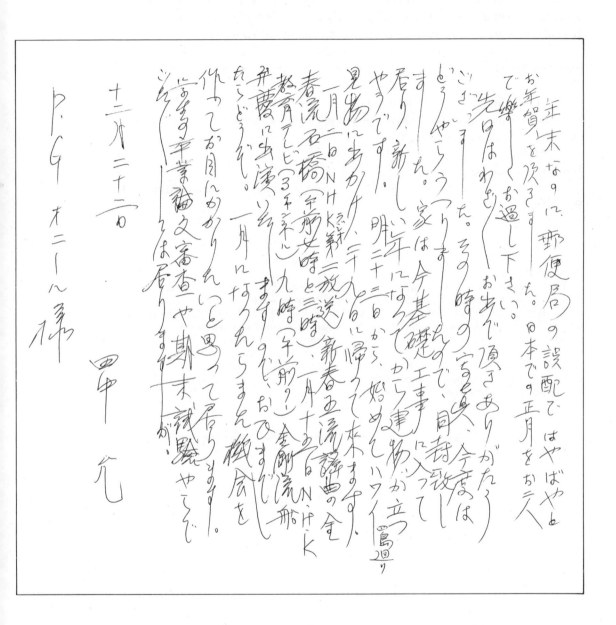

Nenmatsu na no ni yūbinkyoku no **gohai** de haya-baya to o-nenga o itadakimashita. Nihon de no shōgatsu o o-futari de tanoshiku o-sugoshi kudasai.

Senjitsu wa waza-waza oide itadak-i arigatō gozaimashita. Sono toki no shashin, kondo wa dō-yara utsurimashita no de, dōfū itashimashita. Ie wa ima kiso kōji ni haitte or-i, atarashii toshi ni natte kara tatemono ga tatsu yō desu. Myō-nijūsannichi kara, hajimete **Hawai** (yontō-meguri) kenbutsu ni dekake, nijūkunichi ni kaette kimasu.

Ichigatsu futsuka NHK (rajio) Dai-ni Hōsō Shinshun GORYŪ YŌKYOKU no **Konparu**-ryū SHAKKYŌ (gozen shichiji to sanji), ichigatsu jūgonichi N.H.K. Kyōiku Terebi (San-channeru) kuji (gozen?) **Kongō**-ryū FUNA-BENKEI ni shutsuen itashimasu no de, o-hima deshitara dōzo. Ichigatsu ni nattara mata kikai o tsukutte o-me ni kakaritai to omotte orimasu. Gakusei no sotsugyō ronbun shinsa ya kimatsu shiken yara de gota-gota shite wa orimasu ga.

Jūnigatsu nijūninichi

Tanaka Makoto

P.G. **Oniiru**-sama

Notes

a. NHK Abbreviation for *Nippon Hōsō Kyōkai*, "Japan Broadcasting Corporation."

b. GORYŪ YŌKYOKU The *goryū*, "five schools," are the main groups within the world of Nō drama, two of them being the Konparu and Kongō schools mentioned above. *Yōkyoku* are the texts of Nō plays, and since the reference is to broadcast performances of them, the phrase could be translated as "Play Recitals by the Five Schools of Nō."

c. SHAKKYŌ 石橋, "The Stone Bridge," the name of a Nō play.

d. FUNA-BENKEI 船弁慶, "Benkei in the Boat"; the name of a Nō play in which one of the main roles is that of Benkei, the loyal retainer of the famous warrior-hero Minamoto Yoshitsune (1159–1189).

60. Letter from a Man after His Return to Japan

1976年1月10日
東京都練馬区石神井町（しゃくじい　まち）

Dear Professor O'Neill,

新年を迎え、お変りなくお過ごしのことと思います。

昨年11月にお訪ねいたしました折は、御多忙中にも拘らず御親切に御応対下さり、まことにありがとうございました。お陰様で大変有益な知見を得ることができました。

あの後、英国内でもケンブリッジやオックスフォードの美しい田園風景や古い大学を見たり、パリ、ドイツ、ウィーンその他東欧諸国で美しい風景や豊富な文化遺産、遺跡に感激して、12月24日に帰国いたしました。

そんなわけで御礼も大変遅くなりましたが、Dunn教授のofficeでのsnap、現像してみましたところ、どうしたミスか、フィルムがカメラの中で空転していたらしく、1枚も写っていませんでした。まことに残念かつ申訳なく、失礼を深くおわびいたします。Dunn教授にもよろしくおとりなし下さい。

なお、貴学図書館に拙著『中世和歌史の研究』（昭和47年初版）があったかどうか覚えておりませんが、もしおありでしたら同封のプリント御利用下さるようお願いいたします。

取急ぎ御礼とおわびまで。　御自愛下さい。

福田秀一

1976nen ichigatsu tōka
Tōkyō-to **Nerima**-ku
Shakujii-machi

Dear Professor O'Neill,

Shinnen o mukae, o-kawari naku o-sugoshi no koto to omoimasu.

Sakunen jūichigatsu ni o-tazune itashimashita ori wa, go-tabō-chū ni mo kakawarazu go-shinsetsu ni go-ōtai kudasar-i, makoto ni arigatō gozaimashita. O-kage-sama de taihen yūeki na chiken o eru koto ga dekimashita.

Ano ato, Eikoku-nai de mo **Kenburijji** ya **Okkusufōdo** no utsukushii den'en fūkei ya furui daigaku o mitari, **Pari**, Doitsu, **Uiin** sono ta **tō-Ō** shokoku de utsukushii fūkei ya hōfu na bunka isan, iseki ni kangeki shite, jūnigatsu nijūyokka ni kikoku itashimashita.

Sonna wake de o-rei mo taihen osoku narimashita ga, Dunn Kyōju no office de no snap, genzō shite mi-mashita tokoro, dō shita misu ka, firumu ga kamera no naka de KŪTEN shite ita rashi-ku, ichimai mo utsutte imasen deshita. Makoto ni zannen katsu mōshi-wake naku, shitsurei o fukaku o-wabi itashimasu. Dunn Kyōju ni mo yoroshiku o-tori-nashi kudasai.

Nao, ki-gaku toshokan ni **setcho** "Chūsei Waka-shi No Kenkyū" (**Shōwa** 47nen shohan) ga atta ka dō ka oboete orimasen ga, moshi o-ari deshitara dōfū no purinto go-riyō kudasaru yō o-negai itashimasu.

Tori-isogi o-rei to o-wabi made. Go-jiai kudasai.

Fukuda Shūichi

Notes

a. KŪTEN Literally "empty revolutions," this usually refers to "revving" or "racing" an engine which is not in gear, but here means that the spool turned freely without engaging the film.

HIGHER-LEVEL TEXTS

Nos. 61–80

With transcriptions and notes, and uncommon vocabulary in the Glossary.

61. Letter from a Somewhat Younger Man, Known for a Number of Years

拝啓
約三週間の英国訪問を終えて先月
三十一日北極経由にて無事帰国致し
ました。
幸い滞英中は好天気に恵まれ、過去二十
余年に亘って聞かされて参りました、いわゆる
英国の天気を疑いたくなるような日々では
ありました。
その間、北はスコットランド、西はウエールズと駆け足
ではありましたが、一応貴国を拝見致し
その都市の壮重さ、田園の美しさを、更には
幾多の華麗な建造物を心から満喫致
しました。
又貴大学を訪れました折は、御多忙中にも
かかわらず、わざわざ貴重な時間を割いて
下され、種々御配慮を賜り、誠に有難う
ございました。
書中を以て厚く御礼を申し上げます。
日本での再会を心から望みつつ、先生の益々
御多祥あらん事をお祈りします。
向寒の折から何卒お体御大切に。
ダニエル教授にくれぐれもよろしくお伝え下さ
れば幸甚と存じます。
十一月五日
敬具
中里生
オニール教授殿

Haikei,

Yaku sanshū-kan no Eikoku hōmon o oete sengetsu sanjūichinichi Hokkyoku keiyu nite buji kikoku itashimashita.

Saiwai **tai-Ei**-chū wa, **kō-tenki** ni megumar-e, kako nijū-yo-nen ni watatte kikasarete mairimashita, iwayuru Eikoku no tenki o utagaitaku naru yō na hi-bi de wa arimashita.

Sono aida, kita wa **Sukottorando**, nishi wa **Uēruzu** to kake-ashi de wa arimashita ga, ichiō, ki-koku o haiken itashi, sono toshi no sōchō-sa, den'en no utsukushi-sa o, sara ni wa **ikuta** no karei na kenzōbutsu o kokoro kara mankitsu itashimashita.

Mata ki-daigaku o otozuremashita ori wa, go-tabō-chū ni mo kakawarazu, waza-waza, kichō na jikan o saite kudasar-e, shu-ju go-hairyo o tamawar-i, makoto ni arigatō gozaimashita.

Shochū o motte atsuku o-rei o mōshi-agemasu. Nihon de no saikai o kokoro kara nozomi-tsutsu, sensei no masu-masu go-**tashō** ARAN koto o o-inori shimasu. **Kōkan** no ori kara nani-tozo o-karada o-taisetsu ni.

Danieru Kyōju ni kure-gure mo yoroshiku o-tsutae kudasareba kōjin to zonjimasu.

Keigu

Nakazato SEI

Jūichigatsu itsuka
Oniiru Kyōju-dono

Notes

a. ARAN A literary form equivalent to colloquial *arō*, "will/may exist"; thus, here, "(I pray that) you may have."

b. SEI A humble word equivelent to *shōsei* (see 12c) and usable by a man in letters after his name; cf. the use of *hai* under 22g.

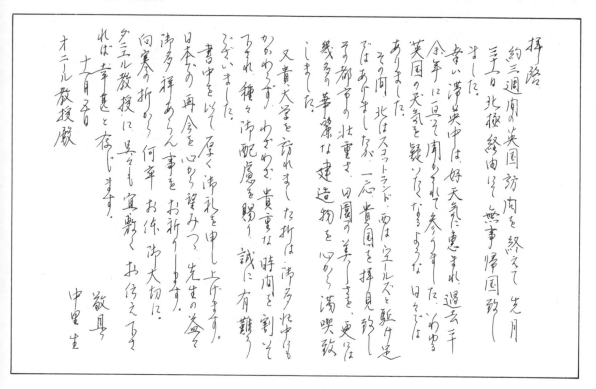

62. Circular Letter from a Publishing House

えいただき、河上肇についての研究を深めていただ
けますよう希望いたしております。
付きましては、内容を紹介しましたパンフレットを
~~同封~~発送させていただきます。
どうかよろしくお願い申し上げます。
一九八二年二月十六日
岩波書店
河上肇全集編集部

Haikei. Kanrei no **kō** masu-masu go-**seishō** no koto to o-yorokobi mōshi-agemasu. Sate, totsuzen o-tayori o mōshi-agemashita go-burei o o-yurushi kudasaimase. **Iwanami** Shoten NI OKIMASHITE, honnen ichigatsu yori, Nihon no kindai-shi ni ōki na sokuseki o nokoshimashita **Kawakami Hajime** no hajimete no zenshū o kankō shi-hajimemashita. Zen-33kan to iu taibu na mono de gozaimasu ga, **sashi-atatte** 26kan o dai-ikki to shite shuppan itashimasu. Watakushi-tachi wa Chūgoku no kakumeika-tachi ni mo fukai eikyō o ataeta kono shisōka no zenshū o Nihon igai no kuni-guni no kata ni mo o-yomi itadakitai to omotte imasu.

Dekimasureba, ki-kenkyū kikan de kono zenshū o o-sonae itadak-i, **Kawakami Hajime** ni tsuite no kenkyū o fukamete itadake-masu yō kibō itashite orimasu.

拝啓　寒冷の候益々御清祥のこととお慶び申し
上げます。
扨て、突然お便りを申上げました御無礼をお許
し下さいませ。岩波書店におきまして、本年一月
より、日本の近代史に大きな足跡を残しました河
上肇のはじめての全集を刊行しはじめました。
全33巻という大部なものでございますが、差当って
26巻を第I期として出版いたします。私たちは
中国の革命家たちにも深い影響を与えたこの
思想家の全集を日本以外の国々の方にもお読み
いただきたいと思っております。
できますれば、貴研究機関でこの全集をお備

Tsukimashite wa, naiyō o shōkai shimashita panfuretto o hassō sasete itadakimasu. Dōka yoroshiku o-negai mōshi-agemasu.

1982nen nigatsu jūrokunichi

Iwanami Shoten
Kawakami Hajime
Zenshū Henshūbu

Notes

a. NI OKIMASHITE The polite *masu* form of *ni oite*, which is a literary equivalent for the colloquial *de*, "in/at (a place)." It thus makes an adverbial phrase, parallel to the attributive *ni okeru* (see 20d).

63. Letter from an Elderly Lady, Known for Many Years

オニール様のお話が出まして 呉々もよろしく
とのことで御座いました
英国で経験する病気も非常に変なもの
で風邪かお腹か リューマチか 何か ちっとも
はっきりせず 無力化した気持で 一日の内
に色々変化するところ 当地のお天気に
よく似ています 医者のお薬も 効くのか効か
ないのか はっきり わかりません とにかく
長くかかりましたが 大分よくなりました
どうぞ 幾重にも 御大切に御願い致します
一寸ご挨拶まで
三月廿日
西
オニール様

Kigi no o-hana ga utsukushiku haru-meite mairimashita. O-genki de irasshaimasu ka. Kajitsu wa o-maneki itadakimashite, hontō ni tanoshii toki o sugoshi, iro-iro to o-motenashi ni azukar-i, kokoro kara orei o mōshi-agemasu. Ōshū e no go-ryokō wa ikaga deshita ka. Mata itsu-ka go-**KŌWA** o uketamawaritai mono da to zonji-agemasu.

Sangatsu jōjun ni **ki-kō** o o-tazune itashitaku yotei shite orimashita tokoro, sono-goro kara nan to naku KARADA no chōshi ga waruku, tō-tō isha ni kakari Eikoku no muryō iryō no go-yakkai ni narimashita. Konna arigatai me ni wa hajimete aimashita. Gakkō wa mō o-yasumi to omoimasu shi, watakushi mo nobi-nobi ni natte ita Yōroppa yuki mo hajimenakereba naranai no de, izure **ki-Ei** shimashite kara aratamete go-tsugō o ukagaitai shozon de gozaimasu. Nigatsu matsujitsu ni Cortazzi-sama no o-taku ni o-maneki itadak-i, **Oniiru**-sama no o-hanashi ga demashite kure-gure mo o-yoroshiku to no koto de gozaimashita.

Eikoku de keiken suru byōki mo hijō ni hen na mono de, kaze ka o-naka ka ryūmachi ka nani ka chitto mo hakkiri SEZU muryoku-ka shita kimochi de, ichinichi no uchi ni

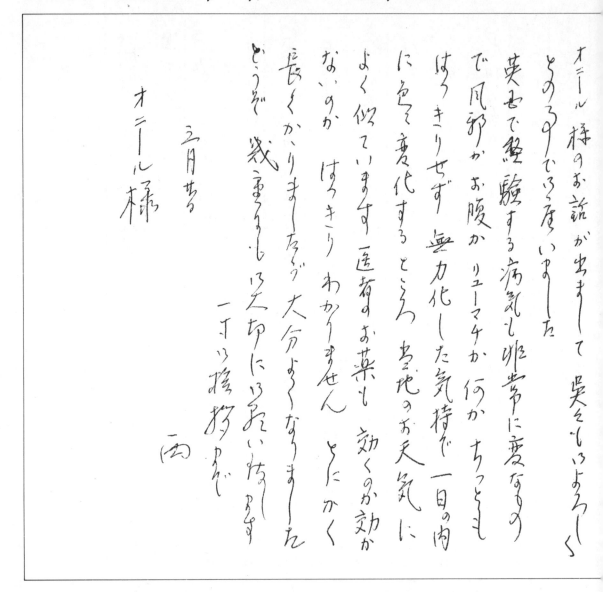

木々のお花が美しく春めいてまいりました
ご元気でいらっしゃいますか 過日はお招き
頂きまして 本当に楽しい時を過し色々と
ごもてなしに預り 心からお礼を申し上げ
ます 欧州へのご旅行は如何でしたか 又いつか
ご高話を承りたいものだと存じます
三月上旬に貴校をお訪ね致し度く予定
して居りましたところ その頃から何となく
身体の調子が悪く とうとう医者にかかり
英国の無料医療のご厄介になりました
こんな有難い国には初めて会いました 学校
はもうお休みと思いますし 私も延び延びに
なって居たヨーロッパ巡りも 始めなければなら
ないので 何れ帰英しましてから改めて
ご都合を伺い度い所存でございます
二月末までに [illegible] 様のお宅にご招き頂き

iro-iro henka suru tokoro tōchi no o-tenki ni yoku nite imasu. Isha no o-kusuri mo kiku no ka kikanai no ka hakkiri wakarimasen. Tonikaku, nagaku kakarimashita ga, daibu yoku narimashita.

Dōzo ikue ni mo go-taisetsu ni o-negai itashimasu.

Chotto go-aisatsu made.
Nishi

Sangatsu hatsuka
Oniiru-sama

Notes

a. KŌWA This reading of the characters gives a respectful word for the talk or conversation of another person. (The reading *takabanashi* for the same characters has the quite different meaning of "loud talk.")

b. KARADA The characters here can also be read *shintai* (see 26i).

c. SEZU A literary negative form from *suru*, equivalent to the colloquial *shinai de.*

64. Letter from a Senior Professor

ることになっていますが、後任の教官には現在の俸給以上が支払えず、最近上京しブリティシュ・カウンシルにお伺いしてイギリスから日本までの旅費等を御補助頂けるかを相談しましたところ、まったく不可能であること判明しました

往復の旅費も支辨できず且また月給五万円では、どうしても貴地からお迎えすることはできないであろうとあきらめているような次第であります。いろいろ理想を抱いても、市立の大學では東京、大阪を除いては十分な教育環境はで

Tsutsushinde nenshi no go-aisatsu mōshi-agemasu. Nihon no go-ryūgaku-chū, **Tōkyō** kara hanare mata kōmu ni tazusawatte iru kankei de nan no o-yaku ni mo tatazu, makoto ni kokoro-gurushii koto ni zonjite imasu. Bannen wa **Tōkyō** de sugoshitaku, futatabi go-**rai-Nichi** no ori ni wa ōi ni go-kyōryoku MŌSHITAKU, tanoshimi ni itashite imasu.

Kanete go-hairyo o itadakimashita hongaku no Igirisu-jin kyōshi no ken ni tsukimashite wa go-kōjō o **shinsha** TSUKAMATSURI-nagara mo tsui go-henji o okurase mōshi-wake arimasen. **Gibusu**-shi wa honnen kugatsu de kikoku sareru koto ninatte imasu ga, kōnin no kyōkan ni wa genzai no sararii ijō shi-harae-zu, saikin jōkyō shi **Buritishu** KAUNSHIN ni o-ukagai shite Igirisu kara Nihon made no ryohi nado o gohojo itadakeru ka o sōdan shimashita tokoro, mattaku fukanō de aru koto hanmei shimashita.

Ōfuku no ryohi mo **shiben** dekizu, katsu mata gekkyūyo goman'en de wa, dō shite mo **ki-chi** kara o-mukae suru koto wa dekinai de arō to akiramete iru yō na shidai de arimasu. Iro-iro risō o idaite mo, shiritsu no daigaku de wa **Tōkyō**, **Ōsaka** o nozoite wa jūbun na kyōiku kankyō wa dekinai koto ga tsūkan SAREMASU.

Haruka ni **Rondon** o shinonde isshō no uchi mo ichido o-ukagai shitai to nenjite imasu. Go-kenkō o inotte yamimasen.

Nigatsu muika

Furuno Kiyohito

Oniiru Hakushi
JISHI

つゝしんで年始の御挨拶
申しあげます　日本の御留
學中、東京から離れま
した公務に携っている関係で
何のお役にもたゝずまこと
に心苦しいことに存じていま
す　晩年は東京ですごし
たく再び御來日の折には
大いに御協力申したく樂し
みに致しています
かねて御配慮をいたゞき
ました本學のイギリス人
教師の件につきましては
御厚情を深謝仕りながら
もつい御返事を遅らせ
申しわけありません。ギブス。
氏は本年九月で帰国され

きないことが痛感され
ます
遙かにロンドンを偲んで
一生のうちも一度お伺
いしたいと念じています
御健康を祈ってや
みません
二月六日　吉野清人
オニール博士
侍史

Notes

a. MŌSHITAKU In addition to their primary meaning of "(humbly) say," both *mōsu* and *mōshi-ageru* are also used as humble equivalents for *suru*, "do," as here. The ending *taku* is here the suspensive form of *tai*, parallel to *imasu*; thus, "I would like (to cooperate . . .) and . . ."

b. TSUKAMATSURI- From its original use as a humble verb meaning "serve," *tsukamatsuru* came to be used as a humble literary equivalent for *suru*, "do."

c. KAUNSHIN The *kana* spelling here was intended for "(British) Council."

d. SAREMASU This passive form of *suru* gives the meaning "is (keenly felt)" and, hence, "I realize only too well that . . ."

e. JISHI A formal, polite term used at the end of letters, through its original meaning of "scribe, secretary."

65. Letter from a Publisher, Known for Many Years

お客様にも大変喜んでいただいて居ります　厚く御禮を
申し上げます
日本は今年万国博覧会で賑やかでございます
又近い内に御来日に成ります様な御予定が
ございましたらお知らせ下さいましたらお待ち申し上げ
て居ります　御家族の皆々様にも宜敷お伝へ
下さいませ
匆々
昭和四十五年四月　桧常太郎

オニール様

Haikei,

Taihen go-busata o mōshi-agemashita. Mina-sama o-kawari mo naku o-genki DE IRAREMASU ka, o-ukagai mōshi-agemasu. Kondo **Shimazaki Chifumi** Joshi ga **ki-koku** o hōmon SAREMASU no de, o-ai itadak-i go-**kōsetsu** o UKETAMAWARASETE itadakereba taihen saiwai ni zonjimasu. Dō-joshi wa **Riidāsu Daijesuto** ni izen o-tsutome ni natte Eigo ga o-jōzu desu. Nō ni mo go-shumi ga fukaku, mai mo o-deki ni narimasu no de, yōkyoku no meikyoku o ikkyoku zenbu Eiyaku suru koto o kikaku shite irare-mashite, watashi no mise de shuppan itashitaku go-sōdan shite orimasu. Yoi o-kangae ga GOZAIMASHITARA, osore-irimasu ga go-kyōji itadake-mashitara saiwai ni zonjimasu. O-kage-sama de **Gaido Tsū Nō** wa sono go mo hiki-tsuzuite shuppan sasete itadaite orimashite Nōgakudō e korareru gaijin no o-kyaku-sama ni mo taihen yorokonde itadaite orimasu. Atsuku o-rei o mōshi-agemasu.

Nihon wa kotoshi Bankoku Hakurankai de nigiyaka de gozaimasu. Mata chikai uchi ni go-**rai-Nichi** ni narimasu yō na go-yotei ga gozaimashitara, o-shirase kudasaimashi-

拝啓
大へん御無沙汰を申し上げました　皆様お変りもなく
御元気でいられますか　お伺ひ申し上げます　今度
島崎千富美女史が貴国を訪問されますので
御會ひいただき御高説を承らせていただければ大変
幸に存じます　同女史はリーダースダイヂェストに以前
お勤めに成って英語がお上手です　能にも御趣味が深く
舞もお出来に成りますので　謡曲の名曲を一曲全部
英譯する事を企畫してゐられまして　私の店で出版
致し度く御相談して居ります　よいお考へがござゐま
したら恐れ入りますが御教示いただけましたら幸に存じ
ます　お陰様でガイドツーノーは其後も引續いて
出版させていただいて居りまして　能楽堂へ来られる外人の

tara o-machi mōshi-agete orimasu. Go-kazoku no mina-mina-sama ni mo yoroshiku o-tsutae kudasaimase.

Sō-sō

Hinoki Tsunetarō

Shōwa yonjūgonen shigatsu
Oniiru-sama

Notes

a. DE IRAREMASU　Since *irareru* is used as an honorific for *iru*, "be (present)," exactly like *irassharu*, the phrase here is equivalent to *de irasshaimasu* (see 20b).

b. SAREMASU　Here used as an honorific, equivalent to *shimasu*.

c. UKETAMAWARASETE　Equivalent to neutral-level *kikasete*.

d. GOZAIMASHITARA　The *kana* spelling of *gozaimasu* and related forms has always been ございます; but since it can also be written 御座居ます and 居る had the old *kana* spelling ゐる *(w)iru*, the writer carried this spelling back into his writing of *gozaimasu*.

66. Postcard from the Proprietor of a Small Hotel

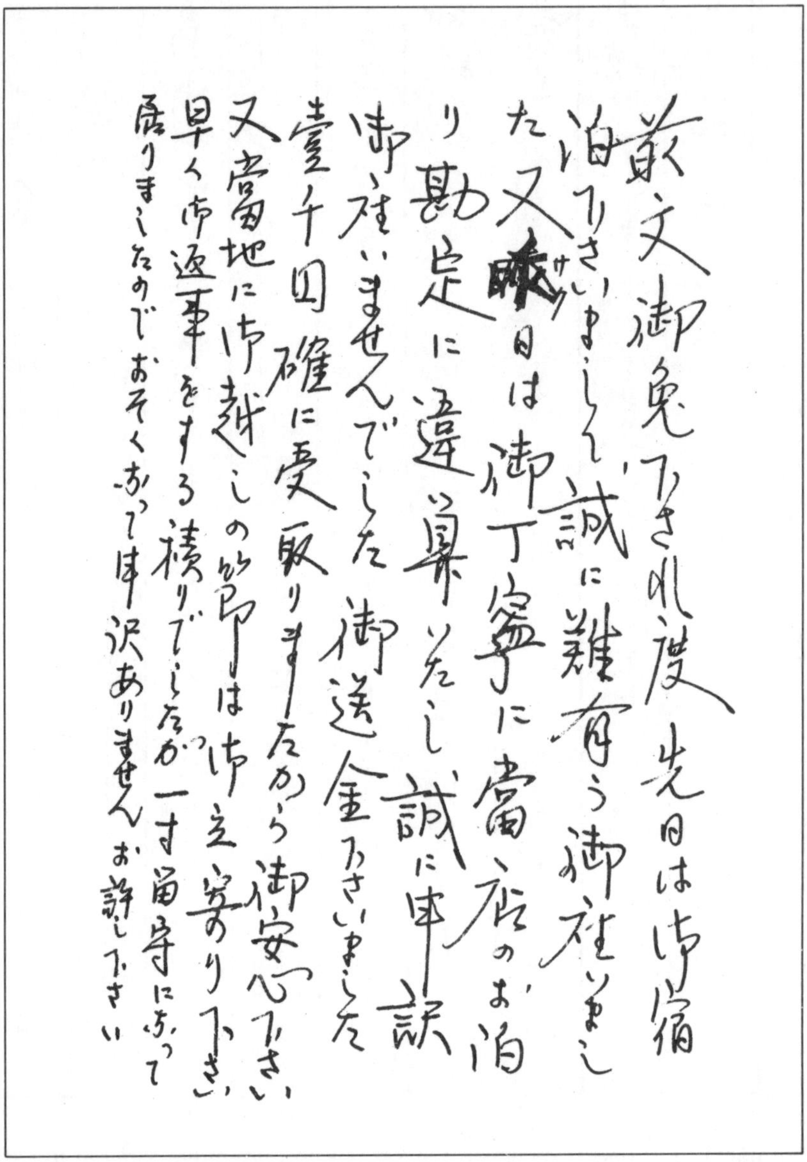
前文御免下され度　先日は御宿
泊下さいまして誠に難有う御座いまし
た又昨日は御丁寧に当店のお泊
り勘定に遺算いたし誠に申訳
御座いませんでした　御送金下さいました
壱千円確に受取りましたから御安心下さい
又当地に御越しの節は御立寄り下さい
早く御返事をする積りでしたが一寸留守になって
居りましたのでおそくなって申訳ありません　お許し下さい

Zenbun gomen KUDASARE-TAKU. Senjitsu wa go-shukuhaku kudasaimashite makoto ni arigatō gozaimashita. Mata sakujitsu wa go-teinei ni tōten no o-tomari kanjō ni **isan** itashi, makoto ni mōshi-wake gozaimasen deshita. Go-sōkin kudasaimashita issen'en tashika ni uke-torimashita kara go-anshin kudasai. Mata tōchi ni o-koshi no setsu wa o-tachi-yori kudasai. Hayaku go-henji o suru tsumori deshita ga chotto rusu ni natte orimashita no de, osoku natte mōshi-wake arimasen. O-yurushi kudasai.

Notes

a. KUDASARE-TAKU This sentence being incomplete, something like *zonjimasu* must be understood after it. Thus, "I would like to have you . . ., I would like you to . . ."

1972. 6. 4.

オニールさんへ

沼本次郎.

先日 あなた宛に参りました郵便物をお送り致して
おきましたが 未だ 到着致しませんか.
その後も Honkong Shanghai Bank などから参りましたが
名宛人は英国に帰国された由記入して差出人に返送
しておきました.
あなたが帰国されましてから日本に於ては"送り仮名"の
用法が若干変りました. 何かの御参考にと思い 本日
スクラップして お送り致します. 朝日新聞に出た全部
です. 最後の批評の通り全く分りません. 尤も私
達は そんなことに無関係に書いております. 法則あっ
ての国語でなく. 国語の中から抽出した共通原則が
文法ですから. この点 我々から見ると異国語の中でも
英語が一番 むつかしい様に思へ 又 例外も多いこと
日本語と同じに思います.
この方が言語のニューアンスが多く含蓄に富んでおる
と思います. 一言にして云へば 科学的の言葉でなく
文学的の言葉であると思います.
世界で最も文学的の言葉であると思います.
学者である貴郎に斯様なことを申上げるのは
"釈迦に説法"と日本では申します. 何卒御諒承下
さい.
どうぞ 益々御元氣で御活躍下さいませ.
当方は本日 どうやら ~~陰鬱な~~ "いんうつな
梅雨の季節に入りました.
皆様によろしく. 何年 何年 御達者で. 又お会い
出来る日があったら 何んと幸福なことでしょう.
乱筆にて御免下さい. 草々

1972. 6. 4.
Numamoto Jirō

Oniiru-san e,

Senjitsu anata ate ni mairimashita yūbinbutsu o o-okuri itashite okimashita ga, mada tōchaku itashimasen ka.

Sono go mo Honkong Shanghai Bank nado kara mairimashita ga, na-atenin wa Eikoku ni kikoku sareta yoshi kinyū shite hassō-nin ni kaisō shite okimashita.

Anata ga kikoku sare-mashite kara Nihon ni oite wa "okuri-gana" no yōhō ga jakkan kawarimashita. Nani-ka no go-sankō ni to omoi, honjitsu **sukurappu** shite o-okuri itashimasu. Asahi Shinbun ni deta zenbu desu. Saigo no hihyō no tōri mattaku wakarimasen. Mottomo, watashi-tachi wa sonna koto ni mukankei ni kaite orimasu. Hōsoku ATTE NO kokugo de naku, kokugo no naka kara chūshutsu shita kyōtsū gensoku ga bunpō desu kara, kono ten ware-ware kara miru to, **ikokugo** no naka de mo Eigo ga ichiban mutsukashii yō ni omo-e, mata reigai mo ōi koto Nihongo to onaji ni omoimasu.

Kono hō ga, gengo no niyūansu ga ōku, ganchiku ni tonde oru to omoimasu. Ichigon ni shite ieba, kagaku-teki no kotoba de naku, bungaku-teki no kotoba de aru to omoimasu.

Sekai de mottomo bungaku-teki no kotoba de aru to omoimasu.

Gakusha de aru KIRŌ ni kayō na koto o mōshi-ageru no wa "Shaka ni seppō" to Nihon de wa mōshimasu. Nani-tozo go-ryōshō kudasai.

Dōzo masu-masu o-genki de go-katsuyaku kudasaimase.

Tōkyō wa honjitsu dō yara "in'utsu" na tsuyu no kisetsu ni hairimashita.

Mina-sama ni yoroshiku. Nani-tozo nani-tozo o-tassha de. Mata o-ai dekiru hi ga attara, nan to kōfuku na koto deshō.

Ranpitsu nite gomen kudasai.

Sō-sō

Notes

a. ATTE NO Literally "there being," this attributive phrase is used after nouns with the meaning "because of the existence of, simply because there is." Thus, here, "it isn't the Japanese language because there are rules."

b. KIRŌ A rather old-fashioned and unusual respectful word for "you," referring to a man; cf. *kiden* under 5e.

68. Letter of Reply from an Older Professor

拝復　早速に御返書賜りありがたく存じます。
御事情を伺えばまことにごもっともでございます。
残念でございますが致し方ございません。当方として、
自然の季節のよいころにこの会を催して来て
おりますが、欧米の方々にとってお出かけになり
にくい時期であることがわかって参りました。
将来においては、この会の時期も考え直さねばなら
ぬかと考えております。
ともあれ、今回はあきらめます。そしてまたの好機を
念ずる次第でございます。お手数をわずらわせまし
たこと、おわび申し上げます。

Haifuku. Sassoku ni go-**hensho** tamawar-i, arigataku zonjimasu. Go-jijō o ukagaeba, makoto ni go-mottomo de gozaimasu. Zannen de gozaimasu ga, itashi-kata gozaimasen. Tōhō to shite, shizen no kisetsu no yoi koro ni kono kai o moyōshite kite orimasu ga, Ō-Bei no kata-gata ni totte o-dekake ni nari-nikui jiki de arimasu koto ga wakatte mairimashita. Shōrai ni oite wa, kono kai no jiki mo kangae-NAOSANEBA naranu ka to kangaete orimasu.

To mo are, konkai wa akiramemasu. Soshite mata no kōki o nenzuru shidai de gozaimasu. O-tesū o wazurawase-mashita koto, o-wabi mōshi-agemasu.

当地

今の所好天が続き、しのぎよい冬でございますが、御地はいかがでございましょうか。御自愛御健安を念じ上げます。寸紙右まで

一九八二年一月七日　小山弘志

オニール様

ちょっとした物を書くのに年を越してしまい、やっと五日に脱稿、そのため賀状も差上げず、この手紙も延引いたしました。おゆるし下さいまし。

Tōchi ima no tokoro **kōten** ga tsuzuki, shinogi-yoi fuyu de gozaimasu ga, **on-chi** wa ikaga de gozaimashō ka. Go-jiai go-**ken'an** o nenji-agemasu. **Sunshi** migi made.

1982nen ichigatsu nanuka **Koyama Hiroshi**

Oniiru-sama

Chotto shita mono o kaku NO NI toshi o koshite shima-i, yatto itsuka ni **dakkō**, sono tame gajō mo sashi-agezu, kono tegami mo en'in itashimashita. O-yurushi kudasaiMASHI.

Notes

a. -NAOSANEBA As the second part of a compound verb, *-naosu* means "(do) again (correctly)," like the English "re-(think, etc.)"; and *-neba* = *-nakereba* (see 24ad).

b. NO NI Here *no* makes a verbal noun form of *kaku* with the meaning of "the writing," and *ni* is the particle meaning "in, to, for." Distinguish this sequence of *no* and *ni* from what can be regarded as the combined *no ni* used as a conjunction with the meaning "although, in spite of" (see 32e).

c. -MASHI An imperative form of *-masu*, like *-mase* (see 8a).

69. Letter to a Younger Man from a Calligraphy Teacher

お元気でいらっしゃいますか
さて　大変お待たせしましたが　写真が出来ま
したので　お届けいたします　お受取り下さいませ
フォトニュースも一部同封いたします　ご高覧下さい
スミス先生から　お送り頂いた玉稿は　本連盟
会報に掲載いたします　会報は　十二月十日頃
完成します　その節また　お送りいたします
それから　先生にお願いがございます　私達は
明後年（一九六七年）に　貴国において　日本書道展
を開催したいと存じます　そして　その時に　元文部大臣
の方や大学教授など約二十名で出席いたし　お国の文
化芸術方面に理解のある方々と交歓して　両国の
理解と認識を深めて　親善関係の増進を
はかりたいと存じております
つきましては　展覧会場の事や　交歓会のことな

どお世話して下さる　貴国文化団体　若しくは　文部
省等　ごあっせんの労を賜わりとうございます
なお　私達二十名の代表団に対して　貴国文部省
または文化団体から招請状をお願いできます
なれば　これに勝る喜びはございません
なお　展覧会や訪問交歓会等に要する費用
はもちろん日本教育書道連盟が全額負担
いたします
貴国訪問の予定は一九六七年八月十二日（午前一〇時
一〇分ロンドン着）～八月十五日（午後二時五分ロンドン発）の三
日間でございます
本来ならば会長名をもって大使閣下あてに
公文書をお送りすべきと存じますが　先に
スミス先生の御意見を承って　その後に公
文書をお送りしたいと考えております

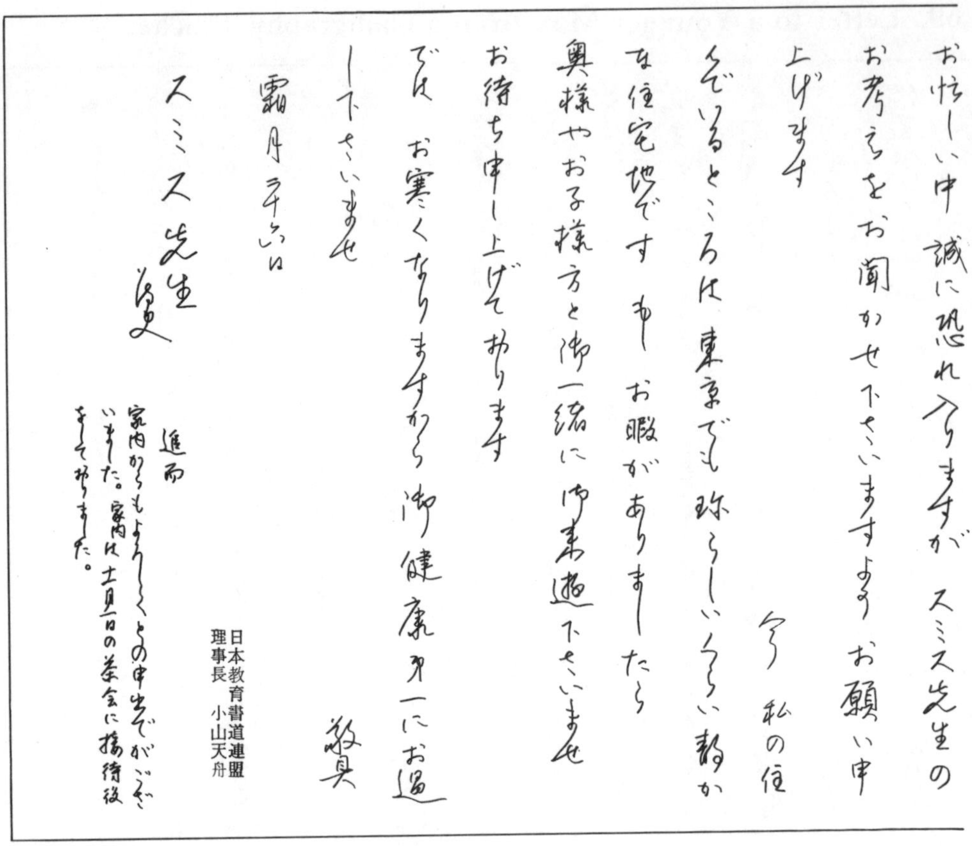

お忙しい中誠に恐れ入りますが　スミス先生の
お考えをお聞かせ下さいますようお願い申
上げます　　尚　私の住
んでいるところは　東京でも珍しいくらい静か
な住宅地です　もし　お暇がありましたら
奥様やお子様方と御一緒に御来遊下さいませ
お待ち申し上げております
では　お寒くなりますから御健康第一にお過
し下さいませ　　敬具
霜月二十六日　　日本教育書道連盟 理事長 小山天舟
スミス先生　侍史

追而
家内からもよろしくとの申出でがござい
ました。家内は十一月一日の茶会に接待役
まして居りました。

O-genki de irasshaimasu ka.

Sate, taihen o-matase shimashita ga, shashin ga dekimashita no de o-todoke itashimasu. O-uke-tori kudasaimase. **Foto** Nyūsu mo ichibu dōfū itashimasu. Go-kōran kudasai. **Sumisu** Sensei kara o-okuri itadaita GYOKKŌ wa hon-Renmei kaihō ni keisai itashimasu. Kaihō wa jūnigatsu tōka-goro kansei shimasu. Sono setsu mata o-okuri itashimasu.

Sore kara sensei ni o-negai ga gozaimasu. Watashi-tachi wa myōgonen (1967nen) ni ki-koku ni oite Nihon Shodō-ten o kaisai shitai to zonjimasu. Soshite sono toki ni moto Monbu Daijin no kata ya daigaku kyōju nado yaku-nijūmei de shusseki itashi, o-kuni no bunka geijutsu hōmen ni rikai no aru kata-gata to kōkan shite, ryōkoku no rikai to ninshiki o fukamete shinzen kankei no zōshin o hakaritai to zonjite orimasu.

Tsukimashite wa tenran kaijō no koto ya kōkankai no koto nado o-sewa shite kudasaru ki-koku bunka dantai moshiku wa Monbushō nado go-assen no rō o tamawaritō gozaimasu. Nao, watashi-tachi nijūmei no daihyō-dan ni tai-shite ki-koku Monbushō mata wa bunka dantai kara shōseijō o o-negai dekimasu NAREBA, kore ni masaru yorokobi wa gozaimasen.

Nao, tenrankai ya hōmon kōkankai nado ni yō-suru hiyō wa mochiron Nihon Kyōiku Shodō Renmei ga zengaku futan itashimasu.

Ki-koku hōmon no yotei wa 1967nen hachigatsu jūsannichi (gozen jūji jippun **Rondon**-chaku)–hachigatsu jūgonichi (gogo niji gofun **Rondon**-hatsu) no mikka-kan de gozaimasu.

Honrai naraba kaichōmei o motte taishi kakka ate ni kōbunsho o o-okuri SU-BEKI to zonjimasu ga, saki ni **Sumisu** Sensei no go-iken o uketamawatte, sono nochi ni kōbunsho o o-okuri shitai to kangaete orimasu.

Ō-isogashii naka makoto ni osore-irimasu ga, **Sumisu** Sensei no o-kangae o o-kikase kudasaimasu yō o-negai mōshi-agemasu.

IMA WATASHI NO sunde iru tokoro wa **Tōkyō** DE MO mezurashii kurai shizuka na jūtakuchi desu. Moshi o-hima ga arimashitara oku-sama ya o-kosama-gata to go-issho ni go-raiyū kudasaimase. O-machi mōshi-agete orimasu.

De wa o-samuku narimasu kara, go-kenkō dai-ichi ni o-sugoshi kudasaimase.

Keigu

Nihon Kyōiku Shodō
Renmei Rijichō
Koyama Tenshū

SHIMOTSUKI nijūrokunichi
Sumisu Sensei
Jishi

OTTE

Kanai kara mo yoroshiku to no mōshi-ide ga gozaimashita. Kanai wa jūichigatsu tsuitachi no chakai ni **settai-yaku** o shite orimashita.

Notes

a. GYOKKŌ *Gyoku*, "jewelled, precious," is a respectful prefix, and *kō* means "draft, manuscript, article"; thus, here, *gyokkō* means simply "your article."

b. NAREBA Although this form of the literary *nari*, "be" (see 14a), also means "since (it is)," here it is equivalent to *naraba*, "if (it is)" (see 3q, 17b).

c. SU-BEKI A literary equivalent to *suru-beki*, "can/should, etc., do" (see 7e). Here it completes a humble form of the verb *okuru*, with the meaning "I/One should (send)."

d. IMAWATASHI NO Although these words introduce a new paragraph, they are written towards the bottom of the page as a sign of humility (cf. *ki-daigaku* under 3k).

e. DE MO In contexts such as this, it is particularly clear that *de mo* is equivalent to *de atte mo*, "even though it is."

f. SHIMOTSUKI This is one of the old poetic names for the months of the year (in this case the eleventh) according to the lunar calendar, and it is used here as an elegant alternative to *jūichigatsu*, "November."

g. OTTE Short for *otte-gaki* 追而書き (or 追って書き), "postscript."

70. First Letter from a Lady to a Teacher in London

拝啓

突然のお便り、お許し下さい。

シェフフィールド大学日本研究センターで日本語を教えていらした氏家洋子先生の御紹介で、御名前を伺いました。

私は現在テキサス大学大学院博士課程言語学科に在籍している学生です。早大一文を七十五年に卒業して以来、オレゴン大学で修士に向けた二年間、カナダのブリティッシュコロンビア大学で過した博士課程の一年目、そしてテキサスでのこの一年、計四年間、言語学を専攻するかたわら、ティーチング・アシスタント並びにアシスタント・インストラクターとして日本語を教えて参りました。将来は日本語教授及び言語学（主に音韻論）の教授・研究に一生を捧げたいと思っております。殊に日本語教授に関しては、強い使命感を感じております。教授法の日々の改善はもちろんのこと、教科書は、私の調べた限りではなかなか満足できるものが無く、近い将来自らの手で作製しなくては、と夢はふくらむばかりです。

将来英国で仕事に就くことを希望しております。本当に唐突で恐縮でございますが、今月中旬から来月上旬迄、そちらへ参ることになりましたので、もしお差し控えありませんでしたら直接お会いしてお話を伺わせて戴きたく、お願いのペンを執った次第です。

おたずね致したいのは左記の点についてでございます。

一、英国での日本語教授職の可能性

一、全体の需要はどの程度か

一、私のような、日本で学士号、米国で修士号及び博士号を取得の者でも英国で職を得る見込みがありますでしょうか。

二、先生の大学では、どの教科書をどのように教えていらっしゃるのでしょうか。又、英国人学生の中に、どのような長所と短所を認めていらっしゃるのでしょうか。

三、五月十四日から六月十日の四週間在英致しますが、この間に出席できる学会、会合（日本語、言語学関係、どんなに小さなものでも構いません）がありますでしょうか。

御参考迄に日・英両語の略歴を同封致します。

英国に着き次第、御都合を伺いに御連絡申し上げるつもりでおりますが、御都合の悪い場合は、御遠慮なくそうおっしゃって下さいませ。

かしこ

五月七日

日暮嘉子

井上英明様

Haikei,

Totsuzen no o-tayori, o-yurushi kudasai.

Shefufiirudo Daigaku Nihon Kenkyū Sentā de Nihongo o oshiete IRASHITA **Ujiie Yōko** Sensei no go-shōkai de, o-namae o ukagaimashita.

Watakushi wa genzai **Tekisasu** Daigaku Hakushi Katei Gengogaku-ka ni zaiseki shite iru gakusei desu. SŌDAI ICHIBUN o nanajūgonen ni sotsugyō shite irai, **Oregon** Daigaku de shūshi ni kaketa ninen-kan, **Kanada** no **Buritisshu Koronbia** Daigaku de sugoshita hakushi katei no ichinen-me, soshite **Tekisasu** de no kono ichinen, kei yonen-kan, gengogaku o senkō suru katawara, tiichingu ashisutanto narabi ni ashisutanto in-sutorakutā to shite Nihongo o oshiete mairimashita. Shōrai wa Nihongo kyōju oyobi gengogaku (omo ni on'inron) no kyōju, kenkyū ni isshō o sasagetai to omotte orimasu. Koto ni Nihongo kyōju ni kan-shite wa, tsuyoi **shimei-kan** o kanjite orimasu. Kyōju-hō no hi-bi no kaizen wa mochiron no koto, kyōkasho wa watakushi no shirabeta kagiri de wa nakanaka manzoku dekiru mono ga naku, chikai shōrai mizukara no te de sakusei shinakute wa, to yume wa fukuramu bakari desu.

Shōrai Eikoku de shigoto ni tsuku koto o kibō shite orimasu. Hontō ni tōtotsu de kyōshuku de gozaimasu ga, kongetsu chūjun kara raigetsu jōjun made, sochira e mairu koto ni narimashita no de, moshi o-sashitsukae arimasen deshitara chokusetsu o-ai shite o-hanashi o ukagawasete itadakitaku, o-negai no pen o totta shidai desu.

O-tazune itashitai no wa saki no ten ni tsuite de gozaimasu.

1. Eikoku de no Nihongo **kyōju-shoku** no kanōsei
   —zentai no juyō wa dono teido ka
   —watakushi no yō na, Nihon de gakushi-gō, Beikoku de shūshi-gō oyobi hakushi-gō o shutoku no mono de mo Eikoku de shoku o eru mikomi ga arimasu deshō ka.
2. Sensei no daigaku de wa, dono kyōkasho o dono yō ni oshiete irassharu no deshō ka. Mata, Eikokujin gakusei no naka ni, dono yō na chōsho to tansho o mitomete irassharu no deshō ka.
3. Gogatsu jūyokka kara rokugatsu tōka no yonshū-kan **zai-Ei** itashimasu ga, kono aida ni shusseki dekiru gakkai, kaigō (Nihongo, gengogaku kankei, donna ni chiisa na mono de mo kamaimasen) ga arimasu deshō ka.

Go-sankō made ni Nichi-Ei ryōgo no ryakureki o dōfū itashimasu.

Eikoku ni tsuki shidai, go-tsugō o ukagai ni go-renraku mōshi-ageru tsumori DE ORIMASU ga, go-tsugō no warui baai wa, go-enryo naku sō osshatte kudasaimase.

Kashiko

Higurashi Yoshiko

Gogatsu nanuka
Inoue Eimei-sama

Notes

a. IRASHITA A past form of the honorific *irassharu*, here equivalent to *ita*. (Other common past forms of the same verb are *irasshatta* and *irasshita*.)

b. SŌDAI ICHIBUN *Sōdai* is an abbreviation for *Waseda Daigaku* 早稲田大学, formed by the regular practice of taking the Sino-Japanese readings of the first characters of each word. The coverage of such organizational terms as *Ichibun*, "First Arts Section," can vary according to the university, but at Waseda the term refers to the daytime courses in the Faculty of Arts.

c. DE ORIMASU In place of a simple *da/desu*, etc., forms of *de (wa) oru/iru/irassharu* may be used when the subject is animate, especially with a few words like *tsumori* (see also 2n).

拝啓
先日は せっかく お目にかかる機会を得て うれしく存じました。
ゆっくりと お話できずに 残念でしたが また ロンドンで 拝眉の
時をたのしみにしております ところで うっかりしていて 名刺を
いただき 名刺の話をしていながら 私の方 名刺をもちあわせず
また 自己紹介もせずに 大変 失礼しました。私は 一九三五年生れで
現在、大阪市立大学につとめております その前に 松平さんと同じ
梅花女子大学というのにつとめておりまして 親しくしておりました。
平安時代の文学を専門にしておりまして、古今集と源氏物語に
関心をもっております。同僚に 能楽を専門にしている伊藤正義氏が
おります。実は 表さんとは 私はまだ お話を交したことが ないのですが
伊藤さんを 通じて 連絡してもらいました。私の大学には 海外
出張の制度があって、三ヶ月、六ヶ月、一ヶ年の 三種類がありまして、
今度、私は 三ヶ月のもので 英国にゆくことになったのですが、日本の
大学の習慣として、外国の大学●研究所 または 図書館などに

受け入れてもらうことが必要でして、私の場合もそのためにケンさんおねがいしました。目的はイギリス各地にある日本文学関係の文献の調査ということになるそうですが、期間も短いことですしそれほど多くのことができるとは思いませんので、半分は各地を見物したいと思っています。もっとも私は英語がしゃべれませんので自由な行動は無理かと思っております。また御帰国になりましたらいろいろと御迷惑をかけることになるかもしれませんが、相談にのっていただければうれしく存じます。先日はおいそがしいところをお邪魔してほんとに失礼しました。

草々

三月四日

増田繁夫（ますだ しげお）

P. G. オニール様

Haikei,

Senjitsu wa hajimete o-me ni kakaru kikai o ete ureshiku zonjimashita. Yukkuri to o-hanashi dekizu ni zannen deshita ga, mata **Rondon** de **haibi** no toki o tanoshimi ni shite imasu. Tokoro de, ukkari shite ite meishi o itadak-i, meishi no hanashi o shite i-nagara watashi no hō meishi o mochi-awasezu, mata jiko shōkai mo sezu ni taihen shitsurei shimashita. Watashi wa 1935nen-umare de genzai **Ōsaka** Shiritsu Daigaku ni tsutomete imasu. Sono mae ni **Matsudaira**-san to onaji **Baika** Joshi Daigaku to iu no ni tsutomete imashite, shitashiku shite imashita. **HEIAN** JIDAI no bungaku o senmon ni shite imashite, **KOKINSHŪ** to Genji Monogatari ni kanshin o motte imasu. Dōryō ni Nōgaku o senmon ni shite iru **Itō Masayoshi**-shi ga imasu. Jitsu wa **Omote**-san to wa watashi wa mada o-hanashi o kawashita koto ga nai no desu ga, **Itō**-san o tsūjite renraku shite moraimashita. Watashi no daigaku ni wa kaigai shutchō no seido to shite, sankagetsu rokkagetsu ikkanen-kan no san-shurui ga arimashite, kondo watashi wa sankagetsu no mono de Eikoku ni yuku koto ni natta no desu ga, Nihon no daigaku no shūkan to shite, gaikoku no daigaku, kenkyūjo mata wa toshokan nado no uke-irete morau koto ga hitsuyō DESHITE, watashi no baai mo sono tame ni **Dan**-san ni o-negai shimashita. Mokuteki wa Igirisu kakuchi ni aru Nihon bungaku kankei no bunken no chōsa to iu koto ni natte imasu ga, kikan mo mijikai koto desu shi, sore hodo ōku no koto ga dekiru to wa omoimasen no de, hanbun wa kakuchi o kenbutsu shitai to omotte imasu. Mottomo, watashi wa Eigo ga shaberemasen no de jiyū na kōdō wa muri ka to omotte imasu. Mata go-kikoku ni narimashitara iro-iro to go-meiwaku o kakeru koto ni naru ka mo shiremasen ga, sōdan ni notte itadakereba ureshiku zonjimasu. Senjitsu wa o-isogashii tokoro o o-jama shite honto ni shitsurei shimashita.

Sō-sō

Masuda Shigeo

Sangatsu yokka
P.G. **Oniiru**-sama

Notes

a. HEIAN JIDAI 平安時代, "The Heian period" (794–1192), during which the cultural and political life of the country centred on the court.

b. KOKINSHŪ 古今集; the first imperial anthology of Japanese poetry, compiled ca. 905.

c. DESHITE The polite *-te* form of *da*, equivalent to neutral level *de*.

み伺いさせて頂きたくお知らせ致します。インタビューは私が英語でさせていただきます。番組の聴取者は一般の英語学習者で特に話すことを身につけたいと会話の勉強をしている人達です。同封のテキストには二月号で、既に放送されているものです。何かの参考にご覧頂ければ幸いです（アメリカ英語で残念に思いますが…）謝礼は一応NHKの規定に従ってなされることとなっております。二万五千円ぐらいとお知らせ致します。よろしくお願い申し上げます。

NHKには渋谷か原宿駅より歩かれるか（約十五分）、渋谷南口からバスでおいでになるのがよろしいかと存知ます。十五、十六、十七、十八番いずれのバスもNHK放送センター前を通るとのことですが、ご乗車の前に一応運転手に確認をしてお乗り下さい。又地下鉄千代田線代々木公園下車徒歩七分ぐらいだそうです。大きな建物ですぐにわかると思っております。万一の場合には四六五ー一一一一番の内線六二八八立入（たちいり）さん（ご連絡下さい。番組担当のディレクターの方です。小生の自宅（お電話下さっても結構です。（四五五ー四五一五）迄す。

Zenryaku,

Senjitsu wa watashi no bangumi e no shutsuen ni go-kaidaku kudasaimashite makoto ni arigatō gozaimashita.

Koko ni tori-isogi tōjitsu no koto ni tsukimashite go-annai mōshi-agemasu to tomo ni kakunin o sasete itadakitaku zonjimasu.

*Nichiji . . . nigatsu nijūichinichi (Sui)

*Basho . . . **Nhk** Hōsō Sentā

*Jikan . . . goji sanjippun–rokuji sanjippun keishoku
rokuji sanjippun–hachiji rokuon

Tōjitsu wa go-mendō de mo **Nhk** Hōsō Sentā made oide itadakitaku zonjimasu. Nishi-genkan no uketsuke nite shōsei ga o-machi mōshi-agemasu. **Nhk** Hōsō Sentā ni wa nishi-guchi no hoka higashi-guchi, shōmen genkan nado ikutsu-ka iri-guchi ga arimasu ga, dono iri-guchi de de mo wakaru yō ni jizen ni tehai o shite okimasu no de, **Nhk** ni o-tsuki ni nareba, uketsuke nite "**Tōgo** no gesuto de kita" to osshatte kudasai.

Bangumi wa jūgofun no nagasa no mono o futatsu rokuon itashimasu. Naiyō wa goku ippan-teki na, sensei go-jishin ni tsuite to, gaikokugo gakushū no koto ni tsukimashite o-

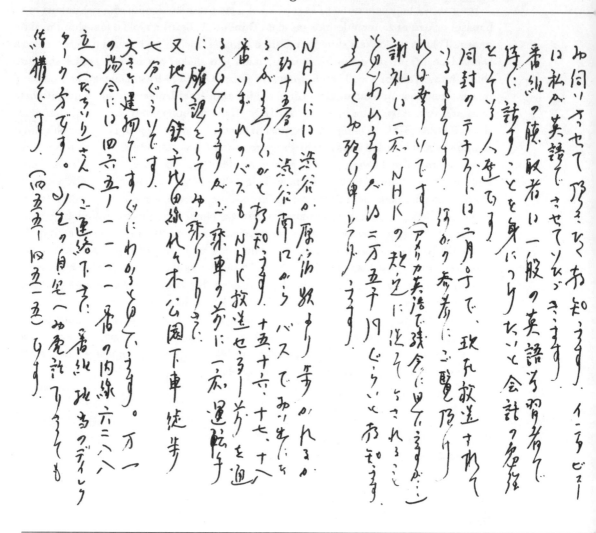

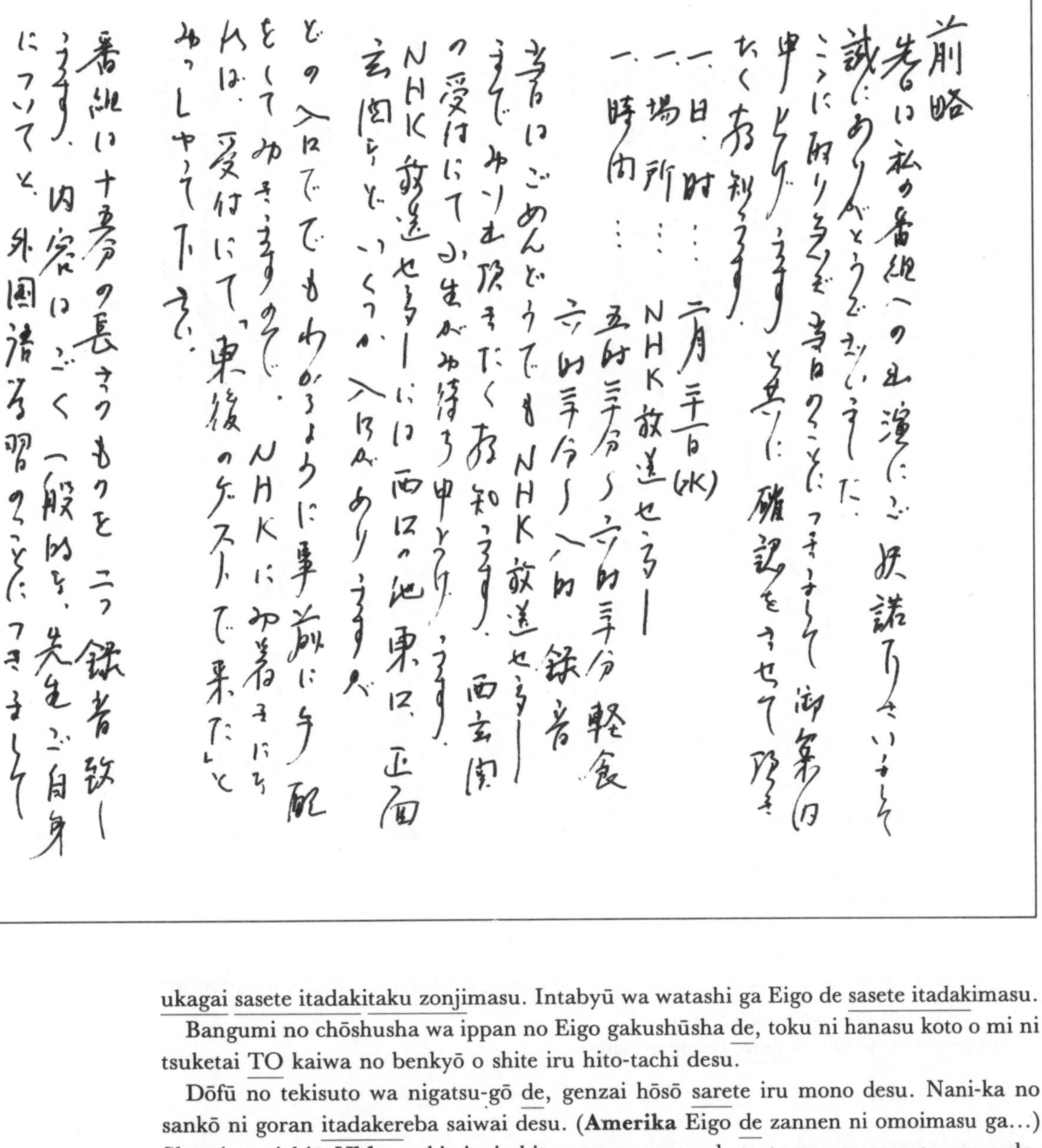
前略
先日は私の番組への出演にご快諾下さいまして
誠にありがとうございました。
ここに取り急ぎ当日のことについてまとめて御案内
申し上げますと共に確認をさせて頂き
たくお知らせします。
一、日時：：：二月二十日(水)
一、場所：：：NHK放送センター
一、時間：：：五時三十分～六時三十分　軽食
六時三十分～八時　録音
当日はごめんどうでもNHK放送センター
までおいで頂きたくお知らせします。西玄関
の受付にて小生がお待ち申し上げます。
NHK放送センターには西口の他東口、正面
玄関など、いくつか入口があります。
どの入口でもわかるように事前に手配
をしてみますので、NHKにお着きになら
れば、受付にて、東後のゲストで来たと
おっしゃって下さい。
番組は十五分の長さのものを二つ録音致し
ます。内容はごく一般的な、先生ご自身
についてと、外国語学習のことにつきまして

ukagai sasete itadakitaku zonjimasu. Intabyū wa watashi ga Eigo de sasete itadakimasu.

Bangumi no chōshusha wa ippan no Eigo gakushūsha de, toku ni hanasu koto o mi ni tsuketai TO kaiwa no benkyō o shite iru hito-tachi desu.

Dōfū no tekisuto wa nigatsu-gō de, genzai hōsō sarete iru mono desu. Nani-ka no sankō ni goran itadakereba saiwai desu. (**Amerika** Eigo de zannen ni omoimasu ga...) Sharei wa ichiō **Nhk** no kitei ni shitagatte nasareru koto to omowaremasu ga, yaku niman-gosen'en-gurai to zonjimasu. Yoroshiku o-negai mōshi-agemasu.

Nhk ni wa **Shibuya** ka **Harajuku** eki yori arukareru ka (yaku jūgofun), **Shibuya** minami-guchi kara basu de oide ni naru no ga yoroshii ka to zonjimasu. Jūgo-, jūroku-, jūnana-, jūhachi-ban izure no basu mo **Nhk** Hōsō Sentā mae o tōru to omoimasu ga, gojōsha no mae ni ichiō untenshu ni kakunin o shite o-nori kudasai.

Mata chikatetsu **Chiyoda**-sen **Yoyogi** Kōen gesha toho nanafun-gurai desu.

Ōki na tatemono de sugu ni wakaru to omoimasu. Man'ichi no baai ni wa 465-1111 ban no naisen 6288 **Tachiiri**-san e go-renraku kudasai. Bangumi tantō no direkutā no kata desu. Shōsei no jitaku e o-denwa kudasatte mo kekkō desu. (455-4515) desu.

ご帰国前のお忙しい時に本当に心苦しく存じますが何卒よろしくお願い申し上げます。
右とり急ぎ用件のみお願いまで
二月七日
草々
オニール先生
東郷勝明

追伸
同封の書式にお書き込みの上ご返送頂ければ幸いです。
テキストに先生のプロフィールということで紹介させて頂く資料にさせて頂きます。もちろん本に出ます前に先生のご承認を頂きますのでよろしくご協力下さい。

Go-kikoku mae no o-isogashii toki ni hontō kokoro-gurushiku zonjimasu ga, nani-tozo yoroshiku o-negai mōshi-agemasu.

Migi tori-isogi yōken nomi o-negai made.

Nigatsu nanuka

Sō-sō

Oniiru Sensei

Tōgo Katsuaki

Tsuishin

Dōfū no shoshiki ni o-kaki-komi no ue go-hensō itadakereba saiwai desu.

Tekisuto ni sensei no purofiiru to iu koto de shōkai sasete itadaku shiryō ni sasete itadakimasu. Mochiron hon ni demasu mae ni sensei no go-shōnin o itadakimasu no de yoroshiku go-kyōryoku kudasai.

Notes

a. TO This is the quotative *to*, equivalent here to *to omotte* (see 15b). Since it is here preceded by the desiderative *-tai*, "from a desire to," with the idea of " would be possible translations.

73. Postcard from a Village Official

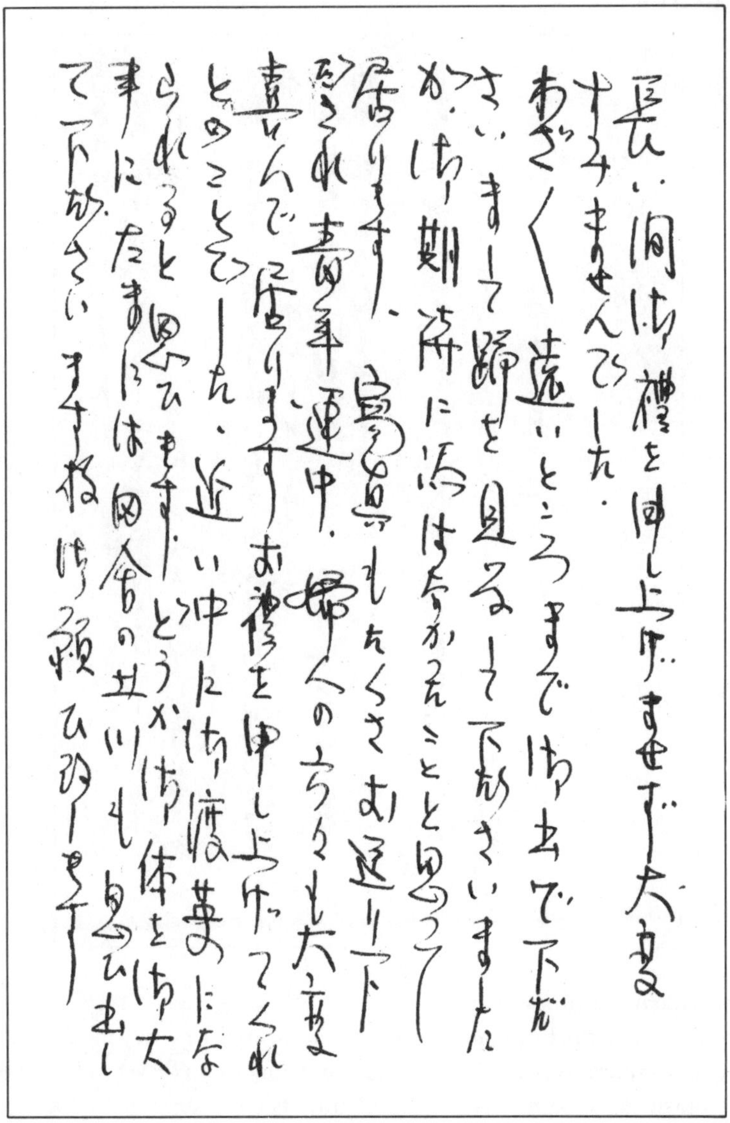
長い間御禮を申し上げませず大変
すみませんでした。
わざわざ遠いところまで御出で下だ
さいまして踊を見学して下さいました
が、御期待に添はなかったことと思って
居ります。寫眞もたくさお送り下
され青年連中、婦人の方々も大変
喜んで居ります。お禮を申し上げてくれ
とのことでした。近い中に御渡英にな
られると思ひます。どうか御体を御大
事に。たまには田舎の井川も思ひ出し
て下さいます様御願ひ致します

Nagai aida o-rei o mōshi-age-masezu taihen sumimasen deshita.

Waza-waza tōi tokoro made oide kudasaimashite odori o kengaku shite kudasaimashita ga, go-kitai ni sowanakatta koto to omotte orimasu. Shashin mo TAKUSA o-okuri kudasar-e, seinen renchū, fujin no kata-gata mo taihen yorokonde orimasu. Ō-rei o mōshi-agete kure to no koto deshita. Chikai uchi ni go-**to-Ei** NI NARARERU to omoimasu. Dōka o-karada o o-daiji ni. Tama ni wa inaka no **Ikawa** mo omoi-dashite kudasaimasu yō o-negai itashimasu.

Notes

a. TAKUSA A pronunciation spelling for standard *takusan*, "many, much."

b. NI NARARERU The original construction here is the *go-* noun *ni naru/nasaru* honorific one explained under 49e, but the *naru* has itself been made more respectful by the use of the *-(ra)reru* form used as an honorific. The three stages of increasing respect are thus *to-Ei suru*, *go-to-Ei ni naru*, *go-to-Ei ni narareru*. For a similar use of the *-(ra)reru* form, see 26b.

74. Letter from a Learned Society to a Japanese Colleague Temporarily in Japan

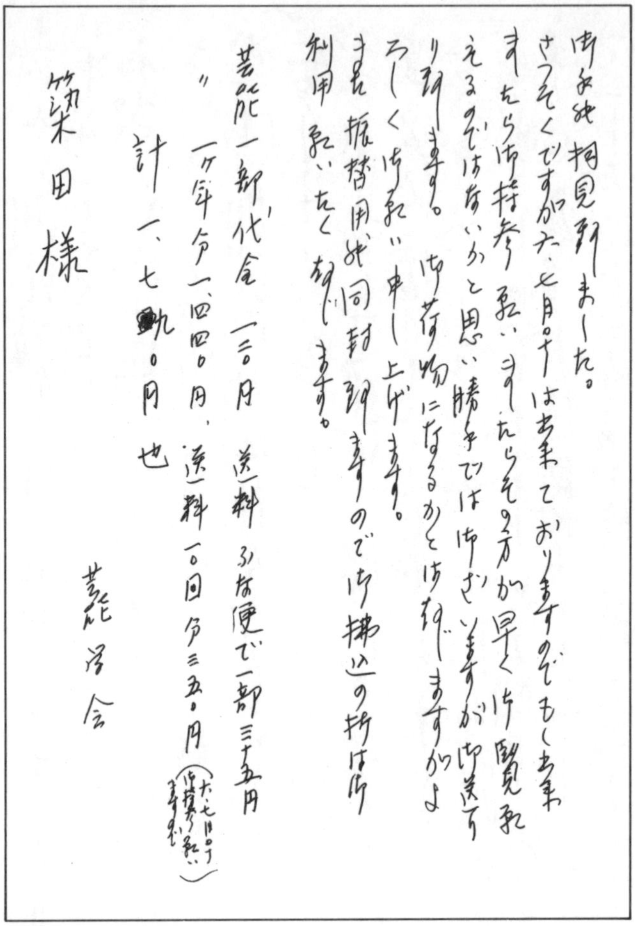
御手紙拝見致しました。
さっそくですが六・七月号は出来ておりますのでもし出来ましたら御持参願いましたらその方が早く御覧願えるのではないかと思い勝手では御ざいますが御送り致します。御荷物になるかとは存じますがよろしく御願い申し上げます。
また振替用紙同封致しますので御払込の折は御利用願いたく存じます。
芸能一部代金 一二〇円 送料 ふな便で一部三十五円
〃 一ケ年分一、四四〇円、送料 十回分三五〇円 (六・七月号御持参願いますので)
計 一、七九〇円也
芸能学会
簗田様

O-tegami haiken itashimashita.

Sassoku desu ga, roku-shichigatsu-gō wa dekite orimasu no de, moshi dekimashitara go-jisan negaimashitara sono hō ga hayaku goran negaeru no de wa nai ka to omoi, katte de wa gozaimasu ga o-okuri itashimasu. O-nimotsu ni naru ka to wa zonjimasu ga yoroshiku o-negai mōshi-agemasu.

Mata furikae yōshi dōfū itashimasu no de o-harai-komi no ori wa go-riyō negaitaku zonjimasu.

GEINŌ ichibu daikin: hyaku-nijūen. Sōryō: funabin de ichibu sanjūgoen.

GEINŌ ikkanen-bun: sen-yonhyaku-yonjūen. Sōryō: jikkai-bun sanbyaku-gojūen (Roku-shichigatsu-gō go-jisan negaimasu no de)

Kei sen-nanahyaku-kyūjūen NARI

Geinō Gakkai

Yanada-sama

Notes

a. GEINŌ 芸能 "(artistic) entertainment"; here the name of a periodical dealing with all kinds of performing arts.

b. NARI Meaning "be" like colloquial *da* or *de aru* (see 14a), this literary copula is commonly retained in contexts like this, where totals and sums due are quoted.

オニール様。　　　　　　　　　　　　7月14日

狂言の原稿有難うございました。たいへん面白く拝読させていただきました。
御指示の項目、新たに追加いたします。有難うございました。

原稿をいただいたばかりで恐縮でございますが、もし御都合よろしければ、Names (2000～3000 wds.) Kowaka (700 wds.) の二項目を御執筆いただきたく存じます。
名前については事典の著者にあれこれ申しあげるのは失礼ですが、幼名、実名、仮名、女の名、諡、字と別号などについて言及していただきたく、地名は、最近いろいろ日本でも地名学の研究が出ておりますので、御参照いただきたく存じます。その上、人名事典、地名事典などを最後に解説していただければ幸です。
幸若は、歴史的なものと、現存する幸若について、前者に重点を置いて書いていただけますれば幸です。文芸としての要素と演劇としての要素とございますが、その割りふりについてはおまかせいたします。
以上御諒承いただけますようお願い申しあげます。

なお、"狂言"の稿料、小切手にて同封いたします。

おるな拝。

Oniiru-sama, Shichigatsu jūyokka

Kyōgen no genkō arigatō gozaimashita. Taihen omoshiroku **haidoku** sasete itadakimashita. Go-shiji no kōmoku, arata ni tsuika itashimasu. Arigatō gozaimashita.

Genkō o itadaita bakari de kyōshuku de gozaimasu ga, moshi go-tsugō yoroshikereba, Names (2000–3000 wds.), KŌWAKA (700 wds.) no ni-kōmoku o go-shippitsu itadakitaku zonjimasu.

Namae ni tsuite wa jiten no chosha ni are-kore mōshi-ageru no wa shitsurei desu ga, yōmyō, jitsumei, **KARINA**, onna no na, okurina, **azana** to **betsugō** nado ni tsuite genkyū shite itadakitaku, chimei wa saikin iro-iro Nihon de mo chimeigaku no kenkyū ga dete orimasu no de, go-sanshō itadakitaku zonjimasu. Sono ue, jinmei jiten, chimei jiten nado o saigo ni kaisetsu shite itadakereba saiwai desu.

Kōwaka wa, REKIshi-teki na mono to genson suru Kōwaka ni tsuite, zensha ni jūten o oite kaite itadake-masureba saiwai desu. Bungaku to shite no yōso to engeki to shite no yōso to gozaimasu ga, sono wari-furi ni tsuite wa o-makase itashimasu.

Ijō go-ryōshō itadake-masu yō o-negai mōshi-agemasu.

Nao, Kyōgen no kōryō, kogitte nite dōfū itashimasu.

Itasaka hai

Notes

a. KŌWAKA 幸若; a type of ballad-drama which was at the height of its popularity in the 16th century.

b. KARINA "Pseudonym"; note that, in other contexts, the reading of these characters would be *kana*, "Japanese phonetic signs."

c. REKI- On this form of the character, see 8e

76. Postcard from a Temple Priest in Reply to an Enquiry

拝復
御手紙拝見致しました。御手紙に依りますれば貴殿は日本民俗
芸能の研究の為、日本に御来航の由誠に御苦労様で御座居ます。
私の寺は一千二百年の歴史を持つ寺で本堂は六百六十五年前の建物
で国宝に成って居ります。私の寺の祭典は一千年の歴史を持つ珍しい
お祭で大蛇退治の儀式と、稚子の行列と稚子の舞が行はれます。
お祭の日時は　五月十四日の午後四時（十六時）より行はれます。
御来寺を御待ち致して居ります是非御でかけ下さい。
敬具

Haifuku,

O-tegami haiken itashimashita. O-tegami ni yorimasureba, kiden wa Nihon minzoku geinō no kenkyū no tame, Nihon ni go-raikō no yoshi, makoto ni go-kurō-sama de gozaimasu. Watakushi no tera wa issen-nihyakunen no rekishi o motsu tera de, hondō wa roppyaku-rokujūgonen mae no tatemono de, kokuhō ni natte orimasu. Watakushi no tera no saiten wa issennen no rekishi o motsu mezurashii o-matsuri de, daija taiji no gishiki to, chigo no gyōretsu to, chigo no mai ga okonawaremasu. O-matsuri no nichiji wa gogatsu jūyokka no gogo yoji (jūrokuji) yori okonawaremasu.

Go-**raiji** o o-machi itashite orimasu. Zehi o-dekake kudasai.

Keigu

77. Postcard from a University Professor of Slight Acquaintance

秋も深くなりました。御かわりなく御すごしのことと存じます。先日は御手紙と桂浜での写真を有難う存じました。丁度旅行出張中で、御返事がおくれまして失礼致しました。御話しのビーズレイ先生の史料コピイの件は五百円でいいと思います。只今高知県立図書館で写して居ります。

関西方面へ御旅行だったそうで、御いそがしいですね。私学会で上京致しました。

十日ひる頃法政大学の方へ一寸行く予定で居ります。(能楽研究所へ)。

Aki mo fukaku narimashita. O-kawari naku o-sugoshi no koto to zonjimasu. Senjitsu wa o-tegami to **Katsurahama** de no shashin o arigatō zonjimashita. Chōdo ryokō shutchō-chū de, o-henji ga okuremashite shitsurei itashimashita. O-hanashi no **Biizurei** Sensei no shiryō kopii no ken wa gosen de ii to omoimasu. Tadaima **Kōchi** Kenritsu Toshokan de utsushite orimasu.

Kansai hōmen ni go-ryokō datta sō de, o-isogashii desu ne. Watashi gakkai de jōkyō itashimashita.

Tōka hiru-goro **Hōsei** Daigaku no hō e chotto iku yotei de orimasu. (Nōgaku Kenkyū-jo e).

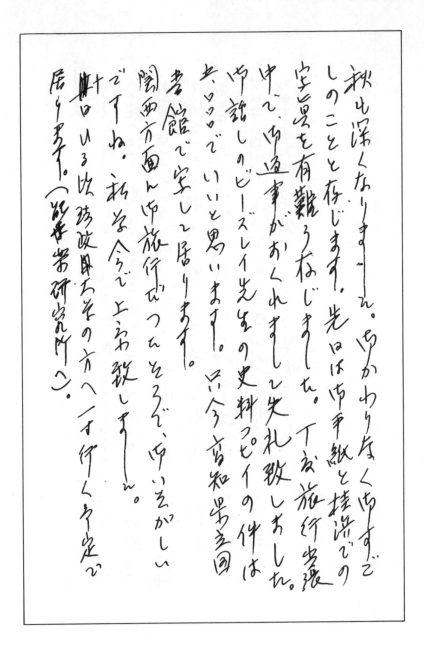

78. Postcard from a Research Student

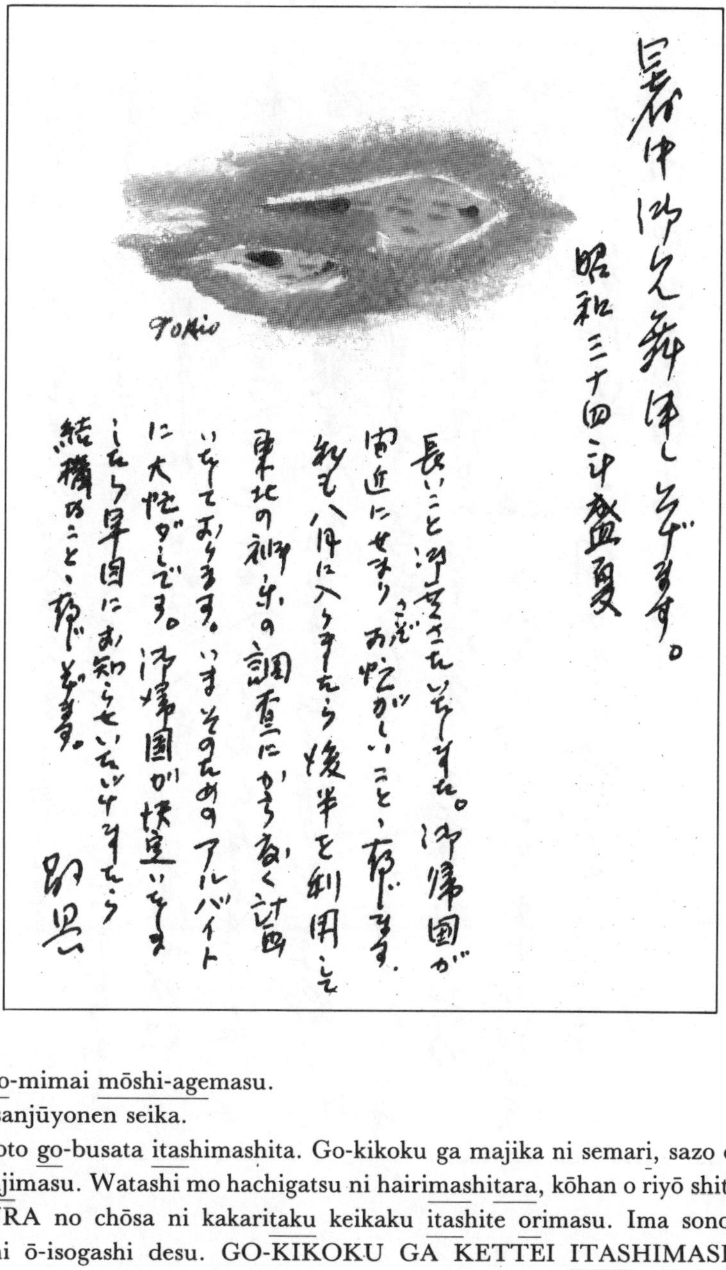

Shochū o-mimai mōshi-agemasu.
Shōwa sanjūyonen seika.

Nagai koto go-busata itashimashita. Go-kikoku ga majika ni semari, sazo o-isogashii koto to zonjimasu. Watashi mo hachigatsu ni hairimashitara, kōhan o riyō shite **Tōhoku** no KAGURA no chōsa ni kakaritaku keikaku itashite orimasu. Ima sono tame no arubaito ni ō-isogashi desu. GO-KIKOKU GA KETTEI ITASHIMASHITARA, hayame ni o-shirase itadake-mashitara kekkō na koto to zonji-agemasu.

Keigu

Notes

a. KAGURA 神楽. It may be hard at first sight to reconcile the handwritten characters with these printed forms, but the second of them is a common simplification for 楽; and although the first may seem to be too complicated to be simply 神, a comparison with the writing of the character 申 for *mōshi-* in the first line will show that this element is common to both.

b. GO-KIKOKU GA KETTEI ITASHIMASHITARA *Kettei suru* is normally regarded as only a transitive verb, so that *Go-kikoku o kettei nasattara/nasaimashitara*, "When you have decided your return home," might have been expected here, but the writer is clearly using it intransitively with the meaning "When your return home is decided"; hence the use of the humble *itasu*.

79. Postcard from a Nō Actor Friend

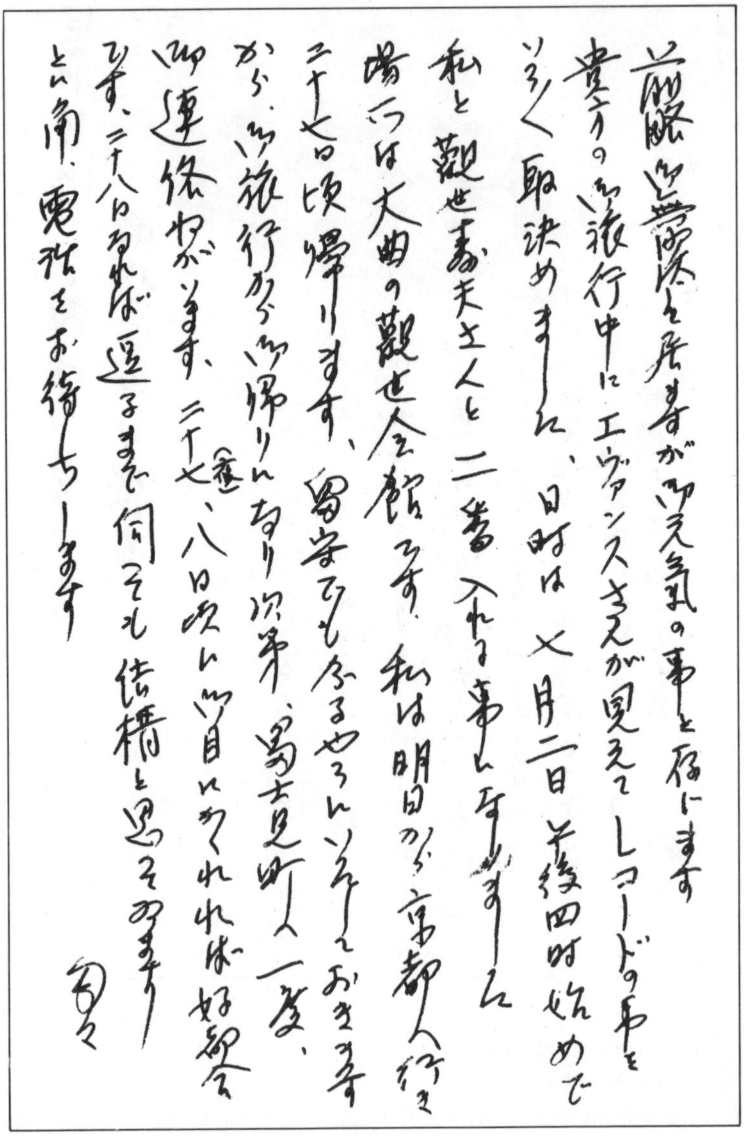
前略 御無沙汰して居ますが御元気の事と存じます
貴方の御旅行中にエヴァンスさんが見えてレコードの事を
いろいろ取決めました、日時は七月二日午後四時始めで
私と観世寿夫さんと二番入れる事になりました
場所は大曲の観世会館です。私は明日から京都へ行き
二十七日頃帰ります、留守でも分るようにいたしておきます
から御旅行から御帰りになり次第、富士見町へ一度
御連絡願います、二十七(夜)、八日頃に御目にかかれれば好都合
です、二十八日なれば逗子まで伺っても結構と思って居ます
とに角、電話をお待ちします
匆々

Zenryaku. Go-busata shite imasu ga, o-genki no koto to zonjimasu.

Anata no go-ryokō-chū ni **Evansu**-san ga miete rekōdo no koto o iro-iro torikimemashita. Nichiji wa shichigatsu futsuka gogo yoji hajime de, watashi to **Kanze Hisao**-san to niban ireru koto ni narimashita. Basho wa **Ōmagari** no **Kanze** Kaikan desu. Watashi wa ashita kara **Kyōto** e iki, nijūshichinichi-goro kaerimasu. Rusu de mo wakaru yō ni itashite okimasu kara, go-ryokō kara o-kaeri ni nari shidai, **Fujimi**-chō e ichido go-renraku negaimasu. Nijūshichi (yoru), hachinichi-goro ni o-me ni kakarereba kō-tsugō desu. Nijūhachinichi nareba, **Zushi** made ukagatte mo kekkō to omotte imasu. Tonikaku, denwa o o-machi shimasu.

Sō-sō

80. Letter from an Older Lady, Known for Several Years

昨夜はプラウライト家で先生御夫妻にお目にかゝり楽しい
ひとゝきを過すことができまして うれしく存じており
ます あのお二人にはとても親切にして頂いて感謝して
おります
昨日は能の神男女狂鬼による分類のことでお話し
合いいたしましたが 芸術新潮芸術辞典の附録に
掲載されております 横道万里雄氏の分類表の
ことは御存知でいらっしゃいますか シテの性格、曲の
内容、夢幻又は現実的、などによって細かく分けてあり
ますが 合理的で 又各流のレパトリーにあるかないか
舞や囃子事、一曲の重点などが 一目で判るように
なっており 大変便利でございます 御参考までに

Sakuya wa **Puraurаito**-ke de sensei go-fusai ni o-me ni kakar-i, tanoshii hitotoki o sugosu koto ga dekimashite, ureshiku zonjite orimasu. Ano o-futari ni wa totemo shinsetsu ni shite itadaite kansha shite orimasu.

Sakujitsu, Nō no KAMI OTOKO ONNA KURUI ONI ni yoru bunrui no koto de o-hanashi-ai itashimashita ga, Geijutsu Shinchō Geijutsu Jiten no furoku ni keisai sarete orimasu **Yokomichi Mario**-shi no bunrui-hyō no koto wa go-zonji de irasshaimasu ka. SHITE no seikaku, KYOKU no naiyō, MUGEN mata wa genjitsu-teki, nado ni yotte komakaku wakete orimasu ga, gōri-teki de, mata **kakuryū** no repatorii ni aru ka nai ka, mai ya **hayashi-goto**, ikkyoku no jūten nado ga hitome de wakaru yō ni natte or-i, taihen benri de gozaimasu. Go-sankō made ni kopii o ichibu betsubin de o-okuri mōshi-agemasu. Moshi o-mochi de irasshaimashitara, nani-tozo tekitō ni go-shobun kudasaimase.

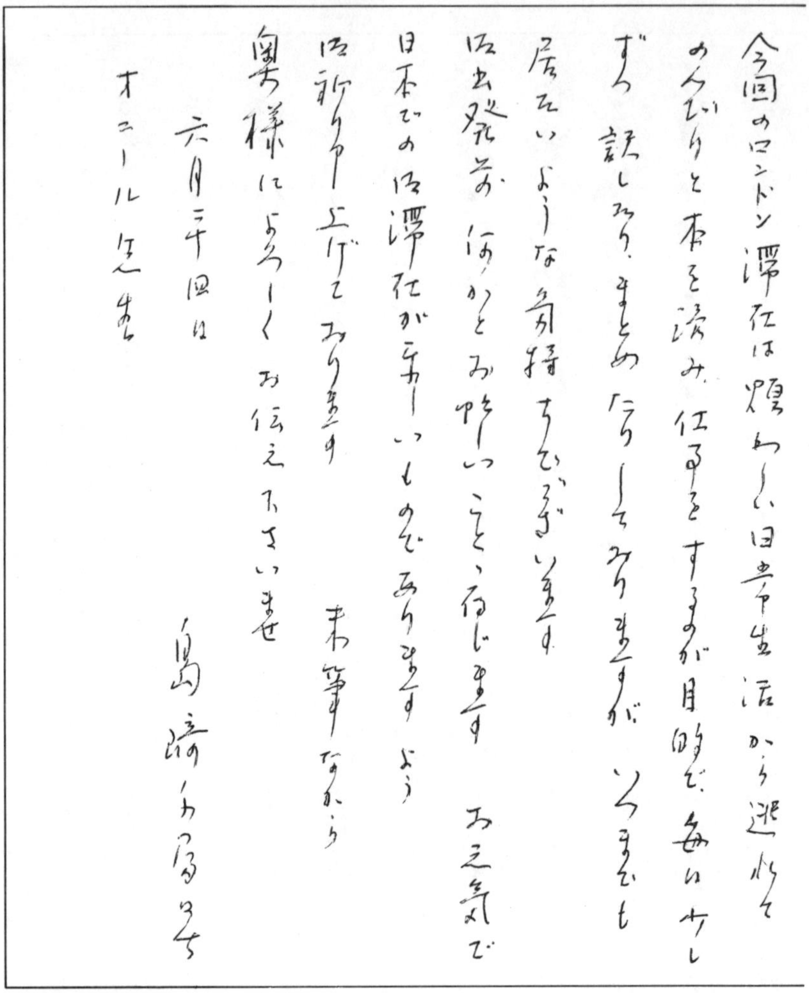

今回のロンドン滞在は煩わしい日常生活から逃れて
のんびりと本を読み、仕事をするのが目的で、毎日少し
ずつ訳したり、まとめたりしておりますが、いつまでも
居たいような気持ちでございます。
ご出発前何かとお忙しいことと存じます。お元気で
日本でのご滞在が楽しいものでありますよう
お祈り申し上げております。末筆ながら
奥様によろしくお伝えくださいませ。
六月二十四日　島崎ちふみ
オニール先生

Konkai no **Rondon** taizai wa wazurawashii nichijō seikatsu kara nogarete nonbiri to hon o yomi, shigoto o suru no ga mokuteki de, mainichi sukoshi zutsu yaku shitari, matometari shite orimasu ga, itsu made mo itai yō na kimochi de gozaimasu.

Go-shuppatsu mae nani-ka to o-isogashii koto to zonjimasu. Ō-genki de Nihon de no go-taizai ga tanoshii mono de arimasu yō o-inori mōshi-agete orimasu. Mappitsu-nagara oku-sama ni yoroshiku o-tsutae kudasaimase.

Rokugatsu nijūyokka **Shimazaki Chifumi**

Oniiru Sensei

Notes

a. KAMI OTOKO ONNA KURUI ONI Also read as *Shin Nan Jo Kyō Ki*, "God, Man, Woman, Madness, Devil," these terms refer to the five groups into which Nō plays are traditionally divided, according to the character played by the main actor.
b. SHITE The term used for the main actor in a Nō play.
c. KYOKU Although its most common meaning is "melody, music," this word is also used to refer to Nō plays, since these consist largely of music and song.
d. MUGEN Meaning "dream, phantasm," this term is used of the common type of Nō play in which a local person is possessed by the spirit of someone who, long before, was closely associated with the place in question.

ADVANCED TEXTS

Nos. 81–100

With transcriptions and notes for all texts,
and uncommon vocabulary for
Nos. 81–99 in the Glossary.

81. Letter from a Younger Scholar

すからよろしく御願い申上げます。
本当に勝手なお願いで恐縮で御座居ます
が呉々もよろしく御願い申上げます。
ヨーロッパで又お目にかかれる事を
楽しみに致しております。
末筆でございますが御両親様の皆々様
によろしく御伝え下さいませ。

敬具

八月十六日

[illegible]田[illegible]

オニール様

Haikei,

Senjitsu wa subarashii o-senbetsu o itadak-i, arigatō gozaimashita. Sobo o hajime kanai ichidō hoto-hoto kanpuku itashimashita. Mattaku watakushi-domo, Nihon o shirazaru Nihonjin to mōsu-BEKU tsuku-zuku hansei o itashimashita.

Sate, kondo watakushi-domo no oji **Sawayanagi Daigorō** mo **Igirisu Doitsu** o hete **Rōma** e MAIRU-BEKU kugatsu nijūichinichi-goro ni hikōki de shuppatsu itashimasu. **Igirisu** ni wa kugatsu nijūgonichi-goro yori tōkakan-gurai taizai itasu yotei de gozaimasu. Nani-tozo watakushi dōyō ni OBOSHI-MESHITE o-sewa kudasaimasu yō ni kokoro kara o-negai mōshi-agemasu.

Sawayanagi wa **Tōkyō** Kyōiku Daigaku no bijutsu-shi no kyōju de, bigaku bijutsu-shi no hō de wa kanari no shigoto o itashite orimasu. **Rondon** de mo bijutsu-kan o hajime sono kankei no shisatsu o suru yotei de gozaimasu. Shōsei no meishi o motte o-ukagai suru to zonjimasu kara, yoroshiku o-negai mōshi-agemasu.

Hontō ni katte na o-negai de, kyōshuku de gozaimasu ga, kure-gure mo yoroshiku o-negai mōshi-agemasu.

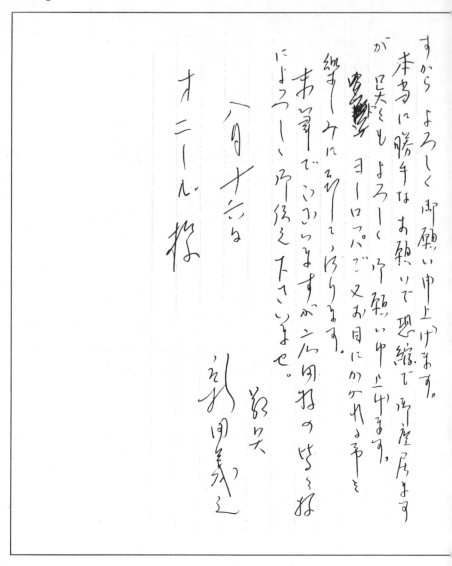

拝啓
先日は素晴らしい御餞別を頂き有難う御座居ました。祖母をはじめ家内一同ほとほと感服致しました。全く私共日本を知らざる日本人と申すべく、つくづく反省を致しました。
さて、今度私共の叔父沢柳大五郎もイギリス・トルコを経てローマへ参るべく九月二十一日頃に飛行機で出発致します。イギリスには九月二十五日頃より十日間位滞在致す予定で御座居ます。何卒私同様に思召してお世話下さいます様に心からお願い申上げます。
沢柳は東京教育大学の美術史の教授で、美学・美術史の方では可成の仕事を致して居ります。ロンドンでも美術館をはじめその関係の視察をする予定で御座居ます。小生共の名刺を持ってお伺いすると存じます

Yōroppa de mata o-me ni kakareru koto o tanoshimi ni itashite orimasu.

Mappitsu de gozaimasu ga, **Hirota**-sama no mina-mina-sama ni yoroshiku o-tsutae kudasaimase.

Keigu

Nitta Yoshiyuki

Hachigatsu jūrokunichi

Oniiru-sama

Notes

a. -BEKU This is the adverbial form of the attributive suffix *-beki*, "which can/should/will/might," and means here "(we reflected) in such a way/to the effect that we should (call ourselves . . .)."

b. MAIRU-BEKU Since *-beku* is here used to indicate probability rather than obligation (see a. above), the meaning is "(he will leave . . .) in such a way that he will go" or, simply, "to go."

c. OBOSHI-MESHITE *Oboshi-mesu* is a very formal honorific equivalent for *omou*, "think, feel," and thus similar to the more common *o-omoi ni naru* form.

82. Letter from an Older Professor Never Met Personally

南向きで、冬も太陽のあたるときは大層あたたかです。
場所は、文京区（小石川）の高台で、東京の山ノ手の中心
にあります。どこへゆくにも便利な場所です。東京大学、
早稲田大学、立教大学、および東京ステーションには、
地下鉄道又は電車を利用して二十分内外で行く
ことができます。
私どもは東京を八月下旬に出発し、ウインに立ち
よってから、九月中旬にロンドンに到着、一カ年間
ロンドンに滞在の予定です。
交換利用を御希望のときは、なるべく
早く御返事を下さい。
まずは右まで。　敬具
一九六五年六月十六日　仁井田陞
P. G. オニール様
なお一階の書庫には小生の書籍、その他を
つめこんでおく、つもりです。右御諒承の
ほど願上げます。

Haikei. **Toicheto** Kyōju kara, rokugatsu kokonoka-zuke no go-shomen no naiyō ni tsuite uketamawarimashita. Chokusetsu, shōsei kara o-tayori suru yō ni to no koto deshita no de, kono shomen o shitatamemashita.

Mada dare to mo shōsei-taku ni tsuite wa, keiyaku o tori-kimete wa orimasen. O-mōshi-ide no yō ni, **Rondon** de o-taku ga haishaku dekimasureba, makoto ni arigataku zonjimasu. Sono kawari ni **Tōkyō** ni oide no toki, shōsei-taku o go-riyō kudasaimasureba, kore mata kōei ni zonjimasu.

Shōsei-taku wa futsū no Nihon-fū no nikai-date desu. Ikkai wa hachijō (ita-jiki, sanpō ni shodana ga tsukutte arimasu no de, jissai no menseki wa hachijō yori sukoshi chiisai), rokujō (tatami-jiki), ichijō-amari (onajiku), shoko, yokushitsu, seiyō-shiki no benjo, sono ta, nikai wa rokujō (tatami-jiki).

Rokujō no ma wa ikkai mo nikai mo tomo ni, tokonoma oyobi engawa tsuki desu.

Minami-muki de, fuyu mo taiyō no ataru toki wa taisō atataka desu. Basho wa, **Bunkyō**-ku (**Koishikawa**) no takadai de, **Tōkyō** no **Yamanote** no chūshin ni arimasu. Doko e yuku ni mo benri na basho desu. **Tōkyō** Daigaku, **Waseda** Daigaku, **Rikkyō**

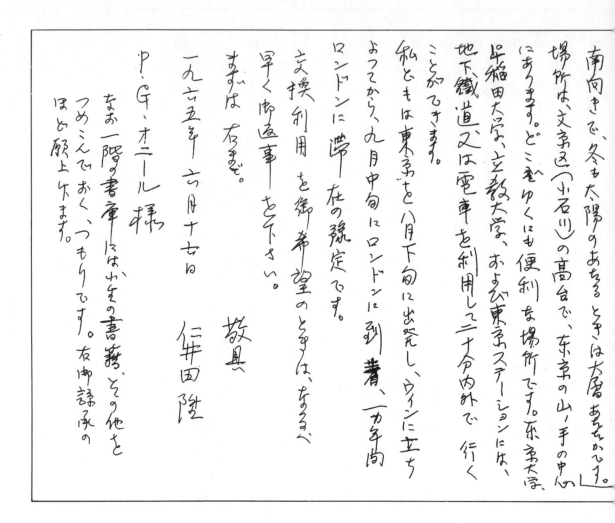

拝啓　トイチェト教授から、六月九日付の御書面の内容について承りました。直接、小生からおたよりするようにとのことでしたので、この書面をしたためました。

また誰とも小生宅については、契約をとりきめてはおりません。お申出のように、ロンドンで御宅が拝借できますれば、まことに有りがたく存じます。その代りに東京においでのとき、小生宅を御利用下さいますれば、これまた光栄に存じます。

小生宅は、普通の日本風の二階建てです。

一階は八畳（格じき、三方に書棚がつくってありますので、実際の面積は八畳より少し小さい）、六畳（たたみじき）、一畳餘（同じく）、書庫、浴室、西洋式の便所、その他

二階は六畳（たたみじき）

六畳の間は一階も二階もともに、床の間および縁側つきです。

Daigaku, oyobi **Tōkyō Sutēshon** ni wa chikatetsudō, mata wa densha o riyō shite nijippun naigai de iku koto ga dekimasu.

Watakushi-domo wa **Tōkyō** o hachigatsu gejun ni shuppatsu shi, **Uin** ni tachi-yotte kara, kugatsu chūjun ni **Rondon** ni tōchaku, ikkanenkan **Rondon** ni taizai no yotei desu.

Kōkan riyō o go-kibō no toki wa, narubeku hayaku go-henji o kudasai.

Mazu wa migi made. Keigu

Niida Noboru

1965nen rokugatsu jūrokunichi

P.G. **Oniiru**-sama

Nao ikkai no shoko ni wa shōsei no shoseki, sono ta o tsume-konde oku tsumori desu. Migi go-ryōshō no hodo negai-agemasu.

83. Letter from a Lady Who Had Been a Colleague for a Year or Two

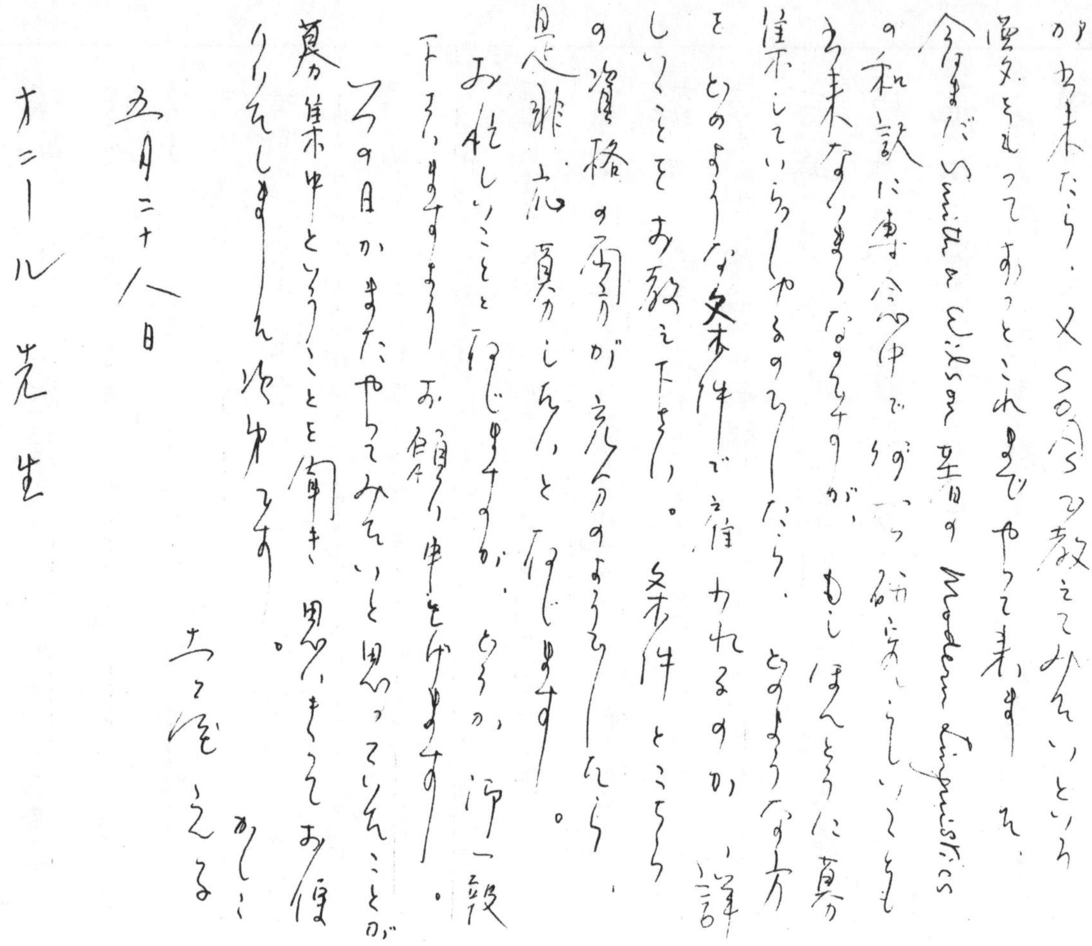
が出来たら、又SOASで教えてみたいという
夢をもってずっとこれまでやって来ました。
今はまだSmith & Wilson 著の Modern Linguistics
の和訳に専念中で、何一つ研究らしいことも
出来ないままなのですが、もしほんとうに募
集していらっしゃるのでしたら、どのような方
をどのような条件で雇われるのか、詳
しいことをお教え下さい。条件というか
の資格の問題が大丈夫のようでしたら
是非応募したいと存じます。
お忙しいことと存じますが、どうか御一読
下さいますようお願い申し上げます。
いつの日かまたやってみたいと思っていたことが
募集中ということを聞き、思いきってお便
りいたしました。
かしこ
[illegible]
五月二十八日
オニール先生

Oniiru Sensei,

Taihen nagai aida go-busata itashimashita ga, sensei wa masu-masu o-genki de go-katsuyaku no koto to zonji-agemasu. Sochira mo haru kara ichido ni shoka to itta kimochi no yoi kisetsu ni NARARE-MASHITA deshō. **Rondon** no itaru tokoro ni mirareru taiboku no midori o omoi-dashite orimasu.

Kochira mo konogoro wa sukkari atsuku natte shimaimashite, hito-bito wa natsu no fukusō desu. Tsui sanshūkan hodo mae, mukashi no **Sutiivun Giru**-san no o-maneki de, **Daian Sukotto**-jō ni mo o-ai shi, hisa-bisa ni **Oniiru** Sensei ya **Dan** Sensei o omoi-dashi, iro-iro tanoshiku kataraimashita.

Ano koro no kata-gata ga takusan **zai-Nichi** shite irasshatte go-katsuyaku to no koto de tanomoshiku mo ureshiku mo zonjimasu.

Sate, tsui sūjitsu mae, **Shingapōru** de oshiete iru Igirisujin no yūjin kara no tayori de, Soas ga Nihongo to onseigaku no kyōshi o boshū shite iru kedo . . . DŌ NA NO? to iu koto deshita. Jitsu wa watakushi no shigoto mo kanari ochi-tsuki, mā-mā manzoku shite iru no desu ga, itsu-ka Nihongo ni tsuite mō sukoshi shirabe, nani-ka matomeru koto ga dekitara, mata Soas de oshiete mitai to iu yume o motte zutto kore made yatte kimashita. Ima wa mada Smith & Wilson cho no Modern Linguistics no wayaku ni sennen-chū de, **nani-hitotsu** kenkyū rashii koto mo dekinai mama na no desu ga, moshi hontō ni boshū shite irassharu no deshitara, dono yō na kata o dono yō na jōken de yatowareru no ka,

オニール先生
長い間御無沙汰致しましたが、
先生は益々お元気で御活躍のことと存じ
上げます。そちらも春から一度に初夏と
いった気持のよい季節になられましたでしょう
ロンドンの至る所にみられる大木の緑を思い出し
ております。
こちらもこの頃はすっかり暑くなってしまいまして
人々は夏の服装です。つい三週間程前
昔のスティーヴン・ヤルさんのお招きで、ダイアン・スコット
嬢にもお会いし、久々にオニール先生のことを
思い出し、色々と懐かしく語らいました。
あの頃の方々が沢山在日していらっしゃって、御活躍
とのことで頼もしくもうれしくもなります。
さて、つい数日前シンガポールで教えているイギリス人
の友人からの便りで、SOAS が日本語と音声学
の教師を募集しているけど……どうなの？……と
いうことでした。実は私の仕事もかなり落着
き、まあまあ満足しているのですが、いつか
日本語についてもう少し調べ、何かまとめること

kuwashii koto o o-oshie kudasai. Jōken to kochira no shikaku no ryō-hō ga jūbun no yō deshitara, zehi ōbo shitai to zonjimasu.

O-isogashii koto to zonjimasu ga, dōka go-ippō kudasaimasu yō o-negai mōshi-agemasu.

Itsu no hi ka mata yatte mitai to omotte ita koto ga boshū-chū to iu koto o kiki, omoi-kitte o-tayori itashimashita shidai desu.

Kashiko

Tsuchiya Motoko

Gogatsu nijūhachinichi
Oniiru Sensei

Notes

a. NARAREMASHITA This passive/potential form is here used as an honorific: the grammatical subject *sochira mo*, "your side too," refers literally to place, but it is so closely associated with the person addressed that the writer felt it appropriate to use an honorific.

b. DŌ NA NO This *no* is an interrogative particle much softer in feeling than *ka* and therefore much used among familiars with the plain forms of verbs and adjectives. Since *na* is the copula equivalent in meaning to *da*/*desu*, etc., the whole phrase is a gentle alternative to *dō da*?, *dō desu ka*?

84. Postcard from a Village Official

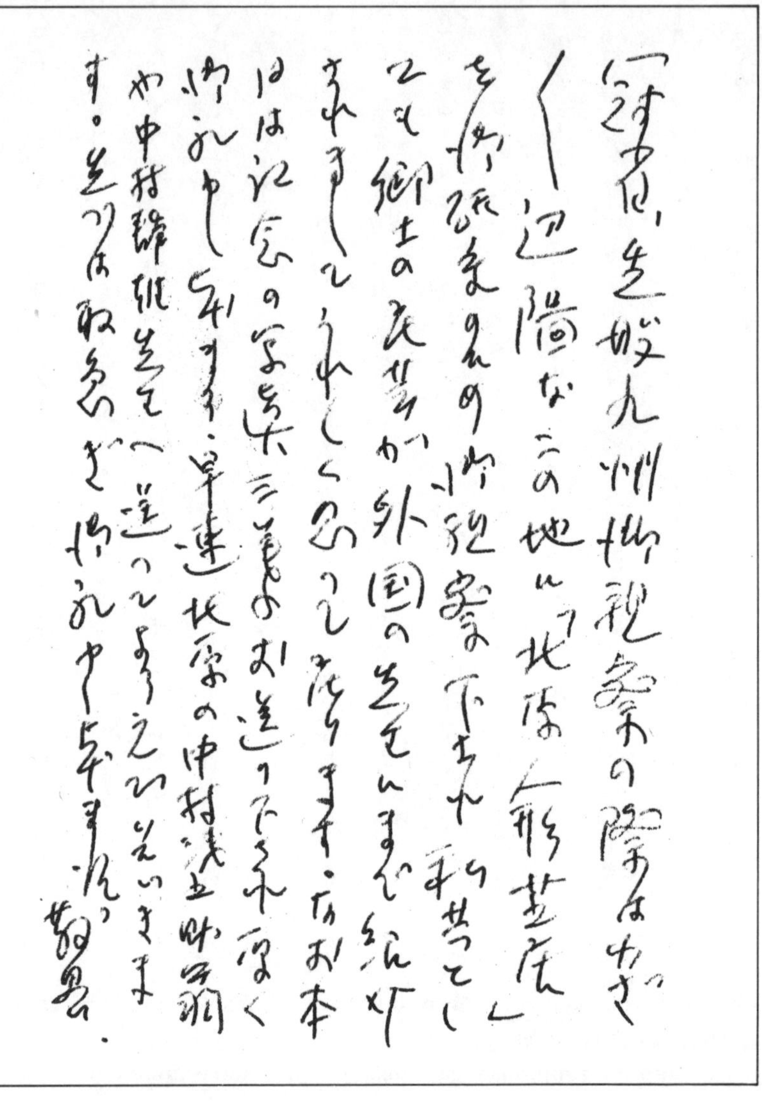
冠省、先般九州御視察の際はわざわざ辺鄙なこの地に「北原人形芝居」を御研究の為御視察下され私共としても郷土の民芸が外国の先生にまで紹介されまして嬉しく思っております。なお本日は記念の写真三葉お送り下され厚く御礼申し上げます。早速北原の中村浅五郎翁や中村静雄先生へ送って喜んでいただきます。先ずは取急ぎ御礼申し上げます。敬具

KASHŌ. Senpan **Kyūshū** go-shisatsu no sai wa waza-waza HENPI na kono chi ni "**Kitahara** Ningyō Shibai" o go-kenkyū no tame go-shisatsu kudasar-e, watakushi-domo to shite mo kyōdo no mingei ga gaikoku no sensei ni made shōkai sare-mashite ureshiku omotte orimasu. Nao honjitsu wa kinen no shashin san'yō o-okuri kudasar-e, atsuku o-rei mōshi-agemasu. Sassoku **Kitahara** no **Nakamura Sengosuke**-Ō ya **Nakamura Shizuo** Sensei e okutte yorokonde itadakimasu. **Mazu wa** tori-isogi o-rei mōshi-agemasu.

Keigu

Notes

a. KANSHŌ "Heading omitted"; like *Zenryaku* (see 2a), a phrase used to apologize for the omission of preliminary greetings.

b. HENPI The second character in this word has its left and right elements reversed, the standard form being 鄙.

c. -Ō A respectful suffix used of an old man; thus, here "(the venerable) old Mr. Nakamura."

85. Postcard from an Older Man Met Once or Twice Before

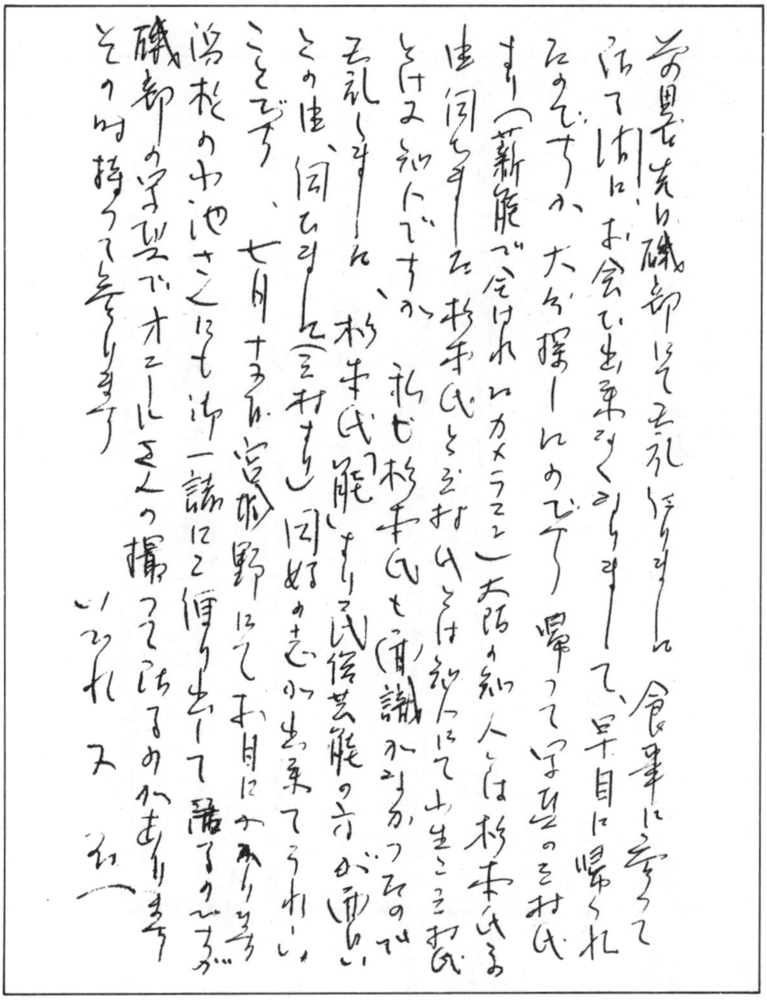

Zenryaku. Senjitsu **Isobe** nite shitsurei tsukamatsurimashita. Shokuji ni maitte iru aida ni o-ai dekinaku narimashite, hayame ni kaerareta no desu ka. Daibu sagashita no desu. Kaette, shashin no **Mimura**-shi yori (**Takigi Nō** de awareta kameraman) **Ōsaka** no chijin to wa **Sugimoto**-shi to no yoshi ukagaimashita. **Sugimoto**-shi to **Mimura**-shi to wa chijin nite, shōsei to **Mimura**-shi to wa mata chijin desu ga, watashi mo **Sugimoto**-shi mo menshiki ga nakatta no de shitsurei shimashita. **Sugimoto**-shi "Nō" yori minzoku geinō no hō ga omoshiroi to no yoshi ukagaimashite (**Mimura** yori), DŌKŌ NO SHI ga dekite ureshii koto desu. Shichigatsu jūgonichi **Miyagino** nite o-me ni kakarimasu. **Hamamatsu** no **Koike**-san ni mo go-issho nite tayori dashite iru no desu ga, **Isobe** no shashin de **Oniiru**-san no totte iru no ga arimasu. Sono toki motte mairimasu.

Izure mata. Fuitsu

Notes

a. DŌKŌ NO SHI "Person(s) of similar taste," the *shi* in this set phrase normally being written with the character 士 "(gentle)man."

86. Postcard from an Elderly Landlady Received While Away on a Trip

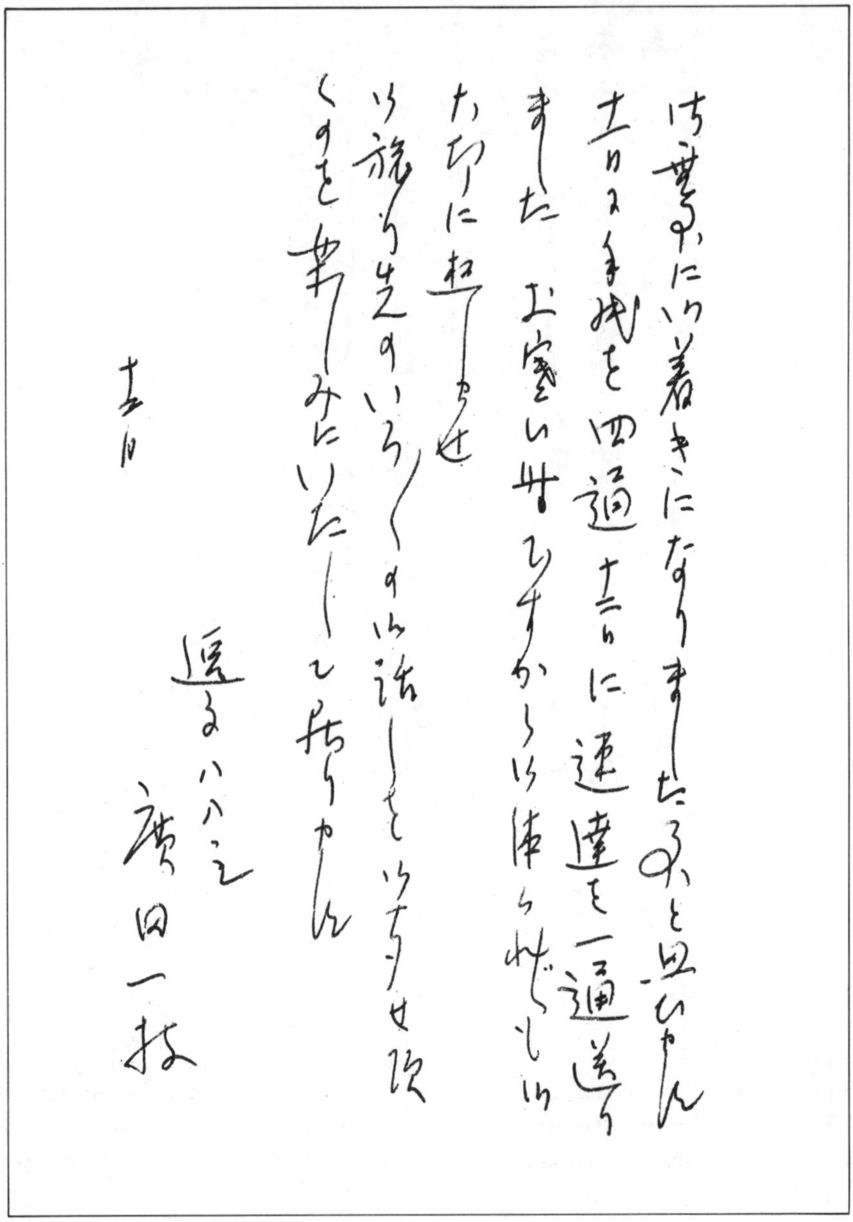

御無事にお着きになりました事と思ひます
十一日に手紙を四通十二日に速達を一通送りました
お寒い時ですからお体くれぐれもお大切に遊ばせ
御旅行先のいろいろのお話しをお聞かせ頂くのを楽しみにいたして居ります

十二日

逗子八八三
廣田一枝

Go-buji ni o-tsuki ni narimashita koto to omoimasu.

Jūichinichi ni tegami o yontsū, jūninichi ni sokutatsu o ittsū okurimashita. O-samui toki desu kara o-karada kure-gure mo o-taisetsu ni asobashimase.

Go-ryokō-saki no iro-iro no o-hanashi o o-kikase itadaku no o tanoshimi ni itashite orimasu.

Zushi 883

Hirota Kazue

Jūninichi

87. Letter from an Older Man, a Professor Specialising in Folk Entertainments

拝啓　さんぞろ祭の方から返事が参りましたか。
しらべてみましたら、これは旧暦の十一月十七日の
やうです。今年の旧暦十一月十七日は、新暦では
十二月二十七日にあたるやうです。
こんどの木曜（二十七日）は、急に福島市の方へ
行くことになりましたので、あいにくながら
休講といふことになりました。
けふ、能楽書林から速達の手紙が参りまして、
貴殿と是非対談をしてはもらへまいかとのこと
でございましたが、御都合はいかがでせうか。
能楽書林の都合のよい日を四日程知らせて参り
ましたが、私はそのうちの二十五日（火）の午後二時
頃から、二十八日（金）の午後四時半頃からの
（二十八日の午後三時半上野着で帰る予定です）

Haikei. **SANZORO** MATSURI no hō kara henji ga mairimashita ka. Shirabete mimashitara, kore wa kyūreki no jūichigatsu jūshichinichi no yō desu. Kotoshi no kyūreki jūichigatsu jūshichinichi wa, shinreki de wa jūnigatsu nijūshichinichi ni ataru yō desu.

Kondo no Mokuyō (nijūshichinichi) wa, kyū ni **Fukushima**-shi no hō ni iku koto ni narimashita no de, ainiku-nagara, kyūkō to iu koto ni narimashita.

Kyō, **Nōgaku Shorin** kara sokutatsu no tegami ga mairimashite, kiden to zehi taidan o shite wa MORA-E-MAI ka to iu koto de gozaimashita ga, go-tsugō wa ikaga deshō ka. **Nōgaku Shorin** no tsugō no yoi hi o yokka hodo shirasete mairimashita ga, watashi wa sono uchi no nijūgonichi (Ka) no gogo niji-goro kara to, nijūhachinichi (Kin) no gogo yojihan-goro kara no, (nijūhachinichi no gogo sanjihan **Ueno**-chaku de kaeru yotei desu) dochira-ka ga kō-tsugō desu. (Nijūgonichi no hō ga, yori kō-tsugō desu.) Moshi ryōjitsu-tomo go-tsugō ga o-warui yō deshitara, aratamete **Nōgaku Shorin** no hō to mo uchi-awasemashō. Nao, watashi no tsugō wa, nijūhachinichi igo deshitara, ima no tokoro jiyū desu.

Nijūsan, nijūyon no ryōjitsu wa, **Iwate**-ken **Waga**-gun no hō ni itte mairimasu. Nijūgonichi no asa ni kaette kimasu.

どちらかが好都合です。(二十五日の方が、より
好都合です)もし両日とも御都合がおわるいや
うでしたら、改めて紀伊國屋書林の方とお合せませう。
あるいは私の都合は二十八日以後でしたら、今のところ
自由です。
廿三、廿四の両日は、岩手県和賀郡の方へ行って
参ります。廿五日の朝帰ってきます。
対談の場所は、大隈会館などいかがかと存じ
ます。はるばるこのことだけのためにおいでいただく
のでしたら、まことに恐縮ですけれど。　草々
十一月二十一日夜　本田安次
P・G・オニール様
おんもと
○沖縄スライドの会は十二月十三日(土)午後一時からになるかと思はれます。

Taidan no basho wa, **Ōkuma** Kaikan nado ikaga ka to zonjimasu. Haru-baru kono koto dake no tame ni oide itadaku no deshitara, makoto ni kyōshuku desu keredo.

Sō-sō

Honda Yasuji

Jūichigatsu nijūichinichi yoru
P.G. **Oniiru**-sama

On-moto

***Okinawa** suraido no kai wa jūnigatsu jūsannichi (Do) gogo ichiji kara ni naru ka to omoimasu.

Notes

a. SANZORO MATSURI An old festival held in a mountain village in Aichi Prefecture.

b. MORA-E-MAI The almost exclusively literary ending *-mai* is a negative one equivalent to colloquial *-nai darō*, "(probably) will not," which is used after the dictionary form of any verb [e.g., *iku-mai*, "(probably) will not go"; *moraeru-mai*, "(probably) will not be able to receive,"] or alternatively after the stem of *-ru* verbs like *taberu* or, as here, *moraeru*. Used here with *ka*, the meaning is thus "(they asked) whether they cannot have me (do an interview)."

88. Circular Letter from a Restaurant

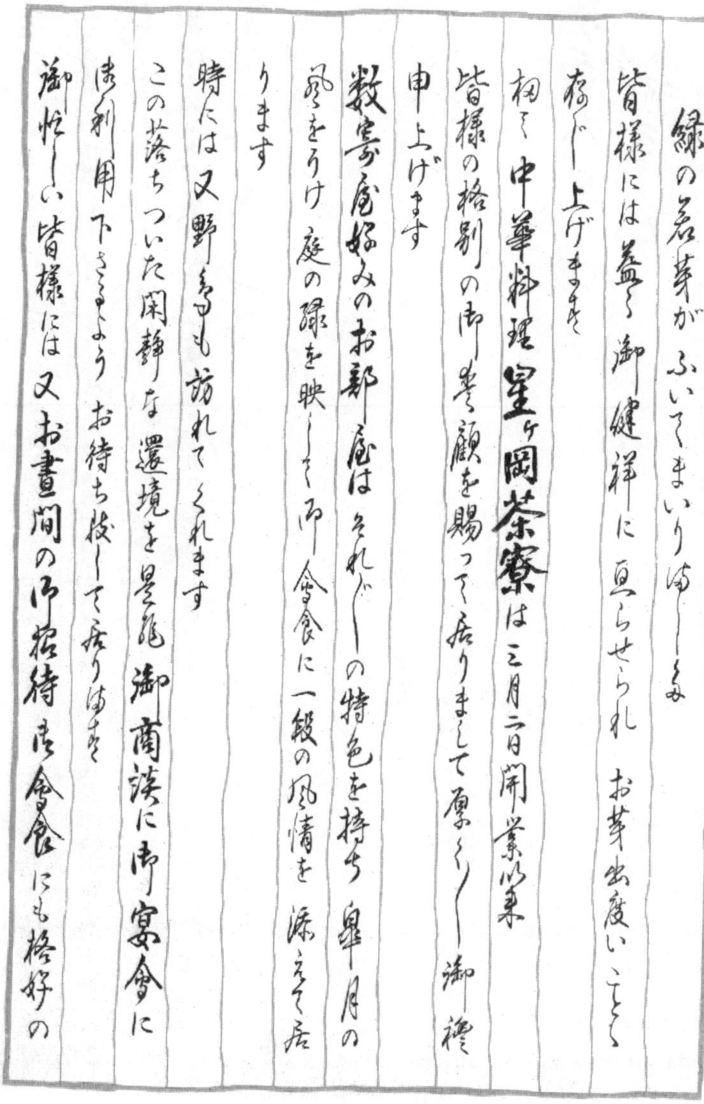

緑の若芽がふいてまいりました
皆様には益々御健祥に亘らせられ お芽出度いことと
存じ上げます
扨て 中華料理 星ヶ岡茶寮は三月二日開業以来
皆様の格別の御愛顧を賜って居りまして厚く厚く御礼
申上げます
数寄屋好みのお部屋はそれぞれの特色を持ち皐月の
風をうけ 庭の緑を映して御会食に一段の風情を添えて居
ります
時には又野鳥も訪れてくれます
この落ちついた閑静な環境を是非御商談に御宴会に
御利用下さるようお待ち致して居ります
御忙しい皆様には又お昼間の御招待ご会食にも格好の

Midori no wakame ga fuite mairimashita.

Mina-sama ni wa masu-masu go-**kenshō** ni WATARASERAR-E, o-**medetai** koto to zonji-agemasu.

Sate, Chūka Ryōri **Hoshigaoka Charyō** wa sangatsu futsuka kaigyō irai, MINA-SAMA no kakubetsu no go-aiko o tamawatte orimashite, atsuku atsuku o-rei mōshi-agemasu.

Sukiya-gonomi no o-heya wa sore-zore no tokushoku o mochi, **SATSUKI** no kaze o uke, niwa no midori o utsushite go-kaishoku ni ichidan no fuzei o soete orimasu.

Toki ni wa mata yachō mo otozurete kuremasu.

Kono ochi-tsuita kansei na kankyō o zehi go-shōdan ni, go-enkai ni go-riyō kudasaru yō o-machi itashite orimasu.

O-isogashii mina-sama ni wa mata o-hiruma no go-shōtai, go-kaishoku ni mo **kakkō** no basho de gozaimasu.

Go-kazoku-zure no go-danran ni mo, mata gaikoku no kata-gata o go-shōtai nasaru baai ni mo kiwamete go-benri de gozaimasu.

場所で御座います
御家族連れの御團欒にも又外國の方々を御招待なさる
場合にも極めて御便利で御座います
眺望のよい高台の園遊会の趣好も亦格別で御座います
是非々々御来駕下さいますよう伏して御待ち致して
居ります

五月　日

赤坂山王台
星ヶ岡茶寮　謹白

英國大使館
領事部　様

Chōbō no yoi takadai no en'yūkai no **shukō** mo mata kakubetsu de gozaimasu. Zehi zehi go-**raiga** kudasaimasu yō fushite o-machi itashite orimasu.

Gogatsu NICHI

Akasaka Sannō-dai
Hoshigaoka Charyō KINPAKU

Eikoku taishikan
-sama
Ryōjibu

Notes

a. WATARASERARE Since *wataraseru* is an honorific verb with a wide range of meaning and it is made even more respectful here by the use of the -*(ra)reru* form, this word can be taken as a very formal and literary equivalent to *oide ni nari* or *o-sugoshi ni nari* at a more modest level of respect.
b. MINA-SAMA On the position of this word, see 3k.
c. SATSUKI A literary and poetic name for May (but originally for the fifth month of the old lunar calendar; cf. 69f).
d. NICHI This being a circular letter, the day was not specified (in such cases, it is common to use the term 吉日 *kichinichi*, "an auspicious day").
e. KINPAKU "Reverently stated"; a formal term usable in letters after the name of the writer.

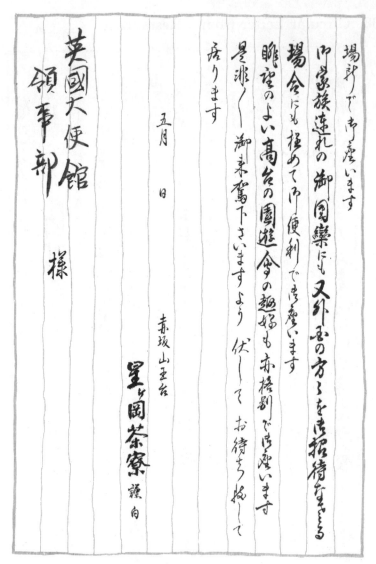

89. Letter from a Somewhat Younger Man Known for Many Years

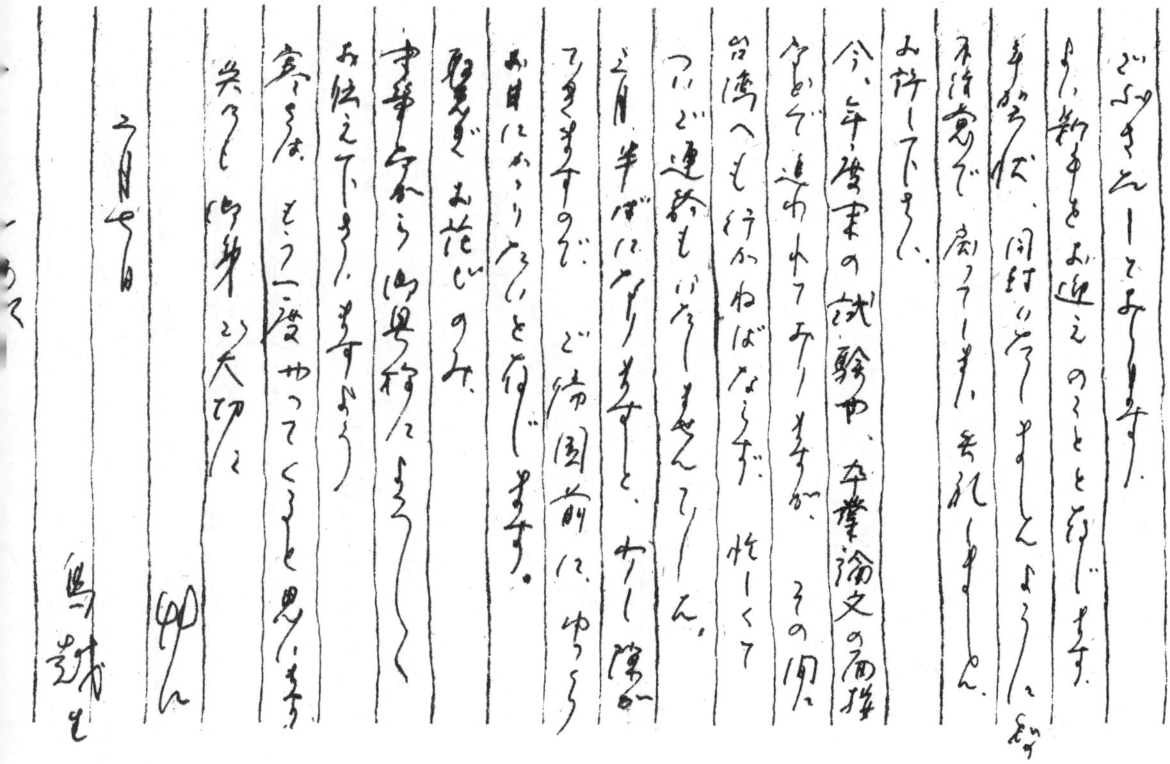
ご無沙汰しております。
よい新年をお迎えのことと存じます。
年賀状、同封いたしましたように
不注意で戻ってしまい、失礼しました。
お許し下さい。
今、年度末の試験や、卒業論文の面接
などで追われておりますが、その間に
台湾へも行かねばならず、忙しくて
つい御連絡もいたしませんでした。
三月半ばになりますと、少し暇が
できますので、ご帰国前に、ゆっくり
お目にかかりたいと存じます。
取り急ぎお詫びのみ。
末筆ながら奥様によろしく
お伝え下さいますよう
寒さはもう一度やってくると思います。
呉々も御身御大切に
二月七日
艸々
鳥越生

Go-busata shite orimasu.

Yoi shinnen o o-mukae no koto to zonjimasu. Nengajō, dōfū itashimashita yō ni watashi no fu-chūi de modotte shima-i, shitsurei shimashita. O-yurushi kudasai.

Ima, nendo-matsu no shiken ya, sotsugyō ronbun no mensetsu nado de owarete orimasu ga, sono aida ni **Taiwan** e mo ikaneba narazu, isogashikute tsui go-renraku mo itashimasen deshita.

Sangatsu nakaba ni narimasu to, sukoshi hima ga dekimasu no de, go-kikoku mae ni, yukkuri o-me ni kakaritai to zonjimasu.

Tori-isogi o-wabi nomi.

Mappitsu-nagara on-oku-sama ni yoroshiku o-tsutae kudasaimasu yō.

Samu-sa wa mō ichido yatte kuru to omoimasu. Kure-gure mo o-mi go-taisetsu ni.

SŌ-SŌ

Torigoe Sei

Nigatsu nanuka

Oniiru-sama

Notes

a. SŌ-SŌ The character here is the 140th radical "grass" itself, used as an alternative to the more common 草 (see 4p).

90. Letter to a Japanese Colleague from an Old Friend

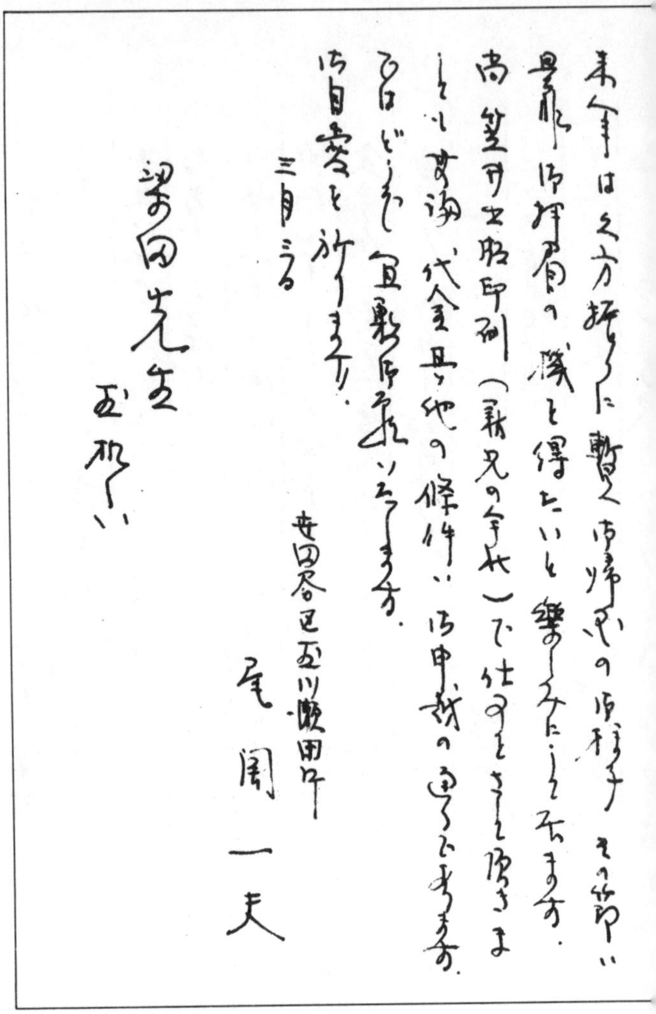

来年は久方振りに暫く御帰国の御様子 その節は
是非御拝眉の機を得たいと楽しみにして居ります。
尚笠井出版印刷（親兄の会社）で仕事をさして頂きまし
ても勿論代金其他の条件は御申越の通りであります。
ではどうぞ宜敷御[illegible]ます。
御自愛を祈ります。
三月三日
世田谷区玉川瀬田町
尾関一夫
梁田先生
玉机下

Go-hensho masa ni haiken itashimashita.

Ichiō wakarimashita no de, dekiru dake go-kitai ni SOU yō ni itashitai to omoimasu. Sassoku tori-kakaru wake desu ga, jitsu wa taihen katte de osore-irimasu ga, watashi no hō ga shigoto ga KONDE imasu no de, watashi no gikei no kaisha de yaraseru koto ni itashimashita. Kono tegami ga kihō ni tsuku to zengo shite gikei no kaisha kara mitsumori-sho, kaisha no keireki-sho, ōbun wabun ryōhō no ga todoku koto to omoimasu. Moto-moto Kokusai Shuppan Insatsusha de zennen ISSHO ni yatte ite dokuritsu itashimashita kaisha de, Tōkyō de mo yūsū na ii shigoto o suru hyōban no kaisha de gozaimasu shi, watashi kara yoku hanashite okimashita kara, go-anshin no ue yarase-te kudasai. Muron, watashi mo sensei to no kankei ni oite wa sekinin o mochimasu. **Kumi-mihon** mo bunsen wa daibu susunde imashita kara, shibaraku shitara o-okuri itasu koto deshō. Go-enryo naku kibō no ten wa o-nobe kudasaimashite go-manzoku no iku made kōsei mo shite itadakitō gozaimasu.

Rainen wa hisakata-buri ni shibaraku go-kikoku no go-yōsu, sono setsu wa zehi go-haibi no ki o etai to tanoshimi ni shite imasu. Nao, **Kasai** Shuppan Insatsu (gikei no kaisha) de shigoto o sashite itadakimashite mo, muron daikin sono ta no jōken wa o-mōshi-koshi no tōri de arimasu.

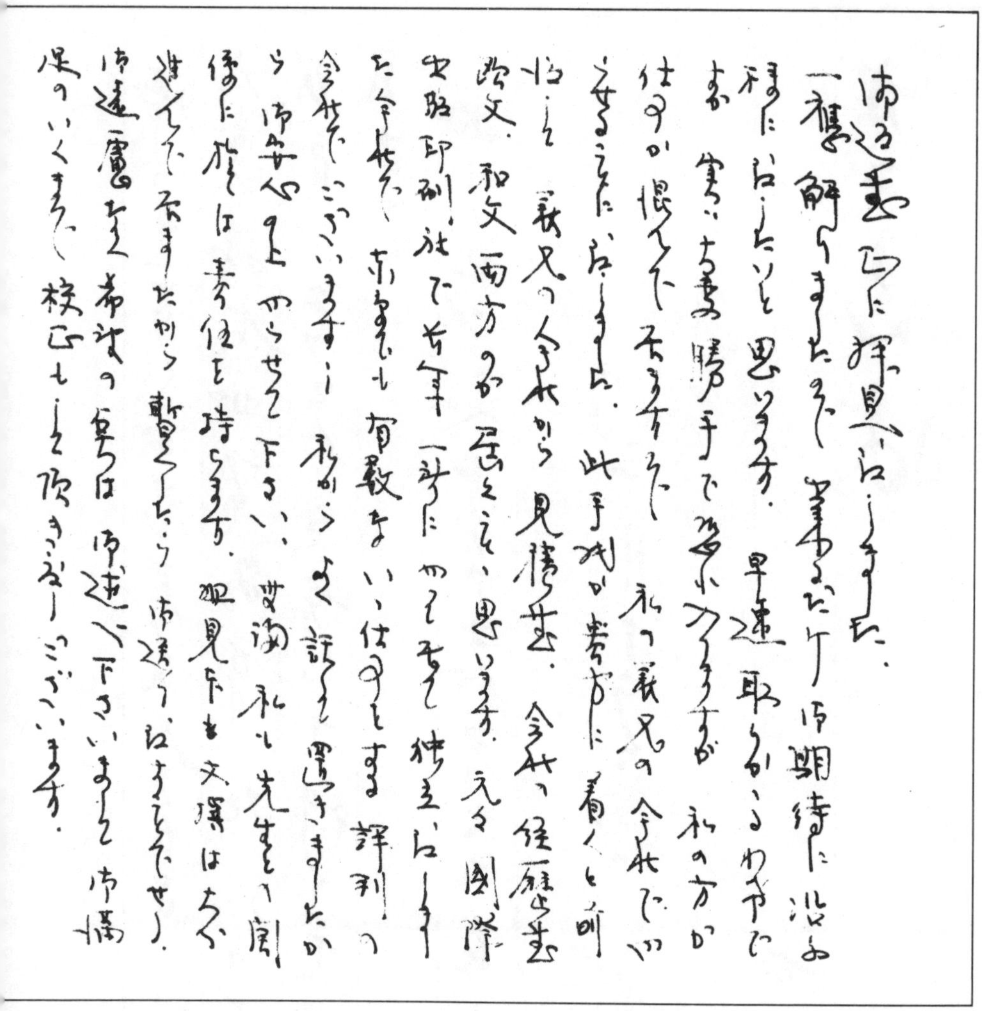
御返事正に拝見いたしました。一様解りましたので出来るだけ御期待に沿う様にいたしたいと思います。早速取りかかるわけですが 実は大変勝手で恐れ入りますが 私の方が仕事が混んで居りますので 私の義兄の今井でいたすことにいたしました。此手紙が貴方に着く頃迄には 義兄の今井から見積書、今井の経歴書、論文、和文両方のが届くと思います。元々 国際出版印刷社で長年一緒に働いて来て独立いたした今井で、本当でも有数な、仕事をする評判の今井でございます。私からよく話して置きましたから御安心の上やらせて下さい。勿論 私も先生の国語に於ては責任を持ちます。但見本も文撰はなく進んで居りますから 暫くしたら御送りいたしますので 御遠慮なく希望の点は御述べ下さいまして 御満足のいくまで校正をして頂きとうございます。

De wa dōzo yoroshiku o-negai itashimasu.
Go-jiai o inorimasu.

Setagaya-ku **Tamagawa Seta**-machi

Ozeki Kazuo

Sangatsu mikka
Yanada Sensei
GYOKUKIKA

Notes

a. SOU The character used here is 沿, but in expressions in which *sou* means "meet/fulfil (a person's wish, etc.)" the character 副 is preferable.

b. KONDE The character 混 found here is normally used only for verbs with the sense of "mixing together," but it is probably used here for *komu*, "be full/crowded," because of the associated idea of "confusion" and because its Sino-Japanese reading KON fits in with the *konde* form.

c. ISSHO Although the meaning of this word here is the same as that written 一緒, the second character used here is 所.

d. GYOKUKIKA A formal concluding phrase in letters, with the same meaning as *gyokuanka* (see 9e).

91. Letter from an Elderly Professor Known for a Number of Years

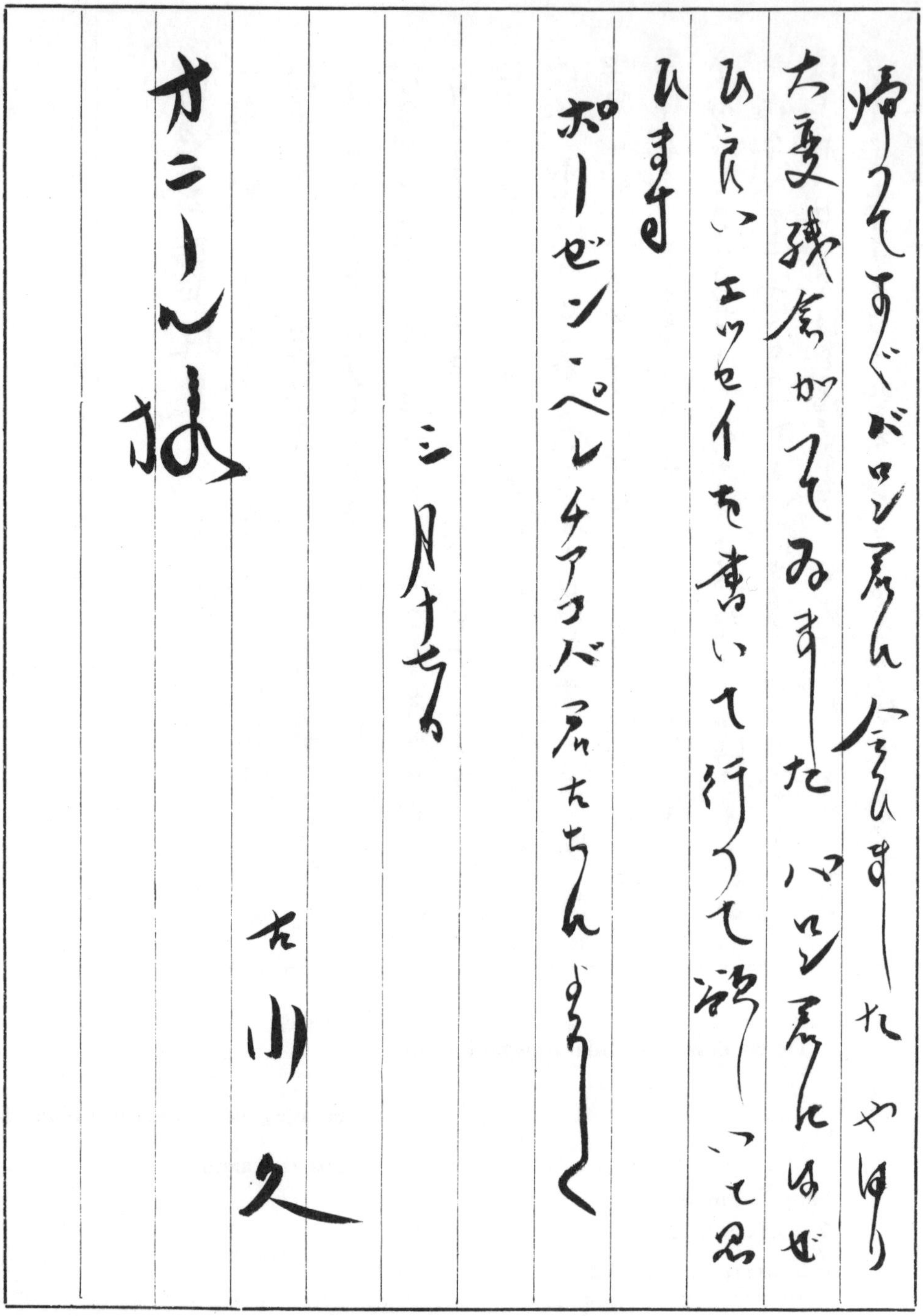

帰ってすぐバロン君に会いましたがやはり
大変残念がってゐましたバロン君はぜ
ひ良いエッセイを書いて行って欲しいと思
ひます
ポーゼン・ペレチアコバ君たちによろしく
三月十七日
古川久
カーレン様

O-tegami arigatō. O-kaze ikaga.

Kondo no tabi no hanbun kurai wa anata ni aeru tanoshimi deshita no de, hontō ni zannen deshita. Shikashi anata no gakusei-tachi ni ae, Kyōgen mo mā seikō deshita no de ureshiku omoimasu. Watashi wa issakunen hajimete **on-chi** o otozureta toki mo sō omoimashita ga, **Pari** yori mo zutto **Rondon** ga suki desu. Kondo mo yukkuri sanpo nado shite ochi-tsuita kibun ni hitarimashita. Watashi wa mō rokujūnana-sai desu kara, sō ikeru chansu wa nai ka mo shiremasen ga, dekireba nando de mo otozuretaku negatte

お手紙有難う　お風邪如何
今度の旅の半分くらゐはあなたに会
つて楽しみにしてゐたので本当に残念でし
た　しかしあなたの学生たちに会へ相
談はまあ成功したので嬉しく思ひま
す　私は一昨年始めて此地を訪れ
時もさう思ひましたが　パリよりもずつと
ロンドンが好きです　今度もゆつくり散
歩などして落ちついた気分にひたりま
した　私はもう六十七歳ですからさう
行けるチャンスはないかも知れませんがで
きれば何度でも訪れたく願つてゐます

imasu. Kaette sugu **Baron**-kun ni aimashita. Yahari taihen zannen-gatte imashita. **Baron**-kun ni wa zehi yoi essei o kaite itte hoshii to omoimasu.

Pōzen, **Perechiakoba**-kun-tachi ni yoroshiku.

Sangatsu jūshichinichi

Furukawa Hisashi

Oniiru-sama

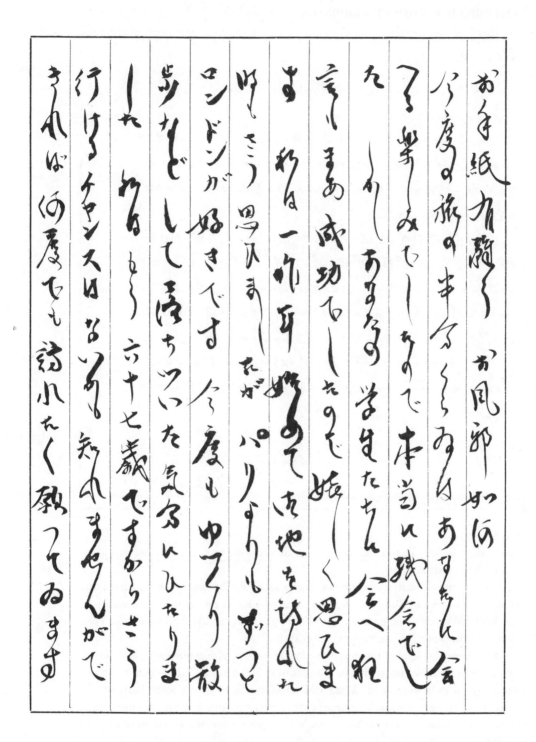

92. Letter from a Former Colleague

O'Neill 先生

ご無沙汰しています。雑誌「言語」誌上ではお目にかかり、ますますご活躍のこと知りました。

さて、今回お手紙さし上げるのは、高橋慶子さんを紹介するためです。この方は、朝日新聞がやっている朝日カルチュアセンターでわたしの生徒です。わたしはそこで、外国人に日本語を教える教師を養成するコースで「日本語の発音」について話しました。

今は国文学関係の出版をやっています。この点から、外国における日本古典文学の受容という問題に興味を持って、能のことなどいろいろ承りたいということです。また上記のコースを受講されたわけですので、日本語教授についても関係をお持ちで、先生の教える者として、またかつて教えを受けた人としての経験などもお聞かせいただければ勉強になると思います。

夏休み中でいろいろご都合もおありと思いますが、もしお時間を少々いただければ、本人も喜ぶことと存じます。お忙しいであろうことは重々わかっていますが何分ともよろしくお願いいたします。

6月6日

野元菊雄

O'Neill Sensei,

Go-busata shite imasu. Zasshi "Gengo" shijō de wa o-me ni kakar-i, masu-masu go-katsuyaku no koto shirimashita.

Sate, konkai o-tegami sashi-ageru no wa, **Takahashi Keiko**-san o shōkai suru tame desu. Kono kata wa, Asahi Shinbun ga yatte iru Asahi Karuchua Sentā de, watashi no seito desu. Watashi wa soko de, gaikokujin ni Nihongo o oshieru kyōshi o yōsei suru kōsu de "Nihongo no hatsuon" ni tsuite hanashimashita.

Ima wa kokubungaku kankei no shuppan o yatte imasu. Kono ten kara, gaikoku ni okeru Nihon koten bungaku no juyō to iu mondai ni kyōmi o motte, Nō no koto nado iro-iro uketamawaritai to iu koto desu. Mata jōki no kōsu o jukō sareta wake desu no de, Nihongo kyōju ni tsuite mo kankei o o-mochi de, sensei no oshieru mono to shite, mata katsute oshie o uketa hito to shite no keiken nado mo o-kikase itadakereba benkyō ni naru to omoimasu.

Natsu-yasumi-chū de iro-iro go-tsugō mo o-ari to omoimasu ga, moshi o-jikan o shōshō itadakereba, honnin mo yorokobu koto to zonjimasu. O-isogashii de arō koto wa jūjū wakatte imasu ga, nanibun-tomo yoroshiku o-negai itashimasu.

Rokugatsu muika

Nomoto Kikuo

93. Letter from a Lady Met Several Times in Japan

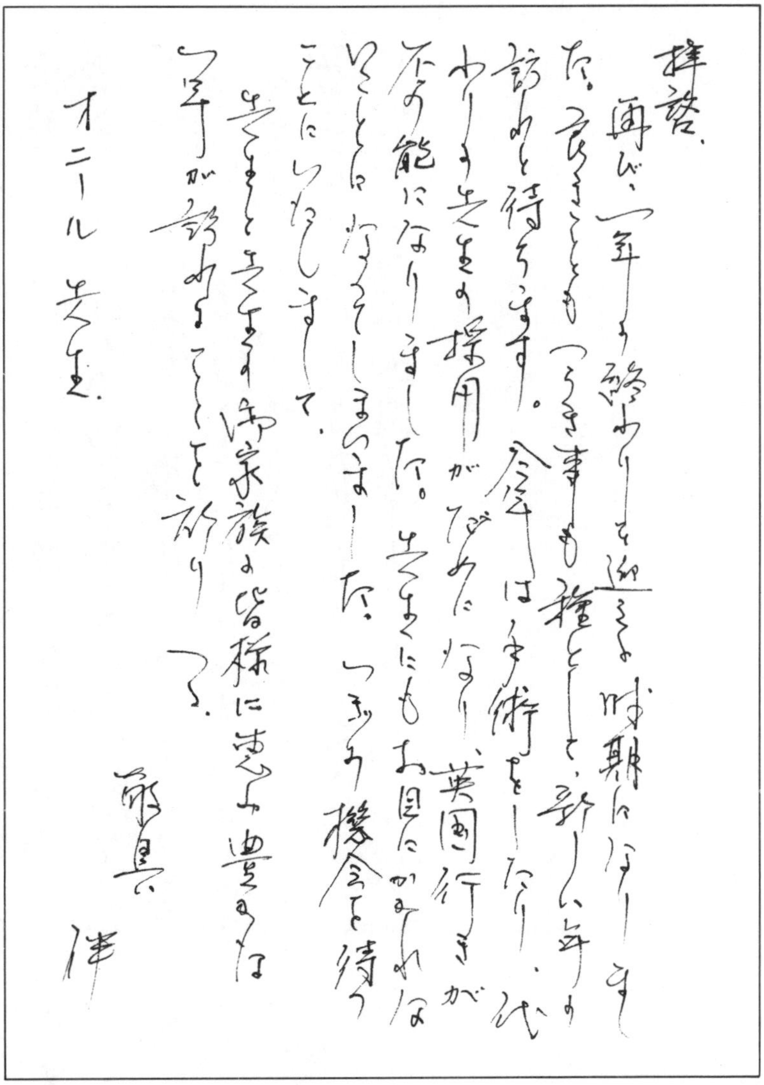
拝啓
再び、一年の終わりを迎える時期になりました。良きことも辛きことも種として、新しい年の訪れを待ちます。今年は手術をしたり、代わりの先生の採用がだめになり、英国行きが不可能になりました。先生にもお目にかかれなくなってしまいました。次の機会を待つことにいたしまして。
先生と先生の御家族の皆様に恵み豊かな一年が訪れることを祈りつつ。
敬具
伴
オニール 先生

Haikei,

Futatabi, ichinen no owari o mukaeru jiki ni narimashita. YOKI koto mo TSURAKI koto mo tane to shite, atarashii toshi no otozure o machimasu. Kotoshi wa shujutsu o shitari, kawari no sensei no saiyō ga dame ni nari, Eikoku-yuki ga fukanō ni narimashita. Sensei ni mo o-me ni kakarenai koto ni natte shimaimashita. Tsugi no kikai o matsu koto ni itashimashite...

Sensei to sensei no go-kazoku no mina-sama ni megumi-yutaka na ichinen ga otozureru koto o inori-tsutsu.

Keigu

Ban

Oniiru Sensei

Notes

a. YOKI . . . TSURAKI The *-ki* ending in these two words being the literary-style attributive ending for adjectives (see 3p), the colloquial equivalents are *yoi/ii* (*koto*) . . . *tsurai* (*koto*).

94. Letter to a Japanese Colleague from a Publisher

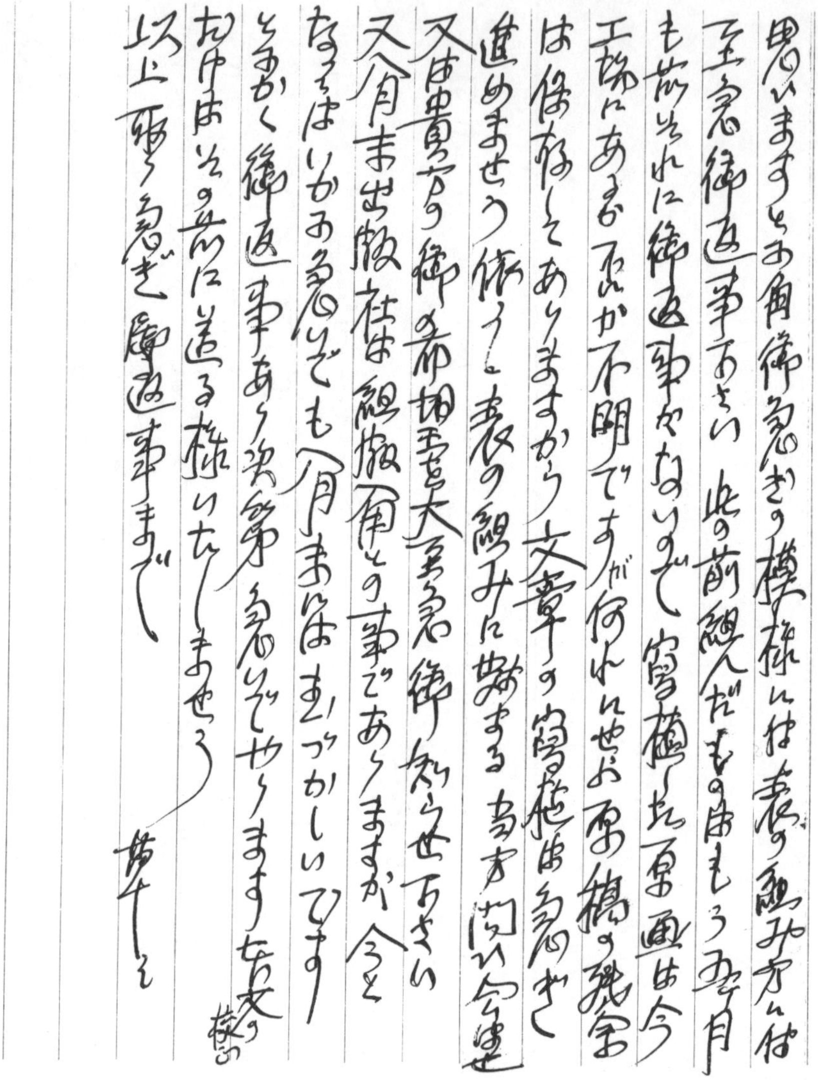

Eikoku **Yanada**-sama **Kasai Tomoyoshi**

Haifuku. Kihō shichigatsu sanjūnichi-zuke **eyā-retā,** honjitsu arigataku haiken itashimashita. Soshite, sassoku-nagara tsugi no tōri henji mōshi-agemasu. Kihō yori watashi-ate ni saru shigatsu tōka, gogatsu mikka nikai ni watari, rei no insatsu ni tsuki go-henji KUDASARESHI yoshi de arimasu ga, watashi wa zannen-nagara sono nitsū-tomo uke-totte orimasenu. Jitsu wa watashi ga dashita kōsei narabi ni tegami wa tashika saru sangatsu muika dashita no desu kara, sangatsu-chū ni wa kanarazu go-henji ni sesshi-uru mono to kangae, katsu tōsha jushin-gakari ni mo sono mune chūi o unagashite okimashita ga, sara ni sono henji ga nai no de mohaya tōho ni wa yōji ga nai to kangaete imashita. Naze naraba, ima made ni yūbin no machigai wa naku, katsu tōsha e wa **Kasai Tomoyoshi Tōkyō** Japan de mo, tada tan ni **Kasai** Shuppan Insatsusha **Tōkyō** de mo kimasu yue, dō shita koto ka to migi nitsū ga todokanu koto o fushigi ni omoimasu. Watashi kara no tegami ni wa **kumi-kata** ni tai-suru meisai o shitsumon mōshi-agete arimasu. Bunshō no hō wa ano **kumi-kata** nite go-manzoku itadakeru to omoimasu ga,

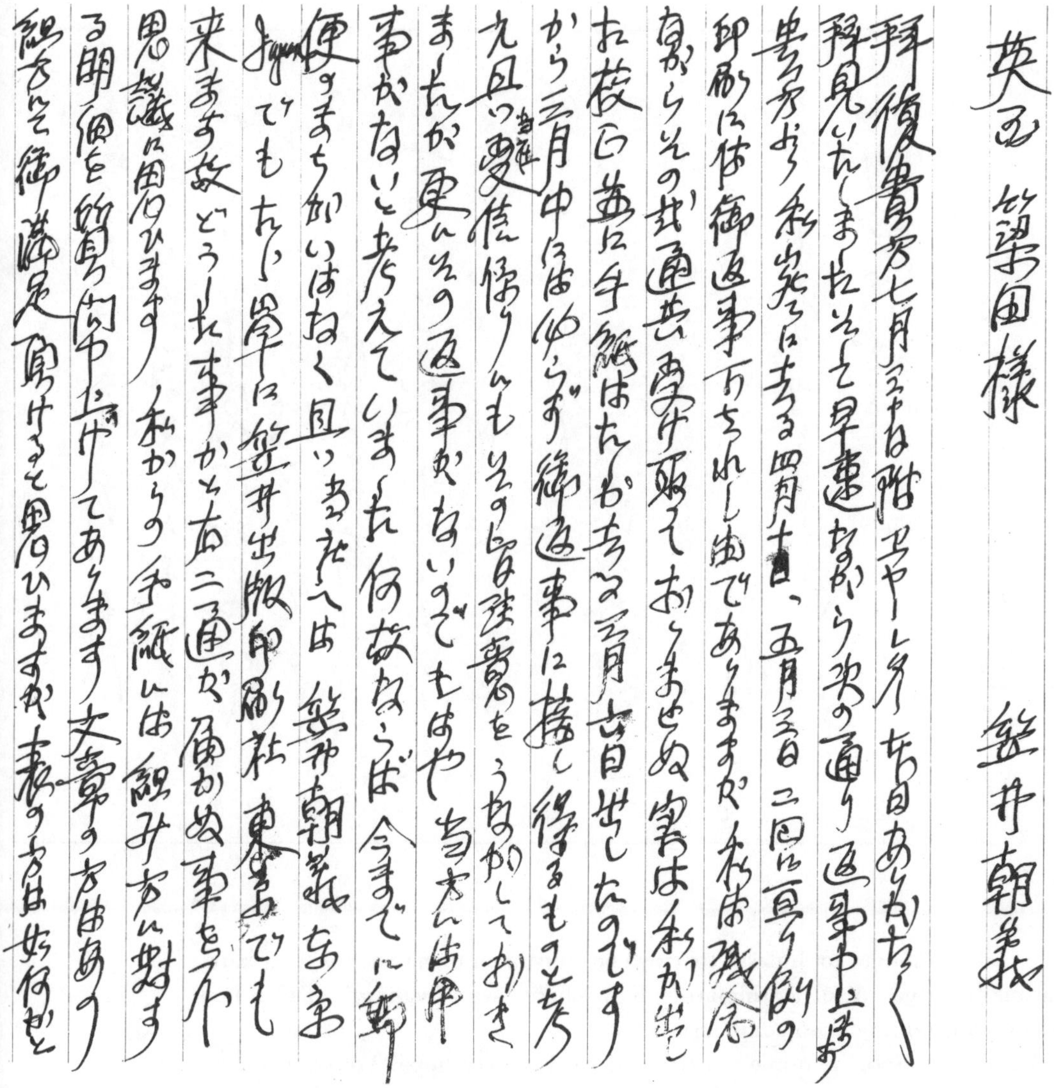

hyō no hō wa ikaga ka to omoimasu. Tonikaku, o-isogi no moyō ni tsuki, hyō no **kumi-kata** ni tsuki shikyū go-henji kudasai. Kono mae **kunda** mono wa mō gokagetsu mo mae, sore ni o-henji ga nai no de, **shashoku** shita genga wa ima kōjō ni aru ka ina ka fumei desu ga, IZURE NI SEYO genkō no zan'yo wa hozon shite arimasu kara, bunshō no **shashoku** wa isogi-susumemashō. Yotte, hyō no **kumi** ni tai-suru tōhō toi-awase, mata wa kihō no go-kibō o dai-shikyū o-shirase kudasai. Mata hachigatsumatsu shuppansha wa **kumi-han** nyūyō to no koto de arimasu ga, ima to natte wa ika ni isoide mo hachigatsumatsu ni wa muzukashii desu. Tonikaku, go-henji ari shidai isoide yarimasu. Honbun no kōsei dake wa sono mae ni okuru yō itashimashō.

Ijō tori-isogi go-henji made.

Sō-sō

Notes

a. KUDASARESHI A literary attributive form equivalent to *kudasareta* or *kudasatta*.

95. Letter from a University Teacher, the Wife of a Friend

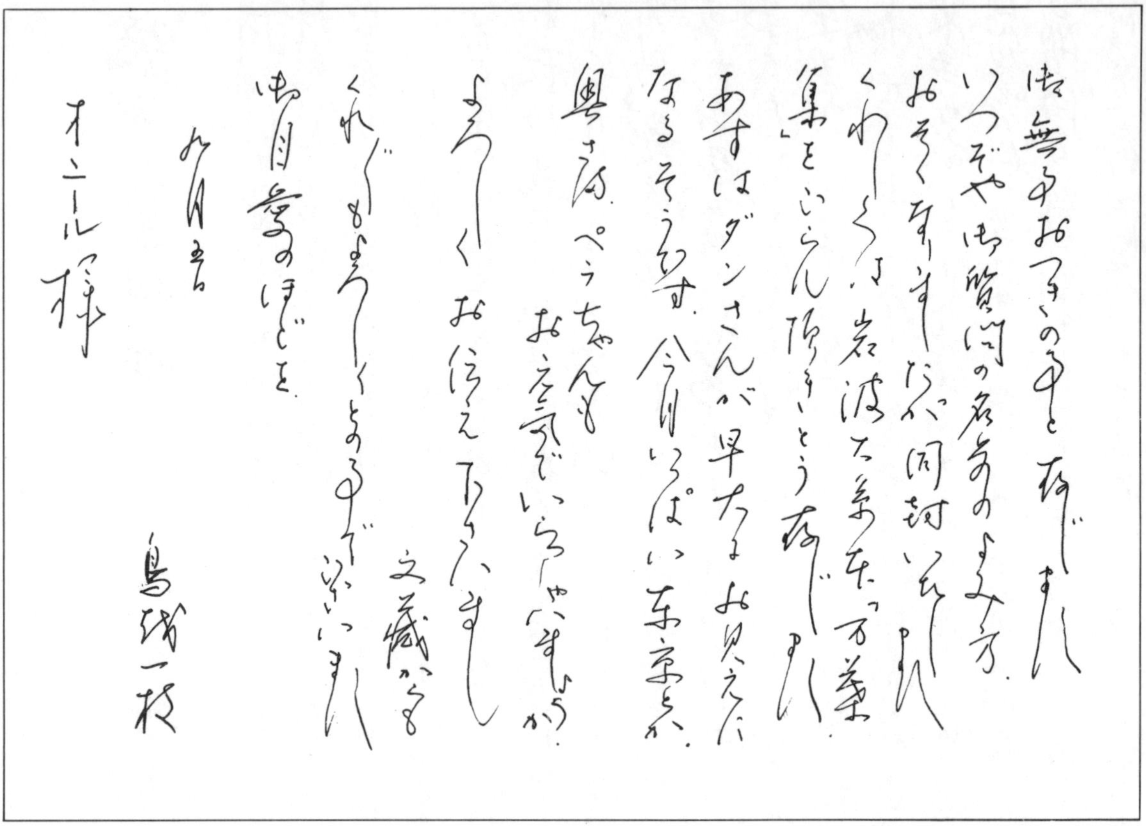
御無事お着きの事と存じます
いつぞや御質問の名前のよみ方、
おそくなりましたが同封いたします
くわしくは岩波大系本「万葉
集」をご覧頂きとう存じます
あすはダンさんが早大にお見えに
なるそうです。今月いっぱい東京とか.
奥さま、ペラちゃんも
お元気でいらっしゃいましょうか.
よろしくお伝え下さいまし
文蔵からも
くれぐれもよろしくとの事でございます
御自愛のほどを.
九月五日
鳥越一枝
オニール様

Go-buji o-tsuki no koto to zonjimasu. Itsuzoya go-shitsumon no namae no yomi-kata, osoku narimashita ga dōfū itashimasu. Kuwashiku wa **Iwanami** Taikei-bon "**Man'yōshū**" o goran itadakitō zonjimasu.

Asu wa **Dan**-san ga Sōdai ni o-mie ni naru sō desu. Kongetsu ippai **Tōkyō** to ka . . .

Oku-sama, **Pera**-CHAN mo o-genki de irasshaimashō ka. Yoroshiku o-tsutae kudasaimashi.

BUNZŌ KARA MO

kure-gure mo yoroshiku to no koto de gozaimasu.

Go-jiai no hodo o . . .

Kugatsu itsuka

Torigoe Kazue

Oniiru-sama

Notes

a. -CHAN A corruption of *-san*, this is a familiar ending associated particularly with children and used with relationship terms and (sometimes abbreviated) personal names. It closely parallels the feeling and usage of the English "-y" ending, as in "Daddy, Billy," etc.

b. BUNZŌ KARA MO The writer puts this phrase beginning with her husband's personal name at the bottom of the column to indicate humility (cf. 69d).

96. Letter from an Elderly Man of Slight Acquaintance

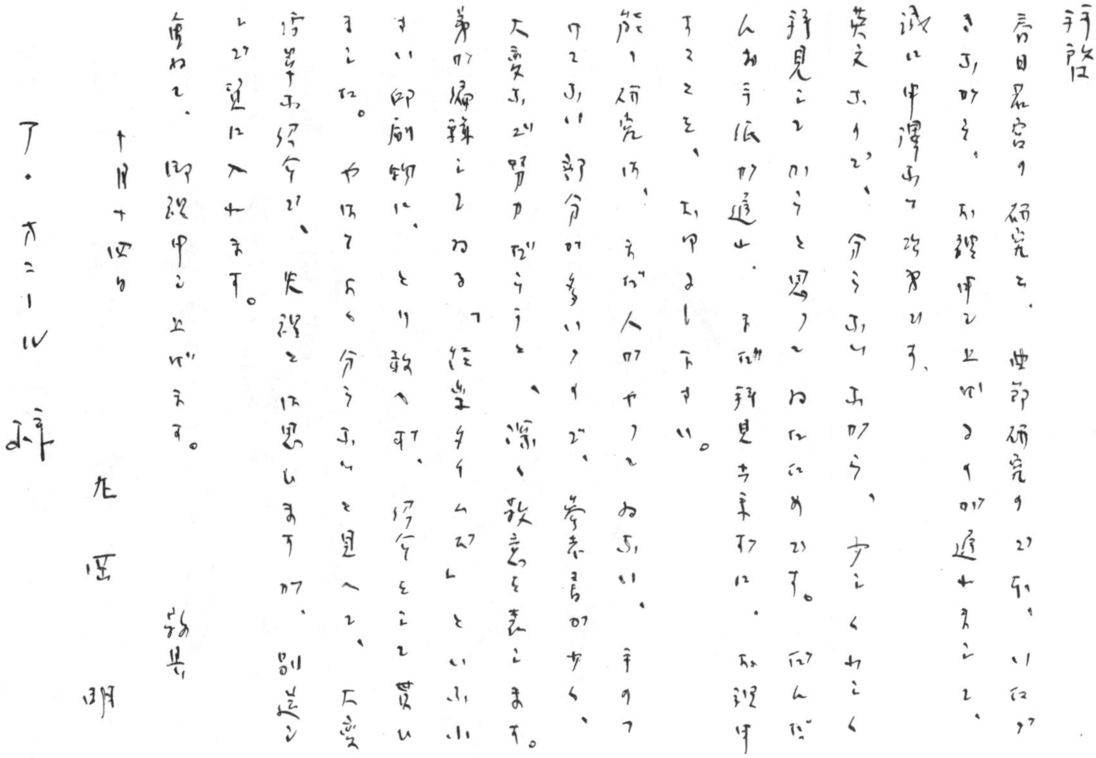

Haikei,

Kasuga Wakamiya no kenkyū to, kyokusetsu kenkyū no go-hon itadaki-nagara, o-rei mōshi-ageru no ga okuremashite, makoto ni mōshi-wake nai shidai desu.

Eibun na no de, wakaranai-nagara, sukoshi kuwashiku haiken shite kara to omotte ita tame desu. Dan-dan o-tegami ga okure, mada haiken dekizu ni, o-rei mōsu koto o, o-yurushi kudasai.

Nō no kenkyū wa, mada hito ga yatte inai, te no tsukete nai bubun ga ōi mono de, sankōsho ga sukunaku, taihen na go-doryoku darō to, fukaku keii o arawashimasu. Otōto ga henshū shite iru ''Nōgaku Taimuzu'' to iu chiisai insatsubutsu ni, tori-aezu, shōkai o shite moraimashita. Yahari yoku wakaranai to miete, taihen kantan na shōkai de, shitsurei to wa omoimasu ga, bessō shite GORAN NI IREMASU.

Kasanete, o-rei mōshi-agemasu.

Keigu

Maruoka Akira

Jūgatsu jūyokka
P. **Oniiru**-sama

Notes

a. GORAN NI IREMASU *Goran* ''(your, etc.) sight/seeing'' indicates respect to another person, and *goran ni ireru* therefore means ''put into your sight,'' i.e., ''show (to a respected person).''

97. Letter of Introduction from an Older Man Known for a Number of Years

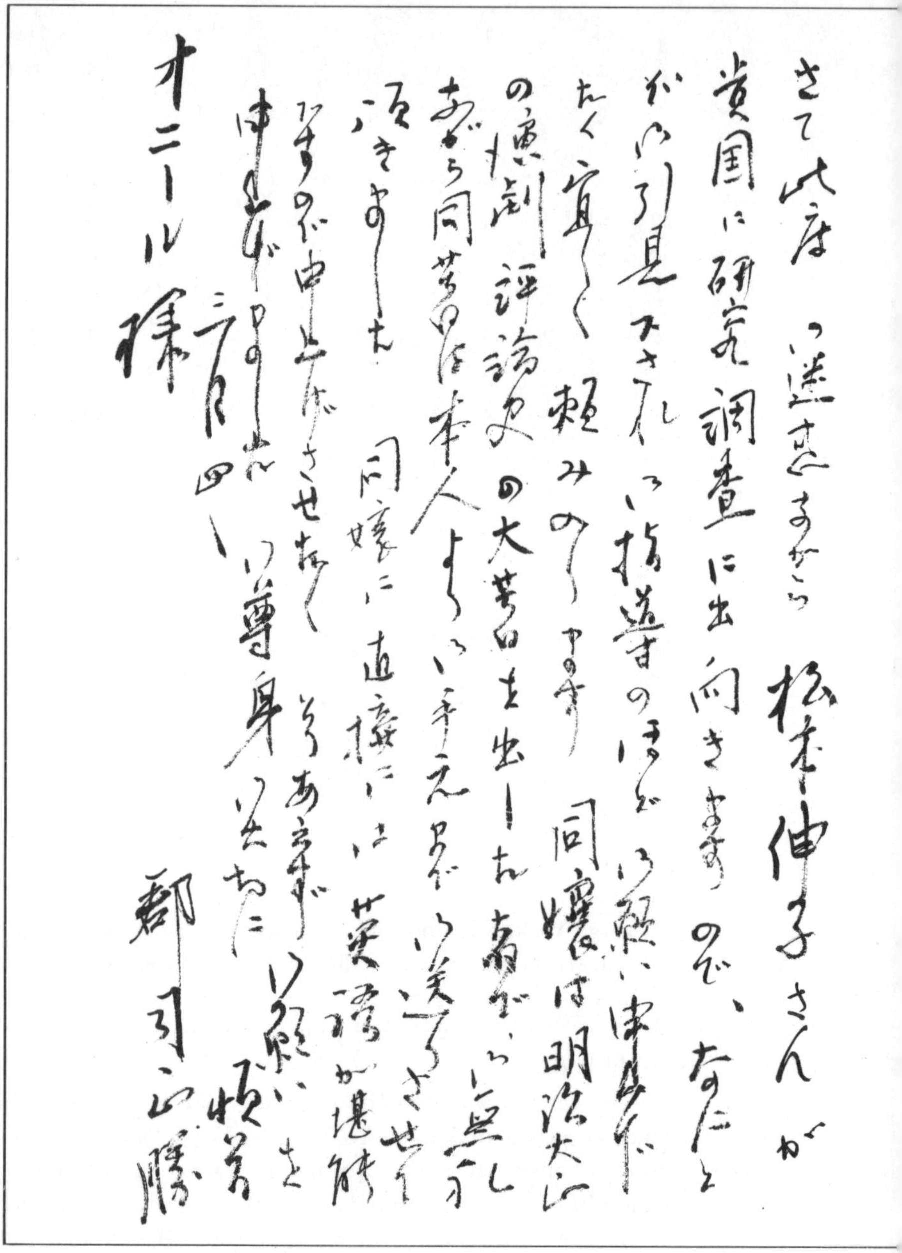
さて此度ご迷惑ながら松本伸子さんが
貴国に研究調査に出向きますので、なにとぞ
ご引見下されご指導のほどお願い申し上げ
たく宜しく頼み入ります　同嬢は明治大正
の演劇評論史の大著を出したもので　ご無礼
ながら同著は本人よりお手元まで

三月四日
郡司正勝
オニール様

Haikei,

Go-buin ni uchi-sugimashite, mōshi-wake gozaimasen. Go-kenkō nite go-shōjin no hodo to haisatsu mōshi-agemasu. Yatto Nihon mo haru o mukaeru kisetsu to natte mairimashita. NISHIURE no **Dengaku** ni go-issho shita koto ga yume no yō desu. Go-tōchi de wa taihen o-sewa ni ai-nari, makoto ni arigataku zonjimasu.

Sate, kono tabi go-meiwaku-nagara **Matsumoto Shinko**-san ga ki-koku ni kenkyū chōsa ni de-mukimasu no de, nani-tozo go-inken kudasar-e, go-shidō no hodo o-negai mōshi-age-taku yoroshiku tanomi-irimasu. Dōjō wa **Meiji Taishō** no engeki hyōron-shi no taicho o dashita mono de, go-burei-nagara dōcho wa honnin yori o-temoto made o-

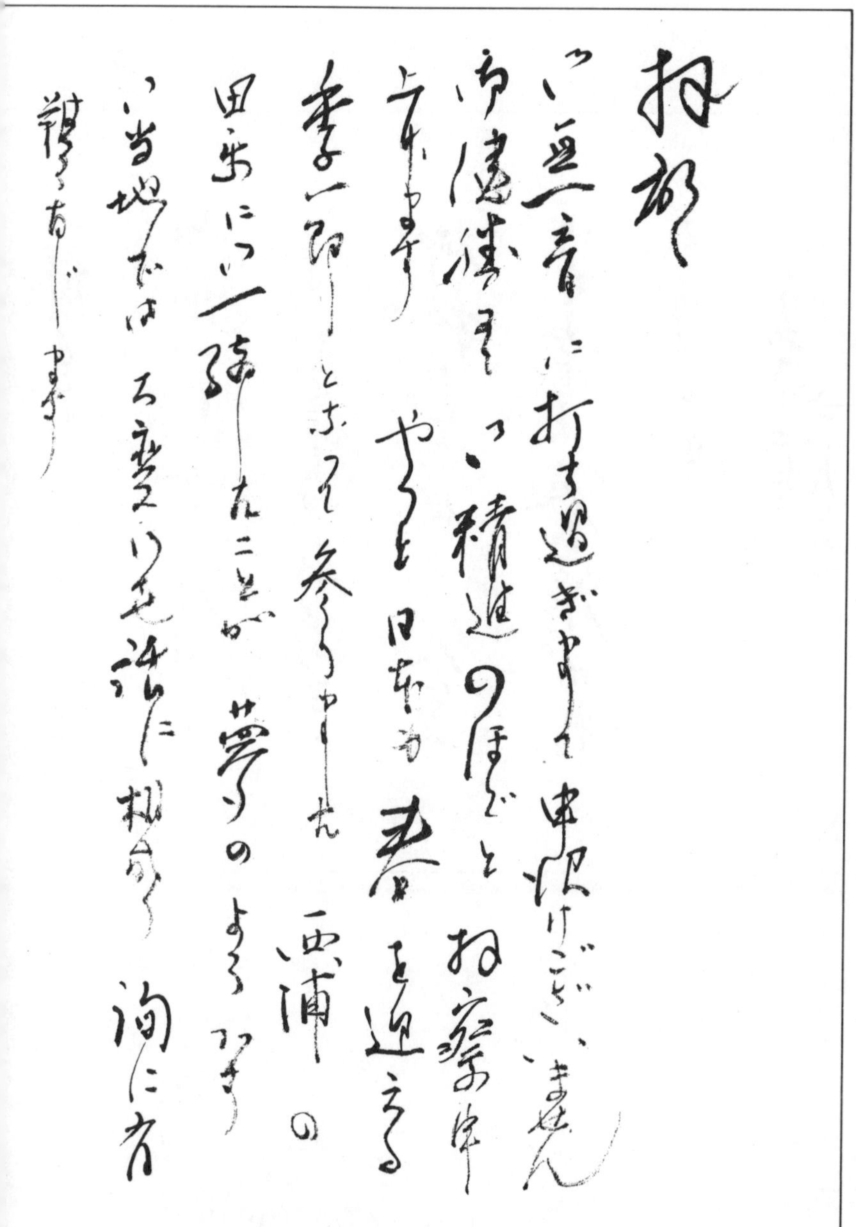

okuri sasete itadakimashita. Dōjō ni chokusetsu ni wa Eigo ga tannō desu no de mōshi-age-sase-taku, tori-aezu o-negai o mōshi-agemashita. Go-sonmi go-taisetsu ni. . .

Sangatsu yokka

TONSHU

Gunji Masakatsu

Oniiru-sama

Notes

a. NISHIURE Although this is the name of the place in question, the usual reading of the characters is *Nishiura*.

b. TONSHU "With bowed head, with respect"; cf. *tonshu saihai* 9c.

98. Letter from an Elderly Man

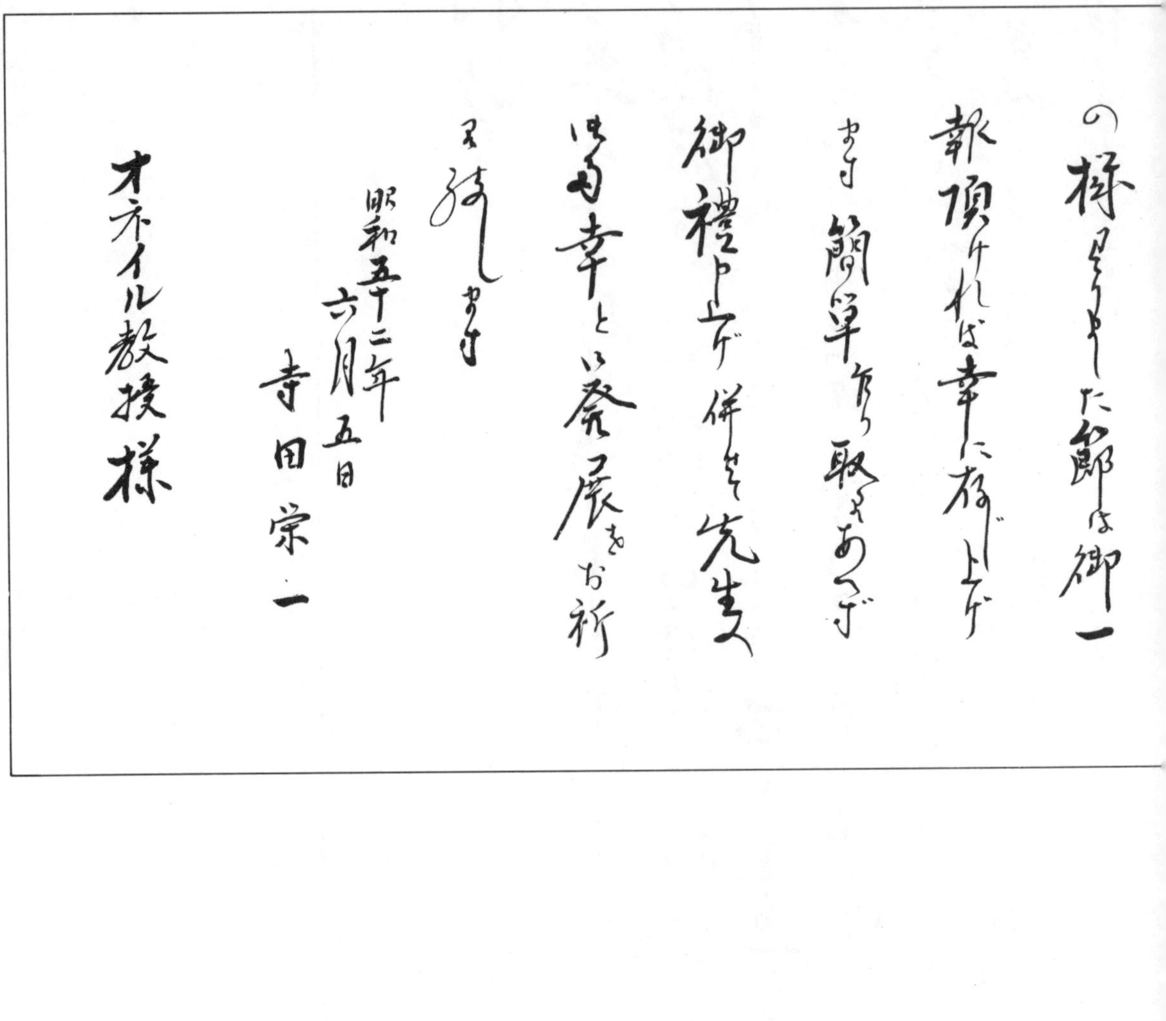

の機ありました節は御一
報頂ければ幸に存じ上げ
ます 簡単乍ら取りあへず
御礼申上げ併せて先生
の御多幸と御発展をお祈
り致します

昭和五十二年 六月五日

寺田宗一

オネイル教授様

Zenryaku

WATAKUSHI-GI

on-chi Rondon ni taizai-chū wa kōshi-tomo ni shu-ju go-kōhai narabi ni hitokata-naranu go-kōjō o KATAJIKENŌ SHI, makoto ni ARIgataku atsuku o-rei mōshi-agemasu. O-kage O MOCHIMASHITE tochū tsutsuga naku buji kikoku itashimashita yue, taji-nagara go-kyūshin kudasai. Sensei go-**rai-Nichi** no ki arimashita setsu wa go-ippō itadakereba saiwai ni zonji-agemasu. Kantan-nagara tori-aezu o-rei mōshi-ag-e, awasete sensei no go-takō to go-hatten o o-inori itashimasu.

Shōwa gojūninen
Rokugatsu itsuka

Terada Sōichi

Oneiru Kyōju-sama

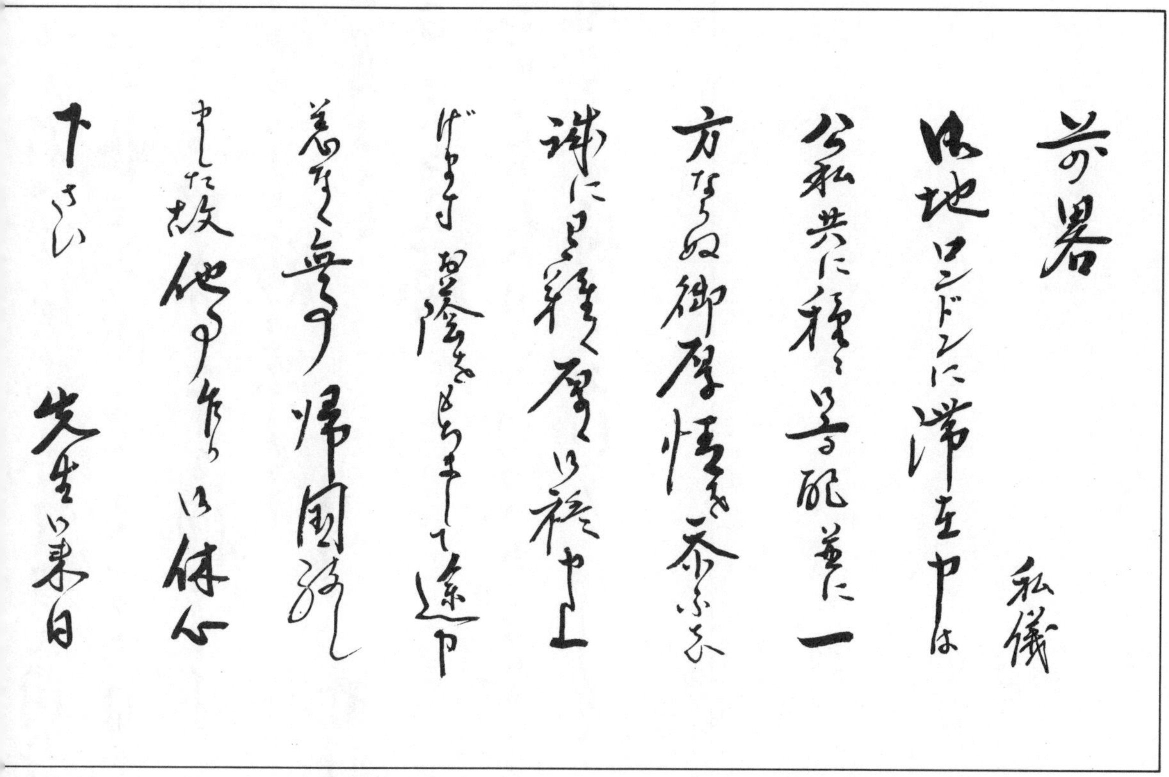

Notes

a. WATAKUSHI-GI On the position of this term at the bottom of the page, see 69d. The literary suffix *-gi* has much the same meaning as (*no koto*) *wa*; thus here, "(As for me,) I . . ."; cf. *-koto* under 20a.

b. KATAJIKENŌ SHI Since *katajikenō suru*, "be favored/honored with," is a contraction of *katajikenaku suru* by the omission of the final k, the correct *kana* spelling of the first word has always been 忝う.

c. ARI The character used here, before the *hiragana* sign for *ri*, is an extreme form of 有; cf. the same form in *arimashita setsu* in line 10 of this same letter, and as a *hentai-gana* for *u* in App. IV.

d. O MOCHIMASHITE The polite *-masu* form of *o motte*, "with, through" (see 30b).

99. Letter from an Older Man of Slight Acquaintance

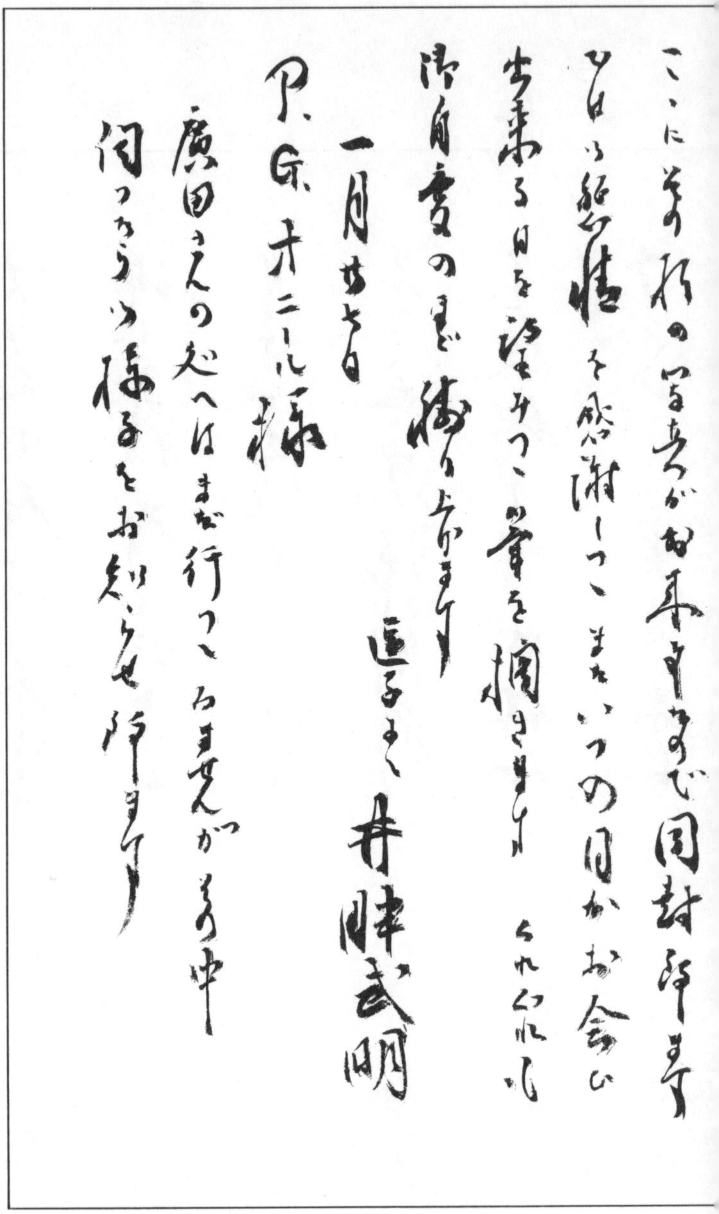
ここにその折の写真が出来ましたので同封致します
御厚情を感謝しつつまたいつの日かお会い
出来る日を望みつつ筆を擱きます　くれぐれも
御自愛のほど祈ります
一月廿三日　　匆々　井畔武明
P. G. オニール様
原田さんの処へはまだ行っておりませんが其の中
伺つてから様子をお知らせ致します

Kahan wa yukuri-naku mo **Rondon** nite o-ai suru kikai o megumar-e, makoto ni ureshiku zonjimashita. O-isogashii naka o waza-waza tōyō bumon no toshokan made go-annai kudasar-e, o-kage o motte tan-jikan de wa arimashita ga, mina-sama no go-kensan no moyō o ukagai-ete shiawase ni zonjimashita. Sono setsu wa KUSE-MAI no kenkyū ni tsuite no ki-ronbun o keizō kudasar-e, arigatō gozaimashita. Watakushi wa nenmatsu ni kikoku itashimashita ga, iro-iro to ato-shimatsu ni bōsatsu sar-e, o-reijō mo sashi-agezu shitsurei shite orimashita tokoro, kaette mata KOI NO OMONI, YUYA no go-hon'yaku o o-okuri kudasar-e, kasane-gasane no go-konjō makoto ni arigataku zonji-agemasu.

Koko ni sono ori no shashin ga dekimashita no de, dōfū itashimasu. De wa go-konjō o kansha shi-tsutsu, mata itsu no hi ka o-ai dekiru hi o nozomi-tsutsu fude o okimasu.

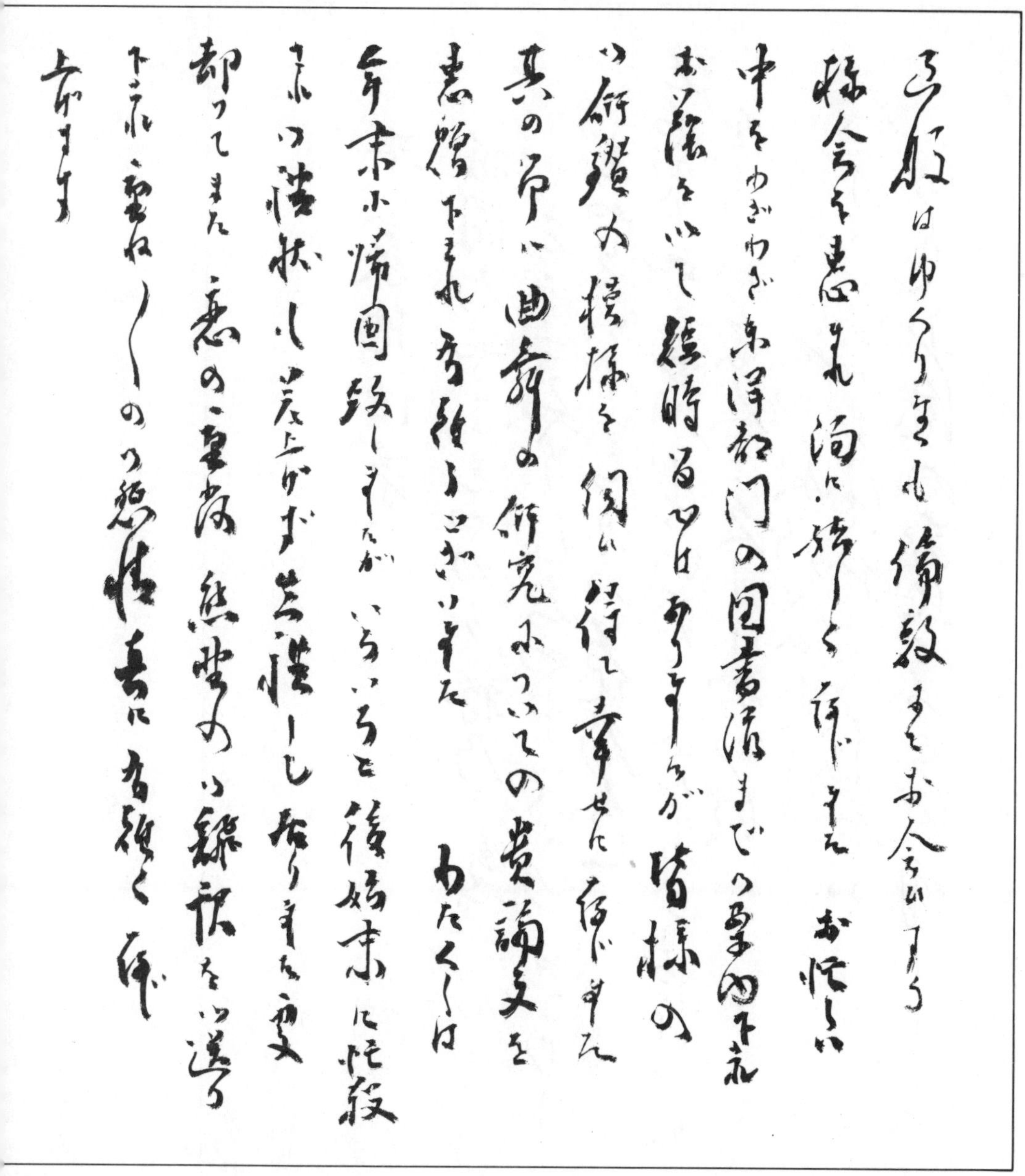

今般はゆくりなくも御縁あつてお会いする
機会を恵まれ洵に嬉しく存じました　お忙しい
中をわざわざ東洋部門の図書館までの案内下され
お蔭をもって短時間ではありましたが皆様の
ご研鑽の模様を伺い得て幸せに存じました
其の節は曲舞の研究についての貴論文を
恵贈下され有難うございました　わたくしは
年末に帰国致しましたがいろいろと後始末に忙殺
されて[illegible]も出来上がらず[illegible]し居りました処
却つてまた恋の重荷熊野の翻訳を送り
下され重ね〴〵の御厚情まことに有難く存
[illegible]ます

Kure-gure mo go-jiai no hodo inori-agemasu.

Ichigatsu nijūshichinichi

Zushi nite

Iguro Takeaki

P.G. **Oniiru**-sama

Hirota-san no tokoro e wa mada itte imasen ga, sono uchi ukagattara, go-yōsu o o-shirase itashimasu.

Notes

a. KUSE-MAI 曲舞; a medieval song and dance form.

b. KOI NO OMONI, YUYA 恋の重荷, 熊野; the names of two Nō plays. "Yuya" is the name of the main character in the second, but the common reading of the characters, as a place-name for example, would be "Kumano."

100. Two Extracts from Classical Literature

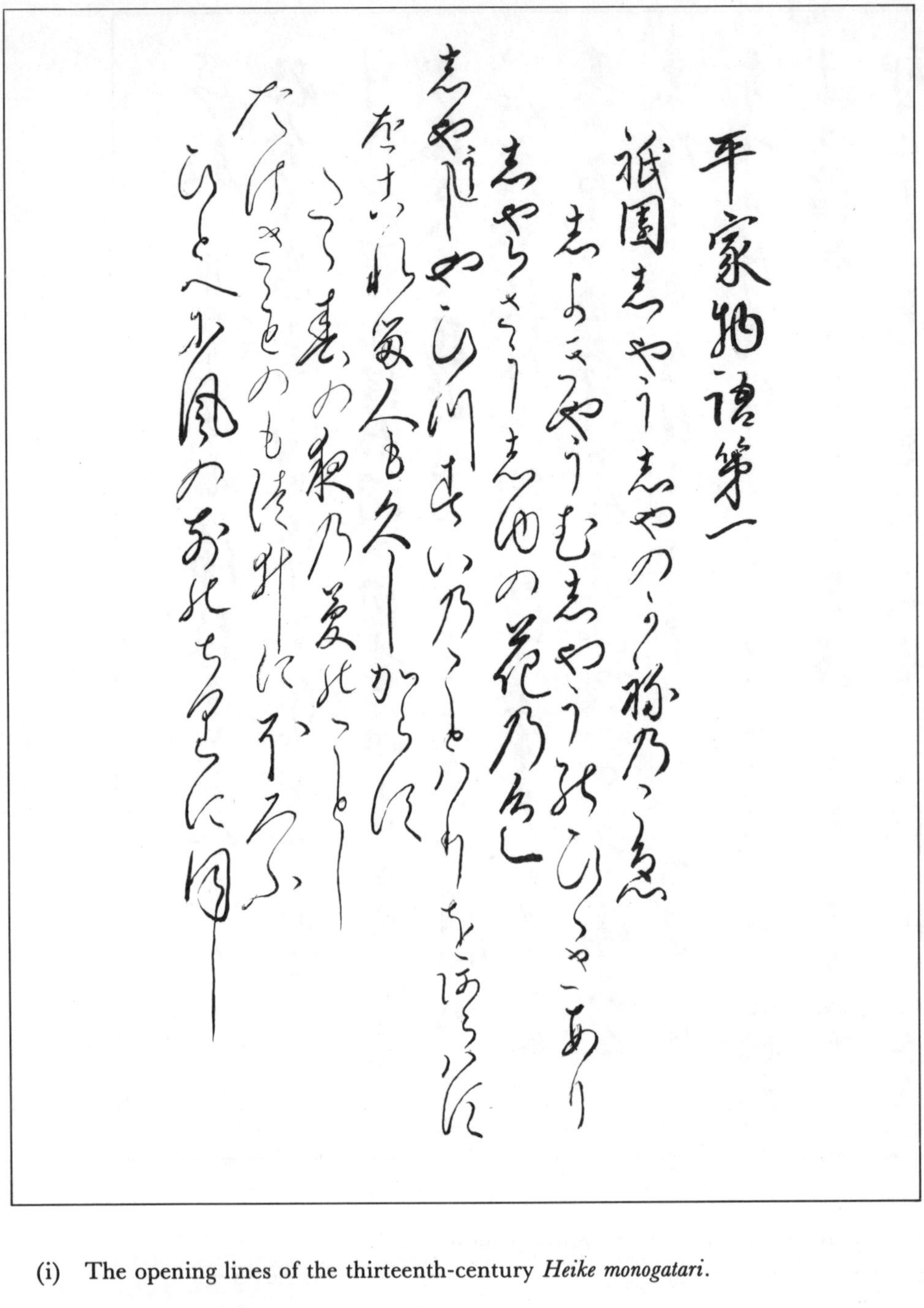

(i) The opening lines of the thirteenth-century *Heike monogatari.*

GION SHŌJA no kane no koe
  Shogyō mujō no hibiki ari.
SHARA SŌJU no hana no iro
  Jōsha hissui no kotowari o arawasu.
Ogoreru hito mo hisashikarazu,
  Tada haru no yo no yume no gotoshi.
Takeki mono mo tsui ni horobu.
  Hitoe ni kaze no mae no chiri ni onaji.

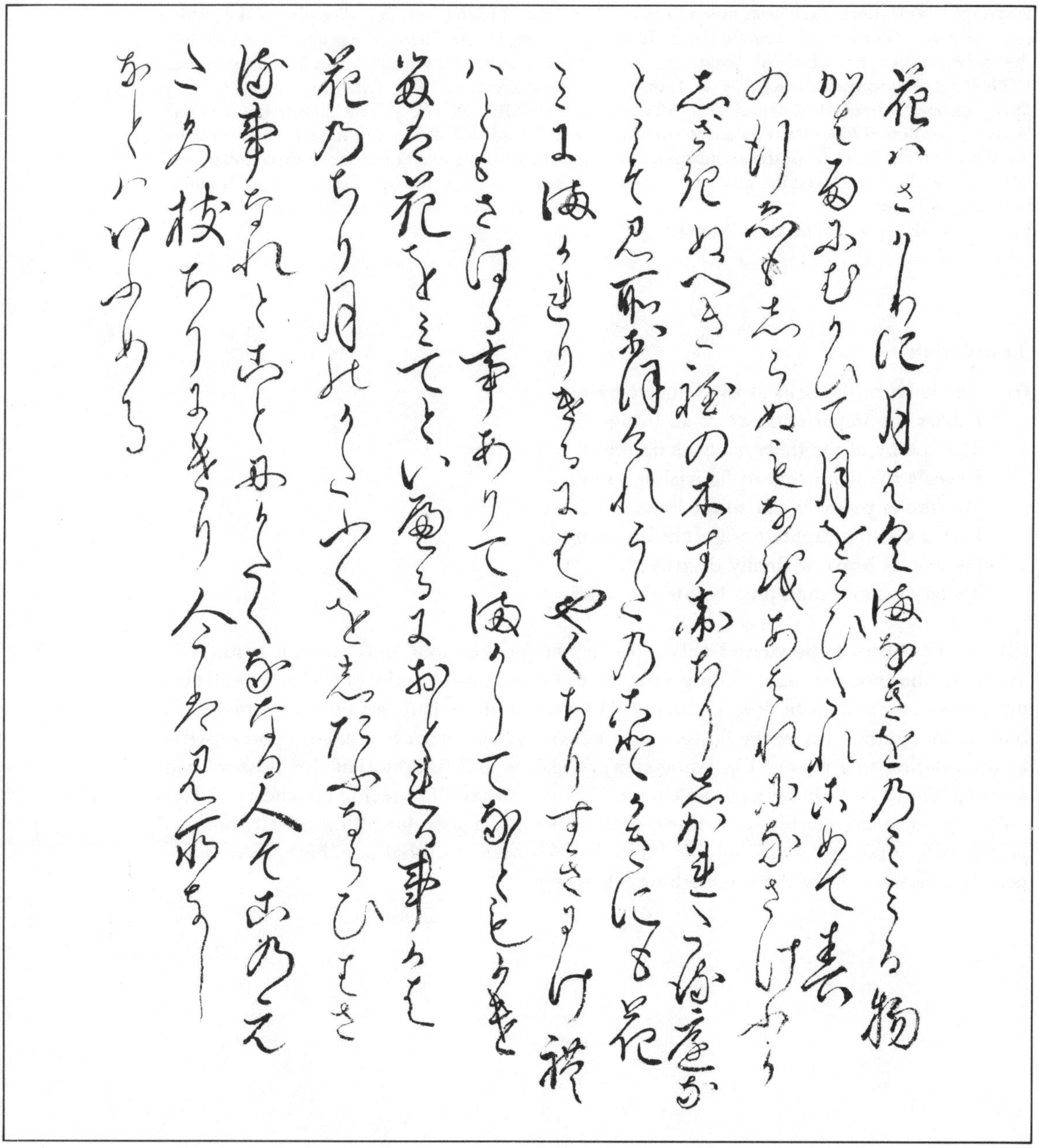

(ii) The opening lines of Section 137 of the *Tsurezure-gusa*, written about 1330.

Hana wa sakari ni, tsuki wa kuma naki o nomi miru mono ka wa. Ame ni mukaite tsuki o koi, tare-komete haru no yukishi mo shiranu mo, nao aware ni nasake fukashi. Sakinu-beki hodo no kozue chirishi karetaru niwa nado koso midokoro ōkere. Uta no koto-gaki ni mo, ''Hana-mi ni makarerikeru ni, hayaku chiri-suginikereba'' to mo, ''Suwaru koto arite makarade'' nado mo kakeru wa, ''Hana o mite'' to ieru ni otoreru koto ka wa. Hana no chiri, tsuki no katabuku o shitau narai wa saru koto naredo, koto ni katakuna naru hito zo, ''Kono eda, kano eda chirinikeri. Ima wa midokoro nashi'' nado wa iumeru.

Notes

a. Since both these passages are in the classical language, translations have been given here instead of notes. (For a self-instructional guide to the grammar of the classical language, see O'Neill: *A Programmed Introduction to Literary-Style Japanese*, School of Oriental and African Studies, London, 1968.) Both passages contain some slight differences from the standard texts, but the handwritten versions have of course been followed here.

b. GION SHŌJA "The Gion Monastery," which was built in Central India by a rich man for the Buddha and his disciples. Like other passages in the *Heike Monogatari*, this opening section is in a rhythmic prose based on a line unit of seven and five syllables.

c. SHARA SŌJU "The double-trunked sal tree," traditionally said to have had two trunks growing out in each of the four directions, and to have been the tree beneath which the Buddha was lying when he entered Nirvana.

Translation

(i) The knell of the bells at the Gion temple
Echoes the impermanence of all things.
The colour of the flowers on its double-trunked tree
Reveals the truth that to flourish is to fall.
He who is proud is not so for long,
Like a passing dream on a night in spring.
He who is brave is finally destroyed,
To be no more than dust before the wind.

(ii) Is the cherry to be viewed only at its height, or the moon only when it is full? To yearn for the moon through falling rain, or to be shut away indoors and miss spring's passing can be still more deeply moving. How much there is to see on branches still in bud, or in a garden where the flowers have fallen and withered. Is it not as good to write as the heading to a poem "On going cherry-viewing and finding that the blossom had already fallen" or "On being unable to go," as it is to say "On seeing the cherry"? It is only natural to feel longing when flowers fall or the moon goes down, but a really boorish person will, it seems, say things like "This branch here, and that one there, have dropped their flowers. Now there is nothing left to see."

APPENDIXES

APPENDIX I

AN OUTLINE OF RESPECT LANGUAGE

The area of Japanese called 'respect language' (*keigo*) or 'levels of speech' is simply a system of showing respect, or a lack of it, to the persons concerned when a statement is made, by using special forms of the language. The persons concerned are primarily the speaker or writer and the person addressed (the 1st and 2nd persons respectively), and often some other person (a 3rd person) who is involved as a topic of discussion, and the forms of language used to express levels of respect depend on the relationships among these three people. This language usage can be as subtle and complicated as these relationships, and reference should be made to other accounts of respect language* for fuller coverage of the system; but the intention here is to provide a basic understanding of it which will be reinforced and supplemented by notes on the forms as they occur in material in this book.

It is important, in any case, not to be frightened by the details of respect language and to remember always that its purpose is very simple: to enable a speaker to be respectful or otherwise to, first of all, the person he is talking *to*, and also to the person he is talking *about*, who is often the subject of his sentence. In fact, one has only to know (i) that *iku* and *ikimasu* are the same in meaning and differ solely in that the *-masu* ending makes *ikimasu* polite to the person being addressed, and (ii) that *irassharu* is an honorific verb (that is, one which shows respect to its grammatical subject), for it to be possible to illustrate the fundamentals of respect language by means of two or three simple sentences:

Tomodachi mo ikimasu "My friend will go too"

in which the use of the ordinary 'neutral' verb *ik(u)* indicates no particular attitude on the part of the speaker towards his own friend, whereas the *-masu* ending shows his politeness to the person addressed; and

Sensei mo irassharu "The teacher will go too"

in which the use of the honorific verb *irassharu* conveys the speaker's respect for the teacher, while its 'plain' dictionary form, without any *-masu* ending, shows that the person he is talking to—a classmate, perhaps—is not felt to warrant any expression of respect.

Sometimes, of course, the person spoken to and the person spoken about will be one and the same, and respect to this 2nd person can then be expressed by a combination of honorific verb and polite ending. For example,

Sensei mo irasshaimasen ka 'Won't you go too, teacher/sir?"

Bearing in mind these two functions of respect language, to express respect to someone referred to in a statement (the referrent), who is often its grammatical subject, and politeness to the person addressed, let us look more closely at how such respect and politeness can be shown.

1. Respect to the Referrent

Essentially, there are three levels of language which can be used of the referrent: a 'neutral' one, like the use of *ik(u)* above, which does not indicate any more respect or

*For example, Gardner and Martin: *Honorific and familiar speech in Japanese*, New Haven, 1952; O'Neill: *A programmed course on respect language in modern Japanese*, London, 1966 and Tokyo, 1983; Miller: 'Levels of speech (*keigo*) and the Japanese linguistic response to modernization' in Shiveley (ed.): *Tradition and modernization in Japanese culture*, Princeton, 1972.

humility on the part of the speaker than "go" does in English; an 'honorific' one, like the forms of *irassharu* in the sentences above, which simply shows the respect of the speaker by elevating the status of the person concerned (the grammatical subject, in the case of verbs); and a 'humble' one, which lowers the status of the person concerned and thereby raises the relative status of someone else who is involved. A simple example of these same three levels is to be found in the common words for 'person' in Japanese: the neutral-level *hito* has the honorific and humble equivalents *kata* and *mono* respectively.

The heart of the system of respect language, however, lies in the honorific and humble verbs which, except for a limited number of special ones, are variants of the ordinary neutral-level verbs such as *kaku*, "write," and *matsu*, "wait," familiar to any student of Japanese.

HONORIFIC VERBS

In any language it is the most common verbs which are likely to maintain their irregularities, and in Japanese respect language a number of these verbs have separate, different-looking equivalents. *Suru*, "do," for example, has *nasaru*, "(kindly) do," and *itasu*, "(humbly) do," as its honorific and humble equivalents.

All other verbs, however, have equivalents formed according to standard patterns. The first and main honorific one consists of a verbal noun in the form of the honorific prefix *o-* and the verb-stem (that is, the stem which takes *-masu*), and the honorific verb *nasaru*, "(kindly) do," (or its alternative *ni naru*), so that the combination *o-* verb-stem *nasaru/ni naru* means literally "(kindly) do a . . . ing." *Matsu*, "wait," thus has an honorific equivalent *o-machi nasaru/ni naru*, "(kindly) do a waiting," that is, "(kindly) wait." Similarly, since *nasai* is an imperative form of *nasaru*, *O-yasumi nasai*, "Good-night," literally means "Do (kindly) rest."

The other standard form of honorific is the *-(ra)reru* passive/potential endings, which can likewise express respect for their subject; for example, *Sensei wa mō kaeraremashita*, "The teacher has already gone home."

HUMBLE VERBS

Since honorific verbs raise the status of their subjects, it follows that any verb in Japanese that can have a person as its subject can have an honorific equivalent, showing the speaker's respect for its subject. Humble verbs, on the other hand, lower the status of their subjects in order to raise the relative status—and thus show respect to—someone else involved in the action of the verb. It is therefore only possible to have a humble form of verb when its action involves some such other person.

When this is so, certain verbs have separate verbs as their humble equivalents but the majority use a standard form, just as in the case of honorifics. The same honorific verbal-nouns (*o-* verb-stem) are used, because of the connection with the other person, but the following verb is the neutral *suru*, "do," or the humble *itasu*, "(humbly) do," giving this standard form a literal meaning of "(humbly) do a . . .ing (for/with the other person)." The humble equivalents of *matsu*, "wait," for example, are *o-machi suru/itasu* "(I, etc., humbly) wait (for him/you, etc.)," and those of *motsu*, "hold, carry," are *o-mochi suru/itasu*, "(I, etc.) will hold/carry it (for him/you, etc.)."

2. Respect to the Addressee

There are certain endings and verbs which are normally used only towards the person addressed. The 'polite' *-masu* endings are the most obvious examples of these and, together with the 'plain' dictionary forms of verbs, provide two levels of respect to the addressee. But there is also a third available for most verbs, which shows the greatest degree of deference for the addressee and can therefore be described as being at the 'deferential' level.

For example, the *o-* verb-stem *suru/itasu* humble form showing respect to a person involved in the action other than the subject has a deferential level which replaces the *suru/itasu* by the very humble verb *mōshi-agemasu*. Thus, while forms of *o-negai* (etc.)

suru/itasu can be used to show respect to any person other than the subject, *o-negai* (etc.) *mōshi-agemasu* is only used to show the utmost politeness to the 2nd person.

Another group of verbs which have a deferential level are those of the *benkyō suru* type where, unlike the *renraku suru* "make contact (with . . .)" type, the action of the verb—"studying" in this particular case—can hardly be thought of as being done for the benefit of, or in connection with, anyone else. To show respect to the 2nd person, this type of verb can take forms of *itashimasu* as the deferential level.

The most common verbs at this level, however, are those complementing the plain/polite pairs *aru/arimasu*, "exist, have," and *da/desu* (equivalent to the more formal *de aru/de arimasu*), "be"; namely, *gozaimasu* and *de gozaimasu* respectively. Thus, whereas *aru*, "There is, I have it/some," indicates a familiarity with, or an absence of respect for the addressee, *gozaimasu* has the same meaning but shows a completely different attitude to the 2nd person.

It must be noted that, because the deferentials are extremely humble forms and lower the status of their subjects in order to elevate the relative status of the addressee, it would make no sense to use them or any other humble verb when the 2nd person is himself the subject. While this is essentially true of the (*de*) *gozaimasu* forms, they offer such a convenient and therefore widely used alternative to *desu* that their range of usage has spread somewhat. The present situation seems to be that, although no educated Japanese would use *de gozaimasu* with a noun referring directly to the 2nd person or anyone closely connected with him—that is to say, *Sensei de gozaimasu ka*, "Are you a teacher?" is not acceptable as an alternative to the straightforward honorific *Sensei de irasshaimasu ka*—(*de*) *gozaimasu* is widely used with adjectives and inanimate objects, even when they relate closely to the 2nd person or his close associates.

The (*de*) *gozaimasu* forms, then, also provide a deferential level for adjectives: with '*na* adjectives,' *de gozaimasu* simply replaces *desu* (e.g., *jōbu de gozaimasu*, "it is strong"); but with the other type of '*-i* adjectives,' *gozaimasu* is used after the long-vowel forms obtained by dropping the *k* from the adverbial *-ku* form (e.g., *takaku*>*takau* = *takō gozaimasen*, "it is not high/expensive"; *ureshiku*>*ureshiu* = *ureshū gozaimasu*, "I am so happy"; and of course *arigatō gozaimasu*, "I am thankful/grateful to you, Thank you."

Incidentally, some of these long-vowel forms may also be found before another deferential verb, *zonjimasu*, which is equivalent to *shiru*, "know," or *omou*, "think, feel, hope": *arigatō zonjimasu*, "I feel thankful/grateful to you," for example, is an even more humble equivalent of *arigatō gozaimasu*, as is the unchanged form *arigataku zonjimasu*.

The following table lists for reference the various neutral, honorific and humble verbs by which the speaker can choose whether or not to express respect for some other person (including the 2nd person), and the plain, polite and deferential levels by which he can choose whether or not to express politeness to the 2nd person only. The variety may at first seem rather daunting, but there are explanations for all the examples in the texts and it will help to remember that all verbs except those listed separately have standard honorific, humble and deferential equivalents, and that these equivalents are easily recognizable because they all use the same kind of verbal noun with honorific or humble verbs meaning "do."

TABLE I: VERBS AND LEVELS USED IN RESPECT LANGUAGE

V E R B S of respect to another person			L E V E L S of politeness to person addressed		
NEUTRAL (No expression of respect or humility)	**HONORIFIC (Respect to subject)**	**HUMBLE (Subject depreciated, for respect to another person)**	**DEFERENTIAL (Marked respect and politeness to 2nd person only)**	**POLITE (Generally polite, with any subject)**	**PLAIN (Used to familiars or subordinates, with any subject)**
All verbs except:	o-vb. stem *ni naru/nasaru*; -*(ra)reru* endings	*o*-vb. stem *suru/itasu*	*o*-vb. stem *mōshi-agemasu* except:	-*masu* forms of any verb	dictionary forms of any verb
aru	*o-ari ni n.*	*(aru)*	**gozaimasu* [*aru*]		
da, de aru	*de irassharu*	*(da, de aru)*	**de gozaimasu* [*no, na, de aru*]		
iku	*irassharu, oide ni n.*	*(iku)*	**mairimasu*		
iru	*irassharu, oide ni n.*	*(iru)*	**orimasu*		
kuru	*irassharu, oide ni n.*	*(kuru)*	**mairimasu*		
iu	*ossharu*	*mōshi-ageru*	**mōshimasu*		
ageru	*o-age ni n.*	'give' only: *ageru, sashi-ageru*			
yaru	*o-yari ni n.*				
au	*o-ai ni n.*	*o-ai s./it.*, 'meet person' only: *o-me ni kakaru*			
benkyō (etc.) *suru*	*go-benkyō nasaru*	*(benkyō suru)*	*benkyō itashimasu*		
renraku (etc.) *suru*	*go-renraku nasaru*	*go-renraku s./it.*	*go-renraku mōshi-agemasu*		
kiru 'wear'	*mesu, o-meshi ni n.*	*(kiru)*			
yobu	*o-yobi ni n., mesu, o-meshi ni n.*	*o-yobi s./it.*	*o-yobi mōshi-agemasu*		
kariru	*o-kari ni n.*	*haishaku s./it.*	*haishaku mōshi-agemasu*		
kureru	*kudasaru*	———	———		
miru	*goran ni n.*	*haiken s./it.*			
miseru	*o-mise ni n.*	*o-me ni kakeru, goran ni kakeru/ireru*			
morau	*o-morai ni n.*				
taberu	*agaru, o-agari ni n., meshi-agaru*	*itadaku, chōdai s./it.*			
nomu	*o-nomi ni n., agaru, o-agari ni n., meshi-agaru*				
shinu	*o-nakunari ni n.*	*(shinu)*			
nakunaru	*o-nakunari ni n.*	*(nakunaru)*			
shiru	*go-zonji ni n.*	*(shiru)*	*zonjimasu*		
omou	*o-omoi ni n.*	*(omou)*			
suru	*nasaru*	*itasu*			

Notes

* = Usable with all subjects (including impersonal ones) except the person addressed and his close associates.

ni n. = *ni naru/nasaru*

s./it. = *suru/itasu*

(   ) When used with a verb, indicates that the verb is used when there is no special humble form.

[   ] Indicates words which replace dictionary forms before nouns, etc.

APPENDIX II

THE OLD AND NEW FORMS OF CHARACTERS

When a list of 1,850 basic characters recommended for general use was promulgated in 1947 under the name of *tōyō kanji*, 740 of them were amendments of the traditional forms, based mainly on common handwritten abbreviations, which were intended to bring closer together the printed and handwritten forms of the most important characters. These amended forms have since become well established as the modern standard ones and were continued without question in the later 1981 list of *jōyō kanji*, "characters for common use," which totalled just under 2,000 in number.

The adoption of more simple forms for basic characters seemed admirable, but it was not without its disadvantages. Apart from the less attractive appearance of some of the amended forms—which in any case are generally a great deal better than their modern Chinese equivalents—readers still have to recognize the traditional forms if they are to read freely anything published before 1947 or the surprisingly large number of words, mostly proper names, which use them even today. Then too, when a phonetic element in a character was amended, the change sometimes made reading and writing more difficult by obscuring the association between a particular element and its Sino-Japanese reading. Also, although the amendments were officially limited to the lists of basic characters, the general public and even publishers and printers understandably extended them by analogy to similar elements in characters outside the lists. The result is that there are now three main types of characters in use in Japan today: the full traditional forms; the officially amended forms of certain characters within the official lists; and the unofficially amended forms of some characters outside these lists.

The offically amended forms themselves are not without their inconsistencies. For example, 來 was amended to 来 as an independent character and usually as a combined element, but 麥 became 麦; 專 was amended in three different ways in various characters; and although repeated elements in such characters as 壘 and 澁 were mostly indicated by pairs of converging lines, as 塁 and 渋, etc., 疊 became 畳 and 參 became 参 .

The situation for the student of Japanese is not, however, as bad as it might seem. Many of the 740 or so present-day amendments are not worthy of special note because they are so trivial that they can hardly cause any problem of recognition: 鑑, for example, is now officially 鑑, 俗 is 俗, and 嘆 is 嘆 ; and what used to be two horizontal lines at the top of a character or component, as in 言 音 商 , etc., now has an official printed form as a dot and a line, as in 言 音 商, etc. Also, in spite of some inconsistencies and illogicalities, the amendments do present generally standard patterns which reduce considerably the problems of equating old forms with the modern amended ones normally learned first. Thus, a familiarity with the most important amendments will, by extension in some cases to similar elements in other characters, cover a large proportion of the old forms that will be met. To this end, a selected list of sixty such characters is given below.

Characters which are amended in their modern forms can conveniently be grouped into four types: (1) those in which elements have been *simplified*, recognizably on the basis of their original forms; (2) those in which elements have been *replaced* by others having no obvious similarity to the original forms; (3) those in which elements have simply been *omitted*; and (4) a very small number of characters with *miscellaneous* other changes, in most cases an added stroke to make a component conform to a more common one. Significant changes in these modern forms have been given in the tables below: the first lists the sixty most important characters which have been amended, and the others illustrate these four types of change, with characters arranged in related groups to show the standard patterns, and up to five examples given for each group.

There is, of course, no need to learn to write the old full forms, unless you wish to do this as a way of familiarizing yourself with them, but it is important to be able to recognize them, both for the considerations mentioned above and because, in the case of handwritten Japanese, they may still appear in the writing of older people and it is from them that many of the cursive forms derive. In the tables below these older forms have therefore been given above the amended ones, so that it is easy to test your recognition of them by covering up the latter. It is recommended, though, that you first go through the list of sixty important amended characters and then, when you are familiar with these, check the tables of grouped characters from time to time until you can readily equate the older forms with their modern ones. In this way, you will soon recognize the standard patterns which account for the majority of the amended forms, and gradually learn also the original forms of the characters which occur only in smaller groups or even singly.

TABLE I: SIXTY IMPORTANT AMENDMENTS

乘	亂	佛	來	假	應	拜	數	會	條	當	發	益	眞	社
乗	乱	仏	来	仮	応	拝	数	会	条	当	発	益	真	社
傳	區	單	勞	國	樂	歸	氣	濱	爭	豫	賣	輕	轉	送
伝	区	単	労	国	楽	帰	気	浜	争	予	売	軽	転	送
圓	圖	團	學	實	禮	縣	缺	聲	臺	醫	鐵	關	雜	餘
円	図	団	学	実	礼	県	欠	声	台	医	鉄	関	雑	余
寫	寶	將	對	廣	舊	萬	藝	號	變	館	驛	體	黑	點
写	宝	将	対	広	旧	万	芸	号	変	館	駅	体	黒	点

TABLE II: SIMPLIFICATIONS

悅	稅	脫	說	銳	券	卷	圈	勝		僧	增	憎	層	贈
悦	税	脱	説	鋭	券	巻	圏	勝		僧	増	憎	層	贈
	咲	送	遂	隊		平	坪	評			黑	墨	默	
	咲	送	遂	隊		平	坪	評			黒	墨	黙	
	半	判	伴	畔		兼	廉	謙			練	鍊	欄	
	半	判	伴	畔		兼	廉	謙			練	錬	欄	
	肖	削	消	硝		益	猛		尊		勳	薰		
	肖	削	消	硝		益	猛		尊		勲	薫

卽 節 旣 慨 槪 即 節 既 慨 概	靑 情 晴 淸 請 青 情 晴 清 請	次 姿 乘 剩 次 姿 乗 剰
鄕 響 爵 郷 響 爵	勸 歡 觀 權 勧 歓 観 権	亞 惡 閒 簡 亜 悪 間 簡
飢 飯 館 飮 飢 飯 館 飲	孃 懷 讓 釀 嬢 懐 譲 醸	兩 滿 帶 滯 両 満 帯 滞
but 食 養 食 養	淺 殘 踐 錢 浅 残 践 銭	爲 僞 灰 炭 為 偽 灰 炭
羽 扇 翌 習 弱 羽 扇 翌 習 弱	來 峽 狹 麥 来 峡 狭 麦	壞 懷 收 敍 壊 懐 収 叙
曜 躍 曜 躍	具 眞 愼 鎭 具 真 慎 鎮	搖 謠 潛 贊 揺 謡 潜 賛
每 悔 梅 海 毒 毎 悔 梅 海 毒	竝 譜 虛 纖 並 譜 虚 繊	曉 燒 象 像 暁 焼 象 像
but 母 母	緣 綠 錄 樣 縁 緑 録 様	嶋 峯 畧 島 峰 略
壯 莊 狀 將 寢 壮 荘 状 将 寝	刃 忍 認 册 刃 忍 認 冊	絕 鬪 溫 絶 闘 温
社 祈 神 禪 福 社 祈 神 禅 福	冐 隋 帽 姊 冒 隋 帽 姉	倂 拜 豐 併 拝 豊
but 祕 秘	愉 諭 輸 囘 愉 諭 輸 回	慌 恆 沒 慌 恒 没
劍 儉 檢 險 驗 剣 倹 検 険 験	揭 渴 謁 硏 掲 渇 謁 研	弦 屆 鷄 弦 届 鶏

TABLE III: REPLACEMENTS		
單 戰 嚴 彈 禪 単 戦 厳 弾 禅	巢 惱 腦 獵 巣 悩 脳 猟	鎖 學 覺 鎖 学 覚

强強 聽庁 歸帰 對対 瓣 據拠 稱称 罸罰 飜翻 攜携 皷鼓 癡痴 嶽岳

辯 (辨 辯 瓣 → 弁)

鐵鉄 寫写 盡尽 黨党 辨 假仮 燈灯 圍囲 壹壱 憇憩 獻献 蠶蚕 竊窃

氣気 關関 晝昼 寶宝 缺欠 雙双 鹽塩 濱浜 衞衛 畱留 爐炉 耻恥 畆畝

戲戯 拂払 轉転 藥薬 縱縦 鑄鋳 樓楼 膽胆 總総 圖図 禮礼 澁渋 邊辺 臺台

靈霊 佛仏 傳伝 樂楽 從従 壽寿 數数 擔担 窗窓

隸隷 壘塁 遲遅 實実

顯顕 繪絵 廢廃 勵励 辭辞 敕勅 瀨瀬 謠謡 瀧滝 款 囑嘱

濕湿 會会 發発 萬万 亂乱 效効 賴頼 搖揺 龍竜 欵 (欵 款 → 款) 屬属 攝摂 遞逓 體体

櫻桜 驅駆 釋釈 繼継 雜雑 舊旧 買買 國国 圓円 當当

營営 毆殴 驛駅 斷断 醉酔 蠻蛮 輕軽 but

榮栄 譽誉 歐欧 譯訳 粹粋 灣湾 經経 陷陥 讀読 鑛鉱 靜静 濟済

勞労 擧挙 樞枢 澤沢 齡齢 肅粛 碎砕 戀恋 徑径 稻稲 續続 擴拡 淨浄 劑剤

區区 擇択 齒歯 卒卆 變変 莖茎 兒児 賣売 廣広 爭争 齋斎

TABLE IV: OMISSIONS

者 者	暑 暑	署 署	著 著	都 都
	突 突	器 器	類 類	淚 涙
	近 近	道 道	巡 巡	進 進
	拔 抜	髮 髪		寬 寛
墮 堕	隨 随	髓 髄		縣 県
專 専	惠 恵	穗 穂		團 団

獨 独	觸 触		郞 郎	廊 廊
德 徳	聽 聴		參 参	慘 惨
曆 暦	歷 歴		藏 蔵	臟 臓
處 処	畫 画 → 画			
聲 声	覽 覧		奧 奥	
醫 医	點 点		號 号	

應 応	價 価	條 条
豫 予	藝 芸	餘 余
疊 畳	盜 盗	騷 騒
擊 撃	壓 圧	腸 腸
貳 弐	蟲 虫	穩 穏
犧 犠		

TABLE V: MISCELLANEOUS

步 歩	涉 渉	賓 賓	鄰 隣
免 兔 → 免		勉 勉	逸 逸

决 決	凉 涼	凖 準

冨 富	冝 宜	糺 糾

APPENDIX III
SEMI-CURSIVE AND CURSIVE FORMS OF IMPORTANT CHARACTERS
(Numbers refer to entries in Nelson's *Japanese-English Character Dictionary*)

LEFT & RIGHT CHARS.											
行 4213			職 3718			音 5110			屋 1387		
待 1609			親 4293			学 1271			道 4724		
御 1628			解 4306			究 3314			何 409		
海 2553			話 4358			祭 3247			島 230		
洋 2550			銀 4855			習 3675			聞 4959		
院 4991			願 255			書 3719			**UNIT CHARACTERS**		
情 1714			館 5174			黒 5403			下 9		
拝 1884			駅 5199			集 5031			上 798		
明 2110			**TOP & BOTTOM CHARS.**			電 5050			生 2991		
物 2857			高 5248			感 1731			申 93		
私 3265			参 850			驚 5229			年 188		
的 3097			安 1283			**ENCLOSURE CHARACTERS**			本 96		
知 3169			家 1311			風 5148			東 213		
致 3847			草 3939			存 1267			事 272		
紙 3510			前 595			国 1037			身 4601		
			思 3001			座 1515			長 4938

APPENDIX IV
VARIANT KANA FORMS

a	ア 阿	i	イ 伊	u	ウ 宇
	安 阿 惡 愛		以 伊 意 移		宇 有 雲 羽 右

e	エ 江	o	オ 於	ka	カ 加
	衣 要 江 緣 得 盈		於		加 可 哥 歌 賀 閑 家

ki	キ 幾	ku	ク 久	ke	ケ 介
	喜 支 木 記 起 幾		久 九 具 求 供 俱		計 介 稀 希 氣 遣

ko	コ	己	許 故 期 古 興 胡 己
sa	サ	散	佐 散 左 狭 作
shi	シ	之	四 師 事 斯 志 新 之
su	ス	須	數 須 壽 春 寸
se	セ	世	瀬 聲 世 勢
so	ソ	曽	楚 處 所 蘊 曾
ta	タ	多	當 他 田 堂 多 太
chi	チ	千	智 池 馳 遲 致 千 地 知
tsu	ツ	川	通 都 頭 津 徒 門

te	テ 天 弖
	亭 傳 帝 轉 弖 天

to	ト 止
	斗 度 登 刀 等 戸 土 東 止

na	ナ 奈
	那 難 奈 菜 名 南

ni	ニ 仁
	二 丹 兒 耳 尔 仁

nu	ヌ 奴
	駑 怒 沼 努 奴

ne	ネ 祢
	寝 念 熱 音 年 根 祢

no	ノ 乃
	濃 農 能 廼 野 乃

ha	ハ 八
	婆 葉 八 羽 半 盤 者 破 頗 波

hi	ヒ 比	火 避 妣 飛 日 悲 非 比
fu	フ 部	婦 風 布 不
he	ヘ 不	嫳 幣 敝 邊 倍 遍 篇 偏 阝部
ho	ホ 保	奉 穗 報 寶 本 保
ma	マ 末	馬 麻 漫 間 眞 滿 万 萬 末
mi	ミ 三	微 民 薇 三 身 見 美
mu	ム 牟	牟 舞 無 无 武
me	メ 女	馬 目 免 面 女
mo	モ 毛	无 裳 茂 母 毛

ya	ヤ 也
	移 屋 哉 耶 夜 也

yu	ユ 由
	柚 游 遊 由

yo	ヨ 與
	容 夜 世 代 余 餘 与

ra	ラ 良
	樂 蘭 羅 良

ri	リ 利
	離 李 梨 里! 理 利

ru	ル 流
	累 類 流 留

re	レ 礼
	麗 連 禮 礼

ro ロ 呂	wa ワ 和	(w)i ヰ 井
楼 婁 路 露 侶 呂	○輪 倭 輪 王 和	位 居 井 遺 爲
(w)e ヱ 慧	(w)o ヲ 乎	n ン
延 衞 恵	越 惡 緒 乎 遠	无

INDEX AND GLOSSARY

This is an index of grammatical points, etc., given in the notes, and a glossary of all words and proper names in Nos. 1–25 and of uncommon words and all proper names in Nos. 26–99. (Vocabulary from No. 100 has not been included, since the passages there are in the classical language.) Alternative words, phrases or characters have been separated by oblique strokes, and elements which may or may not be used appear in parentheses, e.g. *ato (ni)* signifies either *ato* or *ato ni.*

Abbreviations

a. adjective(s), adjectival
adv. adverb(ial)
attr. attributive
caus. causative
conj. conjunction
for. formal
gent. genteel 〔i.e. used as generally elegant language, rather than to show any special respect〕
hon. honorific 〔i.e. indicating respect to subject of v. or, in case of n., etc., to the relevant person〕
hum. humble 〔i.e. indicating humility or lowly status, of the subject in the case of a v.〕
int. interjection
lit. literary
n. noun(s)
neg. negative
part. particle(s)
pass. passive
pn. proper noun/name
pol. polite 〔i.e. indicating respect to the person addressed〕
pot. potential
pre. prefix
pro. pronoun
s. *suru*
su. suffix
susp. suspensive
v. verb(s), verbal
vi. verb intransitive
vt. verb transitive

achi-kochi あちこち adv. here and there
Adamuzu アダムズ pn. Adams
adjective after verb stems 57b
adobaisu アドバイス n. advice
Aerofurōto アエロフロート pn. Aeroflot
agaru 上がる vi. rise, be gained/achieved
ageru 上げる vt. raise, present; see also *-te*, 8k
-ageru 上げる vt. finish . . . ing (humbly) . . .
Aiban Morisu アイバン・モリス pn. Ivan Morris
Ai Bii Emu アイ・ビー・エム pn. IBM
aida 間 n. space, period; —*ni*, —に between, among, while, during
aisatsu 挨拶 n. greeting
ai-sumanai 相済まない vi. be sorry/regretful
Ajia アジア pn. Asia
akachan 赤ちゃん n. baby
akanbō 赤ん坊 n. baby
Akasaka 赤坂 pn.
akeru 開/明ける vt. open, vacate; 明ける vi. dawn, begin, expire (of period of time)
aki 秋 n. autumn, fall
amari (ni) 余り（に） adv. too (much)
ame 雨 n. rain
Amerika アメリカ pn. America
Amusuterudamu アムステルダム pn. Amsterdam
anata 貴方 pro. you
anaunsā アナウンサー n. announcer
ankēto アンケート n. survey, questionnaire
annai 案内 n. guidance, notification, invitation
ano あの a. that, those
aoi 青い a. blue, green, pale
aran あらん vi. 61a
arasoi-goto 争い事 n. dispute
aratamete 改めて adv. again
arata ni 新たに adv. afresh
arawareru 現われる vi. appear
are あれ pro. that; —*kara* —から since that/then
arigataku 有難く adv. with thanks 8c
arigatō 有難う adv. with thanks 8c
aru 在/有る vi. exist, be
aruiwa 或るいは conj. or, alternatively
aruku 歩く v. walk
asa 朝 n. morning
ashi 足 n. foot, leg, step; —*o mukeru* —を向ける turn one's steps, make for
ashita 明日 n. tomorrow 21b
asobasu 遊ばす hon. vt. deign/be pleased (to . . .) 51h
asobu 遊ぶ vi. play, amuse oneself

asoko あそこ pro. there, that place
asu 明日 n. tomorrow 21b
ataeru 与える vt. give
atatakai 暖/温かい, *atataka na* 暖/温かな a. warm
ato 後 n. back, rear, remainder; *—ni/de* —に/で after (wards); —(*ni*) —(に) after . . . ing
atsui 熱/厚い a. hot; 厚い a. warm, cordial, thick
atte no 67a
attributive phrases 14a
au 会う vi. meet
awaseru 合わせる vt. join, fit into/with
Ayako あや子 pn.
azana 字 n. pseudonym, nickname
azukaru 預かる vt. receive (in trust), take charge of, be given 8b

baai n. circumstances, case
Baika 梅花 pn.
bakari ばかり part. only, just, (with numerals) about
Ban 伴 pn.
Bandō 坂東 pn.
bangō 番号 n. number
Baron バロン pn. Barron
basho 場所 n. place
BBC pn. British Broadcasting Corporation
Bei 米 n. & a. America(n) 24b
-beki 可き su. should, ought, can, will 7e, 69c
-beku 可く adv. su. 81ab
bengaku 勉学 n. study
bengi 便宜 n. convenience, benefit; *—o hakaru* —を図る consider/consult (a person's) convenience, accommodate (a person)
benkyō 勉強 n. study
benri na 便利な a. convenient
besshi 別紙 n. annexed/accompanying sheet
bessō 別送 *s.* vt. send separately
betsubin 別便 n. separate post
betsugō 別号 n. another/separate name
betten 別添 n. separate attachment
Biizurei ビーズレイ pn. Beasley
biku-biku びくびく *s.* be nervous/fearful
biru ビル n. building, office block
bōeki 貿易 n. trade, commerce
Boffumu ボッフム pn. Bochum
boku 僕 pro. I 23b
Boruhachitto ボルハチット pn. Ballhatchet
boshū 募集 *s.* vt. recruit, enroll
bu 部 n. section, department, copy (of printed work)
bubun 部分 n. part, section
buin 無音 n. long silence
Bukkyō 仏教 n. Buddhism
bungaku 文学 n. literature; *—-ka* —科 n. literature course
bunka 文化 n. culture
Bunkyō 文京 pn.
Bunsei 文生 pn.
bunsen 文撰/選 n. type-picking/-setting
bun'ya 分野 n. field, sphere
Bunzō 文蔵 pn.
burei 無礼 n. rudeness
Buriti(s)shu ブリティ(ッ)シュ a. British
busata 無沙汰 n. long silence
byōki 病気 n. illness

causative verb forms 1i, 2p, 6i, 7f, 8h
chaku 着 n. arrival
chakuhon 着本 n. arrival of books
-chan ちゃん su. 95a
Chāruzu Bōdon/Dan チャールズ・ボードン/ダン pn. Charles Bawden/Dunn
charyō 茶寮 n. tea-house, restaurant
chi 地 n. land, country
chigai 違い n. difference; *ni — nai* に—ない a. doubtless 61
Chiichi Yuaserufu チーチ・ユアセルフ pn. Teach Yourself
chiisai 小さい a. small
chikai 近い a. near
chikaku 近く n. neighbourhood, vicinity
chikara 力 n. strength
chikuseki 蓄積 *s.* vt. accumulate, amass
chiru 散る vi. fall, scatter
chitto mo ちっとも adv. (not) at all/in the least
Chiyoda 千代田 pn.
chōdo 丁度 adv. just, exactly
chosho 著書 n. book, literary work
chotto ちょっと adv. just, a little
-chū 中 su. while, during, (with)in
chūbu 中部 n. central part
chūmoku 注目 *s.* vi. pay attention
chūsei 中世 n. the middle ages
chūshoku 昼食 n. lunch
chūzai-in 駐在員 n. resident person(nel)
conditionals 3nq, 6v, 71

da だ vi. be
dai- 第/オ pre. -th, -st 5a
Daiana ダイアナ pn. Diana
Daian Sukotto ダイアン・スコット pn. Dianne Scott
Dai-Ei Toshokan 大英図書館 pn. The British Library
daigaku 大学 n. university
daihyō 代表 n. representation; *— torishimari-yaku* —取締役 representative director
daikō-bun 代講分 n. substitute-teaching allocation
Daita 代田 pn.
dake だけ part. only, extent (to which)
dakkō 脱稿 n. completion of draft/ms.
dan 段 n. grade, step, matter 45b
Dan ダン pn. Dunn
dan-dan 段段 adv. gradually
Danieru(zu) ダニエル(ズ) pn. Daniels
danjo 男女 n. man and/or woman; *— o tou* —を問う question/make an issue of (whether) male or female 55c
dantai 団体 n. group, party
-dari, see *-tari*
dasu 出す vt. bring/take/send/put out
-dayū 大/太夫 n. title used for certain professional entertainers 33b
de で part. by (means of), with, in; vi. as *-te* form 6j, 7o, 32c; as susp. 2g, 6ej, 8j, 35a
-de, see *-te*
de arimasu であります vi. be 4h

de aru である vi. be 4h, 7d
Debon デボン pn. Devon
de gozaimasu でございます pol. vi. be 2h
de irareru でい/居られる hon. vi. be 65a
de irassharu でいらっしゃる hon. vi. be 20b, 70c
de iru でい/居る vi. be 2n, 70c
dekiru 出来る vi. be completed/made/achieved/possible
deki-uru 出来得る vt. be able to manage/achieve
de mo でも part. even, say, for example 32c; conj. even so, still; = *de atte mo* 69e
-de mo, see *-te mo*
de motte で以て lit. part. with, by means of
de nai でない vi. be not; see *de aru*
de naku tomo でなくとも 34c
denchū 電柱 n. telegraph pole
Dengaku 田楽 pn. an entertainment originally associated with agriculture and later with Nō
dengonsho 伝言書 n. message, memo
densen 電線 n. electric/telegraph wire
dentō 伝統 n. tradition
denwa 電話 n. telephone; —*bangō* —番号 telephone number; — *o kakeru* —を掛ける vi. telephone
de oru でお/居る hum. vi. be 70c
deru 出る vi. emerge, come/go out, attend
deshite でして 71c
dewa では conj. (well) then
de wa arimasu/aru/gozaimasu/irassharu/iru/oru, see *de arimasu/aru*, etc. and 2h
de (wa) naku tomo で(は)なくとも 34c
dō どう adv. how, in what way
dō- 同 pref. this (same) 45c
dōfu 同封 n. enclosure
Dohatti ドハッティ pn. Docherty
Doitsu ドイツ pn. Germany; — *-go* —語 n. German
dōji 同時 n. same time
dōka どうか adv. somehow; (= *dōzo*) please 6s; (if/whether. . . .) or not
doko どこ pro. where
doko-ka どこか pro. somewhere
Doktorandin n. female doctoral candidate
Doku 独 n. & a. German(y) 24b
Dokugo 独語 n. German language
dōkun 同君 n. this same man 45c
dokutā ドクター n. doctor
Dokuyaku 独訳 n. German translation; — *-bon* —本 n. book translated into German
-domo 共 su. 8f, 22a
donata どなた pro. who 32d
donna どんな a. what kind of; —*-ni -te/-de mo* —に…て/でも 42c
dono どの a. which; — . . . *de mo* —…でも any . . . at all
-dono 殿 su. Esq. 12b
-dōri 通り n. road, way, manner
dōryō 同僚 n. colleague
doryoku 努力 n. effort, exertion
dōyō no 同様の a. same, similar
Dōvā ドーヴァー pn. Dover
Doyō(bi) 土曜（日） n. Saturday
dōzo どうぞ adv. please, kindly 3t

e へ part. to(wards)
-e in susp. forms 1c
Edinbara エディンバラ pn. Edinburgh
Ei 英 n. & a. England, English, Britain, British 24b
Ei-Bei 英米 n. & a. Britain & America, Anglo-American
Eigo 英語 n. English language
Ei-kaiwa 英会話 n. English conversation
Eikoku 英国 n. England, Britain
Emiko 恵美子 pn.
enryo 遠慮 n. restraint, reserve
eru 得る vt. gain, obtain
-eru える pot. ending 4k, 8g, 11i, 47d
Etō Jun 江藤淳 pn.
Evansu エヴァンス pn. Evans
eyā-retā エヤー・レター n. air-letter, aerogramme

foto フォト n. photograph
fū 風 n. way, manner
fuan 不安 n. uneasiness, anxiety
fuitsu 不一 30c
Fujimi 富士見 pn.
Fujita 藤田/多 pn.; — *Kiyoshi* — 清 pn.
Fujiwara Makiko 藤原真貴子 pn.
Fukada 深田 pn.
Fukuda Shūichi 福田秀一 pn.
fukumi 含み n. implication
fukumu 含む vt. contain, bear in mind
Fukushima 福島 pn.
fukyū 普及 *s.* vi. spread, be diffused
fun'iki 雰囲気 n. atmosphere
furatto フラット n. flat, apartment
fureru 触れる vi. touch (on), be contrary; vt. announce, proclaim
Furōrensu フローレンス pn. Florence
furu 降る vi. fall (of rain, etc.)
Furukawa Hisashi 古川久 pn.
Furuno Kiyohito 古野清人 pn.
fusen 不宣 45f
fūshu 風趣 n. purport, elegance, appearance
fu-suru 付/附する vt. attach, submit/commit (to)
futan 負担 *s.* vt. bear, take upon oneself
futari 二人 n. two persons
Futsu 仏 n. & a. France, French 24b
Futsugo 仏語 n. French language
futsuka 二日 n. & adv. second day, two days

ga が part. 2i; before pot. v. 29e;
ga が conj. and, but
Gaido Tsū Nō ガイド・ツー・ノー pn. Guide to Nō
gaikoku 外国 n. foreign country; — *-go* — 語 n. foreign language
gairai(no) 外来（の）a. coming from outside/abroad
gaitōsha 該当者 n. the relevant person
gaiyū 外遊 n. foreign travel
gakka 学科 n. subject, course of study
gakkai 学会 n. conference, learned society
gakkō 学校 n. school
gakubu 学部 n. academic faculty/department
gakuchō 学長 n. (faculty) dean, university president

gakuen 学園 n. college, campus
gakujutsu 学術 n. learning, science
gakunai (no) 学内（の） a. within a university/school/campus
gakunen 学年 n. academic grade/class/year; — *-hajime* — 始/初め n. beginning of the academic year
gakusei 学生 n. student
gakushi 学士 n. university graduate; — *-kai* — 会 n. graduate/alumni association
-garu がる su. 47f
-gata 方 su. 9b
gawa 側 n. side
gekibungaku 劇文学 n. dramatic literature
gendai 現代 n. present age/day
Genji Monogatari 源氏物語 pn. The Tale of Genji 49c
genjō 現状 n. present state/situation
genki 元気 n. good health/spirits
genkō 原稿 n. manuscript, draft
genzai 現在 n. present time
geshuku 下宿 n. lodgings; — *-zumai* — 住(ま)い n. life/living in lodgings
Getsuyō (bi) 月曜（日） n. Monday
-gi 儀 n. su. 98a
Gibuzu ギブズ pn. Gibbs
gijuku 義塾 n. (private) academy
go 後 n. later time; su. after
go- 御 hon. pre.; see also under *o-noun* . . . entries
go-busata, see *busata*
gogakuryoku 語学力 n. language ability
gogatsu 五月 n. May
gogo 午後 n. & adv. afternoon, p.m.
gohai 誤配 n. mistaken distribution/delivery
gōkei 合計 n. total
gomen 御免 n. pardon
go-/o-noun+verb: see under *o-noun* . . . entries
goran 御覧 hon. n. (another's) sight/looking; — *ni ireru* — に入れる show to (another person) 96a
go-reimei 御令名 hon. n. (your, etc.) name
gōri-sei 合理性 n. rationality
-goro 頃 su. about (the time of)
gosei 五世 n. fifth generation; su. (Henry, etc.) V
goshō-guruma 後生車 n. carriage to take one to the (Buddhist) afterlife
gozaimasu 御座います pol. vi. exist, be 2e
gozen 午前 n. & adv. morning a.m.
guai 具合 n. condition, state
-gun 郡 n. country district, sub-prefecture
Gunji Masakatsu 郡司正勝 pn.
Gunma 群馬 pn.
gurai/kurai 位 n. extent; su. about, . . . or so
gutai-teki 具体的 a. concrete, tangible
guttari ぐったり adv. utterly (exhausted)
gyōji 行事 n. event, ceremony
gyokkō 玉稿 hon. n. (another's) ms./article 69a
gyoku- 玉 hon. pre. 69a
gyokuanka 玉案下 n. 9e, 90d
gyokukika 玉机下 n. 90d

hachigatsu 八月 n. August
hagemu 励む vi. be diligent/hard-working
Hagino Kōki 萩野浩基 pn.
haha 母 n. mother
hai 拝 hum. pre. 9a, 27i; hum. su. 22g
haibi 拝眉 hum. n. personal meeting
haibungaku 俳文学 n. haiku (& haiku-style) literature
haichō 拝聴 *s.* hum. vt. (humbly) hear
haidoku 拝読 *s.* hum. vt. (humbly) read
haifuku 拝復 hum. n. 37a
haigu 拝具 hum. n. 24j
haihon 配本 n. distribution of books
haiju 拝受 *s.* hum. vt. (humbly) accept
haikei 拝啓 hum. n. 5c
haiken 拝見 hum. n. (humbly) looking/seeing 9a, 16d
haiku 俳句 n. a type of three-line poem of 17 syllables
hairu 入る vi. enter
hairyo 配慮 n. consideration, concern
haisatsu 拝察 *s.* hum. vt. (humbly) judge, presume 9a
hajime 始/初め n. beginning; (= *o* —) beginning with, and also 6u
hajimeru 始/初める vt. begin
hajimete 始/初めて adv. for the first time
hakaru 図/計る vt. plan, aim at, strive for
hakushi 博士 n. Dr., Ph.D.
haken 派遣 *s.* vt. dispatch, send
hakken 発見 *s.* vt. discover
hakkō 発行 *s.* vt. publish
Hamamatsu 浜松 pn.
hana 花/華 n. flower
hanashi 話 n. talk
hanasu 話す vt. talk, tell
Haneda 羽田 pn.
han'i 範囲 n. sphere, field
happyō 発表 n. announcement, statement, presentation (of report, etc.)
Harajuku 原宿 pn.
haru 春 n. spring; — *-yasumi* — 休み spring holiday
Hasegawa 長谷川 pn.
hashiru 走る vi. run
hataraku 働く vi. work
hatsuka 二十日 n. & adv. 20th day, 20 days
hatsuon 発音 n. pronunciation
Hawai ハワイ pn. Hawaii
haya 早 adv. already, now
hayai 早い a. early, quick
Hayashida 囃田 pn.
hayashi-goto 囃子事 n. instrumental music in a Nō play
Hayashi Takeshi 林武 pn.
hazu 筈 n. likelihood, expectation
hei- 弊 hum. pre. 13c
Heian 平安 pn. 71a
heisha 弊社 hum. n. my/our company
henji 返事 n. reply
Henrii ヘンリー pn. Henry
henshū 編集/輯/修 n. compilation, editing; — *-bu* — 部 editorial section
heru 経る vt. pass (through)
hi 日 n. sun, day
hi- 卑 hum. pre. 3a

-hi 費 su. expenses, cost
Hidaka Minako 日高美南子 pn.
hidari 左 n. left
Higashibatake 東畑 pn.
higoro 日頃 adv. habitually, for a long time
Higurashi Yoshiko 日暮嘉子 pn.
hihan 批判 n. criticism, comment
hihyō 批評 n. criticism, comment
Hiisurō ヒースロー pn. Heathrow
hijū 比重 n. ratio
hikan 卑簡 hum. n. my letter
hiki-shimaru 引締まる vi. become tight/firm/tense
hiki-tate 引立て n. patronage, support
hiki-ukeru 引受ける vt. undertake, take upon oneself
hikōki 飛行機 n. airplane
hina 雛 n. doll; see also *o-hinasama*
Hinoki Tsunetarō 桧常太郎 pn.
Hiraizumi 平泉 pn.
hiraku 開く vi. open, spread, bloom; vt. open (up), develop
hiroi 広い a. broad, extensive
Hiroshima 広島 pn.
Hirota 広田 pn.; — *Kazue* — 一枝 pn.
hito-bito 人々 n. people
hitokata-naranu 一方ならぬ a. unusual, extraordinary 30a
hitori 一人 n. one person
hitsuyō 必要 n. necessity
hō 方 n. direction, alternative
Hoashi 帆足 pn.; — *Banri* — 万/萬里 pn.; — *Tonaji* — 図南次 pn.
hodo 程 n. limit, extent; matter 16e
hōdō 報道 n. information, report; — *kikan* — 機関 the media
hō-Ei 訪英 n. visiting England/Britain
Hōjō Hideji 北條秀司 pn.
hoka 外/他 n. elsewhere; — *no* —の (an)other; — *ni* — に except, besides
hōkoku 報告 n. report
hokorobu 綻ぶ vi. split, begin to bloom
hōmon 訪問 *s.* vt. visit
hon 本 n. book; counter for cylindrical objects, etc.
hon- 本 pre. the present, the . . . in question, this 14d
Honda Yasuji 本田安次 pn.
hongaku 本学 n. this school/university
honkai 本会 n. this society/meeting
hon-no ほんの a. mere, slight
honorific verb forms 6otw, 14b, 26b, 65b, 83a, 88a
honorific verbs 6w, 20b
hontō 本当 n. truth
hōsei 鳳声 hon. n. verbal message
Hōsei 法政 pn.
Hoshigaoka 星ケ岡 pn.
hoshii 欲しい a. desired, wanted 44c
hōshin 方針 n. course, aim, policy
hōshoku 奉職 s. vi. serve, hold office
hōsō 放送 n. broadcast; — *-kyoku* — 局 n. broadcasting station
hoteru ホテル n. hotel
hoyō 保養 n. health, care, recuperation
hōyō-teki 包容的 a. comprehensive
humble verb forms 1ehi, 2c
humble verbs 1gh, 2cf, 3ems, 12e, 13a
hyakunen 百年 n. a hundred years
Hyōgo 兵庫 pn.

-i (in suspensive forms) 1c
i-bunka-kan 異文化観 n. view of other cultures
ichibu 一部 n. one copy (of printed work)
Ichibun 一文 n. First Arts Section 70b
ichido 一度 n. one time, once
ichidō 一同 n. all (of us/them)
ichigatsu 一月 n. January
Ichihara Izumi 市原いずみ pn.
Ichikawa Danjūrō 市川団十郎 pn.
ie 家 n. house, home
Igirisu イギリス n. England, Britain
Iguro Takeaki 井畔武明 pn.
ii 良い a. good
iinkai 委員会 n. committee
Iisutā イースター n. Easter
Iitoyo Kiichi 飯豊毅一 pn.
ikaga 如何 adv. how 4m
Ikawa 井川 pn.
ikebana 生花 n. flower arrangement
Ikeda Tadashi 池田重 pn.
iken 意見 n. view, opinion
ikkagetsu 一箇月 n. one month
ikkō 一行 n. party, group
ikoku 異国 n. foreign country/land; — *-go* — 語 foreign tongue
iku 行く vi. go
ikue ni mo 幾重にも adv. repeatedly, earnestly
ikura 幾ら adv. how much; — *-ka* —か adv. some, a certain extent; — *-mo* —も any number/amount
ikuta no 幾多の a. many, great number of
ima 今 n. & adv. present time; — *wa* —は — adv. at present, nowadays
Imoto Nōichi 井本農一 pn.
Ingurando イングランド n. England, Britain
inoru 祈/禱る vt. pray for
Inoue 井上 pn.; — *Eiji* —栄司 pn.; — *Eimei* — 英明 pn.; — *Tomoko* — 知子 pn.
inshō 印象 n. impression
interrogative word + . . . *-te/-de mo* 42c
ippai 一杯 n. a cupful/glassful; adv. full
ippan ni 一般に adv. in general
ippō 一報 n. communication, word
irarenai 居られない 7g
irareru 居られる 65a
irassharu いらっしゃる hon. vi. come, go, be 6w, 14b, 20b
ireru 入れる vt. put in, include
iri 入り n. entry, beginning
Irie Takanori 入江隆則 pn.
iro-iro na 色々な a. various
iru 居る vi. be (present)
iru 要る vi. be needed
isan 違算 n. miscalculation
Isawa 胆沢 pn.
Ise Sentarō 伊瀬仙太郎 pn.
Isobe 磯部 pn.
isogashii 忙しい a. busy

isogu 急ぐ vi. hurry
Isono Taka 磯野たか pn.
isshitsu 一室 n. one room
issō 一層 adv. (still) more
itadakeru 頂/戴ける pot. v. be able to (humbly) receive 4k, 8h, 17b
itadaku 頂/戴く vt. (humbly) receive 1hi, 2lp, 14f; see also *-te/-(sa)sete itadaku*
Itasaka 板坂 pn.
itasu 致す hum. vt. (humbly) do 1eg, 3o, 4a
Itō Masayoshi 伊藤正義 pn.
itsuka 五日 n. & adv. fifth day, five days
itta see *to* —
ittan 一端 n. one part, a glimpse
iu 言/云う vt. say
iwai 祝い n. celebration
Iwanami 岩波 pn.
iwareru 言/云われる pass. v. be said; (as hon. v. form) say
Iwate 岩手 pn.
izen ni 以前に adv. before, previously
Izu 伊豆 pn.
izure 何れ pro. which 4n; adv. some/one day; — *de mo* — でも 57c; — *ni shite mo* — にしても 4n

jama 邪魔 n. obstruction, hindrance
-ji 時 n. su. hour, o'clock
jidai 時代 n. period
jidōsha 自動車 n. motor-car
jigo (no) 事後（の）a. after the event; — *shōdaku* — 承諾 n. approval/consent after the event
jigō 次号 n. next number/issue
jiin 寺院 n. (Buddhist) temple
jikan 時間 n. time, hour
jikkagetsu 十箇月 n. ten months
jikken 実験 n. experiment; — *-teki ni* — 的に adv. experimentally
jiko 事故 n. accident
jishi 侍史 64e
jissai 実際 n. truth, reality, actuality
jisseki 実績 n. (actual) results/achievements
jisshi 実施 *s.* vt. enforce, carry out
jitsu 実 n. truth, reality
Jiuta-mai 地唄舞 n. a type of dance which grew up in and around Kyōto, accompanied by popular songs and samisen music.
-jō 嬢 su. 33e
jogen 助言 n. advice
jōkyō 状況 n. situation
joshi 女子 n. woman
joshi 女史 n. 42d
jōshi 上司 n. a superior/senior
joshu 助手 n. assistant
jōzu na 上手な a. skilful
jūbun na 充/十分な a. enough, adequate
jūgatsu 十月 n. October
jugyō 授業 n. teaching, instruction
jūichigatsu 十一月 n. November
jūji 従事 *s.* vi. engage in
junbi 準備 n. preparations
jūnigatsu 十二月 n. December
Jurietto ジュリエット pn. Juliet
jūsho 住所 n. place of residence
juyo 授与 n. conferment, award
juyō 受容 n. receipt, acceptance
jūyokka 十四日 n. & adv. 14th day, 14 days

ka か interrogative part.; — *mo shirenai* —も知れない 7h; — *to omou to* — と思うと 7j
-ka 日 su. day (of the month), (period of) days
-ka 化 su. -ize 26d
kabushiki-gaisha 株式会社 n. joint-stock company, Co. Ltd., Inc.
kaeru 帰る vi. return (home)
kage 陰/蔭/影 n. shade, shadow; *o-* — *(-sama) de* 御 —(様)で thanks to (another person)
kagiri 限り n. limit
kai 会 n. meeting, society
kaichō 会長 n. chairman, president
kaigi 会議 n. conference
kaiin 会員 n. (meeting/society) member
kaisha 会社 n. company
kaitei 改訂 n. revision
kakaru 掛かる vi. hang (on/from), take time/money
kakawarazu 拘らず see *ni mo* —
kakeru 掛ける vt. hang/put up, sit, spend; *denwa o* — 電話を— telephone
kaki 下記 a. written below
kakkō 恰/格好 n. shape, appearance; — *na/no* — な/の a. suitable
kakkoku 各国 n. each/every country
kakomu 囲む vt. enclose, encircle
kaku 書く vt. write
kaku- 各 pre. each, every, various
kakui 各位 hon. n. gentlemen 1a
kakuryū 各流 n. each/every (artistic) school
kakushu 各種 n. each/every kind
Kamigata-mai 上方舞 n. a type of dance which grew up in and around Kyōto
Kaminoge 上野毛 pn.
ka mo shirenai かも知れない 7h
-kan 間 su. space of, between
Kanada カナダ pn. Canada
Kanagawa 神奈川 pn.
kanai 家内 n. wife
kanari 可成/也 adv. considerably
kane 金 n. money
kane-gane 予々 adv. previously, before
kanete 予て adv. previously, before
kangaeru 考える vt. consider
kanji 感じ n. feeling
kanjiru 感じる vt. feel
kankei 関係 n. connection
kankō 刊行 n. publication
kankyō 環境 n. environment
kanō 可能 n. possibility
Kansai 関西 pn.
Kansei 関西 pn.
kansei 完成 *s.* vt. complete
kansha 感謝 *s.* vt. be grateful for, appreciate
kanshin 関心 n. concern, interest
kanshō 冠省 84a
kanshū 慣習 n. custom, convention
kan-suru 関する vi. relate to, be concerned with
Kanto カント pn. Kant
Kantō 関東 pn.
Kanzaki 神崎 pn.

Kanze 観世 pn.; — *Hisao* — 寿夫 pn.
kara から part. from, after, since; conj. and so, because; — *suru* — する 29b
karada 体 n. body; wr. 身体 26i
karina 仮名 n. assumed name
Kasai 笠井 pn.; — *Tomoyoshi* — 朝義 pn.
kasaneru 重ねる vt. pile up
kasanete 重ねて adv. repeatedly
kasetto カセット n. cassette
kashi 菓子 n. cake
kashiko かしこ 20i
Kasuga Wakamiya 春日若宮 pn.
kata 方 hon. n. person 3d
-kata 方 su. way of . . .ing 29a
katachi 形 n. shape, form
Katō Hirokazu 加藤裕一 pn.
ka to omou to かと思うと 7j
katsudō 活動 n. activity, movement
katsuji 活字 n. (printing) type; — *ni fu-suru* — に付/附する set up in print
katsuyaku 活躍 n. activity
katte na 勝手な a. selfish, wilful
Kawakami Hajime 河上肇 pn.
kawari 変り n. change, something wrong/different
kawaru 代る vi. change, be substituted for; 変る vi. change, differ from
Kayō(bi) 火曜（日） n. Tuesday
kazoku 家族 n. family, household
keigu 敬具 2q
keihaku 敬白 41b
keikaku 計画 n. plan
keiken 経験 n. experience
keikō 傾向 n. tendency
keisai 掲載 *s*. vt. publish, print
keizai 経済 n. economy
kekkō na 結構な a. fine, splendid
ken 件 n. matter
-ken 県 n. su. prefecture
ken'an 健安 n. health and safety
Kenburijji ケンブリッジ pn. Cambridge
kenbutsu 見物 n. sightseeing
Kenesu ケネス pn. Kenneth
kengaku 見学 *s*. vt. study by observation
-kenka 県下 su. belonging to/coming under a prefecture, prefectural
kenkō 健康 n. health
kenkyū 研究 n. research; — *-jo* — 所 research institute; — *-sha* — 者 researcher; — *-shitsu* — 室 research room/laboratory; — *-sho* — 書 research book/work
kenpoku 硯北 45h
kenritsu 県立 a. prefectural
kensan 研鑽 n. study
kenshō 健祥 n. health and happiness
kenshō 健勝 n. health
kentō 見当 n. estimate, guess
keredomo けれども conj. but, however
ki 気 n. spirit, mind, feeling; — *ga suru* — がする vi. feel
ki 記 su. written (by)
ki- 貴 hon. pre. 3c
-ki き lit. attr. ending 3p, 54a, 93a
ki-chi 貴地 n. your country/land
kiden 貴殿 pro. you 5e
ki-Ei 帰英 n. return to England
kihō 貴方 pro. you
kiipu キープ *s*. vt. keep
kijitsu 期日 n. (fixed) date/day
kika 机下 22h
kikai 機会 n. opportunity
kikan 機関 n. organization
kikaseru 聞かせる vt. cause/allow to hear, inform
kikin 基金 n. fund, foundation
kikō 気候 n. climate
ki-kō 貴校 hon. n. (your, etc.) school/university
kikoku 帰国 n. return to one's own country
ki-koku 貴国 hon. n. (your, etc.) country
kiku 聞/聴く vt. hear, ask
Kikuchi Isao 菊地勲 pn.
kimaru 決/定まる vi. be decided
kinchō 緊張 *s*. vi. be strained/tense
kinen 記/紀念 n. commemoration, remembrance; — *shashin* — 写真 souvenir photograph
kinkei 謹啓 15a
kinkyō 近況 n. recent state/condition
kinō 昨日 n. yesterday 6c, 8d
ki-no-doku na 気の毒な a. pitiable, wretched
kinpaku 謹白 88e
kinshū 錦繍 n. brocade
Kin'yō(bi) 金曜（日） n. Friday
kirō 貴郎 pro. you 67b
kisetsu 季節 n. season
Kitagishi Sukeyoshi 北岸佑吉 pn.
Kitahara 北原 pn.
kitai 期待 *s*. vt. expect, hope for
kitaku 帰宅 *s*. vi. return home
kitaru 来たる *a*. next, coming 4g
Kita-Shirakawa 北白川 pn.
kiyo-zuri 清刷り n. clean printing 46a
kō こう adv. like this; — *iu/shita* — 言う/した a. such (as this) 24e
kō 候 n. weather, season
Kōbe 神戸 pn.
kochi こち n. this direction
Kōchi 高知 pn.
kochira こちら n. this direction
kōdo (no) 高度（の） a. high-degree/-level
kōdokusha 購読者 n. subscriber, reader
kodomo 子供 n. child
kōei 光栄 n. honour, privilege
kōen 講演 n. speech
kōgi 講義 n. lecture
kō-han'i 広範囲 n. wide field/sphere
kōhen 後編 n. second/last volume
kōhosha 候補者 n. candidate
kōi 厚意 n. kindness, goodwill
Koike 小池 pn.
koi-nobori 鯉幟 n. paper-carp streamer
koishii 恋しい a. dear, beloved
Koishikawa 小石川 pn.
kojin 個人 n., — *-teki* — 的 a. individual
kōjin 幸甚 n. great good fortune/favour
kōkai (no) 公開（の） a. public, open
kōkan 向寒 n. approaching/increasing cold
Kokinshū 古今集 71b
kō-kisetsu 好季節 n. fine weather/season

koko ここ n. here
ko-ko 個々 n. individuals
kokonoka 九日 n. & adv. ninth day, nine days
kokoro 心 n. heart, spirit; — *-atatakai* — 温い a. warm, cordial; — *-gurushii* — 苦しい a. painful, regrettable
kokoroyoku 快く adv. cheerfully, willingly
kokorozasu 志す vi. aim at, aspire to
kokorozukai 心遣い n. care, solicitude
kōkūbin 航空便 n. air mail
kokubun 国文 n. Japanese literature/language
kokubungaku 国文学 n. Japanese literature; — *ka* — 科 n. Japanese-literature course
kokubunka 国文科 n. Japanese-literature course
kokugo 国語 n. Japanese language
kokumin 国民 n. a/the people/nation
kokuritsu (no) 国立（の） a. national
kokusai (no) 国際（の） a. international; — *Kōryū Kikin* — 交流基金 n. The Japan Foundation 5b
kokusho 国書 n. national literature/books
komaru 困る vi. be in trouble/difficulty
komeru 込める vt. put/pour in
Komura Hachirō 小村八郎 pn.
Kōnan 甲南 pn.
kondo 今度 n. & adv. this/next time
kongo 今後 n. the future; adv. henceforth; — *tomo* — とも in the future too
Kongō 金剛 pn.
konka 今夏 n. this summer
konna こんな a. this kind of, such 24e
kono この a. this
konogoro この頃 adv. lately, nowadays
Konparu 金春 pn.
konpojishon コンポジション n. composition
konshū 今秋 n. this autumn
kontoku 懇篤 n. kindness, cordiality
Konuma Yoshinari 小沼良成 pn.
kōnyū 購入 n. purchase
korai 古来 adv. from old/ancient times
kore これ pro. this; — *kara* — から from now on; — *-ra* — 等 these
koro 頃 n. time
Koronbia コロンビア pn. Columbia
kōryo 考慮 n. consideration, deliberation
kōryū 交流 n. exchange
kōsei 校正 n. proofreading
kōseki 功績 n. achievement
kōsetsu 高説 n. (your) valued opinion
kōshi 講師 n. lecturer
kosho 古書 n. old book
koso こそ emphatic part. 7k
Kotāchi コターチ pn. Cortazzi
kotaeru 答/応える vi. reply/respond to
koten 古典 n. old literature, classics; — *-ka* — 化 *s*. classicize
kōten 好天 n. good weather
kō-tenki 好天気 n. good weather
koto 事 n. matter, case; — *ni naru* — に成る 5d, 53c; — *ni suru/itasu* — にする/致す 53c
-koto 事 su. 20a
kōtō 高等 n. high grade/class; — *gakkō* — 学校 high school
kotoba 言葉 n. word, language
kotoshi 今年 n. this year
kotsu-kotsu (to) こつこつ（と） adv. laboriously, with a tap/knock
kōwa 高話 hon. n. (your, etc.) talk
Koyama 小山 pn.; — *Hiroshi* — 弘志 pn.; — *Tenshū* — 天舟 pn.
ku 区 n. town ward
-ku く susp. form 4f, 6d, 11e, 51b, 64a
kuchi 口 n. mouth
kudasareru 下される 2d; see *kudasaru*
kudasaru 下さる vt. condescend, (kindly) give 1g, 8k, 20g, 21d
kufū 工夫 n. device, scheme, means
kugatsu 九月 n. September
kumi 組 n. group, class, setting up print; — *-han* — 版 printed/ type-set sheet; — *-kata* — 方 way of setting type; — *-mihon* — 見本 printed/ type-set example
-kun 君 su. 39b
kuni 国 n. country
kurai 位 see *gurai*
Kurainā クライナー pn. Kreiner
kurashi 暮らし n. living, livelihood
kurasu 暮らす vi. earn/make a living
kurasu クラス n. class
kureru 呉れる vt. give 20g
kuri-kaesu 繰り返す vt. repeat
Kurokawa 黒川 pn.
Kurosaki 黒崎 pn.
kuru 来る vi. come
kuwashii 詳/精しい a. detailed, well informed
kyo 居 n. residence
kyō 今日 n. today; — *-konogoro* — このごろ n. these days
kyōfu 恐怖 n. fear, terror
Kyōgen 狂言 20c
kyōhon 教本 n. textbook
kyōiku 教育 n. education; — *-hi* — 費 educational expenses; — *-gaku* — 学 the study of education, pedagogy
kyōin 教員 n. teacher
kyōji 教示 n. instruction, teaching
kyōju 教授 n. teaching, professor; — *-shoku* — 職 teaching post
kyoka 許可 n. permission
kyō-konogoro 今日このごろ n. these days
kyōretsu na 強烈な a. intense, strong
kyōryoku 協力 n. cooperation
kyōsai 共催 n. joint organization/sponsorship
kyōshi 教師 n. teacher
kyōshuku 恐縮 n. hesitation, regret, embarrassment
Kyōto 京都 pn.
kyōzai 教材 n. teaching material
kyūgaku 休学 n. absence from study/school
Kyūshū 九州 pn
kyūyō 休養 n. rest, recuperation

machi 町 n. town, street, sub-ward
machi-nozomu 待ち望む vt. await longingly, look forward to
mada 未だ adv. still; with neg.: not yet
made 迄 part. until, as far as; — *(ni)* —（に） as, for 8n; — *ni* — に by, before

mae 前 n. front (part), time before/ago
Maeno Shōkichi 前野昭吉 pn.
Maezawa 前沢 pn.
-mai まい neg. su. (probably) will not 87b
mainichi 毎日 n. every day
Maintsu マインツ pn. Mainz
mairareru 参られる vi. go, come 6o
mairu 参る hum. vi. go, come 3m, 42a
makoto ni 誠/真/洵に adv. truly
mama 儘 n. unchanged state, just as things are
manabu 学ぶ vt. study, learn
maneku 招く vt. invite
Man'yōshū 万葉集 pn.
mappitsu-nagara 末筆乍ら late (in my letter) though it is, last but not least
Maruoka Akira 丸岡明 pn.
-mase ませ 8a, 68c
-mashi まし 68c
-masu/-mashita ます/ました (as non-final) 1f, 2f, 3n
Masuda Shigeo 増田繁夫 pn.
-masureba ますれば 3n
mata 又/復 adv. also, again; — *no* — の (an)other; — *wa* — は or
Matsumoto Shinko 松本信子 pn.
Matsumura Susumi 松村進実 pn.
Matsuura Satoko 松浦智子 pn.
mattaku 全く adv. completely
mawaru 回る v. turn/go round
mazu 先ず adv. first; — (*wa*) —（は）well (now), then 29g
me 目 n. eye
medetai 目/芽出度い a. happy, auspicious
megashira 目頭 n. the (tear-producing) corners of the eyes
Meiji 明治 pn.; — *jidai* — 時代 the Meiji period, 1868–1912
meiyo 名誉 n. honor; — *kaiin* — 会員 honorary member of a society
men 面 n. aspect
mendan 面談 n. interview
menshiki 面識 n. acquaintance
messēji メッセージ n. message
mi 身 n. body, one's person; — *ni shimiru* — に染みる penetrate/pierce (one)
michibata 道端 n. roadside
midori 緑 n. green (colour)
mieru 見える vi. be visible
migi 右 n. right(hand), the above(-mentioned)
mi-haru 見張る vt. open/strain (one's eyes)
mijikai 短い a. short
mikka 三日 n. & adv. third day, three days
Mimura 三村 pn.
mina 皆 n. & adv. all; — *-sama* — 様 hon. pro. (you) all, everyone
Minato 港 pn.
miru 見る vt. see; *-te* — て 8i
Miruzu ミルズ pn. Mills
mise 店 n. shop
miseru 見せる vt. show
mitai みたい su. like, seems (to be)
Mitsukoshi 三越 pn.
Miyagino 宮城野 pn.
Miyazawa Kenji 宮沢賢治 pn.
mizo 溝 n. ditch, drain
Mizutani 水谷 pn.; — *Kazuo* — 一雄 pn. — *Kengo* — 謙吾 pn.
mo も part. also, even
mō もう adv. by now, already
mochimashite 以ちまして 98d, see *motte*
mōdō 妄動 n. wild/rash action
modoru 戻る vi. come/go back
Moji-dayū 文字大夫 pn.
mokka 目下 adv. now, at present
mokuroku 目録 n. catalogue
mokuteki 目的 n. aim, objective
Mokuyō(bi) 木曜（日） n. Thursday
momo 桃 n. peach
mondai 問題 n. question, problem
mono 物 n. thing
mono 者 n. person 12d
morau 貰う vt. receive 21, 14f
Mori 森 pn.
mōsareru 申される 6o
moshi 若し adv. if 6v
mōshi-ageru 申し上げる hum. vt. (humbly) say/do 1e, 3gs, 4b
mōshi-tsukeru 申し付ける vt. tell, instruct
mōsu 申す hum. vt. say 2f, 64a
Mosukuwa モスクワ pn. Moscow
motenashi 持て成し n. treatment, hospitality
moto 元/本 n. source, origin; — *no* — の a. original, previous
moto 許 n. place, house
moto-genkō 元原稿 n. original manuscript
moto-moto 元々 adv. from the first, by nature
motoyori 元より adv. from the first, naturally, of course
motte 以て vt. using, with, by means of 30b, 45e, 98d
motto もっと adv. more
mottomo 最も adv. most
mottomo na 尤もな a. reasonable, right, natural
Mugendai 無限大 pn. Infinity
muika 六日 n. & adv. sixth day, six days
mukaeru 迎える vt. welcome
mukashi 昔 n. olden/former times
mukeru 向ける vt. turn, direct
mukō 向う n. opposite/facing side, time hereafter/thereafter
muku 向く vt. turn towards, face
mutsukashii むつか/難しい, *muzukashii* むずか/難しい a. difficult
muyami na 無暗な a. thoughtless, rash, excessive
myōnichi 明日 n. tomorrow 21b

na 名 n. name
na な who/which is/are; (*da*) 7o, 83b
nado 等 part. etc., and the like
nagai 長/永い a. long
Nagakawa Reiji 永川玲二 pn.
naga-nen 長年 adv. for many years
-nagara (mo) 乍ら(も) su. (even) while 3r
nai 無い vi. be not
-nai 内 su. within 23f
naiyō 内容 n. contents
naka 中 n. inside, middle
Nakagawa Yukihiro 中川幸廣 pn.

Nakamura 中村 pn.; — *Satoshi* — 聰 pn.; — *Sengosuke* — 浅五助 pn.; — *Shizuo* — 静雄 pn.
naki 無き lit. vi. who/which is/are not 3p
-naku naru なく成る become not, no longer 42b
naku tomo なくとも even though/if it is not 34c
namae 名前 n. name
name readings 2r
Namishō 浪商 pn.
nan-demo 何でも whatever it is, anything
nangi 難儀 n. hardship, difficulty
nani 何 pro. what
nanibun 何分 adv. anyhow, please; — *ni mo* — にも by any means, in any way at all; — *tomo* — とも by all means, please
nani-hitotsu 何一つ n. & adv. nothing/not at all
nani-ka 何か pro. something; — *to* — と in various/many/all ways
nani-mo 何も pro. (with neg.) nothing
nani-shiro 何しろ adv. at any rate, after all
nani-tozo 何卒 adv. kindly, (do) please
Naniwa 浪速 pn.
nani-yori (mo) 何より（も） above all, more than anything 7b
nan nari to(mo) 何なりと（も） 25c
na no de なので 7o
nanoka, *nanuka* 七日 n. and adv. seventh day, seven days
Nanzan 南山 pn.
nao 尚 adv. still, more, further
naosu 直す vt. put right, cure
-naosu 直す vt. do again (correctly) 68a
nara(ba) ならば if it is 3q, 17b
narabi ni 並びに lit. conj. and, in addition to
naranu ならぬ 24d
nareba なれば lit. vi. since/if it is 69b
nareru 慣/馴れる vi. become accustomed
nari 也/なり lit. vi. be 14a. 69b, 74b; — *to(mo)* — と（も） 22e, 25c
naru なる lit. attr. vi. which/who is/are 14a; — *mono* — もの 44b
naru 成る vi. become, turn into
nasaru 為さる hon. vt. do, make 6t, 34b, 49e
nasu 為す lit. vt. do, carry out 6f
natsu 夏 n. summer; — *yasumi* — 休み summer holiday
Natsukawa Shizue 夏川静江 pn.
nayamasu 悩ます vt. afflict, worry
nayamu 悩む vi. suffer, be worried/troubled
ne ね int. I say, is it not so?
-neba (naran[u]) ねば（ならん/ぬ） 24ad, 42b, 68a
negai-ageru 願い上げる hum. vt. request 11-l
negau 願う vt. request, hope for
nen 念 n. feeling, wish; twenty 45g
nen 年 n. year
nendo 年度 n. (financial) year period
nenjiru 念じる vt. pray for, keep in mind
nenrei 年令/齢 n. age, years
nentō 念頭 *n.* mind, thoughts
Nerima 練馬 pn.
NHK pn. (= Nihon Hōsō Kyōkai) Japan Broadcasting Corporation
ni に part. to, at, in, (with pass. v.) by; — *azukaru* — 与る vi. participate in 8b; — *chigai nai* — 違いない be no doubt that, doubtless 6l; — *mo kakawarazu* — も拘らず in spite of 16a; — *oite* — 於て (being) in 62a; — *okaremashite (wa)* — おかれまして（は） 2b; — *okeru* — 於ける (which is) in 20d; — *okimashite* — おきまして (being) in 62a; — *shite mo* — しても even assuming that 4n, 39e; — *suru* — する act/behave as 51c; — *torimashite/totte (wa)* — 取りまして/取って(は) for/to (him, etc.), for (his, etc.) part 29d
nichiji 日時 n. the date and time
Nichiyō(bi) 日曜（日） n. Sunday
nigatsu 二月 n. February
Nihon 日本 pn. Japan
Nihonbashi 日本橋 pn.
Nihongaku 日本学 n. Japanese studies
Nihongo 日本語 n. Japanese language
Nihonjin 日本人 n. Japanese person
Nihon-shi 日本史 n. Japanese history
Niida Noboru 仁井田陞 pn.
nijūyokka 二十四日 n. and adv. 24th day, 24 days
nikai 二階 n. second floor, (British) first floor
nikanen 二箇年 n. two years
ni mo kakawarazu にも拘らず in spite of 16a
ninki 任期 n. term of office
ni naru になる (as hon. v. form) 6t, 49e
ninshiki 認識 *s*. vt. recognize, appreciate
ni oite に於て lit. part. in, at 62a
ni okaremashite (wa) におかれまして（は） 2b
ni okeru に於ける lit. attr. v. (which is) in 20d
ni okimashite におきまして 62a
Nippon 日本 see under *Nihon*
nisatsu 二冊 n. and adv. two volumes
Nishikubo 西久保 pn.
nishin 二伸 n. a postscript
Nishino Haruo 西野春雄 pn.
Nishio Toraya 西尾寅弥 pn.
ni shite mo にしても 4n, 39e
Nishiure 西浦 pn. 97a
nissū 日数 n. the number of days
nite にて lit. part. in, at 12f
ni . . . -te itadaku/morau に…て頂く/貰う 14f, 28e
Nitoguri Akira 仁都栗暁 pn.
Nitta Yoshiyuki 新田義之 pn.
nittei 日程 n. (a day's/daily) schedule/program
no の part. of; (= *ga*) 2i; interrogative part. 83b; — *ka* — か 7n
no の pro. (after v. or a.) 4m; — *de* — で 3f, 7o; — *ni* — に 32e, 68b
Nō 能 n. Nō drama
nobasu 延/伸す vt. extend, postpone
nochi 後 n. later (time), after
Noda Saburō 野田三郎 pn.
no de ので being that and so 3f, 7o
Nōgaku 能楽 n. Nō drama; — *Shorin* — 書林 pn.; — *Taimuzu* — タイムズ pn. The Nō Times
no ka のか interr. part. 7n
nokori-sukuna 残り少な n. small remainder
nokoru 残る vi. remain behind/over
nokosu 残す vt. leave behind/over
Nō-kyōgen 能狂言 n. the Kyōgen comedies associated with Nō drama, Nō and Kyōgen 20c
nomi のみ lit. part. only 11k

Nomoto 野元 pn.; — *Kikuo* — 菊雄 pn.
no ni のに although 32e; for/in . . . ing 68b
noru 乗る vi. be carried/published
noun o . . . ni (shite) …を…に（して） 17a
nozoku 覗く vt. see, peep at
nozomu 望む vt. wish/hope for
-nu ぬ lit. v. ending 24dh
-nuku 抜く v. su. utterly, wholly, fully
Numamoto Jirō 沼本次郎 pn.
nyūbai 入梅 n. the rainy season
nyūshitsu 入室 n. entering a room
nyūyō 入用/要 n. need, requirement

o を object part.: before pot. v. 29e; — *hajime*, see under *hajime*; — *mochimashite/motte*, see under *motte*; — *suru* — する work as 53a
o- 御 pol./hon. pre.; see also under *o-noun* . . . entries
-ō （こ/よ, etc.）う, etc. before *gozaimasu*, etc., 8c, 20fh
-Ō 翁 hon. su. 84c
o-ari おあり v. n. 58a
o-bā-chan お婆ちゃん n. granny
ōbo 応募 *s*. vi. apply for
oboshi-mesu 思し召す hon. vt. think, hope, feel 81c
Ochi Haruo 越智治雄 pn.
ochi-tsuku 落ち着く vi. settle down
odoroki 驚き n. surprise
odoroku 驚く vi. be surprised
oeru 終える vt. finish
ōfuku 往復 n. going and returning, round trip
ōgoe 大声 n. loud voice
Ogura 小倉 pn.
o haiken ni を拝見に 16d
o hajime を始/初め beginning with, and also 6u
o-hinasama お雛様 n. doll (especially for the Doll's Festival)
ōi 多い a. numerous
oide お出で hon. v. n. going, coming, being 21d; — *ni naru* — になる hon. vi. go, come, be (present) 6w
oi-komu 追い込む vt. drive in, corner
ōi ni 大いに adv. greatly, largely
oite 於て : *ni* — に — (being) in 62a
o-jii-chan おじいちゃん n. grandad
Oka 岡 pn.; — *Masahiro* — 昌宏 pn.
o-kage(-sama) de お陰（様）で thanks to (another)
okaremashite (wa) おかれまして（は） 2b
okeru 於ける : *ni* — に — (which is) in 20d
ōkii 大きい a. big, large
okimashite おきまして 62a
ōki na 大きな a. big, large
Okinawa 沖縄 pn.
Okkusufōdo オックスフォード pn. Oxford
okonau 行う vt. carry out, do
okoru 起る vi. arise, happen
okosu 起す vt. give rise to, arouse
oku 置く vt. place, put, leave; *-te* — て — 6q
ōku 多く n. many, most
Ōkuma 大隈 pn.
okurebase 後れ馳せ n. lateness
okureru 後/遅れる vi. become late, fall behind
okuri-dasu 送り出す vt. send off/away
okuru 送る vt. send
oku-sama 奥様 hon. n. wife
Ōmagari 大曲 pn.
o-me ni kakareru お目に掛かれる pot. hum. v. be able to meet 2o
o-me ni kakaru お目に掛かる hum. v. meet 2o
omoeru 思える pass./pot. vi. (can) be thought 47d
omoi 思い n. thought, feeling, wish
omoi-dasu 思い出す vt. recall, remember
omoide 思い出 n. recollection, memory
omoigakezu 思い掛けず adv. unexpectedly 21a
omoi-okosu 思い起す vt. raise thoughts/memories of
Omote 表 pn.
o-moto (ni) 御許/下（に） 52a
o moto ni (shite) を元/本/基に（して） 17a
omou 思う vt. think. feel, hope for
omowareru 思われる pass./pot. vi. (can) be thought, get the feeling 8g
onaji 同じ a. same
onajiku 同じく lit. adv. similarly 19a
on-chi 御地 hon. n. (your, etc.) land/country
onchū 御中 hon. n. Messrs. 1a
Oneiru オネイル pn. O'Neill
o . . . ni (shite) を…に（して） 17a
Oniiru オニール pn. O'Neill
Ōnishi Masao 大西雅雄 pn.
on-moto (ni) 御許（に） 52a
onna 女 n. woman
o-noun (o) itadaku/morau お…（を）頂く/貰う 1h, 4b
o-noun (o) kudasaru お…（を）下さる 1g, 2d, 4b
o-noun ni naru/(o) nasaru お…になる/（を）なさる 6t, 34b, 49e
o-noun (o) suru/itasu/mōshi-ageru お…（を）する/致す/申し上げる 1eg, 3g, 4ab 34b, 43a
onseigakkai 音声学会 n. phonetics association
onseigaku 音声学 n. phonetics
onshi 恩師 n. one's (respected) teacher
opinion riidā オピニオン・リーダー n. opinion leader
orareru 居られる vi. be (present) 6o, 14b, 55b
Oregon オレゴン pn.
o-rei 御礼 n. thanks, recompense
ori 折 n. time, occasion; — *ni furete* — に触れて on occasions
ori-kaeshi 折り返し adv. by return of post
Orivie オリヴィエ pn. Olivier
oru 居る hum. vi. be (present) 2m
Ōsaka 大阪 pn.
Osero オセロ pn. Othello
oshiego 教え子 n. one's pupil/disciple
oshieru 教える vt. teach, inform
osoi 遅い a. late, slow
osore-iru 恐れ入る vi. be fearful/hesitant/apologetic
ossharu 仰しゃる hon. vt. say 28f
-ō to suru/itasu （こ/そ etc.）うとする/致す 11f
otona 大人 n. adult
otozure 訪れ n. visit, news
otozureru 訪れる vi. visit
ou 追う vt. chase (away), follow
o-verb stem ＋ *verb* in hon. or hum. expressions: see under *o-noun* . . .

Owada 小和田 pn.
owaru 終る vt. & vi. finish
Ōya Sōichi 大宅壮一 pn.
oyobi 及び conj. and
Ozeki Kazuo 尾関一夫 pn.

Pari パリ pn. Paris
passive-causative verb forms 7f
passive verb forms 1d, 6f, 8g, 11cj, 14b, 64d
patān パターン n. pattern
pāti パーティ n. party
Patto パット pn. Pat
Pauā パウアー pn. Pauer
peishanto ペイシャント n. patient
Pera ペラ pn. Pella
Peruchiakoba ペルチアコバ pn. Plechakova
potential verb forms 2o, 4k, 7g, 8gh, 11i, 14b, 17b, 29e, 47d
Pōzen ポーゼン pn. Posen
puroguramu プログラム n. program

-ra 等 plural su.
raiga 来駕 hon. n. (your, etc.) coming
raiji 来寺 n. coming to a temple
rainen 来年 n. next year
rai-nendo 来年度 n. next (financial) year period
rai-Nichi 来日 n. coming to Japan
raishū 来週 n. next week
-(ra)reru （ら）れる : as pass./pot., 1d, 2o, 6f, 8f, 11cj, 47e, 64d; as hon., 6o, 14b, 26b, 55b, 65ab, 83a, 88a
rashii らしい a. seem, look (like) 11e, 51b
Rasseru Sukueyā ラッセル・スクエヤー pn. Russell Square
rei 礼 n. thanks, recompense
rei- 令 hon. pre. 4c
reimei: see *go-reimei*
renmei 連盟 n. league, federation
renshū 練習 n. practice, training
-reru れる see *-(ra)reru*
Riidāsu Daijesuto リーダース・ダイジェスト pn. Reader's Digest
Riizu リーズ pn. Leeds
riji 理事 n. a director; — *-chō* — 長 managing director
Rikkyō 立教 pn.
rirekisho 履歴書 n. curriculum vitae
rō 労 n. effort, trouble
rō-fujin 老夫人 n. elderly lady
rokugatsu 六月 n. June
Rōma ローマ pn. Rome
ronbun 論文 n. article, essay, thesis
Rondon ロンドン pn. London
ronjiru 論じる vt. discuss, argue about
rōyaru ローヤル a. royal
rui-suru 類する vi. be like/similar
ryō- 両 pre. both, the two
ryohi 旅費 n. travelling expenses
ryokō 旅行 n. journey, travel
ryokuchi 緑地 n. green land
ryōshō 諒承 n. understanding
ryūgaku 留学 n. study abroad; — *-sei* — 生 n. overseas student

-sa さ n. su. 23a
sadamaru 定まる vi. be decided/fixed
saegiru 遮る vt. obstruct, block
sai 際 n. time
sai- 再 pre. re-, (do) again 24g
-sai 祭 n. festival
saigo 最後 n. finality, the end
sai-hakken 再発見 n. rediscovery
saikin no 最近の a. nearest, most recent
saiko no 最古 a. oldest
sai-shite 際して adv. on the occasion/at the time (of)
saiwai 幸い n. happiness, good fortune
Sakai Kazuya 酒井和也 pn.
sakari 盛り n. height, prime
sakeru 避ける vt. avoid, evade
saki 先 n. (pointed) end, tip, future/previous time
sakujitsu 昨日 n. yesterday 6c, 8d
sakunen 昨年 n. last year
sakura 桜 n. cherry
Sakuragawa 桜川 pn.
sakuya 昨夜 n. last night 6c
-sama 様 hon. su. Mr., Mrs., Miss
samui 寒い a. cold
-san さん su. Mr., Mrs., Miss
sanaka 最中 n. the very midst/middle
sanga 山河 n. mountains and rivers
sangatsu 三月 n. March
sanjō 参上 *s.* hum. vi. pay a visit, go
sanjūnen-kan 三十年間 adv. for thirty years
sankan 参観 *s.* vi. visit and look, inspect
Sankei サンケイ pn.
Sannō-dai 山王台 pn.
Sanzoro さんぞろ pn.
sara ni 更に adv. afresh, furthermore, still more
Sarii-shū サリー州 pn. county of Surrey
-(sa)sareru （さ）される 7f
-(sa)seru （さ）せる 51a, 65c; see also *-(sa)sete itadaku*
-(sa)sete itadaku （さ）せて頂く 1i, 2p, 6ai, 8h
-(sa)sete kudasaru （さ）せて下さる 8k
sashi-ageru 差し上げる hum. vt. offer up, present
sashite さして ＋ neg. 16b
sassoku 早速 adv. immediately
sassuru 察する vt. judge, surmise, sympathize with
sate さて conj. well (then/now)
-satsu 冊 su. (printed) volume
satsuki 皐月 lit. n. May 88c
sawagi 騒ぎ n. uproar, turmoil
sawagu 騒ぐ vi. be agitated/in turmoil
Sawayanagi Daigorō 沢柳大五郎 pn.
sayonara/sayōnara さよ(う)なら int. goodbye
sazukeru 授ける vt. grant, confer, instruct
sei 生 hum. su 61b
seian 清安 n. well-being
Sei-Doku 西独 pn. West Germany
seiei 清栄 n. health and prosperity
seika 成果 n. result, product
seikatsu 生活 n. life, living; — *-hi* — 費 n. living expenses
seiri 整理 n. arrangement, putting in order
seisaku 製作 n. manufacture, production

sekai 世界 n. the world; — *-teki* — 的 a. world (-wide)
sekku 節句 n. annual festival
sekkyoku-teki 積極的 a. positive
Sekushon セクション n. Section
senjitsu 先日 n. and adv. the other day
senkō 専攻 n. special study/research field
senmon 専門 n. speciality
sensei 先生 n. teacher, title of respect for person established in a cultural field
sentā センター n. center
sentaku 選/撰択 n. choice
-seru: see *-(sa)seru*
sesshu 摂取 *s.* vt. take in, absorb
Setagaya 世田谷 pn.
setchi 設置 *s.* vt. establish, institute
setcho 拙著 hum. n. (my) humble work/writing
-sete itadaku: see *-(sa)sete itadaku*
-sete kudasaru: see *-(sa)sete kudasaru*
setsu 節 n. time, occasion 13d
setsu- 拙 hum. pre. 41a
settai-yaku 接待役 n. assistant/server at tea ceremony
sewa 世話 n. care, charge, assistance; — *ni naru* — に成る become obliged (to someone)
sezu せず 63c
sha 社 n. Shinto shrine, company
shadan hōjin 社団法人 n. a corporate juridical person, a corporation
Shakujii 石神井 pn.
shashin 写真 n. photograph; — *-chō* — 帳 photograph album
shashoku 写植 n. photo-setting (of type)
Shefiirudo シェフィールド pn. Sheffield
Shefufiirudo シェフフィールド pn. Sheffield
Sheikusupia シェイクスピア pn. Shakespeare
sherii-shu シェリー酒 n. sherry
shi し conj. and (furthermore) 8m
shi 史 n. history
shi 誌 n. journal, publication
-shi 氏 hon. su. 6m
Shiatā Uākushoppu シアター・ウァークショップ pn. Theater Workshop
shiawase 仕合(わ)せ n. happiness, good fortune
Shiba 芝 pn.
shibaru 縛る vt. bind, fetter
shiben 支弁 n. payment, defrayment
Shibuya 渋谷 pn.
shichigatsu 七月 n. July
shidai 次第 n. sequence, circumstances, reason 22c; (after n. or v. stem) as soon as
shigakka 史学科 n. history course/department
shigaku 史学 n. (study of) history
shigaku 私学 n. private school/college
shigansho 志願書 n. written application (form)
shigatsu 四月 n. April
shigoto 仕事 n. work
shiji 指示 *s.* vt. indicate, denote, instruct; — *-dōri* — 通り as indicated
shika しか + neg. not/nothing but, only
shikai 視界 n. field of view
shikaku 資格 n. qualification
shikashi 然し conj. however
shikiten 式典 n. ceremony
shikumi 仕組 n. contrivance, plan
shikyū 至急 n. extreme urgency
shimau 仕舞う vt. finish, close, put/store away; *-te* — て 7p
Shimazaki Chifumi 島崎千富美 pn.
shimei-kan 使命感 n. sense of mission
shimiru 染みる vi. pierce, penetrate
shimotsuki 霜月 n. November 69f
shinai 市内 n. (inside of a) city
shin'ai 親愛 n. affection
Shinbori Michiya 新堀通也 pn.
Shingapōru シンガポール pn. Singapore
shinken na 真剣な a. earnest, serious
shin-nendo 新年度 n. new (financial) year period
shinpō 新報 n. new journal/publication
shinpojiumu シンポジウム n. symposium
shinsetsu 親切 n. kindness
shinsha 深謝 n. deep gratitude
shinsō 新装 n. new attire/appearance
shiraberu 調べる vt. investigate
Shirakusō 紫洛荘 pn.
shiraseru 知らせる vt. make known
shireru 知れる vi. become known
shiritsu 私立 n. private establishment
shiritsu 市立 n. municipal establishment
shiru 知る vt. know, learn of
shirusu 記す vt. write down, record
shiryō 資料 n. material
shisatsu 視察 n. inspection; — *-dan* — 団 n. inspection group
shisho 司書 n. librarian
shita 下 n. the underneath/lower part; — *no* — の a. lower, younger
shitashii 親しい a. familiar, close
shitatameru 認める vt. write, take/eat (a meal)
shitei 指定 *s.* vt. specify, designate
Shitennōji 四天王寺 pn.
shitsurei 失礼 n. rudeness
shizuka na 静かな a. peaceful, quiet
sho- 諸 pre. the various, many
shō 賞 n. prize
shōchi 承知 n. knowledge, consent
shochū no 書中の a. within a letter
shōdaku 承諾 n. consent
shoin 書院 n. a study, private school
shōka 消化 *s.* vt digest
shōkai 紹介 n. introduction; — *-jō* — 状 letter of introduction
shōkai 照会 n. enquiry; — *-sha* — 者 (personal) referee
shokun 諸君 n. (you/them) all, everyone
shokureki 職歴 n. professional/working career
shomotsu 書物 n. book
shōnō 笑納 n. acceptance (of something unworthy)
shōrai 将来 n. future
shōran 笑覧 n. looking at (something unworthy) 22d
shōsai 詳細 n. details
shōsei 小生 hum. n. I 12c
shoseki 書籍 n. books, publications
shōtai 招待 n. invitation
shoten 書店 n. bookshop
Shōwa 昭和 pn. & era-name from 1926

-shū 州 n. state, county
shujin 主人 n. husband, master
shuju no 種々の a. various, all kinds of
shūkan 習慣 n. custom
shukō 趣向/好 n. plan, idea
shukufuku 祝福 *s.* vt. bless
shūkyō 宗教 n. religion
shuppan 出版 n. publishing; — *-butsu* — 物 n. publications; — *-sha* — 者 publisher
shuppatsu 出発 n. departure; — *-bi* — 日 n. day of departure
shūshoku 就職 n. taking up employment/office
shusseki 出席 n. attendance
sō そう adv. so, like that; — *itta* — 云った 24f; — *iu* — 云う 29c; — *shita* — した 24f
sō そう (before *da*, etc.) it is said that 28g, 43b
-sō そう su. looks/seems like 7a
SOAS pn. 12a
soba 側 n. side, vicinity
sobo 祖母 n. grandmother
sōbō 怱忙 n. busyness
Sōdai 早大 pn. Waseda University 70b
sōdō 騒動 n. disturbance, riot
soeru 添える vt. add, attach
sōfu 送付 n. sending, forwarding
sogai 疎外 s. vt. keep at a distance, hold off
sō itta そう云った 24f
sō iu そう云う 29c
sōken 壮健 n. health
somatsu na 粗末な a. plain, humble
sō-mokuroku 総目録 n. (a general/comprehensive) catalogue
sonna そんな a. that kind of 24f
sono 其の a. that
Sonoko 園子 pn.
sōon 騒音 n. (loud) noise
sora 空 n. sky
sore それ pro. that; — *de wa* — では that being so, well then; — *ni* — に on top of that 48b
sō shita そうした 24f
soshite そして conj. and, then, and then
sō-sō 早々 adv. immediately, early, as soon as; 草々/匆々/忄々 adv. in haste 4p, 89a
sotchoku 率直 n. frankness, straight-forwardness
sōtō na 相当な a. corresponding/appropriate, adequate, considerable
su-beki す可き 69c
subete 全/総て n. all, everything; adv. entirely
Sugimoto 杉本 pn.; — *Hisatsugu* — 尚次 pn.; — *Tōjirō* — 藤次郎 pn.
sugiru 過ぎる vi. elapse; vt. exceed, pass (by/through)
-sugiru 過ぎる su. (do/be) excessively 47h
sugosu 過ごす vt. spend/pass (time)
sugu 直ぐ adv. immediately
sugureru 勝/優れる vi. excel, be superior
sugureta 勝/優れた a. excellent, superior
suikyo 推挙 *s.* vt. propose (for advancement)
Suiyō(bi) 水曜日 n. Wednesday
sukejūru スケジュール n. schedule
sukkari すっかり adv. completely, wholly
sukoshi 少し adv. a little, a few
Sukottorando スコットランド pn. Scotland
sukurappu スクラップ *s.* vt. take clipping (from newspaper, etc.)
sumai 住居 n. house, living quarters
sumanai 済まない vi. & a. be sorry/regrettable
Sumisu スミス pn. Smith
Sumiya Kazuhiko 住谷一彦 pn.
sumu 澄む vi. become clear
sūnin 数人 n. several people
sunshi 寸紙 n. scrap of paper, one's own (poor)/a short letter
sura すら lit. part. even 28b
suri-nukeru 摺抜ける vi. make one's way through, slip away
suru する vt. do, make; serve/act as 53a; *-ō to* — (こ/そ etc.) うと— 11f
suspensive forms: of a. 4f, 6de, 11e, 51b, 64a; of v. 1c, 2dgj, 3h, 6bgj, 8j, 27a, 35a
susumeru 進める vt. advance
sutēshon ステーション n. station
Sutiivan Giru スティヴアン·ギル pn. Steven Gill
Sutorattofōdo-on-Eivon ストラットフォード・オン・エイヴォン pn. Stratford-on-Avon
Sutorongu ストロング pn. Strong
Suzuki Namiko 鈴木南海子 pn.

ta 他 n. another, others
tabi 度 n. time, occasion
tabi 旅 n. journey
tabō 多忙 n. extreme busyness
Tachiiri 立入 pn.
tadaima 只/唯今 adv. (right) now, soon
tadashi 但し conj. but, however
tadashii 正しい a. right, just, correct
Tagawa Chieko 田川知恵子 pn.
tahō 他方 n. the other side/hand
-tai 度い su. want/wish to; — *to omou/zonjiru* — と思う/存じる would like to 3eo
tai-Ei 滞英 n. residence in England
taihen 大変 adv. very, extremely
taikei 大慶 n. great happiness/pleasure
taiken 体験 n. personal experience
Taimuzu Bungei Furoku タイムズ文芸付録 pn. The Times Literary Supplement
taisetsu na 大切な a. important, valuable
Taishō 大正 pn. & era name (1912–26)
taisō 大層 adv. very, considerably
tai-suru 対する vi. face, directed at/toward, (be) against
Taiwan 台湾 pn.
taiyō 太陽 n. the sun
taizai 滞在 n. residence; — *-chū* — 中 during one's stay; — *-hi* — 費 expenses for a stay; *-s.* vi. make a stay
Tajima Kazuo 田嶋一夫 pn.
Takada Makoto 高田誠 pn.
Takahashi 高橋 pn.; — *Keiko* — 慶子 pn.; — *Masao* — 正雄 pn.
Takako Kōnishi 篁子コーニシ pn. Takako Cornish
Takasaki 高崎 pn.
Takatsu Yoshihiko 鷹津義彦 pn.
takamaru 高まる vi. rise, heighten
Takeda 竹田 pn.
takeru 長ける vi. excel, be expert
Takigi Nō 薪能 n. Nō by Torchlight

takō 多幸 n. great happiness
-taku 度く 3eo, 8c, 64a; — *omou/zonjiru* — 思う/
takō 多幸 n. great happiness
-taku 度く 3eo, 8c, 64a; — *omou/zonjiru* — 思う/
存じる 3eo
takusan 沢山 n. many, much, plenty
Tamagawa Seta 玉川瀬田 pn.
tama ni 偶に adv. occasionally
tama-tama 偶々 adv. by chance, occasionally
tamawaru 賜/給わる vt. (humbly) receive, be granted 13a
tame 為 n. benefit, purpose, reason
Tanaka Makoto 田中允 pn.
tanjōbi 誕生日 n. birthday
tanoshii 楽しい a. enjoyable, pleasant
tanoshimi 楽しみ n. enjoyment, pleasure
tanoshimu 楽しむ vt. enjoy
tantō 担当 n. charge; — *-sha* — 者 person in charge
-tara たら 7l
-tari たり 11g
tashika ni 確かに adv. certainly
tatematsuru 奉る vt. present; as su. (do) respectfully 45d
tateru 立てる vt. set up, establish
Tatoru タトル pn.
tayō 多用 n. busyness
tayō 多様 n. variety, diversity
tayori 便り n. news, tidings
tayu-tayu to shita たゆたゆとした a. hesitant, uncertain
tazuneru 尋ねる vt. look for, ask about
-te て v. form 6j
-te ageru て上げる 8l
te-atatakai 手温/暖かい a. cordial, warm
te-atsui 手厚い a. friendly, warm
tegami 手紙 n. letter
-te hoshii て欲しい 44c
-te irarenai て居られない 7g
teishutsu 提出 *s.* vt. present, submit
-te itadaku て頂く 1i, 2p, 6a, 14f, 33h (see also *-(sa)sete itadaku)*
-teki (na) 的（な） a. su.
Tekisasu テキサス pn. Texas
-te kudasaru て下さる 8k
tēma テーマ n. theme, topic
-te miru て見る 8i
-te mo ても : after interrogative 42c
-te morau て貰う 14f
ten 点 n. spot, point, item
tenkirin 天気輪 n. pagoda finial
tenpura 天ぷら n. deep-fried seafood; — *-ya* — 屋 n. a tenpura cook
-te oku て置く 6q
tēpu テープ n. tape
Terada Sōichi 寺田宗一 pn.
-te shimau て仕舞う 7p
tesū 手数 n. trouble, bother
-te (wa) irarenai て（は）居られない 7g
-te yaru てやる 8l, 33fh
-te yatte itadaku てやって頂く 33h
-te yatte kudasaru てやって下さる 33f
Tīchi Yuaruserufu ティーチ・ユアルセルフ pn. Teach Yourself
to と part. and 4i
to と quotative part. 15b, 72a
to と adv. part. 21c, 29f
-to 都 n. metropolis
tō- 当 pre. this, the present, the .... in question 1b
-tō とう : from *-tai/-taku* 8c, 20f
tōchi 当地 n. this place/district
to-Ei 渡英 n. going to England/Britain
Tōgo Katsuaki 東後勝明 pn.
tōhō 当方 pro. I/we (on my/our side)
Tōhoku 東北 pn.
toi-awase 問合せ n. enquiry
Toicheto トイチェト pn. Twitchett
to iu wake de と云う訳で for this reason 51e
tōji 当時 n. & adv. (at) this/that time
toji-komoru 閉じ籠る vi. shut oneself up, confine oneself
toka とか part. and (,say) 4i
tōka 十日 n. & adv. tenth day, ten days
tōkan 投函 *s.* vt. post
toki 時 n. time
toki-doki 時々 adv. sometimes
tokoro 所 n. place, point, stage, aspect 4e, 6h, 14c, 47g
tokubetsu no 特別の a. special
Tokuda Susumu 徳田進 pn.
toku ni 特に adv. especially
Tōkyō 東京 pn.
tomaru 留る vi. stay/lodge (overnight)
tomo とも conj. although 22e, 25c, 34c
tomo ni 共に adv. both, together
tomodachi 友達 n. friend
to no との (= *to iu*) 27g, 43b
tonshu 頓首 97b; — *saihai* — 再拝 9c
Tō-Ō 東欧 n. eastern Europe
toppatsu jiko 突発事故 n. sudden/unexpected happening/accident
tōri 通り n. road, way, manner
tori-ageru 取上げる vt. take up/away/over
tori-atsukau 取扱う vt. treat, handle, deal with
Torigoe 鳥越 pn.; — *Kazue* — 一枝 pn.
tori-isogi 取急ぎ adv. in haste
torimashite (wa): see *totte (wa)*
torishimari-yaku 取締役 n. a director
toru 取る vt. take, gain, obtain
to shimashite (wa): see *to shite (wa)*
to shite (wa) として（は） (in one's role/function) as, for
tosho 図書 n. books; — *-kan* — 館 library; — *-shitsu* — 室 library (reading room)
tōshuku 投宿 *s.* vi. lodge, stay
to suru とする 4l, 39e, 51c
totemo とても adv. very, extremely
totonoeru 整/調える vt. prepare, supply, arrange, buy
totsuzen 突然 adv. suddenly
totte (wa) 取って（は） to, for, in the case of 29d
to wa ie (domo) とは云え（ども） 51f
towazu 問わず 55c
Tōyō 東洋 n. the Orient/East; — *-shi* — 史 Oriental history
-tsū 通 su. sheet, copy
Tsuchiya Motoko 土屋元子 pn.

tsūgaku 通学 n. attending school
tsugō 都合 n. arrangements, circumstance, convenience
tsuide 次いで adv. next, following on
tsuitachi 一日 n. first day of a month
tsuite (wa) 付いて（は） about, in connection/conjunction with
tsūjiru 通じる vi. pass through, be conversant/well informed, be understandable
tsukamatsuru 仕る hum. vt. do 64b
tsukare-kiru 疲れ切る vi. be tired out
tsukareru 疲れる vi. be tired
tsukau 使う vt. use
tsukimashite (wa): see *tsuite (wa)* 1f
tsuku 付く vi. become attached/fixed
tsuku 着く vi. arrive, reach
tsukuru 作/造る vt. make
tsukusu 尽す vt. exhaust
tsumi-ageru 積上げる vt. heap/pile up
tsumori 積り n. intention
tsureru 連れる vt. take/bring along, be accompanied by
tsutaeru 伝える vt. transmit, convey
tsutomeru 勤/務/努める vt. work (as), strive
-tsutsu つつ su. while 2k
tsutsushimu 謹/慎む vi. be circumspect, restrained, reverent
tsuzuku 続く vi. continue, follow on

-*ū*: before *gozaimasu*, etc., 20f
uchi 内/家 n. home, house; — *no* — の my/our (own) 7c
uchi ni 内/中に adv. within, while, during
uchi-awaseru 打合わせる vt. pre-arrange
uchi-sugiru 打過ぎる vi. elapse, pass by
ue 上 n. top; after, following 5f
Ueno 上野 pn.
Uēruzu ウェールズ pn. Wales
Uiin ウイーン, *Uin* ウイン pn. Vienna
Ujiie Yōko 氏家洋子 pn.
ukagau 伺う hum. vt. hear, ask, visit 12e
uka-uka うかうか *s.* vi. be careless/absent-minded
ukeru 受ける vt. receive
uketamawaru 承る hum. vt. hear 4d, 65c
uke-toru 受取る vt. accept, receive
uki 右記 n. the above/previously mentioned
umai 旨い a. delicious, skilful
umareru 生/産れる vi. be born
ume 梅 n. plum tree
umu 生/産む vt. give birth to, produce
un 運 n. fortune, luck
ureshii 嬉しい a. happy
uru 得る vt. gain, obtain
-uru 得る v. su. be able to 22f
usui 薄い a. thin, light, weak
utsukushii 美しい a. beautiful
utsusu 移す vt. move, transfer
utsusu 写/映す vt. copy, reproduce
uwasa 噂 n. rumor, report

verb stems 1ceg; before v. of motion 21; with *-kata* 29a
Verōna no Ni-shinshi ヴェローナの二紳士 pn. The Two Gentlemen of Verona

wa は topic part. as for
wa 和 n. peace, harmony, Japan
wabiru 詫びる vt. apologize for
waga 我が pro. my, our
Waga 和賀 pn.
wajutsu 話術 n. art of conversation, story-telling
wakaru 分/解る vi. & vt. be clear, understand
waku 沸/涌く vi. boil up, be in ferment
warau 笑う vi. laugh, smile
ware 我 pro. I 3j; — *-ware/-ra* — 我/等 we
wariai 割合 n. proportion, rate
warui 悪い a. bad, wrong
Waseda 早稲田 pn.
watakushi 私 pro. I
watashi わたし/私 pro. I
waza-waza 態々 adv. expressly, on purpose
wazuka 僅か n. & adv. a pittance, merely

ya や part. and 4i
yado 宿 n. lodgings
yaku-datsu 役立つ vi. be useful/of service
Yamagata 山形 pn.
Yamanote 山手 pn.
yamu 止む vi. stop, cease
Yanada 簗田 pn.
yaru 遣る vt. do, send; — */ageru* —上げる 8l; see also *-te yaru*
yasumi 休み n. rest, holiday
yasumu 休む vi. rest, take time off
yatto やっと adv. finally, with difficulty
yō 洋 n. & a. the West, Western
yō 様 likeness, way; — *da* — だ 10d, 11d; — *na/ni* — な/に 1cg, 8g; — *ni naru* — に成る 1c, 5d, 53c; — *ni s./itasu* — にする/致す 53c
yō 用 n. business, use, service
yō 葉 n. leaf; counter for sheets of paper
yōbō 要望 n. demand, requirement
yobu 呼ぶ vt. call, summon, invite
yō da 様だ 10d, 11d
yōgo 用語 n. terminology, wording
yoha 余波 n. after-effect, repercussion
yoi 良い a. good
yōka 八日 n. & adv. eighth day, eight days
yokka 四日 n. & adv. fourth day, four days
Yokohagi Michihiko 横佩道彦 pn.
Yokomichi Mario 横道万里雄 pn.
yoku 良く adv. well, often
yokujitsu 翌日 n. next day
yōkyoku 謡曲 n. a Nō text 59b
yōmei/yōmyō 幼名 n. infant/childhood name
yōmei 用命 n. order, command
yō na/ni 様な/に 1cg, 8g
yō ni naru/suru/itasu 様に成る/する/致す 1c, 5d, 53c
yō ni omowareru 様に思われる 8g
yō ni suru/itasu 様にする/致す 53c
yonkakoku 四箇国 n. four countries
yonsei 四世 n. fourth generation
yori より part. than 55a; lit. part. from, since 3b
yorokobu 喜ぶ vi. be glad/happy
Yōroppa ヨーロッパ n. Europe
yoroshii 宜しい a. good, fine
yoroshiku 宜しく adv. well 3t, 6n

yoru 夜 n. night
yoru 依る vi. be based/depend on
yōryō 要領 n. gist, substance, outline
yoshi 由 n. news, matter, reason 10a
yōshi 用紙 n. form
Yoshida 吉田 pn.; — *Saburō* — 三郎 pn.
Yoshihira Yōko 吉平陽子 pn.
yōso 要素 n. element
yōsu 様子 n. appearance, circumstances
yotei 予定 n. arrangement, expectation
yōyaku 漸く adv. gradually, finally, with difficulty
Yoyogi 代々木 pn.
yūbe 昨夜 n. last night 6c
yūchō na 悠長な a. leisurely, casual
yūeki 誘掖 n. guidance
yūjin 友人 n. friend
yuki 雪 n. snow
Yukiko 由紀子 pn.
yuku 行く vi. go
yurusu 許す vt. permit, allow, forgive
yūzā ユーザー n. user

zai-Ei 在英 n. residence in England
zai-Nichi 在日 n. residence in Japan
-zaru ざる 57a
zasshi 雑誌 n. magazine
zasshu 雑種 n. various kinds, mixed type
zehi 是非 adv. without fail
Zen 禅 n. Zen sect/religion
zenkan 全巻 n. complete volume(s)
zenkoku 全国 n. whole country; — *-min* — 民 n. the whole nation
zenpen 前篇 n. first volume, part I
zenryaku 前略 2a
zenryoku 全力 n. whole strength/energy
zenshū 全集 n. complete collection/works
zonji-ageru 存じ上げる hum. vt. know, think, feel 2c
zonjiru 存じる hum. vt. know, think, feel 3e
-zu (ni) ず（に） 16b, 57a
zuibun 随分 adv. quite, considerably
-zuke no 付けの a. dated
-zumai 住（ま）い su. living in
Zushi 逗子 pn.
zutto ずっと adv. right through, throughout, far (more)